U-Knighted We Stand

BOOK OF THE SOUTH

SOPHIA WEST

Written by:
Lady Sophia Key-Raphael West
Adapted from the
Memoirs of Sir Edward-Michael Jagen
1991 – 1996

THIS IS AN **ANGEL KNIGHT PRODUCTIONS** PUBLICATION
When Angels Dream, Book of the North was the first book written, in a
four-part series entitled *Diary of an Angel Knight.*

NOTICE:
U-Knighted We Stand, Book of the South, is a creative non-fiction story
about the life of a courageous human spirit's search for truth. Adapted
from the memoirs of Sir Edward-Michael Jagen, this story is the second
installment in the four-book series, *Diary of an Angel-Knight.* It chronicles
Sir Edward's amazing life adventure from (1991 -1996).

Because many of Detective Jagen's deep undercover police
investigations into organized crime and terrorist organizations still remain
classified, some of the names and genders have been changed,
composite characters created, and time frames compressed, to protect
individual's privacy. This second edition also includes the remaining 24
lessons and 15 Ancient Laws of 'Knowing' from the *Book of Wisdom,* that
Sir Edward channeled from an ascended Master of Atlantis.

Use of all Lessons in the Book of Wisdom is solely the responsibility of
the reader and to be used at your own risk.. Any and all tools and
practices involving meditations, energy work, herbs, crystals, and health
related items should be used only after consulting with your medical
professional.

This book is dedicated to all those who dared
to stand with Sir Edward in the
Shadow of the Spirit of Truth.

Jagen-West

Table of Contents

Prologue by Edward Jagen

As indicated in the preface of *When Angels Dream, Book of the North*, Volume One in the Diary of an Angel Knight series, this book is intended for the 144,000 old souls and earth angels who truly seek to save the world for the Children of Tomorrow. Are you one of them?

If you answered yes, let's cut to the chase. If you don't have peace in your heart, you cannot bring peace to the world. So how then can you help?

Change your thoughts > change your heart > change your world.

The lessons in this book, along with a good honest look at yourself, is the first step towards cultivating the peace that is needed. In the process of reading this book, your ego will be tested to levels that you cannot yet fathom. You will swear in one moment that your opinion is 100% correct, only to have an "aha" moment in the next and realize how your ego tricked you. Don't get me wrong, the ego is a good thing. It helps you stay safe and grounded. But, it usually wants to be the driver. To tame it, you will need to take the reins and control your thoughts, pushing the irrational fears out of your mind that the ego tells you are the truth. Once this is done, you will have a chance to elevate your current understanding and to take action by giving back to the world.

Love, and only love is the answer.

Attention!

Before reading on, be aware that this book is written and compiled by Universal Energy.

After realizing that editors couldn't "just edit" for typos and punctuation because they always felt compelled to change tense and rephrase what Sir Edward or Archangel Michael meant or experienced, I decided to not use their services. Therefore, the story comes out "raw" from the only woman on the planet who knows me. You will read about her later in this volume and more in coming volumes. She is a perfectly clear channel with amazing gifts. One of which is that as she reads my diaries she is transported energetically back to the moments detailed and can experience thought and sensation from all the participants in the conversation. This allows her to scribe perfectly (when appropriate) the missing pieces and transform my memoirs into a creative non-fiction masterpiece.

The dialogue that flows through all volumes of Diary of an Angel Knight is, and was, primarily oral and ancient in origin. Like Thor said in Infinity War "All words are made up." Expanding on that thought, if words are made up, so are the letters that form them. Who made them up? Mankind. And Scholars are the ones who "enforce" their use.

With all of this in mind, if when reading you come across a typo, or grammar mis-use, and you feel it takes away from what you are reading, you may want to just put the book down. Those who feel the energy and have a deeper understanding will either not notice those issues or not allow them to impede their journey to the Greater Understanding.

Apocalypse of Archangel Michael

In 1990, while I was in my third year of channeling the lessons from the lost Atlantean Book of Wisdom, Archangel Michael showed me that in the future, it would be critical for the lessons to be published within two books. The first one with a blue cover and second one red. He also instructed me to tell the story of my life experiences that lead up to my receiving the lessons. And so, I kept a day-to-day diary of events. He told me that modern science had yet to comprehend the full potential of the collective human mind to manifest a more peaceful world.

He explained,

"If humanity used more selfless, positive reasoning in their day to day lives, a new enlightened reality would be revealed. However, currently the human collective consciousness is negatively out of balance. If this mindset continues, it will lead to a world war that will start a chain reaction that will end the human experiment."

Michael closed by saying, "The End of Days will begin when a 'Mad King' becomes an American President and then sides with the enemy of the American Dream."

With the American political environment as it is, it could easily lead one to believe that Michael's prophecy is well underway.

When I asked Michael what could be done, he showed me a vision of thousands of Atlantean descendants scattered around the globe, whose spirit line could be awakened through regaining the lost wisdom of their ancestors. He told me ours is the age of mass communication and to find the best way to get this message out.

He then went on to say, "As the ancient lessons are experienced, humans will relearn how to control their thoughts. Right now, humans, at least the majority of them, do not know how powerful they are because they do not understand what is going on inside of them. There are over ten quadrillion things the brain is managing in the body every second, all without the conscious awareness of the person. This would fascinate people if you gave them this fact about a computer, but telling them it is within their body would confound them because they see their physical form and its limitations. However, the body has only created the impression of being limited. Humans are in actuality limitless and what makes them limitless is their mind. It is the one thing that can attract all good or demolish with all bad. And it is done through the thoughts. The human mind cannot distinguish between reality and what it creates. Take for instance young siblings who just broke a lamp. They immediately start to think up a scenario of what is going to happen to them when the parents find out. The fearful vision and scene they created starts a cortisol response in the body which floods all their cells with negativity thereby lowering the immune system and affecting their health. All the while, mom and dad wind up just being happy the kids weren't hurt. Another example would be parents in fear of an event in their child's future. Their fear is actually creating alternative possibilities for the child instead of the wonderful path that lay before them. Imagine this: Your child is walking in the woods on the way to a beautiful resort (his/her college future). You fear all the different possibilities that could happen in the future and fear he/she won't be a productive happy person or make it through high school. As soon as your fearful thoughts are created it would be likened to building little lean-to shelters (representing the scenarios you think about if the child fails, like dropping out, becoming a vagrant, etc.) in the woods. As the child journeys through the woods he/she now sees the shelters along the way and makes the choice to go stay in the closest one and stop the journey. If you hadn't created those shelters with your mind, they would not exist. Understand?"

I was thrilled that I did understand so I started right away investigating venues to get the word out to the masses to see if the descendants could be found. He told me that if the group could gain the lost knowledge from the lessons and learn to control their thoughts, they would go on the become counterparts aligned with Michael's Angelic Commanders. He said that after that was achieved, I would be given instructions on how to create Crystal Unity Beacons and "Pyramind" (patent pending) devices that the knights would take around the world in order to spread unconditional love and positive reasoning.

On Valentine's Day 2017 the blue book, When Angels Dream, Book of the North, was published by Sophia West as taken from my diaries. The book immediately became an International Best Seller on Amazon. Sophia then created a Facebook page for the book so like-minded seekers of the lost knowledge could ask the authors questions and get answers. We also tested many media platforms to find the Atlantean descendants, but found that even though Facebook had its limitations, it was the place to reach the world. This process opened Pandora's box…literally. We found HOPE with the beautiful spirits of the descendants who have come forward but we also found fire and brimstone thrown at us. Interestingly enough, it wasn't from a religious group, but rather a new age group who labeled us reptilian, among other evil adjectives. Another example of the power of thought. Someone planted an unkind thought and it grew like a virus and affected many people. The group wound up implementing a smear campaign on us. Sadly, all they smeared was themselves by exposing the fact that they were not coming from a place a love rather a place of fear and hate if you didn't do as they said. It was sad to see such hatred well up, so all we did in return was send them love. We learned so much from that social experiment volumes could be written on that topic. The most important thing we learned was that we were on the right track. The evil in this world that wants to keep humanity in the muck and mire used others as pawns against us in an effort to extinguish our light. A CEO in the publishing business told us that it was all actually perfect. "When a book receives this much flack, it's on track.

In spite of that turmoil, we prevailed. Another wonderful group created on Facebook came together to work hard and learn the Atlantean lessons. Several of the positive members from the old group who refused to give into negativity got kicked out and joined our new group. One being Joseph Worker, a retired U.S. Army Ranger, with a gift of being able to test the members who were blinded by ego. It was his job to get members to quit. Much like he did in the military. He was a "Godsend." He deflected the negativity like a champion If there was one true Good and Righteous Man it's Sir Joseph who is a "bad ass" medieval stunt coordinator in Orlando, Florida.

The new group went from 6,300 members to eighty-three as the true descendants and dedicated individuals rose to the top. They have proved themselves worthy due to their tenacity to continue and their pure open hearts. Because of their effort, a channel was opened for me where I learned how to use the elements of gold, silver, copper and clear quartz crystals to make devices that would radiate love and positive reasoning. The ultimate goal is to make 144,000 Crystal Unity Beacon that the 144 Angel-Knights will distribute. around the world by burying and submerging 72,000 Crystal Unity Beacons marked with an "E" as tributes to Mother Earth for the paradise we have been given to live upon.

The other 72,000 Beacons will have a golden bell attached and a number from 1 to 144 on its bottom. The number represents the Archangel Commander and the 1,000 Angels of Light in that battalion. Those Beacons are to be gifted as tribute to people who need love and positive reasoning. When the person shakes the crystal, it will release the positive energy of the angels inside.

I was also shown that the time would come when I would outfit the Angel-Knights with War Shields and copper "White Light" meditation pyramids. The War Shields are to be tablets with ten posts connected with gold and silver wires to form the Kabbalah, or Tree of Life. Using special Crystal devices and an internal lighting system the Knights, working in concert, would be able to send positive thoughts to the Crystal Beacons that were being placed around the world. The "White Light" pyramids would be used to remotely heal tensions in the world, divert weather systems from harming life and damage to property. I also saw that it would allow Astral Project through different dimensions while in an awakened state of mind. Called "Pyraminds" because they were fueled by thought I got the feeling that they were much like the legendary "Fountain of Youth" because of the electromagnetic "White Light" healing energy that is stored inside the structure. It was a most amazing vision but I had no idea where to start. I would have to depend on Archangel Michael's guidance for that.

We now have a second Facebook Group page called, Good Knight University. The members attend live online bi-Monthly Master Studies Program where Lady Sophia covers the lessons and contemporary topics as well. Members are living all over the world on six continents. The challenge with time zone difference is alleviated by using the War Shields that transcend time and space.

The only prerequisite to join the class was that members must set aside (not get rid of) what they think they know so they can gain the knowledge they need to put into action. Our philosophy is, "If you think you know you don't, and if you know you don't you do!"

ADDENDUM--As of this publishing, the Angel-Knights in Good Knight University have each been equipped with at least one War Shield and a "White Light Pyramind" that they are learning to operate. To date they have spread over 3,000 Crystal Unity Beacons infused with love and positive reasoning around the world, with an emphasis on the United States. The Angel-Knights link their love and the power of their mind to the growing grid lines of crystals to affect positive change. Reports are coming in every day documenting the miraculous changes happening in the lives of those who have been gifted a beacon; illnesses are being reversed, financial burdens are lifting, relationships are healing and potentially catastrophic weather events are weakened

Now it's time to seek the remaining 144,000 Light Bearers of Legend to help seed the world with Crystal Unity Beacons so the collective consciousness of the earth can balance into the Universal "Christ" Consciousness. Archangel Michael says it's the only way of breaking free of all of the lies and misinformation that holds humanity in the grip of the forces of darkness that abounds.

How about it? Want to join the movement of love and positive reasoning?

If you want to learn more about our global effort to balance the consciousness with crystals radiating unconditional love and prosperity to all who come in contact with them visit us on Facebook at Crystal Unity Beacons.

Chapter One

She Isn't Coming

It's so cold in here. This space was once alive with energy and vibration, and now it's completely devoid. I can't even remember anyone ever standing on these knighting pods. Wow, why can't I remember? Why can't I see? I felt more alive when I drowned and was in Connie's presence.

Michael, are you here?

I can't feel anything. I feel absolutely nothing. I can't hear him, her, anyone or anything. Please sweet baby! Please talk to me.

She isn't coming. It's over. I've failed.

What am I doing on the floor in the middle of the knighting circle? When did I leave my chair?

With my elbows on my knees, I rest my head in the palms of my hands and weep. "Just breathe. Just keep breathing," I feel like I'm going to pass out. Memories and visions of my life are dancing in front of me; a life review? My mind is swirling…

Other worldly chimes ring out all around me. I feel a presence. The center of my forehead is pulsating. "What? What's going on? Who's there?" I cry out.

No answer.

I must have fallen asleep. Someone has come into the Castle. I get up and go into the hallway in search of the origin of the chimes. There's no one here. That's weird.

The chimes ring out again. I turn in their direction, towards the knighting circle where I was just sitting. How can that be? As I walk back into the room, the chimes ring out again. I look up at the full-sized mannequin of Connie, *Mother Earth*, hanging above the knighting pods. I feel my face contorting with bewilderment - why does the noise seem to be coming from her? And I remember the day I hung her there. I didn't install a sound mechanism in *or* around her.

"Why do you fret fine Sir?" an otherworldly voice asks.

Shaking my head back and forth as if it will actually clear the fog in my head, I think, wow this is one trippy dream. I swear that mannequin just talked.

Laughter.

I step back. It's laughing now?

"Why do you accept so easily My Michael speaking with you as real and not the voice of your Mother?" the melodious voice asks.

"Mom? It doesn't sound like you" I say.

"I think I sound *just* like me," she responds.

"Uhhhmmm, so, who - are - you?" I ask.

"I told you already silly boy. I am your Mother," she says with an etheric giggle.

"Are you Mother Earth? Connie?"

"Connie is your sister. I am her Mother as well. I ask you again, what is troubling you son?"

"I, uh, I hung that mannequin to represent Connie. I'm confused."

"Why do humans always think that what they do matters more than what they are? Confusion is as confusion does. Everything is in flux. The only thing on your earth that never changes is that change will always happen. Wrap your thoughts in one ball and when it breaks, so do you," she replied.

I feel like my head is expanding like a balloon. Maybe I just died again? If so, I think I liked the first time around better. Connie was comforting. This chick is trying to mess with my mind. Although her voice is far more enchanting than anything I've ever heard. It's like she is Michael, the Hierophant, and Master ERU rolled into one.

"Chick? I am no chick. And all will be known when your waiting is full. The pieces are moving on dimensions far beyond your current level of understanding and awareness. It's not over. Not everything is as it seems and nothing is as you plan. Now I ask you one last time, what troubles you my love?" she probes.

"Great! You too with the 'waiting being full thing.' I guess you know Master ERU? Okay, well, here it is: everything seems to be falling apart. And since you know I called you chick in my mind why don't you know everything else like Michael, he always knows what I am thinking" I ask.

"It is true I know everything about you, inside out and upside down. I am here to empower you. If you lend your own voice to your concerns in

My presence, then there I AM, and you will find a way to un-concern yourself. If I tell you what to do, you will never *do* it on your own," she replies.

I sighed and relented to the fact that this maybe some sort of angelic therapy counseling session.

I told her, "My staff is freaking crazy. They cat-fight and can't apply the lessons the Hierophant gave me to teach. I can't see how humanity is going to make a shift if my **own** people, Angel-Knights for God's sake, can't get it right. I feel like I am failing Michael and now..."

I break down and start sobbing.

"...and now she's not coming. I can't hear her anymore. What did I do wrong?" I plead.

An etheric sound swirls in the room. Tingles come up my left leg and then rush through my whole body.

"You mean my baby girl? She is very much here and at the same time very much on her way. There is no greater Love in the Universe than She and that LOVE cannot be stopped."

"*Your* baby girl? Who are you again?" I ask.

"Aaaada...my Ada," a faint whisper blows over me like a breeze. I feel my face being held in a tiny little pair of hands.

Cuil, a ann-thannath
Cuil na-happui
Cuil na-near
Cuil na-cuil
So n-glad
Cin'll happui dai
Buut near uns too
Ha's in I balant
Cin must dorth-true
Cin must dorth hunmble
Cheb- cin
Chin or- ar
Een thoubh cin stumble
Chase cin carin goodbye
Guin- cuil na I fullest
N- yourself
Cuil na-happui
Cuil na-near
Cuil na- something
I'I maki cin glad...

Everything went black.

My eyes flew open and I gasped for breath. What the hell just happened? As I pulled myself together I realized my sorrow was gone. Echoes of a sweet little voice delivering a rhythmic poem ran through my head. Whatever just happened breathed new life into me and gave me the strength to forge on.

Chapter Two

Angel and the Freemasons

January of 1991 was very cold. Due to energy within the charity and the weather outside I was feeling the chill deep down to my bones. Home wasn't so great either. Smack dab in the middle of massive snowy days, Linda found herself looking for a new job. Fairfield Farm Kitchens, a division of Marriot, had been sold. And all the employees had either hired by the new company or moved on within the corporation. Marriott built a new Distribution Center in Savage, Maryland, but it was too far away for Linda to travel. She loved working for Marriott and the people, so she was sad to leave. After a few months of job hunting, she was offered a position as the Benefits Administrator for Embassy Dairy in Charles Country, Maryland. Linda immediately fit in and had a new work family. Her boss, Andy Moss, was a great guy, and took an instant liking to the charity, believing in what the Good Knight Network was doing to protect and empower children.

One day while I was visiting Linda at work, Andy donated two thousand white T-shirts to the charity which were left over from a "Got Milk?" campaign several years earlier. Lady Bonnie Gabriel had a friend in the printing business who silkscreened the cover of *A Good Knight Story* on to the front of the T-shirts. We gave them away to any newly dubbed "Good Knight" kids during our programs, who promised to teach what they learned to others.

Meanwhile, I spent my days presenting safety programs at schools. It was very rewarding to see those little innocent eyes staring back at me, all the while knowing what I was about to tell them could save their lives; if not at least a lot of heartache.

But by and far though, most of my days were focused on designing and creating exhibits at East Wing Castle. It was such an amazing experience to have Michael show me a vision, and then to go to work almost unconsciously, finally stepping back to see what "we" created together. It often made me think of the movie Xanadu with Olivia Newton

John, where the muses came to Earth and inspired artists. I was definitely inspired…and then some!

I was really excited when Lady Bonnie told me we had received a donation of five hundred children's books from a local book store that was going out of business. This gave me a reason to create a bookshop at East Wing Castle, to house the donated books as well as our own "A Good Knight Story" for sale. I decorated the inside of the shop like a magical fairy land with glitter everywhere. And the kids loved it!

One weekend Linda and I stopped at East Wing to drop off my armor after a program, and she had a brilliant idea. "Instead of buying statues of fairies and knights to decorate the bookstore, why don't we make them out of ceramics ourselves and sell them too? That way the families who visit can buy something of meaning that is unique to us. And it can actually become more of a gift shop then."

"That's why they pay you the big bucks!" I teased her.

Michael told me Linda was onto something here; something even bigger than she realized at the time.

So, from that weekend on, my evenings were spent helping Linda clean greenware ceramic pieces for firing. We displayed her creations in the gift shop and among the scenes of the exhibits. The second part was actually brilliant, because people who visited the Castle to take the tour would fall in love with the statuary and then see similar pieces in the gift shop. Of course, everyone wanted them! We actually started taking orders on some pieces. Linda did all the work and split the profit 50/50 with the charity to help pay the bills. It was a win-win situation!

The pieces were beautiful because Linda really did have a flare and artist's touch with the painting, but Michael let me in on a little secret. While I was cleaning the green ware for her to have fired, my energy and DNA was going into the clay of each piece. When he told me that, I was like, "What?"

Michael went on to explain that, "Every human leaves a little DNA everywhere they go. Whether it's strands of hair dropping off heads or the sloughing off of skin cells."

That last part grossed me out to really think about.

He gave me a flash vision of my cleaning the green ware and some of my cells embedded themselves in the clay. Then he told me that the energy coming from my hands was vibrating into the clay and changing the matrix of each statue's energy. It was something that I immediately "knew" was correct. It was one of those times that others would label déjà vu. I knew it already from some time and space long ago.

The First Wednesday Club members were the first to clamber to buy Linda's pieces. They were her absolute best customers. I know they were energy sensitive so it proved the point that these pieces were fused with my DNA which was charged with Michael's energy. As soon as Linda would finish a piece, one of the members would be there to buy it. She refined her work and started specializing in Angels and Fairies, which led to us calling the shop "Angel Wings and Other Things."

The charity was now surviving on the sales of my book and Linda's crafts. This allowed me some more breathing room to tend to some work Michael had been setting up elsewhere.

Michael said that one of the most enlightened civic organizations in the world were the Masons, and that we should try to set up a meeting with their hierarchy in the hope of garnering support for our Child Empowerment campaign. Dr. Peterson had attended high school with one of the Grand Masters of Lodge Number One in Washington, D.C., so he touched base with his old friend, Tomas Milestone. Quicker than I could say "done" and Michael, in his armor (via my legs), was standing before a gathering of 33 Degree members, in their Scottish Rite Temple on Sixteenth Street NW. It was one of the most powerful structures I had ever entered. I could feel the wisdom of the ages when I walked through the front door. Talk about spirits, the building had more spirits hanging around than a graveyard!

My Grandfather Morris had been a Freemason, but he never talked to me about what they did during meetings. Michael told me that they had pretty much turned into a club that businessman join in order to pass out their contact cards to other members, but that their inner sanctum still held true to the belief of the transference of enlightenment and wisdom.

As I stood in the middle of their main ceremonial room, flanked on both sides by men seated in specially carved wooden throne-like chairs, Michael spoke through me. I never heard a word of what he said. I got the feeling that Archangel Michael was explaining to them his plan to protect and empower a generation of children that would serve as Sons of Light, illuminating the darkness that ignorance breeds in the world. When Michael was finished talking, I became aware again. He simply bowed my head and we walked out of the building. I guess it must have been the customary thing to do, I was clueless.

That evening I had merely been Michael's legs and the coat rack for his sacred armor. All I could tell was that he was speaking to some of the wisest men on the planet, way above my pay grade or understanding. And I felt so very small.

Chapter Three

Love is the Answer

Lesson Thirty:

Queen of Spades, received January 8ᵗʰ, 1991 Book of Wisdom, channeled from Hierophant:

In this lesson, I learned about love, and that energy generated by a human during their life can remain long after the person has died. This goes especially for the extremes in love, as well as in the energy of hatred. I also gained knowledge about hauntings and apparitions, and about how to free human spirits who are trapped between this world and the afterlife.

SEE APPENDIX FOR ENTIRE LESSON

While the channel of the lesson was still open I was shown a vision demonstrating that our current human understanding about demons is wrong:

We have been told that fallen Angels became demons on Earth after they rebelled against God in heaven. I was shown that all of God's creations were made out of love. When Angels were created, they were not given free will. Their purpose was only to serve the will of God. With that understanding how could they rebel? When humans evolved and gained self-awareness, we rose above the animals on the planet. That's when we acquired an immortal, celestial spirit and a reasoning mind with the power to co-create. With reasoning, God gave us the best and the worst gift possible, the gift of "Free Will." We were given the choice between selflessly co-creating within God's love or to destroying creation out of our selfishness. Angels were then sent to help guide humans to a reasonable balance of serving oneself, family and environment while also nurturing the light of our celestial spirit. After death, our spirit returns to the heavenly realms for eternity.

This is where it seems to get tricky for most humans to comprehend though.
I was shown Jesus saying, "In my father's house there are many mansions." Then

Archangel Michael explained that meant there are different "levels" to Heaven. And the spirit can only enter levels based on the understanding it has gained and the life the human has lived. A selfish greedy person who dreamed of living in a glorious castle on a fluffy white cloud overlooking the Ocean of Forever would normally wind up in the lower level living in a gloomy shack on a dismal swamp. A man who lived in a gloomy shack and selflessly helped his neighbors would wind up in the palace after death.

So, began the great Human Experiment. Choice became too much for many of the newly minted minds and many chose the path of selfishness and destruction, which darkened their spirits. The selfish actions of humans became so dark that there was no place for them in heaven. These dark spirits were trapped between this physical, third, dimension, and the spiritual, fourth and fifth, dimensions. Over time those dark sprits grew to number in the billions. Merging their energies together as powerful forces of evil, the religious hierarchy started giving them demonic names such as: Lucifer, Satan, Beelzebub, and Mephistopheles. So, it appeared with our ability to co-create, we humans created all the demonic darkness in the world through the choices we made. Michael said that there was never any rebellion in heaven because the angels never had the freedom of choice to rebel only the purpose of service. "Fallen Angels" are just a myth, passed down through the generations, covering up man's fall from grace.

I was then shown what Michael called the Demonic Agenda. Since the dark spirits, or demons, were now doomed to reside on Earth, they began influencing the minds of man. They used our human physical urges and emotions against us. Since they couldn't gain entrance to the heavenly realms, they didn't want other spirits to evolve either. Their agenda was to create such an imbalance in the Human Collective Consciousness of Earth, that man's selfishness would spread like a fungus destroying the environment and all human life on earth.

God saw this happening and offered help. To counter the effects of these Dark Spirits, Light Spirits who were already in Heaven, who wanted to improve their status were given a chance to return to this dimension as "Spirit Guides," helping the living negotiate through the darkness of life. If the human follows the guidance offered, both the human and the spirit guide can elevate in the afterlife. If the human turns evil or full of hatred and becomes a Dark Spirit, the Spirit Guide is bound to the Earth as well. It is a risk worth taking though.

To balance the Collective Consciousness and rescue the trapped Spirit Guides, Archangel Michael and his legion of 144,000 Warrior Angels of Light return to Earth every 500 years in the hope of merging with humans who are willing to help to round up as many Demons and Dark Spirits as possible during a given timeframe. The Dark Spirits are then transported to the Great Red Spot on the planet Jupiter to remain for all eternity.

After channeling this lesson, Angel Michael told me that I should start sending the lessons in the Book of Wisdom out to seekers who couldn't physically show up to become members of the First Wednesday Club. He said everyone needed the opportunity to gain the "Knowing" because his legion needs 144,000 humans of the light with a highly elevated mental understanding and enough courage to put it into action.

I immediately got that all too familiar feeling of impossibility and thought that this was going to be another hard task. It was once again my knee-jerk reaction, so, I took a deep breath, relaxed and asked, "Where am I to find these seekers?"

Of course, no response came.

That night I had a dream I was reading the Washington Post newspaper looking through the want ads. In the miscellaneous section I came upon an ad that read:

Attention Seekers: If you wish to change your life and become a more successful person, you must gain the forbidden secret knowing from the lost Book of Wisdom. Send $5.00 and a SASE on the 1st of every month for a monthly lesson to: Master Hierophant P.O. Box 00000

I **thought**, oh, okay Michael, I get it. Thanks for the answer.

So the next day when I arrived at the castle I sat down at my desk and typed out the ad as I remembered it from the dream. Then I started researching all the newspapers in major cities where I could place the ad. My first targets were Washington, D.C., Baltimore, Chicago, New York and Atlanta.

It was going to be interesting to see if anyone answered the Hierophant's ad.

In January, our meeting of the First Wednesday Club had to be pushed off a bit because of a snow storm. So, Dr. Peterson contacted everyone and asked them to write a short summary of what love meant to them and instructed them to have it prepared for the next class. Since we were all both students and teachers of one another everyone had to write a summary - even me. What people wrote, told us a lot about the person.

When we finally got together, we could have talked all night about everyone's perspective on love. Each was as different as the individual. Many people cried because the lesson showed a side of love that they had never thought of before. I felt compelled to share with them my quest and view of love as well.

Before I read them what I wrote, I told them that when I was growing up my philosophy was, "Never love more than you can afford to lose." My perspective probably was based on losing my father and my brothers taking everything I had that I held dear at such a young age.

I told them, "I am happy to say I am not as guarded now as I was then. Linda opened my heart to love again!" The whole room in unison let out an awwwww!

Then I shared my summary titled "My Quest to find God's Love."

Dear Fellow Students and Teachers:

This is my answer to our current assignment "What is Love?"

As is always the case, understanding changes with each and every day. This is my understanding today as I review the question. It may even change as I write and further ponder this deepest of human emotions we call, LOVE.

When Michael set me on this Divine Quest, he told me that it would eventually lead me to the "true meaning of love." I can't say, for all I have experienced so far in my 42 years, that I have found it.

Funny, as I just wrote that Michael whispered, "Well I guess you have to keep looking cowboy." I'm glad he has a sense of humor!

What I have actually found through the years is: love is costly! Real love demands sacrifice that can't be found in self-centeredness. I could give without loving, but I could never love without giving. Sacrificial love requires that I give what I value most: my heart, mind, soul, and all the strength of my being.

I found that real love does not always follow our natural way of thinking; it is not an impulse from feelings as most people believe.

In my interactions with others, I did find a lot of "like" in this world, but not a lot of "love." People seemed to confuse the two! I have found that most everyone who is looking for love doesn't know how to love, so how can he or she recognize love if they found it? I have found that the path to true love is through sacrifice. True love is finding the strength to set aside my ego and become a better person.

Unconditional love is the ultimate action of loving. It is firmly rooted in the heart which then sends signals to the brain and not the other way around - with the brain sending signals to the heart. Asking what is love is like is like asking: "What is running? What is breathing? What is seeing?" We all know what those actions are. We also know what love looks like and we know when we are just playing at it. In short, when we are loved, there is tangible proof. It's not an abstract thought or feeling it's concrete and evident. You see it, taste it, and feel it, but most of all you "Know" it. Love truly is the Creator's greatest gift to me.

On that note, I am often asked why I call God, "The Creator." My answer is simple. After spending a lifetime with the Archangel Michael consciousness buzzing in my mind, it was obvious to me that God created man in His image.

What is His "image?" It's the action of creation or ability to create. Therefore, man also has the ability to create or destroy. The first thing man created was a God in *man's* image. Then man built religions around that image. Now when someone says, "Let's pray to God." The first question asked is, "Who's God are we praying to?" Therein lies the problem! God is a metaphor for man. My "Creator" is a metaphor for Love.

As King Solomon wrote in his Book of Proverbs (27:19), "As water reflects a man's face back to him, so is the heart of one man to another." To me this means, when you are treated with love and in the presence of love, your heart feels that love and "Knows" that love. According to the Holy Books, our Creator commands us to love as in Deuteronomy (6:5), "And you shall love the Lord your God with all your heart, with all your soul, with all your strength and love your neighbor as yourself."

This precept leads us to voice that age-old question, "How can we be commanded to feel an emotion?" You can't! Either you feel it or you don't, right? In fact, within that quote, Archangel Michael tells me, we are not being ordered to feel a feeling in the abstract sense, rather, the command is for us to behave lovingly toward all things, since all things are part of our Creator. In that light, "And you shall love…." actually means, "You shall perform acts of love." As in the acts of love our Creator has shown toward us.

In closing, I feel love is just something that happens to us, but I am still on the Divine Quest to find the true meaning of LOVE. I know I will "Know" it, when I see *her*.

Chapter Four

Mail Order Teacher

I made it a habit to stop at the post office every two weeks to check what I called "The Hierophant's P. O. Box." There wasn't anything there the first time I went, but on my second trip I was surprised to find forty-seven people wrote back requesting lessons! Unfortunately, only sixteen had followed the instructions.

I was going to go ahead and send Lesson One out to all forty-seven, but Michael told me not to because people who didn't follow the instructions were just looking for another freebie. Even if I sent it, they wouldn't use or apply the lesson. He told me one of the greatest lessons for humanity was – energy output, gets energy back. It is actually a crucial ingredient for the cycle of life and growth. Those who give, receive and those who receive must give. Those with hands out all the time will receive of course, but it will be meaningless. This concept had to apply to seekers of wisdom, so that their investment in the lessons would compel them to at least apply the knowledge to their lives.

I replied back to him, "Well *I* didn't pay for the lessons."

Michael quickly quipped back at me, "*You* paid a price dearer than currency. You have paid with your life. You have paid with your devotion to my mission. You have paid with your selflessness. You have dedicated yourself to these lessons and followed instructions to practice. Although I don't tell you this too much, because I don't want it going to your head, you are quite the devoted vessel. If you don't do as told, you know too well the Hierophant will discontinue the lessons. You are the child with a parent who has held true to their word of removing privileges if work is not completed."

"Thank you, Michael, of course, you are right. I did pay, and of course I am a great vessel!" I said with laughter at the second part of my sentence.

Again, there was just silence.

"Okay, okay, I was joking of course. Where's your sense of humor?" I added.

I noticed on the second month, many of the same people wrote again, but this time followed my instructions. Before I knew it, I had over five hundred mail-order students asking for monthly lessons. It was becoming a nightmare keeping track of recording which student needed which lesson next.

Dr. Peterson helped me create files for each student, both the mail order ones and those we worked with in person. We organized the files according to start date and lesson progression. Some mail order students became impatient and wrote us demanding more than one lesson a month. We took the class very seriously, regardless of whether they "attended" via mail or in person, so we created an admission process with "requirements." The requirements included a list of questions that the individual needed to answer even before the application was reviewed.

Due to some of the, shall we say, unstable, letters we received, Michael said the mental state of these individuals needed to be evaluated prior to acceptance and sending out the lessons.

This of course felt a little overwhelming to me as I am not that type of administrator. I can tell you what to do (actually Michael can tell you what to do through me) but I don't excel at the paperwork stuff.

Dr. Peterson was on sabbatical while doing research for the University, so he agreed to organize everything and then train a few members of the First Wednesday Club who volunteered to help out.

Lo and behold, our "Enlightenment University" was off and running.

It was such a blessing to be able to hold the First Wednesday Club gatherings at the charity's East Wing Castle. Being in such a loving, magical place made people feel free, secure and open. Even the air felt accepting. The members found it easy to share their private inner most feelings that sometimes bubbled up from going through the lessons together.

As I channeled, taught and learned from month to month I was given a vision of what actually happens while we are "going through the lessons." In my mind's eye, I saw a spiral staircase. As I stood on step "1" and looked around the spiral, I noticed numbers on each stair. The numbers were on the top, bottom and sides of each step. When I looked directly above me I saw the number "1" again, just like the one I was standing on. When I stepped up and stood on "2," I looked up and directly above me was "2" as well. This continued all the way to "53" when I have made 1 full rotation around the pole. As I looked upward again the staircase seemed to continue to climb upward - to infinity and beyond – repeating the numbers.

Michael described the concept to me in his "language" for which there are no human words. My best translation of the concept would be "perpetual motion learning." The lessons, as a whole, build upon one another cyclically. But even deeper than that, each word builds mathematically upon each prior word, in a multi-dimensional sacred geometric grid. He went on to tell me that there would come a day when the details of my life and work would need to be written down. "Save your diaries and these journals you have been keeping since childhood. A special woman will come into your life and know how to arrange your words in a sacred manner. Like the True Love you seek, you will know this one when you see her."

"Really?" I thought. "Who the hell would want to read about my life?"

I took a deep breath and let his words sink in for a moment. Not to sound disrespectful, but when I channeled some of the lessons from the Hierophant I couldn't help but to think, "Wow that's a snoozer. How boring!" All of a sudden, I got a little twinge of nervousness about the pressure to actually do more with this information than just teach it. What if people didn't want it? What if it sucked? Who would be able to take it all and make it into what Michael and the Hierophant intended it to be? I knew that I did not have the gift for sacred writing as Michael described. "Was it someone in the group already?" I asked myself.

"Just let it go and stop harping on it." Michael snapped. "It is far off in the future and nothing can be done about it now anyway! Concentrate on NOW!"

Michael's statement startled me so much that I actually felt like I jumped out of my skin. I had to laugh out loud at my surprise when he snapped at me. Seriously? At this point in my life you'd think I would have learned that he "hears" everything I think!

Chapter Five

Let's Get Stoned

Lesson Thirty-One:

Jack of Spades, received February 8th, 1991 Book of Wisdom, channeled from Hierophant:

In this lesson, I learned all about the stones, rocks and crystals that make up the "Treasures of the Magi." I gained knowledge on their powers and how to use them to enhance the power within me. I was fascinated by the different effects that occurred when I put certain stones together. I also learned grid formations that really amped up the power of the stones.

SEE APPENDIX FOR ENTIRE LESSON

After channeling lesson thirty-one Michael saw all of the things I was practicing to program certain crystals. He immediately "upgraded" the information from the channeled lesson to give me a higher level of instruction. He said I was a natural with crystals. The lesson integrated so well with my vibration that he showed me some focused meditations he wanted me to teach to the class, if they were able to grasp the first level as I had.

Immediately he flashed visions and detailed instructions on how to drop programed crystals in negative places to change the energy of the area and how to divert weather situations with mental focus upon crystal grid lines. I was so excited to see crystals used this way and was hoping beyond hope that the members would "get it" the way I did so we all could do the exercises that Michael had shown me.

That month when I stood in front of the members of the First Wednesday Club gathering, I felt like a rock star. Literally! When I announced the lesson was on crystals, I swear the squealing screams coming from the class reminded me of working patrol at an Elvis concert. This time though, the squeals were coming from the men as well as the women. I was clueless that so many people loved rocks! If the announcement wasn't enough, I fully expected someone to pass out from excitement when I gifted everyone a water-clear quartz point. I thought, "This must be what the Ice Cream man feels like when he hands treats out to little kids from his truck!" After everyone settled down, I told them about all the different ways I practiced had with crystals since the lesson was given to me.

One member raised his hand, and while bouncing up and down in his seat like Horshak from *Welcome Back Kotter*, asked "Can we please try the one experiment you did? The one you called mind over matter?"

Michael told me this was an excellent night for exactly that purpose. He had me take everyone outside, with crystal in hand, to the field next to East Wing Castle. It was quite cold and a slight drizzle had begun to fall. Michael guided everyone through the progressive relaxation exercise. When all members were ready he said, "Now focus on the rain hitting your body. Focus harder! Now, keeping your eyes closed, look up and let the rain hit your face. Tell it to stop, NOW! Breathe…" He paused for a few moments and the rain suddenly stopped. He then said, "Now hold your crystal up to the sky and focus on the air getting colder. The colder it gets the warmer you will get. When you are nice and warm the rain will turn to snow. Breathe…"

It was beautiful to observe. From my vantage point I saw everyone breathing in unison and I swear I could see them all thinking too. They were truly one mind. Everyone was linked together. Michael did his magic!

Within five minutes the snow came down. We celebrated like kids waking up to a snow day off from school. After much laughter, amazement and hugs all around, we all went back inside the building to finish the class.

The members had no doubt they made it snow that night. The power of the mind is incredible.

Since the entire class grasped the lesson with such amazing acuity, Michael told me to give them the exercise I'd seen in the vision as their homework for the month.

I asked if anyone in the class would be traveling during the month leading up to the next gathering. Several people raised their hands. Two were going to Virginia together traveling through Skyline Drive. One was heading to North Carolina for a wedding and one was going to Pennsylvania. PERFECT! I gave them each four crystals. I told them once they reached their destination to leave the crystals somewhere they were guided to, and in a place where no one would remove them. I also told them to mark the location of each crystal on a map and to bring the map back to class.

We formally ended class with a circle meditation but no one wanted to go home. It was such a peaceful joyous feeling. Dr. Peterson went down the hall to the kitchen and made up a batch of hot cocoa. Then we all went back outside and had a snowball battle. It was so nice seeing everybody enjoying their new found "Knowing." They were like little kids again. And it made me happy.

Chapter Six

Treasure of the Magi Completed

Lesson Thirty-Two:

Ten of Spades, received March 8th, 1991 Book of Wisdom, channeled from Hierophant:

In this lesson, I learned the powers of the remaining minerals, rocks and crystals in the "Treasure of the Magi" collection and how to use them as well. Now came the hard part. We all had to start locating the minerals on the list!

SEE APPENDIX FOR ENTIRE LESSON

Standing before the class I announced, "This month's lesson is actually like a 'part two' of last month's…" and before I could get out the remainder of my sentence about it being a continuation on the topic of crystals, the room erupted! They were so excited to learn more about crystals. I thought, wow, who could have guessed there were so many secret rock hounds in the world?

Before we began the next lesson, I had the volunteer "crystal planters" tell about their experience during the month and about where they created their section of the crystal trail. I also had them share their map with us, showing where the crystal grid points were. Interestingly, when I connected all the dots where the crystals had been deposited on the map with a marker, it formed a straight line up the mountain range!

I wondered, how do "They" do that? Amazing!

One of the members was so excited to see that straight line and tell about her experience, she actually trembled while sharing it with us. She said almost as soon as she crossed the North Carolina line she felt the vibration of the crystals change. And when one wanted to be "planted" she heard the crystal guiding her. Each of the volunteers who took crystals on their journey had had similar experiences. Needless to say, the excitement of this new-found modality of working with crystals amped up the anticipation of this month's lesson.

As fate would have it, a little nuisance snow storm was heading our way by the end of the week. Michael said, "This is it. The perfect opportunity to try out the lay line of crystals."

I had the class set an intention to have the storm hit the mountain range and lose power so that when it made its way to us it would be little more than a dusting or would curve away from us to a less populated area.

Sure enough, the storm fizzled and all we saw were some picturesque flurries on that Friday afternoon.

Michael said, "This is just the beginning of a world-wide crystal grid you and your knights will lay over the next thirty-three years. In time, you will use this network of crystal grids to do far more important things than change the course of clouds. You will change the course of humanity."

Shuddering chills went up my spine.

I "Knew" this was getting real, or more real, as the case maybe.

After finishing the lesson that evening, Michael spoke to the gathering, "This completes your list of special magical stones. You should try to collect as many of them possible. Put them in small plastic bags and label them. Place your collection in a box and call it 'Treasure of the Magi.' There will be great power coming from the box as the elements come together. Be aware however, in this age of man many of these stones will be impossible to find. But, because of the power and presence of the mind, you, a true seeker of the 'Knowing,' possesses the power to create any missing stone. All you need to do is write the name of the missing stone in gold ink on the surface of a clear quartz crystal. Through thought and alchemy, the quartz will transform into the properties of the missing stone. This proxy stone can be used in any meditation or grid as you are called upon to use it. Now that you know about these stones, know there are Crystal Healing Practitioners in the metaphysical world who use them. They work with the properties of the stones and honor the Will of the Creator to help remove blocks, or ailments, and align the energy systems of the body. The powers won't work for everyone though. If that is the case, it could be Karma or God's Will to be so. Also know this, the power of these stones, in no way totally eliminates the need for a medical doctor. Modern medicine can override the Will of God sometimes, so I must recommend that the opinion of a personal doctor be sought after every medical issue. Consulting with a medical doctor can give you a better insight and understanding of the nature of the illnesses you wish to cure. Always use every resource at your disposal. We have come very far in the evolution of the medical sciences. Don't discount anything; use it on an as needed basis. That is the true Wisdom of the Magi. Be open-minded to everything!"

And, a reminder warning: Once again, these stones, as with all the powers you are attaining, can only be used for and with positive purpose. Remember, the power of the Ancient Magi Masters is still in everything; even the names of these stones have power. That is why the Hierophant felt that it was important for you to have this list of 'Power Stones.' Be respectful at all times."

Although the powers of the stones in the "Treasure of the Magi" collection cannot be measured by science, the mere fact that the Ancient Masters once held them sacred is what gives power to them today, especially in the hands of a truly empowered believer. It is the power and focus of the practitioner's mind that wields the "Powers of the Universe." Your powerful will and focused desire, through your mind and third eye gives strength to any form of matter you wish to empower. Some bits of matter, such as quartz crystal can help the practitioner amplify that projected desire and will echo thoughts for long periods of time.

Chapter Seven

The Devil's Work

March was a particularly sad month for the Good Knights. Dr. Peterson received a call from the Grand Master of the Masonic Lodge. Apparently, there was a murder in Virginia Beach of two students who attended the same elementary school as his niece. A high school student who was practicing satanic rituals was the suspect in custody. He went on to say that the entire population of fifteen hundred students at the school were terrified. His lodge had voted to immediately respond by sending the Blue Knight and his staff to the school to present the Good Knight Child Empowerment Network's "ABC's of Safety" program.

The talk Archangel Michael gave at the Masonic Lodge in DC several months earlier came flooding back to my mind. The dots were now beginning to connect for me.

A few days after receiving the call, Dr. Peterson, Lady Bonnie, Linda and I found ourselves driving to Virginia Beach. Instead of stopping at the hotel to check-in, Michael told me to keep driving and go straight to Bird-Neck Elementary School.

When we walked through the doors it was like piercing a thick energy veil. The three of us looked at each other quizzically as we walked into this surreal environment. The air was charged with dark energy. Even the hairs on Linda's forearms and neck were standing up.

Everyone was somber. The students wouldn't look us in the eyes. When a stray glance did happen our way, it felt as if we were staring into the eyes of zombies.

When we got to the Office, the police investigators and Administration were there together. They wanted to know more about our program and about what topics we would teach. The investigator in me of course wanted to know more details about the case. After walking them through the core of our program one of the investigators, Detective Bannon, said, "Chief Oaken would like to brief you on the specifics of the case down at the station, but I don't think the ladies should attend." Linda and Bonnie were all too happy not to learn the gory details, plus they were tired from the drive and wanted to go to the hotel. Detective Bannon said he would drive me to the station and then drop me off at the hotel afterwards, so the ladies could go on their own way. Linda was a little unnerved by the weird energy in the school, but Michael assured me everything was fine. I told them to go and have a drink in the hotel bar and I would join them soon. This appealed to Linda and Bonnie, so off they went.

On the way to the station Detective Bannon told me that the suspect, sixteen-year-old Shea McCellan, had a devil fixation. He believed that Satan wanted him to sacrifice "lifeforms" to prove his devotion. Shea's parents and neighbors confirmed Shea's strange behavior and the progression of his rituals. They told the police he first started by killing birds. When the neighbor who lived behind the MCellans found a circle of twelve dead black birds next to a shed in his yard, Shea said he did it to keep them away from his mother's garden. But then, dead cats were being found in the woods around the neighborhood. One neighbor even called 911 after seeing Shea carrying a crate of cats into the woods. Since it wasn't an emergency, the police came the next day to take the report. Upon search of the woods they found a circle of rocks with the dirt inside soaked with blood. No sign of the crate or cats. Unfortunately, there was no proof that Shea did anything other than being seen carrying a crate of cats. The case was of low priority so no one ever took a blood and dirt sample. Soon after, family dogs in the community went missing. Shea's mother reported that she found clothes with blood and fur on them so she confronted him. Shea reasoned away the red flag that popped up in her mind by saying he and a friend went hunting and the friend's dad showed them how to skin and clean the animals.

I shook my head while listening to all of this and thought, "There were signs everywhere for those who wanted to see." Unfortunately, when it comes to parents, it is tough enough to think your child could do anything so macabre, but its even more difficult to report it. By the way, this type of psychological turmoil is the very thing which keeps many criminals free to do harm.

In this situation however, the psychosis elevated. Shea wasn't getting the same kill-thrill with animals. This time, children were offered up to the "Darkness."

Once at the station, I met Chief Oaken.

"Detective Jagen, a pleasure!" he said while shaking my hand.

"I'm retired from the force Sir, but in a sense, once a detective always a detective," I replied.

"Yes, I am aware of that," he said. "And exactly why I asked Detective

Bannon to bring you down here. Because there really is no explaining what you will see on the video. We could've told you what Shea said, but it's more than that, as you will soon see." Oaken went on, "During interrogation, Shea admitted to luring seven-year-old Tommy Whiteling and nine-year-old Dennis Howel into the woods. It wasn't what he said but more how he said it. It gave all of us the creeps. It didn't feel like a teenager sitting there. It felt like evil."

Detective Bannon led the way to a viewing room. He put in the VHS tape and on the TV screen popped the image of "the red-headed devil lover" - the nickname Michael whispered in my ear.

"It was a cake walk. All I had to do was promise to show them a hunting knife an old Indian gave me," he said while flippantly using both hands to make the "quotes'" signs in the air. "I just told them the old Indian put a curse on it so I could only let one other person at a time see it. Idiots! I stood Tommy next to the tree," he said leaning forward for emphasis and throwing his hands up in the air, "he didn't even question me about it. Then I took Dennis to the clearing. I chanted the words Master told me to and held the knife up high for Master to bless it. Those idiots didn't think nothing of it 'cause they thought it was Indian words. They never knew what hit 'em," he said, as he smiled the most sinister smile I ever saw. Then, while pointing at the camera lens and laughing, he announced, "Master wants you to know the bloodletting from slittin' their throats is a win for the Darkness…Michael. You know. You know who is coming!" Looking at the monitor I saw the face of evil. After all the years I'd been on the police force, of the things I saw, this, THIS sent shivers down my spine.

This boy was an instrument of the darkness. Led astray yes, but of his own free will was acting out his dark beliefs.

The video ended and we all just sat there frozen like mannequins.

Chief Oaken broke the silence, "Now you know why I wanted you to see it. We are dealing with more than a murder here, I believe."

I stood up and shook his hand and nodded. There really wasn't much more anyone could say. He was right, there was more here than a murder.

Detective Bannon dropped me off at the hotel and I joined the ladies in the lounge for a drink. After what I just seen, it was a welcome distraction.

The next day before the program, we met with more school officials and briefed them on the day's programs. The school was from Pre-K to Eighth grade so we were planning to split the classes and do two presentations. I felt that we should work with the older kids first, as they might not take the program as seriously as the younger children. The staff agreed but there was a special request from the teachers of the two slain boys. They wanted to know if the Blue Knight would come to their classrooms to meet with their students first before the program. I thought that was a great idea as they were more directly affected than the rest of the children.

Lady Linda helped me strap on the armor, while Lady Bonnie and Dr. Peterson went to the classroom where the teachers had combined the entire second grade so they could read *A Good Knight Story* to the kids. When I came in, I could tell the kids were uplifted. I told them that I was sorry that the bad man hurt their friends, but our job now was to make sure we protect other kids from being hurt.

We gave each child *A Good Knight Story* book and answered questions. Of course, a lot of the kids wanted to know was how the bad man killed their friends. I told them, "What's more important to know than that, is *how* Dennis and Tommy were tricked into the woods. He used the 'B-Trick.' He bribed them with the promise of showing them his new knife. There are ten tricks in all that bad people use to hurt children. Just like the Jester did in the *Good Knight Story,* remember?"

Then Archangel Michael came through to test them, "What trick did he use?"

One little boy named Michael yelled out, "The B-trick Bribes!"

"That's correct! Great job Sir Michael! I see you becoming a protector of all children." Addressing the entire second grade Angel Michael asked "Now, do you want to learn the more about the rest of the tricks?"

The entire classroom erupted with excited yeses!

I led the second-grade class into the auditorium where the sixth, seventh, and eighth grade classes were already seated.

Glancing around the auditorium, Michael told me it was going to be a rough crowd with a lot of showoffs and hecklers. However, that piece of information wasn't the least bit of preparation for what awaited me.

When I took the stage, it started with someone yelling out "Birdman!" Then someone else yelled, "No it's Kentucky fried Chicken Man!" Then the whole room erupted into hilarious laughter. Even the teachers were laughing.

I noticed Dr. Peterson and Lady Bonnie going over to the teachers to get them to calm the kids down, but the place was totally out of control. Then I saw Linda sitting at a table where she planned to fill out the certificates of knighthood. Her eyes were like saucers filled with tears, ready to cry. I could tell she felt bad for me. I felt like I was being tarred and feathered by the crowd, just like the Blue Knight was in *"A Good Knight Story."* The only ones who weren't laughing were the second graders; they started crying at seeing the Blue Knight being humiliated.

I drew on the strength of those children for courage.

To them I was a champion, come to save children, but to the rest of the audience I was a foolish clown. I held up my hand to calm the room and the laughter just increased, but I stood my ground.

Michael said, "Let's go."

I walked off the stage and a few seconds later the laughter stopped, but everyone was still talking. In the area behind the curtain Michael had me pick up two small wooden chairs, then return to the stage. When I did, while holding the two small wooden chairs, Michael said through me to the audience in a loud commanding voice, "I didn't come here for you!"

The room fell silent.

The energy shifted. It was palpable even to those who are usually obtuse. Every eye was transfixed on the Angel in Blue armor who took control of the room. His presence was overwhelming.

Michael had me place one chair on my right, then one on my left as he continued, "I came for Sir Dennis who is sitting here," pointing to the right chair, "and Sir Tommy" pointing to the chair on my left. Michael went on, "The rest of you can go back to your classrooms now. I just wanted you to see me apologize to Dennis and Tommy for my arrival here being too late. If I had come a month ago, they would both still be alive. You see, I'm just a messenger sent to teach children the tricks that bad people use to bully, kidnap, abuse or murder them. I call it the "ABC's of Safety." A strange hush came over the room as all those bodies exhaled at once. It sounded like the earth took a breath.

Michael asked, "Does anyone know what trick Shea McCellan used to murder your schoolmates?" Everyone in the audience seemed stunned and just looked at one another as if to say, "Who is this guy? A few seconds earlier we were laughing this fool off the stage and now he's touching us in places we didn't know existed."

The second grader, little Michael's hand shot up quickly.

I called him up on stage while saying, "Now that's a brave knight! Out of all the smart kids sitting in this auditorium there are only three who know what trick the devil used on that dark day." I stood little Michael between the two small chairs.

Archangel Michael asked in the microphone, "And who are those three kids?" The Blue Knight then handed little Michael the microphone and began walking to the edge of the stage. Just before he stepped off the six-foot high stage the great Angel said, "Dennis, Tommy" and when he hit the ground with chains and armor plate jingling, he pointed up at the child on the stage he added, "And little Michael here."

Turning to the little boy standing tall between the two empty, wooden chairs the Blue Knight said, "What trick was used to kidnaped your friends Michael?"

I felt Angel Michael's confidence, but oh man, was I praying this child would remember.

My memory is etched with the look in that little boy's eyes when he replied, "The devil used the B-trick, bribes! Shea promised to show Tommy and Dennis his new knife. They followed him into the woods, and then he killed them with it."

When I turned to face the audience, there wasn't a dry eye in the house. I looked back at little Michael who was beaming with pride. For the rest of the program those sixth, seventh and eighth graders hung on every word we said with that same pride. They were told that if they promised to teach the "ABC's of Safety" to all the other little kids then bad people couldn't trick them anymore.

When I was ready to flame the sword and start the knighting ceremony, I called little Michael back on stage to help me. Being my lifesaver that day, he certainly earned the honor. As the flame reached the tip of the long sword I could see in the attentive eyes of every student, they got the message.

After the assembly, many teachers and students came forward to apologize to me for the rude behavior of the audience.

I said, "Everything was as it should be, if they didn't laugh, I wouldn't have been forced to call Tommy and Dennis' spirits to the stage to strike the chord inside of them. This will be a day none of us will ever forget. Something special happened here today."

The second assembly for Pre-K through fifth grade was a lot easier. Those ages typically don't tarnish from peer pressure like the middle schoolers. This group was in wide-eyed wonder and hadn't lost their childhood innocence yet. Michael and I gave them a magical ride through the "ABC's of Safety." In their minds, they were in Eagleton helping the Blue Knight save the children. They especially loved when it was time to flame the sword of Tenacity. When the fire rose up the blade the entire audience gasped with a whooshing sound.

After I knighted all the children I bid them adieu and I went behind the curtain to remove the armor. Linda came back to help unbuckle me and pack up my gear as the auditorium quickly emptied.

I walked back on stage to retrieve those two chairs Michael carried out so I could put them away. When I looked up I had noticed a well-dressed man with a neatly trimmed white beard, wearing a gray trench coat and a camera around his neck. I had noticed him earlier at both programs that day. Each time I saw him he was taking notes or pictures of the assemblies. He glanced my way but then turned around and left. While loading our bags in the car he came out of nowhere and approached us.

He said, "Mr. Jagen, uh, I mean, Sir Blue Knight! My name is Fred. I was sent as an observer and historian of sorts from the Masons. I was a previous Grand Master of a local Masonic Lodge so our brothers from DC contacted me to come here to the event today." He paused and took a deep breath that said, went "What I witnessed today was truly humbling. I really thought when you left that stage you weren't coming back. And then when you did, well…I witnessed the biggest transformation of illumination I have ever seen in my life. It was awe inspiring. When you came back through those curtains, I had to do a double take, you were not the same person that walked off that stage."

I replied, "If Shea McCellan could channel Satan and the Sons of Darkness to do his bidding, it's only fair that I be permitted to channel Archangel Michael to champion the Children of the Light."

Fred said, "That is only fair, I agree, But one question. How do you know what to say when you're on stage? I watched both programs and they were completely different. No script, but yet you covered the concepts perfectly."

I replied, "It's a long, crazy sounding story that I have been journaling for years. I'm told someone will come around one day who can put it all together into a book. Just know for now that all I do is open my mouth sometimes and what needs to be said comes out."

"I sure hope I'm still around to read it. What you did today blew me away," Fred said.

I added, "Today I've shown that if we are going to win the battle against the darkness that haunts this area, it can only come through the light of truth. The darkness took those children, and only the light could bring them back."

"I bet you have some stories to tell. I would love to learn more," while winking he said, "just in case I'm not around to read that book. Would you and your knights honor me by coming to dinner tonight at my house so we could talk more?"

After looking at Linda and the ladies and seeing them nodding yes, I replied, "It would indeed be our honor."

Fred gave us his address and directions and we agreed upon dinner at 6pm. We went back to the hotel to get cleaned up and rest for a bit. After being in the armor, a nice hot shower felt like heaven.

Later that evening, we all gathered at Fred's beautiful home on the ocean. He began by serving us cocktails on the beach. As we sat there in the sand chairs, listening to the surf, I thought how different Virginia Beach felt compared to our beaches in Maryland. Regardless of the difference, It was nice to relax by the water after the accomplishments of the day.

During dinner, I basically told Fred my life story and about how Angel Michael guided me to the spirit of a Magi from Atlantis, who was currently dictating fifty-three lessons from the ancient Book of Wisdom.

Linda kept trying to get me to shut up about the spiritual stuff and just talk small talk. Typically, this is her job. Keeping me grounded about Michael and my mission. I know it and she knows it, and it is a little game we play, until it gets real and Michael says, no more screwing around, do what you have to do and say what you have to say. Remember, Linda is not into metaphysical stuff. Kind of ironic, isn't it? Me who channels an angel, and not just *any* angel, lays his head on a pillow at night next to a woman who is elemental fairy folk.

This time, however, all of my words were being absorbed like water droplets into a sponge. It turns out Fred was a little bit more than just an observer sent by the Masons.

His full name was Dr. Fredrick Lord, and he was a retired Unitarian Minister and Professor of Angelology.

Seriously I wondered again - how do they do that?

He said, "I study angels and demons. It is my business. One of the main reasons why I settled in the Virginia Beach/Hampton Roads area was because there were many dark cults concentrated in this energy grid."

I said, "I respect everyone's right to believe what they want as far as religion or practice, even the Satanist, but when their 'deity' tells them to harm someone, they must be stopped." I explained, "Michael told me Angels were created by God and demons were created by humans."

He said, "That's not how the Bible reads."

I said, "I'm sure there is a lot of truth missing from the Bible. Remember the Bible was inspired by God but written by many scribes over hundreds of years. As in any writing its meaning is left up to the interpretation of the reader or minister, or translator as in the case of the Bible. There are threads of truth in all of the holy books and there are common threads between them as well. They are the same stories told from different perspectives or with different intent, to control the believers of that doctrine. The one common point the Bible and all other holy books talk about is a third book or testament being written before the end of days which will be based on the Book of Life."

Dr. Lord looked confused and changed the subject saying, "How do you know you're not being guided by Jesus, instead of Michael?"

I said, "Jesus was a Jewish Rabbi who studied the Kabbalah Illuminati which is all about working with God's angelic hosts. When Jesus called on protection he asked his Father to send Angel Michael. I believe the Father and Son sent Michael to earth on a mission. Along the way, Michael found this poor kid that he felt he could groom into a fitting pair of legs and a coat rack for his armor."

I wasn't sure if I was making my understanding known. He said he was following me and understood. I knew I was treading in areas that were beyond his belief system, but he wanted to know what made me tick so I jumped in with both feet.

I continued, "My experience and understanding is that God is much more than the old man in the sky we pray to, or curse if we don't get our way. He/She is an electro-magnetic energy consciousness that can't be described in human words. God is the stuff our souls are made of. Through me, he has my soul manifest in Michael's armor serving his one true charge, His children. When I was guided to create, and then to wear the armor something happens to me. Michael seems to be able to take better control and get more done. He told me that I could only wear his armor for seven years, and then I would have to create my own armor and wear it for seven years. Then I would spend another seven years in white robes delivering the Book of Wisdom to seekers of the "Knowing" in order to finish a twenty-one-year cycle. Therefore by 2014 we will be done with His Divine Quest."

Dr. Lord sat back in his chair and just stared at me saying, "You have such a great story to tell. I hope someday you write a book about your adventures with Angel Michael. I think it would help open people's eyes to the way they can become closer to the powers that exists around them."

I said, "How in the world could I ever explain what you saw today at the school, let alone all the other things that have happened?"

Dr. Peterson, Lady Bonnie and my wife Linda continued to talk about things they had seen and experienced over the years. I ended the evening by telling everyone how I could see the way in which Michael and the Hierophant's Book of Wisdom lessons were fitting into everything we were doing. It was like OJT, On the Job Training, on steroids. "If it weren't for me being able to feel the emotions of those children and bring them to tears, today would have been a disaster for the Light and another victory for the Darkness. The day Shea McCellan murdered those two little boys the energy of Satan was served; today the energy of the Creator was served.

Chapter Eight

The Price of Doing Business

Lesson Thirty-Three:

Nine of Spades, received April 8th, 1991 Book of Wisdom, channeled from Hierophant:

In this lesson, I learned about Precognition, which is the direct knowledge or perception of the future, obtained through extrasensory means. I was given several tests to help elevate my mental awareness.

SEE APPENDIX FOR ENTIRE LESSON

The First Wednesday Club members were really cooking now. After thirty-two lessons under their belts, they could all see how much their mental powers were growing for those who really practiced and were there "for the right reasons."

It was easy to tell which members were coming for the lessons and which members were just coming for the good feeling they received by being at the East Wing Castle. And as is the case with many groups, there were some with underlying motives that were of less than pure in their intent. Every month, Dr. Peterson, or Sir Gregory, as he was now known, and I both stressed how important it was that everyone use the month to practice each lesson and review prior ones as well. We emphasized that was the only way the power within would grow.

There were budding relationships happening and and even flirting happening during class. I could see the auras of individuals change from month to month. Once there was a male across the room and a female on the opposite side. In the air above the class there was a pink and green arc-like rainbow. Each month the two would find themselves closer and closer together. Then eventually they started sitting next to each other. A case of kismet you ask? Maybe!

Whenever I would feel the impression of someone attending class for reasons other than learning, Michael would always remind me: "That's the price of doing business. Each one represents a portion of society that will benefit if that human vessel wakes up and elevates. They will either get it or leave. Don't waste your time in judgement over it."

I did as Michael suggested and shrugged it off and moved on. I opened this month's gathering by telling everyone the lesson would incorporate simple tests to gauge their abilities to remote view and to project energy. This would help them determine a base line of their powers and possibly which natural gifts they were born with in their "Psychic Toolbox."

I instructed them to pick a partner. Dr. Peterson handed out a deck of Zener cards, paper and pencil to each "team." The Zener cards had designs on them; a circle, a square, a plus sign, wavy lines, and a star. I told them while Sir Gregory was handing out the decks to please decide who was going to be the receiver and who was going to be the sender. I explained, "The sender will pick a card and mentally project the image of the chosen card to their partner who would try to receive that image. You will create a tally sheet on your paper to record the number of correct and incorrect visions. The members were so excited to try this, they reminded me of little kids bouncing in their chairs.

Once they started, there were some struggles and frustration. I reminded them to breathe, let go, and above all not to force something to happen. Michael suggested I get some essential oils out of my briefcase to use with those who were frustrated. Remarkably it worked like a charm for all except one, who refused to try it.

After each team member took their turn projecting and receiving, we asked for volunteers to tell us how many correct visions they received. We had a wide variety of answers for a wide variety of reasons. I found it fascinating that some really gifted tapped in individuals struggled while others excelled.

Now mind you, part of the success was due to the ability of the sender, not just to the gifts of the receiver.

I walked to the chalkboard and lifted the cloth I had pinned to the wall. It was covering the rating chart below for the card test. Immediately upon doing so I felt a deep seeded hurt coming from someone in the room. I said nothing, just looked around. Then I said, "Look at the chart and compare your score. Don't take anything too seriously, whether you did very well this time or you didn't."

Number correct	Rating
1– 5	Laws of Chance
6– 7	Possible Ability
8–14	Workable Ability
15–25	Definite Ability

Michael had me scan the room as the members reviewed the chart and were chatting amongst themselves.

He said, "Watch well. A psychological experiment is unfolding. We will gather great information into the minds of mankind tonight."

I took a deep breath and opened my senses even further. I could actually sense egos flaring. Ones that felt defeated and ones that were over inflating. It was such an amazing thing to experience. Michael was right.

One member's aura was sparking red flares. She had historically tried too hard in class. I thought maybe once again, she was beating herself up about not getting very many correct answers. Earlier, I had seen her struggling while she was interacting with her partner. She was also someone known for "jockeying for position," or trying to be someone else in the group other than who she was.

After just about everyone else in class shared their response tally, she shot up out of her chair with purse and notebook in hand and started to leave.

Michael interrupted her strides towards the door by saying, "Where is your ego having you run my child?"

"I am not running anywhere and I am **NOT** your **child!**" She yelled.

A very silent but yet very heard mental "uh oh" shot through everyone's mind in the group. It was as if faint whispers carrying hushed voices were blowing through all our minds like a breeze.

Here we go I thought. The ball is on your court Michael. What's next? I smell a lesson coming on and it isn't one that I channeled and typed from the Hierophant.

Before Michael could even speak through me, Lady Katrina turned and faced me with tears rolling down her cheeks. "Why can't I ever do as good as everyone else? What makes them so much better than me? Why can't I be like Sherry? She is so perfect!" she barked.

"Why would you want to be anyone else other than your perfect self?" Michael asked.

"I'm, not perfect. Everything I have ever done, EVERYTHING, has been wrong. You, you are so controlling and always telling me what to do and that I am never good enough!" she cried out.

I thought, "What the H, E double hockey sticks is she talking about?"

Her screaming sent shock waves of energy through the group. I could see the more sensitive empaths struggling and taking on her pain. One younger male member of the group, Ken, who was typically quiet and reserved stood up. "Katrina, I am so sorry you are feeling the way you do. Can you do something for me? Please take a breath. From my point of view, as an observer, it appears you are projecting on Sir Edward maybe some latent childhood issues with your father? I think if you come sit back down, the group could help you with a different perspective of whatever is bubbling up right now. It feels as if you are in crisis mode and I know we would all like to help."

Katrina's energy immediately shifted and she started back towards her chair to sit down.

I thought wow, "Who is this guy?"

Michael said, "Just watch…and learn."

And so, I did. I watched as the entire group seemingly hugged Katrina with their auras of compassionate love and energy. I saw her enveloped in a bubble of healing as each member took their turn to speak or share a tidbit of love.

After it was said and done, Katrina apologized to me and the group. "I am so sorry." She continued by revealing the root of her pain, "I was so severely beaten as a young child by a demonic alcoholic step-father. There was literally nothing I could do to please him. Nothing. If I did it my way, I got beat. If I did it the way he told me, it was still not good enough, I got beat. I've been struggling with PTSD since I was thirty-four. It surfaced when I was with my fiancée and he started acting like my step-dad. All these memories would flood back in from when I was little and I started having panic attacks. The doctors are treating me with medicine but it hasn't helped. When I saw that chart, it reminded me of a time when my step-dad compared me to my perfect half-sister and when my numbers weren't like hers he stripped me down and beat me while I was naked in front of my mother and sister. And no one came to my rescue."

She broke down and sobbed for 7 minutes straight. Everyone in the room was holding a sacred space for her. I could see their chakras all lit up like a Christmas tree. The energy was grounding her and the room. Compassion and healing were washing over her.

When her convulsive sobs stopped. All went still. The air in the room was lighter. She looked up and smiled. Her eyes sparkled as she spoke, "It's gone! I'm free. I don't feel its presence anymore."

Ken, who I later found out had a double major in theology and clinical psychology, asked, "What presence?"

Katrina responded, "Failure."

"Well," I silently said to Michael, "that was unexpected."

"Not for me," he responded.

We ended the evening with a little bit of light conversation about practicing the lesson for the month. We wanted to keep Katrina's healing held in a sacred space. We felt further talk would not have us achieve that goal. Ken suggested a prayer and Michael told me to get everyone into a circle and hold hands. Left palm up to receive energy with right palm down to give.

I asked, "Ken, do you have a prayer in mind?"

"Yes, the Serenity Prayer," he said.

We bowed our hands and began:

*"**God grant me the serenity**
to accept the things I cannot change;
courage to change the things I can;
and wisdom to know the difference.*

Chapter Nine

Remote Viewing

Lesson Thirty-Four:

Eight of Spades, received May 8th, 1991 Book of Wisdom, channeled from Hierophant:

In this lesson, we revisited Psychogenesis and then I moved on to be tested on Telepathy, the communication of thought or ideas by means other than the known senses. I also gained insight in Remote Viewing, the practice of seeking impressions about a distant or unseen target using extrasensory perception or "sensing with the mind."

SEE APPENDIX FOR ENTIRE LESSON

It was another great class; the club members were really getting the hang of using their special powers. We all discussed our practice throughout the month and I told the class that these tests would become a great reference and aid in the future. Developing these skill sets personally helped me as a private investigator to find lost or missing items as well as the location of people of interest.

I also told the class that it was a good idea to find other individuals who had developed their skill sets outside our group. Utilizing the projecting energy skill, they could draw people to themselves. And, working with individuals stronger than themselves would elevate their skills just by being connected.

I said, "Ask questions of the others you meet so that together you may expand the 'Knowing' that is developing in each of you. This is very important. Ask how they feel during a display of their ability, and be sure to express your feelings and sensations with them. Since many of us sense our abilities in different ways, learn how others perceive the same abilities. It is this type of exchange that helps us all grow. And journal everything you do as well as the answers you get.

At the end of class Ken raised his hand to address the elephant in the room, or better yet, the elephant that wasn't in the room. "Where is Katrina? Do you know? he asked. "We were all looking forward to hearing how her life has been after the beautiful release she had last month."

Dr. Peterson and I looked and each other for the answer and we both shrugged our shoulders and shook our head "no" to Ken.

Sadly, Katrina never showed up to class or even called to let us know how she was doing.

There was an unspoken worry for her, but more importantly there was the knowing that it was also the end of the line for her in regards to the class. She missed a lesson. She was done.

The next day, Dr. Peterson called me. He said when he got into work that morning there was a message on his answering machine. It was from Katrina. She apologized for not letting him know sooner, but she couldn't bring herself to come back anymore. She admitted to feeling great when class was over and feeling relief. But then over the course in the coming days and weeks of that month, her thoughts were chattering to her. Peterson held the phone next to the answering machine so I could hear some of it.

"You both threw me under the bus. Everyone was examining me. I can't possibly come back to class. I feel too exposed. My therapist said it isn't positive for me to ride that kind of roller coaster. Goodbye," she said.

"Goodbye indeed," Michael said. "And so goes most of humanity. They cannot control their thoughts which is sad. But even more heartbreaking is knowing that they don't really want to. They are comfortably numb-brained, living in their illusion and pain."

Chapter Ten

Walking Dead of Atlantis

Lesson Thirty-Five:

Seven of Spades, received June 8, 1991 Book of Wisdom, channeled from Hierophant:

In this lesson, I learned about how people view the world around them in different ways, and about why it was so important for me to wear the blue and gold armor at this stage in my life. I also gained more insight on the story of Atlantis and the Walking Dead that still roam the Earth today.

SEE INDEX FOR ENTIRE LESSON

I saw this lesson as an omen that things were about to change. The East Wing Castle was an enchanting place, but Michael didn't feel we were reaching the masses and that we needed to do more. Lady Bonnie and I were the only Good Knights doing programs at schools and knighting the children. Archangel Michael was all about knighting the children. I could feel the empowerment of the child and the angel whenever we leveled a sword to a shoulder. I knew that something was up and I didn't have to wait long to find out what.

During my meditation the next morning, Michael had me tap into another Archangel, Metatron, a laser focused, bull-like, strong energy that gets jobs done. A builder. He was to help guide me while creating sets at East Wing Castle.

All the week he was by my side. I felt like I was on intravenous caffeine. I had so much energy I literally didn't stop each day until Metatron was satisfied with the work I had completed.

At the end of the week as I was decorating a set, Sir Gregory, walked in. He worked at the Maryland Renaissance Festival for six weekends every summer portraying Gregory the Great, a court entertainer and teller of fortunes. I noticed that the Metatron's consciousness suddenly was becoming more and more interested in Sir Gregory. I felt him leave me and go to Gregory.

Immediately I got the impression that Metatron was not satisfied with the work I was doing inside a building. And I saw him reviewing the vibration of Sir Gregory.

"He's attracted to the outdoors," Michael said. "The fake dirt, plastic flowers and statues don't resonate with his vibration."

I laughed out loud thinking, "What a 60's hippy-dippy type of Angel he must be."

I was then given a vision of Metatron building structures on a large property. He wanted real trees, real dirt, flowers, plants, rain, snow, sunshine, waterfalls and rocks to climb on. Well you get the picture.

Metatron rushed back to me with a whoosh. He whispered something about building a special kingdom to protect "The Child of Victory." Then added, "Dr. Peterson has the key to where you need to go. Michael assigned me to him, but I'll report back."

I just sat there for a moment to let all this sink in. Okay, so now I am having Angels report to *me?*

Michael said, "Yes, and no. They are really reporting to me. But you will start to have to work with them all."

"All?" I asked. "What do you mean by all?"

"Well, let's just say for now, there are 144 aspects of God and they are the angelic battalion leaders. They are all under my, our, command," he responded.

The new information put my entire biological system on overload. My stomach immediately churned and I heard it begin gurgling. Then I re-heard what Michael had said.

As my panic rose I asked, "There will be 144 energies like you talking to me? And by the way, I thought there were only 7 archangels? And I thought you were only seeking twelve others to help bring down the archangel commanders? And why haven't you told me this before?"

"First of all, everything is plastic. Everything is dependent on the wild card humanity carries called 'free will' Second of all, I have you on a need to know basis, because things change so rapidly. At a minimum, yes, there will be 144 angels. That is the goal. Who told you there were only seven; was it part of your religious training by men who twisted the word of God to fit their power-hungry needs? And twelve is the minimum number of commanders." Michael sternly said.

I thought, "I must be going crazy."

Obviously, he heard me because the response was, "Knock it off. You have been victorious through far worse with just me by your side. The reinforcements are on their way now. It's all going to work out. Don't sweat the small stuff and by the way…it's all small stuff."

(Note from the author—you will read in book three of the Diary of an Angel Knight series, that in early 1996 a book was published with an extremely similar statement above. When I read Sir Edward's memoirs with that last line I questioned him, "You do know about that book don't you?" He said, "Yes. When I said something to Michael about it and how the money made from it could've helped the charity, he said, "Well, it's wisdom. Wisdom has a life energy force and if you don't do something with the wisdom you receive, someone else will."")

Meanwhile, back at the ranch…

Metatron's consciousness was working with Dr. Peterson. He was trying to get through to Peterson to encourage an impulse to ask the Maryland Renaissance Festival management if they would donate a small piece of land on the festival grounds so that the charity could build a Good Knight Castle outpost. Michael told me that it not only was the perfect atmosphere for Metatron to build, it was exactly what we needed to reach more children. Hundreds of kids would come to that festival every year with not a lot to do except ride the ponies.

Dr. Peterson had some remnants of ego that tended to get in his way at times, but when he was in character as "Gregory the Great" he heard very well! That weekend at the festival, was perfect timing. Metatron projected a vision in an open space across from the fortune telling booth. Sir Gregory saw The Blue Knight on horseback riding up to his camp, dismounting and walking over to a line of thousands of children waiting to be knighted. He couldn't wait to get home that night to call me about his vision.

"That is fantastic," I said, "you heard well."

Sir Gregory called the management team and they loved the idea. The festival brought in about a half a million guests every summer, but few children because they didn't have a lot for kids to do. We organized a meeting at East Wing Castle so to give them a taste for who we were and what we were doing. The Ren-Fest staff fell in love with all the scenes and artifacts we had on display. They agreed it was a great match for both organizations. The staff said that they would take the matter up with their board and get back to us in a few weeks. The festival was juried which meant that all the vendors had to vote on any new vendors coming in. It sounded like a done deal.

Chapter Eleven

U-Knighting

Lesson Thirty-Six:

Six of Spades, received July 8, 1991 Book of Wisdom, channeled from Hierophant:

In this lesson I learned about Mysticism, the Mystical and Mystics - a person who seeks by contemplation and self-surrender to obtain unity with or absorption into the Deity or the absolute, or a person who believes in the spiritual apprehension of truths that are beyond the intellect. I gained a greater understand as the Hierophant was preparing me to create the Philosopher's Stone.

SEE APPENDIX FOR ENTIRE LESSON

This lesson was an interesting one. It appeared that we were all to become "Philosopher Stones;" living, breathing magical beings of light.

"Now that is going to be interesting," I thought!

I could see that Thomas, Gwen, Jackie, Eleanor, Leah, Barbara, Tray, June and Susan were already showing remarkable improvement over the thirty-six months of study. And combined with Lady Bonnie, Sir Gregory and Lady Judah I felt we had the first twelve "Good Knights" Michael was seeking in order to bring down his archangel commanders. Things were definitely progressing in the right direction and everyone was elevating. Many of the members also wanted to join the Good Knights as volunteers helping to protect and knight children.

Later that week we got the call from the Renaissance Festival manager. He said over three quarters of the vendors voted for the charity to have a space at the festival starting the end of August. We were thrilled! That gave us only three weeks to build our Good Knight Campsite though.

"I sure hope Metatron jumps back in the game," I told Michael.

He said, "I don't think there is too much of a chance we could keep him away." He went on to say, "This opportunity has a great chance to start attracting more potential volunteers for the charity and possible seekers of the "Knowing" for a new group to start."

So we started to rally the troops in more ways than one. We called for a special mid-month gathering of First Wednesday Club Members at East Wing Castle. Michael had me dress in armor for the gathering. I knew something big was about to happen. Just as he had done at Maryland University in the beginning, but without the armor, Michael opened a gateway to heaven. Again, he had us create the blue mist in the center of our circle. Orbs of white light started appearing around certain First Wednesday members. The orbs were Michael's Commanders - or top-level angelic spirits.

He asked, "How many of you feel ready to have an angel assigned to you to help further the Divine Mission? This is the called the "Aligning." Reach deep down inside and ask. You will 'Know' if you are ready, or not. The angel whose vibration matches yours will align with whomever has the best chance of successfully maintaining the angelic frequency."

Of course, everyone announced they were ready, even though I knew some were not. I was wearing Michael's Armor. I went and stood on the center pod in the knighting circle.

The woodland scene that I had built around the outside of the circle seemed to come to life. The lights on the Tree of Life were pulsating. The blond-haired angel dressed to represent Mother Earth "flew" above the knighting circle. When I had created her, I made her wings out of chicken wire covered with white fiber batting and several hundred white feathers hot-glued to the fiber. I mounted a circulating fan behind a boulder in the rear of the exhibit so as the fan turned toward the angel the air blew the wings making them flap. Tonight, with all the orbs of energy in the room it felt like she was really alive!

Michael directed the members to come sit around the circle on the floor with their hands cupped at their chest. He explained, "If one of the orbs floating in the mist lowers itself into cupped hands, please stand and quietly walk into the knighting circle and taking a spot on one of the seven pods.

Around the circle, you could see mouths dropping open as the first three orbs floated right down into the cupped hands of Dr. Peterson, Bonnie and Judah. I watched as they approached the knighting circle. Their faces were all aglow. Three more orbs descended into the cupped hands of Eleanor, Barbara and Leah. They came forward and took their places on the pods.

Michael and I worked in concert within the armor for the "U-Knighting" ceremony. He pulled a short sword from a sheath attached to the armor on our right leg. Piercing the orbs with the sword, he drew its energy into the sword, one after the other. Then we touched the sword to the member's crown chakras. Speaking some words in Latin, which I did not understand, he then said, "I dub thee an Angel-Knight Lady Leah-Israfel" Moving down the line one by one he continued, "I dub thee Lady Eleanor-Haniel. I dub thee Sir Gregory-Metatron. I dub thee Lady Barbara-Raphael. I dub thee Lady Bonnie-Gabriel, and last I dub you Lady Judah-Anael"

Those six were then asked to stand outside the circle as three more orbs descended into the cups of three additional students, who rose and took up positions in the knighting circle where Michael repeated the same Latin verse, pierced the orbs with the sword then touched the crown saying, "I dub thee Angel-Knight, Lady Gwen-Batque. I dub thee Sir Thomas-Sachiel and last, I dub thee Lady June-Zigzagael.

All nine Angel-Knights were then asked to stand inside the circle as remaining members gathered around the outside. As I looked out over the rest of the students, the remaining orbs disappeared. The "Aligning" had ended. I could see that it was setting up as a test for their egos. Many of them couldn't understand why some of the newly dubbed Angel-Knights were picked over them.

Michael spoke, "These first nine represent everything that is right and everything that is wrong within humanity. They have strengths and they have weakness. We will help them become stronger, wiser and work in unison with their angel. Let us bow our heads and pray that they can surrender their egos and elevate to the understanding of the angel that now guides them."

"Anyone here who feels that they were worthier of this status than any one of the nine, should know that thought is why you are not standing as one of the these first nine." He paused and looked into the faces of the disappointed then continued, "If you think I am talking to you I'm probably not, if you think I am not talking to you, I probably am."

Michael, at times, could be pretty blunt which I could see got under certain peoples' skin. But, I was constantly reminded, this wasn't a personality contest and it certainly wasn't even anything I hadn't seen in the army or on the police department. The only problem here was, none of these people had ever been a part of a disciplined organization. I knew Michael would test people on purpose. He wanted the people who had entitlement issues and who didn't want to get over them, to leave because they would just weaken the core group of knights. Michael was playing for keeps and some of them were just playing.

To clear up any confusion, Michael spoke more on that topic, "I know some of you are looking for a snuggly spiritual cult that makes you feel all warm and fuzzy. You want to be in that 'Army of Goodness' that has the beachfront condos or co-op communes. Well this is not a cult and I can't let any of you turn it into one. It's also not a social hangout club. The road ahead will be riddled with darkness and hard work. If I can make you angry with me or if something I say pisses you off, you should think about quitting now. Remember, I can't hurt your feelings. Only you can hurt your feelings. I'm here to help you not hurt you, but if you are overly sensitive and get your feeling hurt easily, you will not like this path. Many of you lie to yourself. I can't let you do that anymore. I want to save you the time and aggravation of just hanging around if you are going to quit anyway. I must mentor those who stay to attract one of God's Holy Commanders and the only way to do that is to earn their respect. Whining and crying won't get it."

"Ouch," I thought. I knew it needed to be said and tough love is obviously, well…*tough*!

(Note from Sir Edward: Over the years, I have heard Michael repeat parts of that same warning to every new group of people who would step forward. He didn't want any one fool trying to turn his mission into something it wasn't. His command is much like the military Special Forces. Michael will push and poke and ring them out. Elevation of an individual is often like grinding off the rough edges of a diamond with a buzz saw sometimes. If a person stays after all of that, they were meant to be there. If not, they leave. Michael is seeking the best of the best and he settles for no less.)

One of the club members who was surprised he wasn't claimed was, James Gray. James rode with an outlaw motorcycle gang called the "Pagans." He was the one during Lesson 9 - "Seven of Hearts, April 8, 1989" - who thought about quitting when Michael brought in the Hierophant through the blue mist. The experience both freaked him out and made him a believer all in one fell swoop.

Sir James asked, "You said we have to earn their respect, exactly how do we do that Sir Edward-Michael?"

Michael replied, "By making the lessons you've been given part of your daily understanding. You must live the Ancient Laws of Wisdom. Over half of you haven't even practiced any lesson outside of the classroom."

Eyes got big and everyone looked at each other as if to say, "How did he know?"

Seriously?

They forget who they are dealing with in a blink of a blink of an eye.

Before we dismissed class that evening, I reminded everyone of the Hierophant's word to me, "The lessons are going to go deeper reach higher at the same time. You must practice and live the lessons in order to keep moving on."

I also told them Michael wanted everyone to do some form of community service once a month if they were going to continue. He felt it was important for people to be a part of selfless service. It was a vehicle to help open their eyes wide enough to see past their own ego. We already had several of the First Wednesday Club members volunteering at the East Wing Castle. Some full time, but most whenever they could fit it in. I offered the rest of the class a chance to help the Good Knight Network as well, but if they didn't feel drawn to do so, then another non-profit would do. Michael said it was "food for their souls."

Some of them knew that the charity had been accepted as a vendor at the Maryland Renaissance Festival and asked if they could volunteer there. I told them we could use some help building the Good Knight campsite and help filling out knighting certificates for the children who visit on the weekends. It was a perfect answer to Michael's request!

In the days following the "aligning" ceremony, I noticed significant changes in the members who volunteered at East Wing Castle during the day *and* who had been assigned an angel. Ones who usually quarreled or didn't like playing on a team, suddenly seemed to "get it" and began controlling their egos. The most apparent shifts were in "Sir Gregory-Metatron" and "Lady Bonnie-Gabriel." Gregory-Metatron wasn't as grouchy as his human counterpart, Dr. Peterson, had been in the past and Bonnie-Gabriel wasn't as bossy as usual. I liked the change. The feeling in the air was lighter.

I also watched another manifestation of the merging unfold. Lady Judah-Anael, who was our procurement officer for the charity, used to struggle to get donations. Now that Anael was aligned with her, she was easily able to gather all the building supplies we needed for the festival. I listened to her on the phone with vendors. Everything she said sounded so smooth and clear. No one could say no to her. She now seemed to have been given the gift of persuasion. Even when she couldn't get an in-kind donation of building supplies, businesses would offer a cash donation to the charity instead. Everyone she contacted loved our work to keep kids safe and wanted to help.

I truly was in awe of the changes that I began to see in the charity's volunteer staff.

Over the next few weeks, a hardworking dedicated team of First Wednesday Club volunteers gathered at the Maryland Renaissance Festival. I formed groups and assigned tasks, broken down into categories of what needed to be accomplished in order to be ready to open.

We started by putting up a split rail fence around our small 40'x40' encampment. The construction group then worked with the art group to build and decorate an old wooden cart. The plan was to use it to display our Good Knight T-shirts, books and some of Linda's ceramics. They made a hinged plywood "lid" that could be closed and locked down at night or if it rained, to protect the wares. Next we made a maze out of bales of straw for the kids to play in, and put up flags, planted flowers and bushes. Then we erected a large blue medieval tent as a place to read "A Good Knight Story" just in case it rained. One of the volunteers who had a woodworking hobby created a sign to hang over the entrance to our space. It was a long thick wooden sword with "The Blue Knight's Camp" painted on it. I couldn't believe how much the knights had gotten done in such a short time. I was so proud of them.

When the festival opened, we hit the ground running - literally! We stayed busy from opening to closing doing safety programs and knighting the children. Even adults wanted to be knighted and become Good Knights on a quest to protect children. There was a constant flow of people coming to us. While the volunteers took shifts signing knighting certificates and manning the gift shop cart, the "Blue Knight" was always on. Our camp was right out in the sun so Michael's blue and gold armor shone bright like a beacon of hope for everyone to see. It was just as Michael wanted it. He was thrilled to see everyone feel the pull to the light. Of course the sun combined with Michael's armor made me feel like a Maryland blue crab steaming in a pot! Being in the armor in that ninety-five-degree heat for twelve hours each day was somewhat of a challenge. I sweated out so much that even the leather armor became saturated.

I had Linda buy me four pair of boots. Mid-day Saturday, I would change my socks and put on the second pair of boots. Sunday, I would do the same with pairs three and four. All week long, we would leave them out on the sun porch to dry so I could do it all over again the next weekend.

Linda was always worried I would dehydrate. I'd say, "How can I dehydrate when one of the 54 volunteers is always shoving a cup of water in my hands?" And just to lighten things up and lessen her fears I would tell her, "It helps me keep my girlish figure! Look at it this way, at least now I don't have to sit in the sauna during the week."

All kidding aside there were obvious challenges, but the rewards far outweighed any difficulty. The looks on the faces of the children were worth all the blood, sweat and tears we collectively shed to create the space. We were so popular that all the T-shirts the Embassy Dairy donated were sold out in the first weekend. Patrons just couldn't get enough of the Good Knights.

When I got the chance, I loved walking through the festival grounds in Michael's armor and seeing everyone else in period dress. It was like being in a time machine. The actors were incredible at bringing to life the age of King Henry the VIII. Michael told me that most of the actors weren't acting, that some of them were actually re-living the lives of their ancestors. This time in a more positive and controlled atmosphere. He said that this was the closest thing to crossing into another dimension many of us would ever experience and that we could affect a lot of good through this venue. I didn't know what that meant, but I could only hope that I was helping him. His was a great and noble burden and I was humbled to be of service.

Despite all the joyful experiences, I could also sense some negativity directed towards our Good Knights encampment. I noticed that some of the vendors and paid actors were not pleased with our seemingly overnight success at RenFest.

This was confirmed by Sir Gregory. When Greg was "on" he was on, and I mean angelically tapped in. When he was "off" in his lower self, watch out. He couldn't help but bring all the trash talking about us back to the camp to infect all the volunteers. I noticed it was almost like he got off on doing so. Like a rush of dopamine. Michael told me that, believe it or not, there was an aspect to Sir Gregory, present in humankind as well, that actually enjoyed the turmoil. Spreading negativity and putting others down helped them in some twisted way to rise up and feel better about themselves. For some, like Gregory, it was an unconscious addiction that he was unable to see or keep under control at this point.

Sadly, this kind of negativity always put a damper on the positive experiences we were having. It was like a virus. Every weekend it was the story of someone else who had a problem with us for yet another reason.

I could see now why the old Indian medicine man gave me the "No Bull Shit" leather rawhide that I used to create Michael's armor. It took the meaning of protective armor to a whole new level.

Chapter Twelve

Your Focus Needs More Focus

Lesson Thirty-Seven:

Five of Spades, received August 8th, 1991 Book of Wisdom, channeled from Hierophant:

In this lesson, I began to learn about the use of herbs in healing. It connected with the lessons I'd been given on rocks, stones and crystals. There was so much to learn and my head was swimming with knowledge.

SEE APPENDIX FOR ENTIRE LESSON

During the First Wednesday Club gathering, Michael pointed out that all the cures for what ails us could be found growing on the Earth and the human body can produce any drug found at the local pharmacy. He said that the problem with western medicine is that doctors are often too quick to prescribe a pill, not letting the body's natural healing systems kick in. Pills typically suppress the issue, treating the symptoms while not curing anything. He added that this leads to a weakened immune system that can contribute to other medical problems later on in life. That is one of the reasons cancer has become so prevalent in humans.

Dr. Peterson had an extensive background in herbal medicine and essential oils. He spoke at great length about the use of essential oils in homeopathic healing.

It was an eye-opening talk and one that, of course, led to more questions. The important thing that everyone walked away with that evening was a new level of awareness. Awareness that there are other options out there, the importance of exploring those options, and knowing that ultimately only you know what is right for your body.

After the lessons were complete, several of the members started a conversation about the wonderful work we were doing at the Renaissance

Festival to teach kids how to stay safe from predators. The rest of the class got charged up about it and said they wanted to help.

It was heartwarming to feel the excitement coming from the members. They truly wanted to help children stay safe. The cadre of Good Knight volunteers was growing rapidly. We had help on the weekends at RenFest and during the day at East Wing Castle. A commitment was forging and a new kind of awakening was surfacing in each member. They all started to see that if we could keep the innocence of the current generation intact, they would grow into adults who were more stable and aware. All of our efforts were for the Children of Tomorrow.

Now… if we could just keep everyone's mind focused on what was important and not who trying to date one another!

Working that close weekend after weekend, day after day, social relationships were beginning to form. Small groups of volunteers would go out to dinner after RenFest, or out for drinks after a week of work at East Wing. Little cliques and larger ones grew a life of their own. There was the "pretty girl club" and the "smart girl club" and then the boys who followed them like a pack of wild dogs.

As an observer of it all, I could see the handwriting on the wall. The close personal relationships could very well get in the way of service and studies.

Michael flat out said to me one day, "I'm not running a dating service. You need to step in."

"Me?" I asked. "Why me?"

He never really responded, but he guided me into a position one day so that I would stumble across the "answer." I was heading down the hall of East Wing Castle to leave for the day. Michael told me to go into the storage closet. I asked, "Why? I don't need anything in there that I can remember."

He said, "Just do it and when you get in there you will see what you need."

So, I turned tail and headed for the closet. Now mind you, this closet was more like a room. We dumped costumes, décor and supplies in there that I used to create exhibits. It was not organized and neat. All I could think was, "what the hell does he think I need and if it is in there, how am I going to find it?"

When I opened the door and turned on the light, I saw two of the volunteers in the act of personifying what I said earlier about "forging a commitment." Unfortunately, what I witnessed was not the kind of commitment forging I was hoping to see.

When I asked Michael about personal relationships in the group all he said was, "What did I tell you when I left you in Augsburg, Germany?"

I got his point loud and clear.

I wrote a memo to the entire group of volunteers. I think they got my point…hopefully.

The following weekend at RenFest everyone was on their best behavior. It was a joy to see everyone work together in and around all of the magical people at the festival. But the two members I'd seen in the closet were not fooling me. I could still see their auras and the connection between them. It was okay for them to bond. I just had to put them on notice that there was a level of respect for place and timing of said "bondings" and that their choices could affect the mission for everyone.

Lady Linda Fortunata and Sir Edward-Michael at RenFest

Getting caught up in the moment at RenFest was easy. It was one big party. There was magic everywhere and the food…the food was amazing! My favorite thing to eat there was the 16th Century world famous Turkey Leg. It was ginormous and a meal in itself.

One of the characters at the festival was Mrs. Gobbler, the Turkey Plucker. She walked around with a rubber turkey that had pure feathers sticking out of it. You could always tell where she had been from the trail of feathers she'd leave behind. Mrs. Gobbler loved to hang around the Good Knight Camp harassing the children and trying to tickle them with her feathers.

That weekend Mrs. Gobbler gave a little girl named Victoria a white wing feather. I noticed Victoria patiently waiting in line to be knighted with the most beautiful smile on her face. After I knighted her she said, "You're an angel, right?"

I said, "No, I'm a knight."

Handing me the white feather she said, "No, you are an angel and this is for your wings."

I was humbled, shocked and very honored. I told her that I would put her feather in my black cape to remind me of her goodness. Other kids who saw what Victoria had done, picked up feathers from the ground and gave them to me as well when it was their turn to be knighted. Before you knew it, kids started harassing Mrs. Gobbler every weekend asking for white feathers to give to the Blue Knight.

I kept my promise to little Victoria and the rest of the kids. Every Monday morning when I returned to East Wing Castle, I would hot glue or sew the feathers into the lining of Michael's black wolf fur cape. In a few short weekends, I had five hundred feathers on each side. They formed a pair of white angel wings hidden beneath the cape.

Mrs. Gobbler ended up changing her character the last weekend of the season because it was getting to expensive trying to keep up with the feather demand! She became Mrs. Ratly the Rat Catcher. She would walk around with rubber rats in a cage asking kids if they had a mouse or rat problem at home. It was very funny watching her chase imaginary rats around the grounds trying to catch them in her butterfly net. She would run past our campsite yelling, "Blue Knight! Keep watch on your cape! Rats love to eat turkey feathers."

I felt bad for Mrs. Gobbler, uh, Mrs. Ratly, but those feathers were a great way to keep track of how many children Michael had knighted that first year.

Subsequently, our resident wood carver made a huge plywood feather. We tallied each child knighted by coloring in the gauge within the feather. It looked somewhat like a thermometer that we would color in as we knighted a child. Since the first thousand feathers completed Michael's wings, I started creating fancy peacock feathered broaches to represent an additional one thousand children knighted. I pinned the broaches to the inside of Michael's cape and soon I had fourteen broaches. Michael said that was enough broaches and he told me to add a gold medallion with pearl beads to represent every five thousand kids reached. By the end of that first year the cape represented that eight thousand children had been knighted.

I'd say that was quite an accomplishment!

Chapter Thirteen

Echo into Eternity

Lesson Thirty-Eight

Four of Spades, received September 8th, 1991
Book of Wisdom, channeled from Hierophant:

In this lesson, the Hierophant told stories that really made me think and he clarified the transformations our bodies undergo. He also gave me the Laws of Wisdom and left me with some additional food for thought he called, Wisdom of the Ages. I could see how he was using up-to-date references to help me understand his ancient views of knowledge.

SEE APPENDIX FOR ENTIRE LESSON

In preparation for the September First Wednesday Club gathering, Michael told me to have Sir Gregory contact the members and tell them to read *A Good Knight Story* ahead of time. He wanted them to see how the lessons I had received from the Hierophant played out in the book.

When the members gathered, they discussed the psychology in the book. They were able to recognize how so many people in life, as in the story, let a lie become their truth.

"It was coming through loud and clear, and that is what led to the Blue Knight being condemned by the people," Thomas said. "They let a lie become their truth."

"Yes, Thomas that is correct," I said.

I explained again about how the story came to me. "Remember, Michael said that the book would take on a life of its own and then within the first month of publishing the story it would save a child's life?"

Since all of the members had now been to the Renaissance Festival and seen Michael's armor at work with the kids, I could tell the story made a deep impression upon them.

RenFest was wrapping up for the season and many in the group wanted to know where the quest was going from here. I said, "Michael has shown me a vision of a video that illustrates the tricks in the book being acted out so that children have a visual to permanently imprint on their minds. He also showed me that eventfully a Hollywood producer would see the value in the story and turn it into a feature film. But, we have millions of children to reach before that can happen." After saying that I silently thought what an impossible feat to knight even one million kids would be.

Michael spoke up and said, "This life saving message will catch fire over the next ten years reaching millions, and with the proper people in place the feature film will reach billions worldwide. We will not stop until the *"ABC of Safety"* is second nature to all children. Those tricks are adults' weakness that the Sons of Darkness use to defile God's children. We cannot let this human ignorance continue."

Chapter Fourteen

Meet the Queen of Hearts

Lesson Thirty-Nine:

Three of Spades, received October 8th, 1991 Book of Wisdom, channeled from Hierophant:

In this lesson, I learned that the Constant Walker (the spirit I met when I drowned) is one of the Seven Celestial Sisters, a divine daughter of the Creators. We focused on childhood memories in the hope of learning how to distinguish between the good and the bad. I was taken to a mystical Labyrinth of Miracles and met Queen Kei Sophia Pistis of Atlantis who taught me many things. I also learned about the Nine Dimensions of Existence.

SEE APPENDIX FOR ENTIRE LESSON

During this lesson, we all wrote down the good and bad things that happened to us in our lives. During a guided meditation, we all journeyed to a labyrinth and held audience with the Queen of Wisdom. This labyrinth was other worldly. It felt like a connection between heaven and earth.

For the first time in my life, I was free from the hatred that had attacked Frankie and me, the abuse from the "good Christian" baby sitter, the torment from my brothers and every other clash I've had with people who tried to stop me from growing and finding happiness. In the presence of The Queen, there was an overwhelming sense of a type of love I had never felt before. All the turmoil in my life now made sense. I realized that if it weren't for those times, I wouldn't be the man I was rapidly becoming and the hero of my own life's story. She gifted me that insight.

When the meditation was over, Michael also spoke to the First Wednesday Club members about the balance of male and female energy in the human body. He said that, just as our brain is divided into the right and left hemispheres, so are our bodies also male and female within our electro-magnetic fields. He went on to say that humanity has become unbalanced. Men and women both have become far too masculine which has created aggressive tendencies in many. When we are passive, our bodies produce the feminine hormone estrogen and when we are aggressive our bodies produce the hormone, testosterone. Like the Yin and Yang, the balance that runs through everything in life, we must also bring our hormones under control in our bodies if we ever stand a chance at finding real happiness.

In order to give us a greater understanding of this concept, Michael had everyone go into a relaxed meditative state of being. He had all students focus on their feminine sides. He had all the women shed any feelings of masculine aggressiveness that was brought on by a male driven society. He did the same with the males in the class. He guided everyone toward having the perfect view of a female body, dressed in whatever clothing that made us feel feminine.

Staying in a relaxed state with those feelings mind, he instructed everyone to write down how they felt on a sheet of paper. Then he brought them back to center and took them into their masculine sides. Michael then guided everyone toward having the perfect view of a male body, dressed in whatever clothing made them feel masculine. He asked everyone to write down how they felt.

Once everyone was finished, Michael brought the class back to a normal state of mind and asked for volunteers to read what they wrote.

People were laughing and seemed more at ease. Everyone shared how pleasant they felt as a loving woman, but how dominant they felt as a man.

Lady Georgia said, "I was having trouble walking. I kept tripping over my penis."

We all laughed.

Most of the men said they felt better than they had felt since childhood.

Michael explained, "One of the reasons for this exercise is that I am going to attempt to bring down the Seven Celestial Sisters to earth and align them with an earthly counterpart as I did with the angels who have aligned with the Angel-Knights. "I am seeking volunteers to step up and see if you can attract a sister like some have attracted an angel. If you are interested in trying this, you will need to prepare for the next class. In order to bring about the required balance, you will have to reverse your clothing for gathering. Men will have to be dressed as a women and women will have to be dressed as a man. You can come dressed or arrive early and dress at the castle." Michael ended by pointing out, "My Armor is the perfect outward likeness for the masculine/feminine balance. Whenever Sir Edward suits up, he is in drag insofar as the breastplate was formed around a pillow that supported one of Linda's stuffed bras. Beneath the breastplate is a blue "mini-skirt" of dragon scales. Below that are blue and gold leather leg bracers or "panty hose" and then 3" high heel western boots. The male in the armor and the feminine energy of the armor brings the two together. That is the only way I can align with him as one. Sir Edward is not the Archangel Michael, but when he's in the armor we are one in the same."

I was shocked. Everyone was interested in the transformation exercise. They were all buzzing about how wonderful they felt releasing the burden of the stereotypes. And for the first time, it all made sense and I saw the armor as the perfect blend of masculine and feminine energy. No wonder I felt so different when I put it on.

As we prepared to leave, Michael suggested that everyone take advantage of Halloween later in the month since it was the only time of the year cross-dressing was acceptable. He said that the girls should help the boys with their female clothing and makeup. Most women's shirts and pants have been more masculine since the 1930's, so it would be easier for the women to become male than the men to become female.

He closed the evening by saying, "If you ever expect to have an audience with the Creator, you must enter the temple balanced and childlike."

Chapter Fifteen

In the Presence of God

Lesson Forty:

Two of Spades, received November 8th, 1991 Book of Wisdom, channeled from Hierophant:

In this lesson, the Hierophant began preparing me to approach the Temple of Wisdom where the Creator dwells. It was going to be a lot harder than my journey to visit the feminine side of the Godhead. I could see now why Michael guided me to several transsexual informants on the police department to help me better understand the energetic balance present inside of their minds.

SEE APPENDIX FOR THE ENTIRE LESSON

November's First Wednesday Club gathering was a hoot to say the least. Nearly everyone dressed as the opposite sex. Michael did a balancing ceremony to help everyone maintain the energy. Sir Thomas already had long brown hair so it wasn't too far of a jump for him to access his feminine side, but Sir James was having a bit of a hard time with it. It is not all that easy to go from biker dude to biker chick in just the blink of an eye.

As an anchor for the evening's activities, Michael had me share the details of an undercover investigation I conducted on the police department when someone was slashing and stabbing hookers on 14th St. Northwest in Washington, D.C.

Back in 1978 during my undercover days. I dressed as a transvestite and walked through the parks and back alleys for weeks. The surveillance team looking for volunteer undercover investigators liked screwing with me and said "At get-go you are an ugly man, but you make an even uglier woman."

No one else would volunteer for the assignment so I told those investigators that beggars can't be choosers. No one was beating down the door to take this assignment. I didn't even want to do the investigation because I felt foolish, but Michael said that it was important for my growth and it would all make sense later in life.

He has said that a lot over the years.

With no one else volunteering, the surveillance team chose me for the assignment. The station's clothing closet didn't have anything in my size, so I had to go to the Goodwill. It wasn't fun let me tell you. And embarrassing, wow! Try finding size 13 high heels. When I got home and put it all on Michael told me, "Dressed as a woman you are a firecracker when you need to be a stick of dynamite."

I asked, "What do you mean by that?"

He responded, "In other words, you half-ass look the part, but you no-ass feel the part. Look in the mirror." Then he asked, "Would you, date you?"

I said, "Uh, nope!"

He told me to contact my old friend and informant Ruby Begonia. After the IRA gun running investigation that hit the news, she found out that I was a cop. She told me she had suspected I was a cop after rescuing her from the rapist in that ally. Nevertheless, we remained friends through the remainder of my time on the force. She would feed me information every once in a while, when it benefited her business.

I called Ruby and I told her that I had to go undercover as a she-male hooker. All I heard on the other end of the phone was laughter - that lasted an uncomfortably long time. I didn't take it personally because I knew the image of me dressed up as a woman she had conjured in her head. Let's face it, who wouldn't laugh at that?

I knew Ruby would do anything for me as long as it didn't interfere with her business. Ruby said, "I'll arrange for you to meet up with some girls who can help you. But mind you, and hear me well, I don't want any of this traced back to me."

"That's perfect. I will make sure of it and thank you!" I said.

Ruby gave me the name and number of a girl who introduced me to another girl, who introduced me to a gay guy, who introduced me to a transvestite, named Princess who lived with a group of girls in an Upper Northwest mansion in Washington, D.C.

Now try to follow that lead. I was pretty sure my promise of anonymity to Ruby was secure.

Princess and I hit it off right away. She introduced me to her friends; the seven hookers, five women and two transsexuals who she lived with.

The seven of them worked together as high-price call girls when needed for Ruby Begonia. These were not your run of the mill "streetwalkers." They all lived together in a large historic mansion on upper Connecticut Avenue. Michael told me I would never be able to attract the culprit until those seven girls saw me as fully feminine. They would be my litmus test so to speak.

After a few days of hanging around with them I revealed that I was really an undercover D.C. cop investigating the stabbing of the three girls in the parks off of 14th St. earlier that month. I was looking for the person that people in the area were calling "The Butcher."

Princess just smiled at me and said, "No shit, Sherlock. Did you actually think we thought you were anything else? I mean you ain't even tried anything with any of us. We don't have 'friends' that just hang out with us."

I asked them if they would please help me.

They all agreed and then Amanda, one of the transsexuals, who took a clear liking to me said, "It's going to take work on your part, honey. You have to embrace your inner feminine." When she looked at me I felt that she could see right into my very soul. Then she said to me, "Remember this about me, I don't ever lie. That's why I took the name Amanda. It tells everyone up front what I'm all about, if they have the common sense to hear me out."

We locked eyes and I felt like I was in a trance. I must admit it was hard to see a male while looking at her. She had this natural feminine beauty. Then it hit me, her name was A-**MAN**-DA. Ha, got it! A man, duh!

Amanda was a gorgeous light skinned black woman. I could not see any hint of male in her, other than a slight Adam's apple when she lifted her chin. She assured me that she still retained her manhood, but kept it safely tucked away from view.

I do believe I may have blushed when she said that!

Even though this was going to be a challenge for me, in more ways than one, Michael had definitely guided me in the right direction. I soon learned that "The Sisters Seven," as they called themselves, were a practicing "Voodoo Sacred Circle of Power." Amanda, who was from Haiti, was their High Priestess. I always thought that Voodoo was black magic, but Amanda explained that it was actually a mixture of African and Catholic religious beliefs. She said that it was Hoodoo that was the magic of darkness.

These seven ladies taught me so much about the power of the word and the mind's ability to manifest the word into solid form. They pretty much adopted me as part of their sacred circle. I needed help not only looking like a girl but putting off the feminine vibe, the latter being the more difficult task to accomplish. And while they were helping me I served as a straight man's energy they could draw on since they were either gay or lesbian.

After they told me about the ability to manifest the word, I asked, "Can you come up with the words to help me manifest into a vision strong enough to lure the 'Butcher' to me." The Butcher had just slashed another girl the night before and the street workers were in a panic. The stakes had just gone up, I had to move fast.

Princess said, "There has to be a balance of male and female energy in everyone in order to function properly in the world. I know you have it in you. We will help you find it, but you have to work at it too."

Amanda said "This guy who is slashing the girls is totally feeding off of his male side and fear of his female side is driving his aggression against women." She handed me a book, "Here read this. It's about the practice of Voodoo and the constellation Pleiades. You can refer to it later. It will help you make sense of what we are going to show you tonight."

I shook my head as I couldn't believe a transvestite hooker was teaching me such deep esoteric beliefs.

Michael reminded me, "Remember, our teachers wear combat boots, high heels, sneakers and sometimes bare feet. Learn from everyone. Each person is a walking, talking, living textbook."

"Okay. Good point," I responded.

The Sisters Seven then took me into their sacred ceremonial room where I was placed in a chair surrounded by eight lit candles of different colors. They all sat around me and hummed various vowel sounds.

I thought, "I've done some crazy stuff in my life, but really Michael?" It was a little scary when a white mist started to rise up around me as they hummed. They told me it was the Breath of God.

Amanda said, "Saint Michael and the Virgin Mary are standing on either side of you. They are here to keep you in balance." The humming stopped and Amanda continued, "If you follow our instructions a transfiguration will occur and you will attract the fiend who you seek."

After the ceremony, we all sat around and had a cup of tea. One of the other "sisters" wanted to know why the Archangel Michael seemed to be so strong around me. So, I told them the story about my near-death experience and the angel guiding me since I was a child.

Amanda jumped in and said, "Go now and read the book I gave you. It will answer many questions for you. Don't come back until you finish it."

It took me two days to read that book. I began to see why the world had gotten so out of balance. With my new-found knowledge, I now felt I was ready to continue.

When I arrived back at the mansion several days later, the girls were ready for me. I was escorted into a lush bathroom where they had prepared a hot bath with specially treated oils, salts, and holy waters. The sweet smell of incense permeated the room.

Honey, a beautiful long-haired blonde transvestite instructed, "Strip down and soak in the tub. When it was time, someone will come back for you." She hit the button on the wall and the Jacuzzi jets started bubbling.

A brief thought of "what the hell is this?" shot through my mind.

"Michael?" I pinged.

No answer. Of course!

I took a deep breath and the twinge in my gut was gone. I had the immediate impression all was okay and to just go with the flow. Also, I thought, I'm a big boy, I can handle myself!

After soaking for two hours I was apparently ready for the makeover to begin. Princess came knocking on the door. She took me to a boudoir type parlor. There were dressing screens and makeup tables just like you'd see in the old-time movies. I was guided to sit down in front of a makeup table.

"What, no mirror?" I asked.

No one answered me. I imagined this was what it would be like, being around a group of monks on a mission, except these gals were the 180-degree opposite of a group of monks.

One sister did my make-up and eye lashes. One put long red fake fingernails on me, while another sister prepared a long blond wig and fitted it to my head. The fourth sister supplied me with hose and under garments, while the fifth put me in a corset to give me a slender waist. I gasped as she pulled (remember she, is a he, with the strength of a bull). My ribs felt like they were being crushed and said, "I've had a woman take my breath away before, but this is ridiculous. Ba-dump bump!"

Not a word. Not a smile. I got nothing. Tough crowd.

The sixth sister completed the "package" when she helped me slide my body into a tight-fitting blue dress. I felt an awful lot like Cinderella getting ready for the Royal Ball.

Since there wasn't a mirror in the room I didn't know what I looked like, but…oddly enough I *felt* pretty. I was then taken into the grand ballroom where they had set up candles everywhere. I was expecting some kind of "woo-woo" ceremony, but was surprised to find Amanda standing there with a glass of champagne and a pair of size thirteen black stiletto high heels.

She said, "To be a lady you must first walk a mile in the ladies shoes."

I asked, "And the glass of champagne?"

She smiled, pinched my nose and said, "That's for me to drink while I watch you walk, silly girl."

I sat in the chair they had set up for me in the center of the large circular room, while Honey slid on my high heels.

Amanda motioned Honey away and then said, "Start walking darling. You have a lot of ground to cover. Go outside to the pillars and begin walking the Void of Nothingness."

"You mean the black marble area?" I asked.

Amanda just smiled and nodded her head.

The floor of the ballroom where she was sitting was white marble. Eight pillars held up the domed ceiling above her with a large crystal chandelier hanging down in the center. The floor beyond the pillars was black marble that had gold lines running through it. Walking in the heels was difficult on the white marble, but when I crossed through the pillars and walked on the black marble, it wasn't as bad. My ankles were wobbly, but I got the hang of the stride after a while.

As I walked the circular path, I noticed that there were eight large gilded frames with their centers covered in black fabric hanging on the walls between the pillars. I wondered why they were covered. I thought there was no use in asking because apparently, they were the only ones who could talk.

I walked and I walked. I bet that I walked for two hours as the Sisters Seven sipped on champagne, ate cheese and fruit, played music, talked and danced.

I was getting tired. Heels are not easy to walk in and it made me appreciate what women must go through every day. My calf muscles were now aching, but I felt like I had mastered it, or rather "mistressed" it, pardon the pun.

I got up the courage to speak and asked, "When am I going to see myself?" As soon as the words came out of my mouth, I turned to see who said them. It didn't sound like my voice, even though I knew I formed them in my mind. My voice had changed. I no longer sounded like myself. I had a sweeter higher sounding woman's voice. In fact, oh geez, I sounded like my mother!

Amanda said, "You are no longer Edward. You are Constance, our eighth sister and you are the perfect embodiment of a balanced spiritual human being of light." The Seven then raised their glasses to toast their new sister.

Amanda explained "You are now an illusion. Your image should only be seen for the first time as reflected in the waters of a clear pond."

I was then taken outside to their rose garden. In the center of the garden was a large reflecting pool where they stood me on a stone platform. I looked down at the surface of the pond. When I saw the face that was looking back at me I was stunned. It was the face of the Constant Walker who saved me from drowning as a child. It was the face of Mother Earth.

Amanda said, "There is only one Earth Mother, she just wears many faces."

A realization came over me. It was true, we can manifest as anything we want to be.

"Our imagination is our only limitation," Amanda reminded me.

The Sisters Seven took me back inside to the ballroom. The black cloth had been removed from the the frames. They were mirrors! And I saw my complete transfiguration for the first time.

I…was…gorgeous!

Amanda asked, "Connie, would you date you?"

I said, "Absolutely."

They did a short ceremony where they put a "Zone of Protection" around me, giving me a talisman on red parchment to shield me from evil and harm. They then turned their focus to willing the "Butcher" to seek me out that night. I thanked them for all their help and left feeling like Saint Joan of Arc ready for battle.

I called Detective Bender who was the head of our surveillance team that night and told him I had gotten some help to look more like the bait that would attract the "Butcher." The entire team couldn't wait to see what I looked like. When I arrived at the rendezvous point, neither the men nor the women detectives could believe it was me. However, standing close to seven-feet-tall in high heels, I was the tallest woman they had ever seen.

Sgt. Carmichael yelled, "Damn Jagen, you make a better-looking woman than you do a man.

I jokingly said, "Well, my mother always said that I should try to be more like my sister Kathy."

The surveillance team then moved into position and I started walking the blocks where hookers were known to operate. I walked and I walked. Now I truly knew what being the "Constant Walker" was all about. Up and down 14th Street from Logan Circle over to Scott Circle to Thomas Circle and back again. I then moved over to Farragut Square at Connecticut and K Street.

I felt like a fishing boat trolling for the big one. I was getting some pretty evil looks from the resident prostitutes who felt threatened by a newcomer. I was getting a lot of whistles, catcalls and guys soliciting prostitution, but no Butcher. I definitely got the feel for what it's like to be a woman on the D.C.'s streets with a bunch of horny men hanging around. It was a scary sensation, even with knowing I had a gun and a six member back up surveillance team watching my every move.

I paused the telling of my story to get a drink of water. Glancing around the room I could see the First Wednesday Club members were hanging on my every word. Plus, since I was dressed for the class wearing the same outfit I had described in my story it truly was like the old detective me materializing before their eyes. They could see it was real, with the exception of the mustache I was still sporting.

"Okay, so are you going to tell us how it all ended?" Jim asked.

The whole room chimed in at once asking for me to go on. Everyone wanted to know how the investigation turned out.

And so, I continued. It was getting late, about 3:00 o'clock in the morning, and the streets were becoming deserted. Detective Bender radioed that we were running the surveillance until 3:30 a.m. and then we'd call it a night. I was making my last pass through Farragut Square, which was a large park just a couple blocks from the White House. One of the females on the surveillance team came on the radio headset saying that she was observing a white male who looked like he had been trailing me for several blocks.

Carmichael spoke up through the headset and told me to sit on a park bench to see what the man's next move would be.

A short muscular white male with a crew cut, wearing a blue hooded jacket started walking toward me. I slid my pistol out of my purse, put it in my lap, crossed my legs and waited for his next move. I had already made up my mind about what I was going to do. I'd seen the photos of the slashed faces of the girls.

"If I see a knife, I'm dropping this dude," I thought.

He walked right passed the bench and never once looked at me. That made me feel like he knew I was a police decoy or was just a normal citizen walking home. I could hear the chatter in my earpiece from the surveillance team as the man moved away and out of sight. Detective Bender called it a night and said we would pick up the surveillance again the next evening.

My legs were killing me. All I wanted to do was get off them. As I was returning to my vehicle parked at 12th and K Streets I had to walk through Franklin Square, another park which was outside of the surveillance area.

Michael said, "Stay alert. You are in danger. I quickly popped my earbuds back in. Just as I was radioing Detective Bender of my location, a dark hooded figure jumped out of the bushes to my right.

Without even thinking, I went on autopilot. All my martial arts training as a kid and in the military, came back to me.

The dark figure yelled, "You fucking whore!" as he ran toward me waving a long knife.

Not even thinking about the gun in my purse, I jumped and high kicked burying a six-inch stiletto heel in his chest. It knocking him to the ground. The knife flew from his hand into the bushes.

I pulled my pistol and said, "Police, asshole! Stay down."

He said, "Fuck you," then got up and started running. How the hell he could run after a high heel went into his chest was beyond me.

What I would have given for a set of my bolas right about then, but it wasn't in the cards. I kicked off the heels and a foot race ensued. Lucky for me he was a slow, short-legged guy who couldn't run very fast. I tackled him and held him down. I heard a myriad of feet running my way. Detective Bender get there first with Carmichael and a few others close behind. I kept him down until the cuffed him. My rescuers! I thought.

"Wow," Bender said, "You are a mess. Guess the department will have to buy you new panty hose Jagen.

Looking down I saw runs in both my stockings, a ripped dress and three broken fingernails. But, hot diggity, I got my man!

That night I gained a greater respect and appreciation for our policewomen and women in general.

The class enjoyed my story and from it they felt more comfortable allowing their own opposite masculine or feminine side to shine through.

Michael and I then helped guide the First Wednesday Club members in preparation for their journey to the Great Temple of Wisdom. Since we could only prepare them for the journey and not conduct a guided meditation two the temple, only twelve members made it as far as the inner doors. Everyone documented their journeys and we were all amazed at how closely each individual's experience matched everyone else's. Michael told all members to review all the lessons they had completed to date before the next lesson, in the hopes that we would be able to move all the way through the doors to the realm of Creator.

Chapter Sixteen

The Day I Made God Laugh

Lesson Forty-One:

Ace of Diamonds, received December 8th, 1991 Book of Wisdom, channeled from Hierophant:

"The more you know, the more 'Knowing' will come to you." ERU.

My Dear Brother Hermit and Teacher,

In the past lesson, you reviewed the Ancient Laws of Wisdom. They need be carved deeply into your memory. They are the seeds of your personal powers and the means by which you should live your life, if you choose to stay on this "Path of the Magi."

Please take this time to review the past forty lessons once more to see if there is any additional information on any subjects you may have forgotten. Be sure to reread it all. It is important that you be prepared for the remaining thirteen lessons. If you haven't gained an adequate level of understanding and proficiency with the first forty lessons by now, you will be lost.

Like my teacher, Master ERU told me, *"It is not enough that you 'know' this knowledge, you must become the Wisdom of this Knowledge if you are to succeed."*

SEE APPENDIX FOR THE ENTIRE LESSON

In this lesson, I was prepared for an attempt to enter the Temple of Wisdom in hopes of gaining an audience with the Creator. I was told that I could say nothing or ask up to two questions. As I approached the outer doors, a female voice asked me to describe the meaning of the two pillars standing on either side of me. I responded, "By the Will of the Creator, his angels have brought down the Great Laws of Wisdom to bring order to the universe."

The doors opened and I entered. I put on the white tunic resting on the table to my right and chose a red belt from the many colors on the table to my left. In front of me was a massive set of black doors. In the center of the doors was an Ankh carved in gold. It glowed with a brilliance that is indescribable.

I pounded on the door and it felt ice cold. I pounded a second time and the door was so hot that it burned my hand. I was afraid to pound a third time. I felt ashamed and unworthy to enter - plus what if the doors didn't open? I gathered my wits, closed my eyes and prepared for the worse. I let my fist go with my last pound on the door, but when my hand reached the surface of the door it was no longer solid. The force of my swinging arm propelled my whole body through the formless doors and I fell to the ground, landing on my knees.

When I looked up I saw another huge golden Ankh with a brilliant white light burning in the center of the upper loop. It was so bright that I was unable to look directly at it. Around the outside of the bright red cross-shaped altar that the supported the Ankh, were twelve large boulders. As I walked around the circle of boulders feeling the different energy of each one, I noticed that the Ankh always appeared to be facing me - but it wasn't turning. It didn't seem to have a side or back, only a front.

After walking completely around the circle, I chose to sit upon boulder number four. I looked up to the ceiling and it was swirling with white clouds, filled with angels singing the most beautiful melodies. I felt so much peace and love all around me. I pondered what my two questions would be - but realized I already knew what they would be before I even entered the room.

I heard a commanding voice come from the White Light of the Ankh. It said, "Why would you ask a question of 'Me' which you already know the answer to?"

I was not prepared for that. I jumped from the rock and laid face down on the blue marble floor. I couldn't speak, but in my mind, I thought, "Confirmation Father. That would be the only reason to ask such a question."

In a beautifully calm voice the Creator said, "Because my children want to feel close to 'Me', but no one religion that they create feels right for everyone, and that's a good thing. Unfortunately, they look for me in all the wrong places. You have traveled inside to reach me. They must do the same. There are many on the outside who claim you must go through them to reach me. That is not true, but there are people in your world who feel they can't reach me on their own so the righteous people like you step up to help, but there are also the deceivers from down under that prey upon the weak minded."

When I heard "down under" I asked, "Do you mean 'down under' like in Australia?" It was no sooner off my lips when I realized He was referring to Hell.

I heard God laugh out loud.

I couldn't believe it. I made God laugh. Then I thought about it. Watching humans and the silly things we think and do sometimes must be funny. All the stuff we humans get ourselves into then pray to God to get us out of made me wonder even further how we are viewed.

When the Creator stopped laughing he asked, "Now I have a question for you my young knight. Who is guilty? The deceivers or the people who let themselves be deceived over and over again just to fit in to the accepted norm in the world?"

Shielding my eyes, I looked up at the White Light and said, "The deceivers Lord; for preying upon the innocent."

The voice replied, "The deceivers are just doing what deceivers do. How can they be guilty of anything? And are the innocent really innocent or just lazy in their life's journey for truth and understanding?"

I didn't know what to say. That was a hard question to answer. I knew as an investigator I question everything where most people accept what people tell them as truth.

My head felt like it was going to explode so I tried to think of a second question. All that came to mind was, "Why is there so much pain and suffering in the world?"

The Creator quickly answered, "That question has been asked of me since the beginning of time and my answer has never changed. On earth, all thriving life feeds on other life forms in order to grow and fulfill its needs. In doing so, something must experience pain and suffering. When the anteater consumes the inhabitants of the anthill, the ants experience pain and suffering. When the fox kills and eats the anteater, again there is pain and suffering. When man shoots the fox to keep it out of the chicken coop there is pain and suffering. Just as there is pain and suffering when a man kills the chickens to feed his family. The only difference between the Animal Kingdom and the World of Man is that man doesn't stop with satisfying his need for nourishment. Using his free will, Man seeks to dominate everything, and from that selfish impulse, comes most of the pain and suffering in the world. In order for me to do something about the pain and suffering I would have to remove man."

There was a short pause and the angels above me started swooping down around the Ankh as the Creator continued, "Another perspective on your question could be, imagine a world where everything was perfect. A world where man's every need is fulfilled and he wants for nothing. How long do you think it would take before boredom would set in? Without the struggles in life, your life would have no meaning. Negative people do what they do and positive people do something to counter it. In the end the struggles you endure in life become your story. Some are proud of their story and some are not, but nevertheless each human leaves a story for all to view in the end."

With that the walls opened up all around me. I was surround by billions of orbs that were like spherical motion picture screens. Each orb was a human life in a constant state of "play/review." As soon I looked directly at one, I knew person's whole life story; the good, the bad and the indifferent. Everyone was the same, yet different. I realized that this was where we come when we die. While watching all of the "lives" reviewing themselves, I could see what Michael meant when he said, "Heaven can be a Hell for some when they finally reach it." In the orbs and in their constant reviewing of individual lives, I could feel the pangs of regret coming from most. They were reliving the things each individual had chosen, but when they got to the things they wished they had done, the pangs were more intense.

The walls closed again. I knew it was time to leave so I said, "Thank you Father for answering my questions. I will try harder to live a better life." Shamefully I bowed my head and backed out the room. I knew I'd be thinking about those questions for the rest of my life. I just hoped that when it was my time to return to the Creator, I would have a greater story to share.

There were other things that happened to me inside of the Temple of Wisdom, but they were of a personal nature between my Creator and me. If you practice these lessons and make it into the Temple of Wisdom you will understand. All I can tell you is that it was an experience that changed my life forever. I learned from Michael afterward that a human being can only enter the Temple of Wisdom once without dying, so make sure you are truly ready before you make your attempt. I hope you will be more prepared than I was.

In the days leading up to the First Wednesday Club gathering I shared pieces of my lesson forty-one experience. Word quickly spread and everyone was anxiously awaiting the class. That night, Michael and I had all the members sit on the floor in a circle in the great room at East Wing

Castle and everyone was instructed to hold hands. Next we put them into a relaxed state of being. Then we started a sequential hand squeezing pattern to bind our energy together as one. Unlike previous attempts at this energy exercise, everyone was well attuned and no one skipped a beat. The Alpha-Omega Cloud, or Breath of God mist began to form in the center of the circle as we continued to squeeze hands.

Michael cleared my vision so that I could see what he saw. I watched as each of the members approached the temple. Out of the remaining twenty-two club members that had made it this far, all but five made it into the Great Temple of Wisdom and held an audience with the Creator. During their time in the temple I could tell that their consciousness no longer occupied their bodies.

Because this was a very personal experience, when they returned to their bodies we did not talk about it. I also didn't want to make the five who weren't able to make it in feel uncomfortable. The five said that they knew why they were not ready to enter and that they would try again in the privacy of their homes. This was very empowering for them, and a wise decision as well.

After that we all went home exhausted, to ponder the "Sacred Event." I thought, "Wow, it truly is amazing what a well-balanced group of open-minded people can do when they put their minds to it. The mind is truly the doorway to the soul."

Later that month to celebrate the coming Christmas season, Lady June-Zigzagael came up with a great idea to launch a new tradition for the Knighthood. She called it the "Knights before Christmas Event." The concept was for our gathering to do something special for area families in the month leading up to Christmas.

Lady June asked us each go to a dollar store to buy trinket presents for kids to give to their parents and kids presents for parents to give to their children. We wrapped all the presents and marked them accordingly, i.e. father, mother, boy or girl. We then would make the rounds to some of the homeless shelters in the Baltimore/Washington metro region. We would dress in full regalia and present the "ABC's of Safety" program for the families. After the program, we would have the kids select presents for their parents from a big Santa-type bag brought in by elves.

While the kids were up front talking to the elves, some of the knights would be in the back of the room helping parents select a gift for their children. We would bring both groups together in the center of the room in a big circle to sing Christmas songs and make the exchange of presents. Many of the parents would cry because they knew it was the only present their child would receive that year. The new event was a big hit and became a long-lasting Good Knight holiday tradition.

Due to the success of the Knights Before Christmas Program and the Ren-fest that fall, by year's end Michael's cape showed that 15,000 children had been knighted. When we celebrated New Year's Eve at East Wing Castle I was especially thankful for the deeds of this circle of Good Knights. We had truly had an incredible 1991.

The New Year started off with a blast of frigid air and winter was exceptionally bitter on Solomon's Island. The Chesapeake Bay was frozen over so Coast Guard ice cutters were constantly moving in an effort to keep the shipping lanes open. All of their work resulted in a great wall of ice running straight down the center of the bay. One evening after a heavy snowfall, I walked out on to the beach. The site nearly took my breath away. Snow-capped mountains of ice appeared to line both sides of the bay. The stunning beauty also reminded me of a time when Michael showed me the view of a lush tropical island from the air, and then when I landed on the beach there was a tiger charging out of the jungle to eat me. I ran into the sea just to find myself surrounded by man-eating sharks. It was his warning to me that just because there is beauty; danger could be lurking just around the corner.

Indeed, potential annihilation was located right around the corner. From where I was standing on the quiet snowy beach, I could see the Cove Point lighthouse to my left. Right around the bend, not a half mile away, was Calvert Cliffs Nuclear Power Plant. The reality of disaster with a nuclear power plant is grim, but it gets better. Right next to Calvert Cliffs is the location of Columbia Gas Company's liquefied natural gas (LNG) platform - just off shore from the Cove Point Lighthouse.

Talk about a recipe for disaster. When ships would come in to off load the LNG everyone living in the Cove Point community would hold their breath. We learned that if any of the LNG material were to hit the water it would cause a huge explosion that would blow up the ship. The ship explosion would then blow up the power plant, which would level everything within a five-mile radius. Not to mention the fallout resulting from the explosions.

When I was on the anti-terrorist taskforce, undercover gathering intelligence information, I heard rumors that certain terrorist groups were discussing having divers plant underwater explosives on a ship coming into offload their LNG. The terrorists felt that if the wind was blowing in a northern direction toward Washington D.C., blowing up Columbia Gas plant would also blow up the Calvert Cliff's Nuclear Power Plant which would act like a dirty bomb spreading radioactive material straight up the Chesapeake to contaminate the Baltimore/Washington corridor for over one hundred years.

Right! And Michael had us buy a beach house at this potential ground zero! The things we do!

Having Archangel Michael in my consciousness has definitely kept me on my toes. He thinks and sees seven moves ahead of everything. That's a good thing; it has kept me this side of the dirt so far. It's not that I worry, but with Michael guiding, I do wind up in some of the oddest situations. Like living near ground zero.

All kidding aside, the beach cottage was a wonderful place to live. And live we did! Linda and I discussed making the most of every moment we had in this life and we wanted to do it with as much style as we could. With that said, Linda decided to start a new tradition of throwing a party on "Little Christmas", or the Epiphany, January 6th of every year. We decided to make it the party to honor the Good Knight volunteers and all the work everyone had done for the charity. And since the Epiphany was said to be the day that the Magi who were following a bright star were led to a special child, I thought that it was fitting that the First Wednesday Club members who were working so hard to stay on the "Path of the Magi" would be invited as well. Most of the First Wednesday Club members were now volunteers as well so it served both purposes.

Linda really loves Christmas so it gave her a chance to set out her large fairy and angel collections in a magical Christmas wonderland. As I was helping her arrange the figurines to decorate our "Sand Castle" I thought about how lucky I was to get to work with my angels year-round.

Linda cooked for days preparing for the event, and when the knights arrived they felt truly honored. We made it a grand black-tie gala celebration. Everyone cleaned up real nice! If you had chanced upon this gathering you would have sworn it was a Hollywood soiree. As I looked around the room, I was truly amazed at how much the members had all grown over the past forty-two months.

We ended the evening on the beach with a roaring bonfire. To my surprise the Coast Guard Lighthouse Keeper went out on the point and shot off a couple of fireworks and rockets. I thought how cool it was and wished I could do it as a tradition to end our yearly feast to honor the Magi of old and new.

Wishes do come true you know…

Chapter Seventeen

Full Moon Ceremony

Lesson Forty-Two:

King of Diamonds, received January 8th, 1992 Book of Wisdom, channeled from Hierophant:

In this lesson, I learned a new perspective on good and evil. I realized that no matter how much good someone tries to do in this world, there are still "good people" who will proclaim them evil. It does make you wonder if self-proclaimed good people are really good or are they just envious of others' goodness. It all comes down, to so called, "good people" judging the goodness of others. Really good people don't need to judge anyone. In this lesson I also learned about the Full Moon White Light Ceremony.

SEE APPENDIX FOR ENTIRE LESSON

By the end of January 1992, McCarthy's ego was flaring. He was taking issue with the charity because it had changed its name to the Good Knight Child Empowerment Network. Denny wanted to continue investigating missing children cases, but Michael wanted us to reach the kids before the predators ever got to them. Denny liked adventure and thrills. An investigation was exciting when the was racking down the clues and gathering intelligence. It was like playing a game and locating the final answer was the ultimate prize. Unfortunately, this game had living "game pieces" who were getting hurt. Finding dead bodies wasn't part of Michael's plan.

Denny was also a party guy; a James Bond type lover of the ladies. Personal issues began surfacing that he refused to deal with. The things that haunted him were just too scary to face. He started drinking heavier than normal and Lady Judah-Anael stopped seeing him romantically. I presumed it was because she didn't want to be just another one of his girlfriends. This was all setting up to come to a head. I just didn't know where or when it would happen, so I pressed on.

Our private security agency, Two Eagles International Inc., still had a well-paying yearly contract. Our current detail was to secure a large friendly "World Series of Poker Tournament" held every January. It was hosted by a multi-millionaire we code-named "Mr. Mon E. Bags." One of his many companies held the contract to supply all the hamburger meat to one of the world's largest fast food hamburger chains. Leading up to the big event each year, Mr. Bags' staff personnel would mail out fifty-two playing cards to his business friends and associates from a special deck of playing cards to serve as the invitation to his winter home in the suburbs of Baltimore, Maryland. The cardholder was required to bring a $25,000 cash buy-in to the World Series Poker Club in order to participate in the yearly event. The rules of the tournament were simple; dealer's choice; five or seven card stud; the ante triples every hour; when you're $25,000 runs out you're out of the game. The cards were dealt until one man wins it all. There was also no splitting the pot at the end.

However, when you found yourself out of the original game you could move to the bar or other gambling amenities set up in the huge rec-room complex on the lower floor of Mr. Bag's castle-like mansion that over looked the city. Mr. Mon E. Bags was a class act when it came to setting up his casino. It was modeled after a private casino in Las Vegas where several of his "Rat Pack" buddies used to take him back in the day. Rumor has it, he was very close with Dean Martin, Joey Bishop and Peter Lawford.

Needless to say, because of the guidelines, the final pot for the tournament was always a monsterous $1,300,000. After the last hand was dealt, and the cash and trophy handed out, the real gambling began. There were millions in cash floating around that house during the night.

Over the years holding this contract, I was getting more and more worried. The more years the tournament was held, the more talk happened throughout the year. That was a lot of cash in one place - and you never quite knew who else knew about it. McCarthy and I felt it was just a matter of time before a group of stick-up boys would try to take the house down. So each year we added more guards to the detail.

Admiral Zumwalt had recommended us for the job years before, because he knew we would keep things peaceful, safe and secure. I was bound and determined to live up to that recommendation, and of course, have things stay "nice-nice."

During the evening event, everyone in our detail wore classic black-tie tuxedoes and was armed to the teeth. We made what we were carrying well known, mostly for the benefit of the players. We needed the word to get out that if you messed with us, someone was going to get hurt. This was real life, without the clout of the police department. We had to depend on our wits because there would not be any back-up coming. Thank God, I had Michael on our side. He would always have us out doing our rounds whenever suspicious people were rolling through the neighborhood.

Michael was a great look out.

Curiosity from neighbors spread like wildfire when all the expensive cars and limos parked down the lane where Mr. Bags lived. It was a neighborhood with homes that started at five million dollars. His home, sat on two acres, was valued at over seventeen million. Naturally Mr. Bags had an elaborate security system for the house and there was a viewing room where monitors were set up. We stationed two guards in there and we also set up additional portable infrared cameras and alarm sensors around the perimeter of the main house and property that would sound a loud beep if someone broke the beams. Denny definitely knew his craft. When it came to securing high-level executives and their homes his Secret Service expertise was priceless.

This year's tournament began just like all the previous World Series of Poker gatherings. It was our seventh time securing the event, so we knew most of the guests. However, my attention was drawn to one new person who came late. I watched him play for a while. He didn't fit in at all. After a while he excused himself to go to the restroom or "check the scales" as he put it when he passed by me. I radioed Ben in the security room to watch him. Ben recorded this guy roaming around from room to room looking out of various windows on one side of the house. He radioed me back the info.

Mr. Bag's policy from the get-go was "hands off." He told us that he didn't want his guests hassled in anyway, and to just make a note of anything out of the ordinary. I complied with his request in this case as well. I did most of my surveillance from outside looking in and from the outside looking further out. Follow that one.

I told Denny to cover the table area while I went to see Ben in the security room. I watched this guy go over and close the blinds on one of the windows in a side guest bedroom that faced the woods. He then returned to his designated seat at the card table. Obviously, it didn't take a genius detective to tell that something wasn't right. The guy was acting very suspiciously.

I walked back into the table room and McCarthy told me he struck up a conversation with the guy. He found out that his name was Tim Bucktutu and he was from the Middle East.

I looked at Denny in amazement while shaking my head and asked, "Really? Tim Buck Tutu? Like Timbucktu? Is this a joke?"

Denny shrugged his shoulders and said, "I don't know man. I'll go ask around." Twenty minutes later and Denny reported back that no one seemed to personally know him, but one guy said that Tim was a friend of a member that couldn't make it.

All I knew was, I didn't trust him.

One of the players who overheard Denny asking about this guy, came up to me and said, "It's pretty damned risky letting someone into such a high stakes poker tournament whom no one knows."

That night McCarthy was off his game. Letting people hear him blatantly try to get intel wasn't like him and he shrugged me off when I questioned an obviously bogus name. He was definitely bothered about something more than normal, but he wasn't sharing. He also was drinking, which he never did on detail before. I knew that Lady Judah had broken off their relationship, so I thought maybe that was on his mind. I felt split and doubly burdened now with watching Mr. Timbucktoo and Denny.

About 2:00 a.m. an alarm sounded on one of our motion sensors set on the northeast perimeter of the house. By the time McCarthy got to it, he reported nothing appeared out of the ordinary. Denny was just going through the motions, dismissing the alarm as being caused by a wandering deer, dog or raccoon passing through the beam.

I wasn't so sure. I had an uneasy feeling about it. I told McCarthy that he had to get his mind on the business and off of whatever personal problems were distracting him. His energy was off and he needed to snap back into reality and tend to his responsibilities.

I stepped up my game to cover the slack created by Denny. During one of my patrols around the outside of the house, I noticed the shadow of someone at that same bedroom window where Tim Buck Tutu closed the blinds. As the blinds reopened I saw Mr. Timbucktoo gaze out and then walk away. I went over to the window and looked out across the property to see what he was looking at. All I could see was a clump of trees across the street. I radioed McCarthy and asked him to check it out. When he did, he found that the leaves had been disturbed under the trees and that there were several fresh cigarette butts laying on the ground. It was now obvious that someone was watching the place.

Now we had to determine if it were the good guys, such as cops who were planning to bust the place, or bad guys planning to rob it.

It was time to present my case to the establishment. I knew there was a hands-off policy but something was about to go down. When I asked

"Mr. Bags" about Tim Buck Tutu, and he said, "He's a friend of a friend who couldn't make it tonight. My friend passed his invite to this guy."

I replied, "This has all the signs of a robbery being setup."

All Mr. Bags said was "Handle it Jagen. That's what I'm paying you guys for."

I told Denny that we were on our own and to keep his eyes out while I did some recon.

Michael told me to take a drive around the neighborhood. When I did, I noticed a silver panel van parked on the next street over with a man behind the wheel smoking a cigarette. A few minutes later a second man walked out of a wooded area carrying what looked like a short barrel shotgun. He got into the van.

I radioed McCarthy telling him about the situation and my observations. That they didn't act like cops on surveillance, and that I was sure they were setting up to hit the Mr. Mon E. Bags home. We decided to let the local police sort it all out. The last thing we wanted was an earlier morning shootout in this quite upscale Baltimore neighborhood.

McCarthy called the Baltimore Country Police. He told the dispatcher that he was retired U.S. Secret Service Agent working private security and during his rounds he observed two suspicious men in a silver van casing the homes in the neighborhood. He went on to say that one of the men appeared to have a short barrel shotgun and he was sure it was a crew looking to do a home invasion.

We returned to the party. A few minutes later it rained cops. McCarthy went over to talk to the police official on the scene to let him know he called the tip in. There were guns, ski masks, maps and other implement of crime recovered from the van. Both men were arrested, without incident. Since it all went down discretely a street over from our client's house no one at the World Series of Poker club even knew what happened. The important thing was, they were no longer in danger of being robbed.

When we advised Mr. Bags of what had happened, I told him that I felt Tim Bucktutu was signaling the crew outside on when it was clear to attack the house.

He said, "It's over, say nothing to him."

Denny said, "You're the boss."

As the night went on Tim Bucktutu began acting nervous. He kept going to the window and looking out. I walked up to him and said, "You know they're not out there anymore, don't you?"

He said, "I don't know what you're talking about."

I laughed saying, "I'm talking about you being the luckiest guy at the party tonight, but the police have a full report on your involvement. I'd leave if I were you and never come back. It's time I walk you to your car."

He started to sweat saying, "That won't be necessary."

I said, "Yes, it is necessary. I want you to get home safely."

Denny and I walked him out.

Around 4:30 a.m. the event ended. McCarthy and I walked all the members to their cars. A few were too drunk to drive so we took their keys and called cabs to take them home or back to their hotels, since Mr. Mon E. Bags was responsible for their condition. The guest didn't like it, but understood it was all part of the service of keeping them safe.

When we got back to the house Mr. Bags thanked us for keeping everything under control without having to make a police report or disrupt his party. It would have been hard to explain the mini casino and all that cash to police. He reached into his pocket and gave us each five hundred dollars as an over and above the call of duty tip. He then invited us to stay for a drink and a Cuban cigar while his staff cleaned up.

As we sat at the bar, I noticed Denny wasn't sipping the cognac. He shot three snifters down in the time I drank just one. He was really bothered about something. I knew whatever it was, it was bubbling up to the surface. I didn't have long to wait before I found out what.

We said good night to our host and walked to our cars. McCarthy stopped in the middle of the street and said, "My father promised me a pony when I was a kid. You know I never got that fucking pony."

I said, "Do you really want to talk about this now Denny."

He just looked at me.

I said, "Denny I never promised you a pony, nor am I your father. And if this is about the Macaroni mouse being McCarthy that's not the case." Macaroni was the name of a white mouse I had when I was a kid, but in the story, he did turn into the Blue Knight's white pony.

The effects of the drinks were showing on him. I said, "Let me drive you home brother. We'll come back for your car in the morning."

McCarthy replied, "Ed, have you lost your fucking mind? going to Congress wearing that ridiculous suit of armor? It's an embarrassment to us, are you crazy?"

This conversation was picking up the same place it left off over a year earlier. He just couldn't let it go. I said, "Denny the Governor didn't think it was crazy when he asked me to receive the Public Safety Volunteer of the Year Award. And HE requested that I appear in armor."

Denny quickly responded, as if he was waiting for me to mention the award, "Governor Schaeffer is crazy too!"

He walked away from me then turned back around.

I said, "Right, he's crazy like a fox." I continued, "There are two types of undercover methods I've found that have helped me to succeed, covert and overt. For years, I fought crime in the covert form, wearing the style of clothing that helped me fit in to the environment I was working in. Now I'm wearing an overt fashion, a suit of armor, to help awaken the hero inside of children." I paused to gather my wits then continued, "Michael showed me that I should bring the Good Knight Story to life. Plus, the governor wanted me in the armor. That was the only reason it was made in the first place."

Of course, I couldn't tell Denny the real truth about why the armor was made. At least not at this moment in time. He was in no mental state to hear me.

McCarthy erupted, "There are no fucking angels talking to you Jagen. That's what I mean. Are you crazy?"

McCarthy walked a few feet away then continued, "No angels talk to me, so why would one talk to you?"

I replied, "It's probably because you wouldn't listen to them any more than you're listening to me now." I paused again then said, "People say that Jesus, God and even a dead relative talk to them all the time. I don't have that. I don't even have a real conversation with Michael. I just think a question and if he's around I get an answer."

Denny was talking, but my attention was focused on a vision that McCarthy would betray me within a year. There was nothing I could say. He was drunk, tired and hurt.

I said, "Brother I love you, but I'm afraid we are going down two separate paths."

He walked to his car and drove away. On the ride home, I asked Michael what was to become of Denny. I was shown that Denny was focusing all his frustration with life on me and the Good Knights because he felt he no longer fit in. Denny's negative thoughts were like a cancer that would eventually eat him alive. I felt sad and helpless. I called McCarthy several times over the next few months, but he never returned my calls.

Chapter Eighteen

The Serpent of Fire

Lesson Forty-Three:

Queen of Diamonds, received February 8th, 1992 Book of Wisdom, channeled from Hierophant:

In this lesson, I learned about the seven Chakras. The seven Chakras are the energy centers in the human body through which energy flows. The word "chakra" is derived from the Sanskrit word meaning "wheel." Literally translated from the Hindi it means "Wheel of spinning Energy." The chakra is a whirling vortex of powerful energy. In this lesson I also received a warning about awakening the Kundalini, or Serpent of Fire, within the body.

SEE APPENDIX FOR ENTIRE LESSON

After channeling lesson forty-three I thought, "Okay, now it's getting scary." What in the world is the Hierophant going to be teaching me that could cause so much harm. Michael told me not to worry and try not to spook the First Wednesday members unnecessarily. He promised he would set up safeguards. Easier said than done - I was the one who had to read the lesson to them.

I decided to throw caution to the wind and told the class about this month's lesson and next month's warning. I found the class was more curious than sacred and that was a good thing. We all spent most of the class memorizing the chakra points.

Michael came through and explained that, "The Kundalini is a concentrated force field of intelligent liquid White Light and Divine Fire within the spine that is vital to human development. When awakened, the Serpent of Fire allows a union of Human Will, Knowledge and Action to create an intense psychological and physiological process of transformation within the mind."

Michael then took everyone into a guided meditation where we traveled through our own chakras, following the path that the Serpent of Fire would take the following month.

He said, "I will show you why you don't want the Serpent of Fire to dip below the Umbilical Chakra or the solar plexus in the direction of the Root Chakra."

Michael had everyone lay on his or her back on the floor. He had us all use our right index finger to touch each of the seven-chakra centers on our bodies. Starting with the Root working toward the Crown, he moved us through each center slowly. Then he said, "Imagine the end of your index finger is a glowing red sparkling light. Now, starting at your Crown slowly work your way down the spleen and stop. Do not go any lower than the spleen."

He brought everyone's focus to the red spark of light pulsating at the end of our fingers. As we moved down we all felt a warm tingling sensation radiating around the area it touched, by the time I got to the Spleen Chakra all I could think about was ending the class and getting home to be with Linda. An overwhelming feeling of sensuality came over all of us. Michael asked us all to imagine the red spark turning blue and begin moving it back up through the Chakra Centers to the Crown. Then he asked us to turn off the blue light and stand up.

After everyone was standing Michael said, "Now you know why this is not a game. If that little red spark could arouse your Root Chakra without even touching it imagine fully awakening the Serpent of Fire that you can't control, moving throughout your body." He then told everyone to go home and be with a loved one.

I jokingly added, "Or take matters into your own hands."

Everyone laughed as we said good night and headed for the door.

Chapter Nineteen

Yoga is the Bomb

Lesson Forty-four:

Jack of Diamonds, received March 8th, 1992 Book of Wisdom, channeled from Hierophant:

In this lesson, I learned more about the Serpent of Fire. Even after channeling the lesson and going to sleep, I was awakened by Michael and instructed to re-contact the Hierophant for further instructions. I do warn everyone reading this lesson to take it very seriously and to not approach it from a sexual standpoint as it can drive you mad and fill you with feelings of insatiable lust.

SEE APPENDIX FOR ENTIRE LESSON

During the First Wednesday Club gathering on lesson forty-four, the Hierophant put the fear of God in most of the members. Most of them were afraid to participate in the practice session for fear that the Serpent of Fire would move down instead of up. Michael had to return to the Father, so he wasn't there to help us as he did in our last class.

One of the First Wednesday Club members, Sir Tray-Zadkiel was a Yoga Master and he walked everyone through the raising of Kundalini through the Chakra Centers. I was so glad he was there and I now could see what a powerful group Michael was putting together. It was a very interesting experience.

The whole class could feel the power moving up through their bodies. It was different then when Michael did it. Michael was more commanding. Sir Tray did warn us all again to the fact that we should never let the power drop below our navel or Umbilical Chakra. He said that most of the people that do, become sex addicts and the passion of sexuality turns more negative in to lust.

I asked Sir Tray to show the class a few yoga positions that would help us all to improve our balance and peace of mind. I never thought the body could bend the way he did in some of the poses he taught us. I must admit it was a bit alarming to see just how out of shape and off balance we all were. We really needed this…all of us!

From that night forward, I was determined to incorporate Yoga into the class. Beginning each month's lesson with a ten-minute yoga exercise seemed like a brilliant idea to me. Unfortunately, Sir Gregory-Metatron wasn't crazy about the Yoga training. He was heavyset and had body image issues. He refused to even try the positions. When I shared my idea of doing this every month he lost it and barked at me, "That's not what I'm here for!"

I reminded the good doctor of what I had said a few months earlier, that "You will leave when this path no longer fits your fairy tale."

He laughed.

I didn't.

I could see this was the beginning of the end for him. We were rapidly reaching his personal limits. As we said good bye for another month I reminded the entire class that to be an Angel-Knight means to do whatever it takes to better ourselves and to rise above any limitations we think we have. Our thoughts were all that holds us back, nothing more.

As those words echoed in my mind, I couldn't help thinking about Denny not being able to stay open to a new direction in life. It just felt odd that McCarthy would have so many problems with the Blue Knight persona. I mean what was the big deal anyway? I couldn't put two and two together to make any sense of it, but I also couldn't afford to waste time worrying about it either.

The next day I got a call from Admiral Zumwalt.

He said, "Good news Ed, the ladies who started Child Help U.S.A., the largest child protection non-profit in the country, want to honor the 'Blue Knight' with their 'For the Love of a Child Award' during a Black-Tie Gala in Washington D.C. this summer." He went onto say that they were using the Good Knight Child Safety Awareness Program at their facilities across the country and giving out information through their 24/7 national hot line.

"Well Admiral, McCarthy is going through a bit of depression and is having a real problem with me bringing the *Good Knight Story* to life by wearing the armor," I sadly said. "I don't know if he will agree to attend with me, just FYI."

The Admiral laughed and said, "It takes a lot of guts to parade around in a suit of armor, but its your passion that gets the attention of children and adults." He paused to take another call that came in. When he came back on the line he finished by saying, "Sir Edward, you are the Blue Knight! What you are doing is commendable and the ladies of Child Help U.S.A. agree. You have inspired us all. Don't worry about what a few thinks. If someone has a problem with you, after learning about your background, then *they* must have a personal, or mental problem. Keep up the good work. You do the charity proud!"

His words were bittersweet to me. It was great news about Child Help award, and I felt good that the Admiral thought well of me and what I was doing, but I still had pangs of sadness when thinking of Denny and his attitude toward me.

Chapter Twenty

Telepathy and Hypnosis

Lesson Forty-Five:

Ten of Diamonds, received April 8th, 1992 Book of Wisdom, channeled from Hierophant:

In this lesson, I learned more about the Serpent of Fire and how it could increase my Telepathic abilities. I also received information on the history of Hypnosis and instructions on how to activate the chemical dopamine in the brain. The Hierophant ended by giving me a better understanding of the size and relationship between the earth and moon.

SEE APPENDIX FOR ENTIRE LESSON

Many of the First Wednesday Club members wanted to start additional practice sessions during the week at East Wing Castle since the Hierophant and Michael were teaching more complex lessons that required more concentration. It was nice to see them studying while Michael and I were working on perfecting the scenes in the Great Room. It also gave Lady Bonnie added helpful support when school field trips came to the castle for child safety awareness programs.

Hearing the sounds of children enjoying themselves in this magical setting was music to my ears. Teachers and chaperones would approach me as they left the presentation and asked if I had ever thought about recording the Good Knight "ABC's of Safety" lecture on VHS so they could take it back to their classroom for positive reinforcement.

I thought, "Why didn't I think of that?" It was a great idea! So, we met that week with charity volunteers and outlined a plan of action. We formed a video production committee who would share the tasks and bring the project to completion. Their overview described various activities to be spread across the next several months. We needed to gather a team of experts in psychology, education and film making. Together they would develop the best method to share the charity's message. Lady Bonnie and I got busy bringing the script to life and drafted an advertisement for volunteer actors and actresses to fill the roles. We calculated that this project would take at least 6 month to complete. The ultimate goal was to sell the *Good Knight ABC's of Safety* video in the gift shop for ten dollars, to raise funds for the charity's outreach efforts. It seemed to be the perfect companion to the *A Good Knight Story* book for a generation hooked on TV.

On April 26th, 1992 Sir Gregory had booked the Good Knights to perform a knighting ceremony at the Montgomery County Fairgrounds. Two weeks prior to that event a special request also came in for me to do a program at a Unitarian Church on that same morning. Lady Bonnie-Gabriel and Sir Thomas-Sachiel had been at the church the week before reading "*A Good Knight Story*" during its annual Easter children's festival. After the story telling they sold books and videos with the promise that the Blue Knight would pay the kids a visit the following Sunday. Being in the armor all day and traveling from one location to the other was going to be a bit taxing. We would also have to send some volunteers ahead to the Fair and some would go with me to the church. I was really wrestling with all my details.

Sensing my vacillations, the Pastor of the church called me. "Mr. Blue Knight!" he said. "Our children are so excited you promised to knight all of them with the flaming sword and to autograph their books. I can't wait to meet you myself!"

My decision was made. I agreed to do both events because I didn't want to disappoint the kids in the congregation. And how can one go back on a promise made to kids?

Most of the volunteers who signed up for the day went straight to the fairgrounds. My lovely wife, Lady Linda, Lady Susan-Zapiel and I headed to the church. When we arrived, Linda first helped strap me into the armor and then went to set up some of her ceramic angels for sale to the congregation as a fundraiser. I went back stage in the Parish Hall to prepare for my talk about the "ABC's of Safety." Lady Susan-Zapiel set a table up at the back of the hall so she could fill out Certificates of Knighthood at the end of the event.

After I was introduced, I came from behind the curtains in Michael's Armor. There was a surge of joyful energy flowing up and on to the stage. I could just feel an outpouring of love from every member of the congregation. It was always nice when the audience knew the story of the quest before I arrived. When a performance was set up this way, there was excited anticipation to see the character in the book come to life in front of them. Every pew was full and there was standing room only along the walls. A feeling of grace and pride came over me as I took the podium to talk about the importance of protecting all God's children from the Sons of Darkness who seek to destroy their innocence.

The audience was hanging on Michael's every word. When we finished reviewing the *ABC's of Safety* I unfurled the Angel-Knight, "Love Thy Children" standard (banner).

Michael asked "Does anyone want to join our Divine Crusade to help teach and protect the children?"

Every hand in the audience went up.

Michael picked up the Sword of Truth. As he drew the sword out of its blue sheath to reveal it gleaming blade he said, "Make the angel wings over your heart and flap them. Now focus *all* your goodness into this sword and ignite the "Flame of Truth.""

The entire room gasped when the sword burst into flames. And I was no exception. It's one of those things that never ceases to amaze me and one of the things I'll miss most when my time in Michael's Armor comes to an end.

When Michael's armor was made, he said it could only be worn for seven years, then I would have to create another armor to finish the quest. I knew that day wasn't too far off in the future and the clock was ticking. Every moment I had I was grateful for.

Looking similar to a line for communion, every person in the church came forward single file to feel the power of the sword leveled to their shoulder. It was one of the most humbling days of my life. I remember when we got to the car to leave telling the minister, "If this was my last day on Earth, this is exactly how I would like to spend it."

He said, "Sir Edward let us pray that this is not your last day on Earth. You have a lot of God's children to reach on your quest." That gave me comfort and made me feel good - that someone else really saw and felt my mission.

On the way out of the church, I told Lady Linda that I would drive. But she said, "No you need to save your energy for the long day ahead at the county fair."

Lady Susan agreed with her saying, "That was a great program, Sir Edward. So rewarding, but it took a lot out of you. Why don't you get some rest? You still have more kids to see soon."

Since I wasn't driving, I left the lower half of the armor on so when we got to the festival all I had to do is slide into the breastplate and cape.

An uneasy feeling came over me as we drove out of the parking lot. I had a feeling of dread, but I couldn't understand why. I remember feeling this way before in my life when something bad was about to happen. I reached out to Michael, but I didn't hear anything back.

My mouth opened and spoke, "Take it slow Linda." I didn't think those words so I assumed it was Michael's way of responding to me.

Lady Susan moved over behind Linda and told me, "Linda's a good driver Sir Edward, just lay your seat all the way back and relax. It's going to be about an hour drive to the fairgrounds."

I relaxed back in the seat and the baby cherub angel swinging from the rear-view mirror caught my eye. It was quite hypnotic watching it swing back and forth. I closed my eyes falling to sleep listening to the ladies talking about the nice people at the church and how they wanted us to come back again next year.

Right as I drifted off I was dreaming about falling. Before I felt the "hit" I sensed danger and made myself wake up. I sat straight up and saw we were driving down a steep hill toward an intersection. We had the green light, but I saw there was another car coming from the opposite direction with its left turn signal on. The memory of the night when our black police cruiser was struck from behind came flooding into my being and I suddenly connected the dots on that familiar feeling of dread I had.

In a split second, everything went into slow motion as we entered the intersection. I was out of my body and all over the place in time and space simultaneously. The images I saw looked like a motion picture filmed being shown one frame at a time. "It's the Matrix. Hang on," Michael shared.

I watched as the other car did turn left into oncoming traffic. It was as if the driver didn't even see us coming.

Now you have to remember, back in 1992 most cars on the road didn't have seat belts. And if the car did have them, most people didn't wear them. Many were afraid of being trapped in the car.

I snapped back into my body and looked over and saw that Linda wasn't wearing her seatbelt and that I had unhooked mine when I put my seat back. I knew we were in trouble. A head-on collision was just milliseconds away. We were about to die. We were driving about forty miles an hour coming down that hill.

As our vehicles collided I said, "Please Michael save Linda and Susan, they shouldn't die because of this quest." I felt Michael's strength enter my arms. My left arm shot across Linda's chest to hold her back from crashing into the steering wheel and windshield. Then my right arm shot up to the windshield and visor to create a wedge that would hold both of our bodies in place. Something hit my right eye hard.

The impact was so great that Lady Susan shot forward smashing her face on the back of Linda's seat. Thank god, she was wearing her seat belt. I don't think even Michael could have held her full weight back as well as Linda's. Even if he had, my arm would have been crushed by the steering wheel.

When the cars came to rest, the dashboard and steering wheel of our car was pushed back on top of us. The blow I took to the head had left a gash above my right brow. I could feel the blood running down my face into my eye. I noticed my right-hand little finger was broken and hanging sideways, but I didn't feel any pain.

I asked Linda and Susan if they were okay. Both said yes. They tried their doors to get out but they were jammed and would not open. Mine did so I crawled out of the car and came to my feet. I felt a familiar snap in my lower back, however, I was operating on pure adrenaline by that time and didn't feel the pain. I ran over to the other car. The driver was stuck under her steering wheel but turned around looking for something in the back seat. She was frantic. She couldn't speak English. Later I found out she just immigrated from China. Even though I couldn't understand her words, I understood she wanted me to help her get something in the back seat. When I moved to the back window I saw what she was looking for. An elderly lady (her grandmother) had been propelled forward and was now lodged halfway under the front passenger seat. She was still alive, but I was sure there were broken bones.

Michael said she shouldn't be moved until the ambulance arrived.

Just then the first fire truck rolled up.

I ran back to my car on Linda's side. Linda looked out of it. Susan had crawled out of her window and said that Linda was complaining that her foot hurt. She was trying to help her get out of the window but Linda was trapped under the dash and couldn't move. I pulled a piece of broken dashboard back and saw that Linda's right sandal had been ripped off. There was no blood, but I could see that her right foot was broken in half at the arch. The whole top of her foot and toes were pointing sideways. Resting on top her broken foot, like a little reminder from above, was the angelic cherub from the mirror, still trying to protect her.

I ran over to the fire truck and identified myself as a retired police officer. I advised that there was a very old woman trapped under the front seat of the white car and that my wife had a crushed right foot and was trapped in the blue car.

Michael told me, "Quickly! Tell Lady Susan to safeguard the Sword of Truth."

I asked, "Right now? In the middle of all this? Why?"

In an instant I found out the answer.

Just as I turned to Lady Susan, two paramedics grabbed me. I was strapped to a backboard and a collar restraint was put around my neck.

I yelled to Lady Susan as they took me away, "Don't let the sword out of your sight!" I was put in the back of an ambulance. I kept telling the crew that I was okay and had to get to my wife, but I could see they were also on a mission to safeguard the Blue Knight.

The female EMT said, "Now I've seen it all. What did you do, make a wrong turn at Sherwood Forest?"

Glancing down, I realized I was still in partial armor from the hips down, which might have been what saved my feet and legs from harm.

At the hospital, my leg armor and boots were removed and left on the gurney in the hall. I was in a curtained ER "room" lying on a table while the doctor stitched up my head and then set my little finger. My thoughts kept going back to that little angelic cherub sitting on Linda's broken foot.

Even if you don't believe in angels it's little things that have to make you think, we are truly never alone. However, most people miss these signs, because they are too caught up in what happened and not looking at the bigger picture of what could have happened. No one died that day and I, for one, knew our number was up.

When the police officer investigating the accident, came in to talk to me I told him I was an ex D.C. cop. We made some police brotherhood banter and then he said, "You all had the angels working overtime today, Ed. Judging by the total damage of both vehicles everyone should be wearing toe tags in the morgue. Other than your wife, it was just minor injuries."

Just then I heard the voice of a child outside the room scream, "Oh no Sir Edward is dead!"

When the police officer went out into the hall he found that several of the Good Knight volunteers from the festival we were on our way to had arrived with their children. They saw my blue armor and boots lying on the gurney and everyone was sobbing. I got up and walked out to greet them and their sadness turned to joy.

Just then I heard the loudest scream of pain I'd ever heard in my life. I knew it was Linda having the broken bones in her foot set.

True to form, this day was a real ping-pong match between the ups and downs of energy.

Later while in the waiting room, a nurse told us the doctor who set Linda's foot was the best in the country. Unfortunately, he didn't believe in numbing the patient before he manipulated the bones back into alignment. It was a ridiculous statement to me, but I wasn't the clearest I could be at the moment either. The doctor who stitched me up ordered pain medicine before he set my finger, so I was a little loopy. As the volunteers sat with me in the waiting room we heard poor Linda scream for over thirty minutes in agony. All we could do was send "White Light."

I was released that day, but Linda was admitted and stayed for two days. She had to have screws placed in the foot to hold the bones together. When she was released, she was in a cast all the way up to the knee. No pressure was to be placed on her foot for two months, so she was confined to a wheel chair. The beach house had a lot of steps so I would have to carry her from place to place. I felt so bad for her. But at least we lived to tell the tale.

Chapter Twenty-one

How I Stopped Smoking

Lesson Forty-Six:

Nine of Diamonds, received May 8ᵗʰ, 1992 Book of Wisdom, channeled from Hierophant:

In this lesson, I was taught the proper way to hypnotize someone to help them stop smoking. It was amazing how easily the mind could be controlled under hypnosis. I had been to comedy shows over the years where hypnotists have put all types of strange suggestions into people's minds, so I could see how easily certain people could be convinced of almost anything.

SEE APPENDIX FOR ENTIRE LESSON

At the end of this month's class, I had several First Wednesday Club members, who had smoked for years, come forward and ask me to help them stop smoking. They all tried to stop on their own at one point or another, but just couldn't stick with it.

I told the class that when I joined the police department I didn't smoke, but I was immediately put into a patrol car with a chain smoker. My partner was so bad that he'd have one cigarette in the ashtray burning, one in his left hand hanging out the window, while he stuck a third cigarette in his mouth to light. I couldn't get him to stop smoking, so like an idiot I started smoking in self-defense. And by the end of the year I was smoking two packs of cigarettes a day.

Smoking served me well when I went undercover because everybody smoked in the bars. When I moved into private security, Michael wanted me to quit. He said smoking was the worst thing someone could do to their bodies. I tried and tried to stop smoking but couldn't. Michael gave me a guaranteed recipe for success using herbs and pure will power. I had the class practice on each other using the hypnosis lesson, but they learned it was very hard to kill a craving. So, I gave them Michael's recipe.

As in everything I've passed on to you, consult a physician before you experiment, then do so at your own risk.

Michael's Stop Smoking Recipe

1. Michael said I would need an "Under Pain of Death" reason to quit smoking. That means if you smoke again expect the end is near. You will have to come up with your own reason, other than the fact that you are killing yourself with every puff. Write your reason down on a 3' x 5' card.

2. Take a fresh pack of your brand of cigarettes and empty half the tobacco out of all the cigarettes in the pack. Divide the loose tobacco into two piles. Put one of the piles back into ten of the cigarettes and seal the end with a twist to keep the tobacco from falling out.

3. Cut up: four leaves of white "smudging" sage up into small pieces; four strands of sweet grass; and four long hairs from the head of the person who wants to stop smoking. You will need about 6" of hair in all.

4. Mixed everything in step 3 into the second pile of tobacco and then refill the remaining ten cigarettes. Twist the ends like you did with the first ten.

5. Mix up all twenty cigarettes so you can't tell which ones contain the special blend.

6. Put the pack of cigarettes in the freezer until you are ready to quit smoking.

I wasn't ready when Michael wanted me to quit, but I made up my package of smokes as instructed and then put them in the freezer until I was ready.

As is always the case with Michael, I didn't have to wait long.

The evening after I made my stop smoking recipe cigs, Linda and I went to dinner on Solomon's Island at our favorite restaurant, Harbor Lights, on Back Creek. While we were sitting there watching the boats going in and out of the harbor our attention was drawn to one boat in particular that was built a lot like our 25' Sports Craft the *Meghan-V*, named after my granddaughter, Meghan Victoria.

The boat was about fifty yards away from us when we saw two guys running around on the back deck. All of a sudden, there was an explosion and the two guys were blown into the water. Before the Fire-Rescue boat could arrive to put out the fire, the vessel had burned to the waterline and sunk.

We found out a few days later that the two guys suffered third degree burns and were still in the hospital. I also learned that the two guys had borrowed the boat from a friend and didn't know to turn on the engine blowers before starting. There was a gas leak in the engine compartment below deck so when the engine got hot an electrical spark ignited the flumes and the boat blew up.

That was scary. I must admit I didn't always remember to turn on the blowers on the Meghan-V, but it was always the first thing I did from that day on.

A couple of months passed. I was taking Linda, her mother Hester, Dawn, Spencer and baby Meghan, who was still an infant, out on the Meghan-V. The first thing I did was turn on the blowers, then the engines and then I moved from piling to piling untying the lines.

As always, I had a cigarette hanging out of my mouth. While pulling out of the boat slip and cruising down the creek, Hester said she smelled gasoline. When I went back to investigate, I got down on my knees to open the engine compartment. I was immediately hit in the face with gas flumes. I could see that a line had broken and it was squirting gas everywhere and there I was with a lit cigarette in my mouth. The long ash was ready to fall into the gas filled engine compartment. How we didn't blow up from my stupidity is beyond me.

Time seemed to stop when I said to myself, "God please protect everyone on board from harm. I promise I will never smoke again if you keep them all safe."

I stood up, shut off the engine, threw the rest of that pack of cigarettes in the creek. Using the anchor and rope, I inched my way back into the boat slip. Everyone on board counted their blessings that day, knowing full well what could have happened.

With the fear still present enough I could smell it, I got through that first night without a cigarette. It was easy because I also think I was still in shock. But the next morning, man, I had the craving. I promised not to smoke, but I didn't know how long I could hold out. After Linda went to work that morning Michael told me to get the pack of doctored cigarettes out of the freezer.

He said, "Light one up and smoke it to the filter."

I replied, "I can't do that. I promised God I wouldn't smoke."

Michael said, "The Creator will understand as long as this was the last pack of cigarettes you ever smoke."

I took one out and lit it. It was one of the good ones. When I was finished, he said to light up another one.

"Really?" I asked. "Because I really don't want another one…yet."

"Yes, really," he barked back.

This time I was not so lucky. It tasted weird, but not bad. There was a very odd taste and smell, but I finished it.

Michael said, "Smoke another."

To make a long story short, by the time I had smoked eight cigarettes they all tasted like crap; even the good ones. I was done with smoking. To this day, I still remember the taste and smell of the altered cigarettes.

Michael said, "Mark and remember that taste and smell. It's important. Your hair is the key element in this recipe. Because you smoked your own DNA a chemical reaction happened in the air sacks of your lungs. It then mixed with the white corpuscles in your blood and went to your brain. It was a type of pseudo self-cannibalism. You have the rest of your life to finish that pack of cigarettes, if you do, God help you."

I never had another cigarette craving, ever again.

I have helped many people over the years stop smoking using the "doctored pack of smokes" method but it all boils down to the fact that the person must have a compelling reason to quit. I thank the Creator every day that the "Meghan-V" didn't blow up. I could not have lived with myself if anyone had been hurt that day because of my stupidity.

Chapter Twenty-two

Two Buzzards atop a Cake

Lesson Forty-seven:

Eight of Diamonds, received June 8th, 1992 Book of Wisdom, channeled from Hierophant:

After the serious topic of the last lesson, the Hierophant wanted to keep this one light. In this lesson, I learned about casting lots and using color frequencies to heal the body. I also gained knowledge of the use of color lasers which are used in surgery today.

SEE APPENDIX FOR ENTIRE LESSON

As word spread about the classes, we were receiving more and more interest from curious seekers. Sir Gregory and I had to begin an additional class due to the demand. Since we already had the forty-five lessons typed, taught and practiced, I felt comfortable teaching multiple classes during the month. We had to sit down with the charity members to outline a schedule because there also was a surge of interest in using East Wing Castle for birthday parties and private events, along with the already booming field trip experience.

Sir Gregory fielded a call from a couple who wanted to have their wedding in the castle. We set a time to meet with them so we could discuss details.

They were a very nice couple, who were a *little* on the dark side. They wanted to have their wedding at the castle, because they wanted to be married in "Heaven" by the Archangel Michael since they live with "Satan in Hell on Earth;" their words, not mine.

"We heard that East Wing Castle is the closest thing to Heaven on Earth, and that we could find Archangel Michael here," the woman said.

Before I formulated the question, Michael gave me the answer but told me to ask them anyway. "How did you know that I perform weddings? I've never told anyone, except my wife, that I became an ordained minister?" I asked.

In unison, and as if on cue, they both responded, "The Dark One told us to seek out the Knight in Blue Armor. The man within holds the consciousness of Archangel Michael and he is the only one who could marry you two."

"Well, that's interesting," I said as the hairs stood up on my arms and the back of my neck.

Michael told me to calm down and to tell them I would l do it, but with one condition.

Reluctantly, I gave in and said, "I will perform the ceremony on one condition. I will pronounce you 'married' and then pronounce you 'divorced' in my next breath."

They laughed thinking I was joking. But when they realized I was serious they actually loved the idea. I just shook my head and thought, "Michael, man you really get me into some bizarre situations."

The date was set for the eve of the summer solstice.

As the wedding planning unfolded it further proved that these two went in for everything that broke with tradition. They showed us a mock-up drawing of their cake. The only thing traditional about it was the background of white icing. It had two buzzards on top, was drizzled with red icing to look like dripping blood, and was covered in small plastic black widow spiders.

Talk about appetizing!

On the day of the wedding loud Punk Rock music was playing up until the hall doors opened to reveal the bride. Their wedding march was *Tiptoe through the Tulip's* by Tiny Tim. Sir James Gray drove the "bride," Robby, and his mother, who had the largest boa constrictor around her neck, down the aisle on the back of his motorcycle - to the cheers of all in attendance. Even the snake was dressed as well, wearing a black bow tie. Robby wore a black mini skirt wedding dress. And yes, he exposed much that day to all in the hall when getting off the bike. The "groom," Cherry, wore a white short-sleeve tuxedo. One of their guests described their piercings and blue fish scale tattoos as looking like a couple of catch and release bass.

During the ceremony, Michael spoke to the couple, "You are soulmates who have gotten lost in each other's weirdness. Not that there is anything wrong with that, as long as nobody gets hurt. Life and love should be fun." He then said, "Edgar Cayce once wrote, 'A soul mate is an ongoing connection with another individual that the soul picks up again in various times and places over lifetimes. We are attracted to another person at a soul level not because that person is our unique complement, but because by being with that individual, we are somehow provided with an impetus to become whole ourselves.' However, Edgar didn't go far enough with his statement. You will find later on in life that the soul only lives once and that it is the spirits around you, who you are sensing when you feel a connection to a different life, time or place."

"Do you understand that?" He asked.

A huge swoosh of air blew through the room and the energy shifted. Everything went calm, like a placid lake. A moment of pure clarity came over them and they both nodded their heads, while a simple and humble "yes" came out of their mouths.

"Okay, turn and face each other. I now pronounce you husband and wife. You may kiss the bride," Michael said.

I took a breath after Michael finished and then kept my promise. "And I now pronounce you Divorced!"

At the reception, I learned it was Sir James Gray, the biker student from First Wednesday Club, who had referred the couple to the Good Knight Network. When I asked him why he referred them he said, "I just wanted to see how you would handle them. And you did real good brother. Most of what they say and do is for attention. They don't worship Satan or live in Hell. They like messing with people."

"Well I knew when Michael told me to marry them that there was more to it than what they said. They felt the acceptance here today and will live their lives now without the need to shock everyone in order to gain control and guard their hearts. It was a very healing ceremony for all," I replied.

The reception was great and the forty invited guests were very respectful of the castle exhibits. Most said the castle made them feel like a kid again. Everyone danced and sang the night away. When it came time to leave several of the guests asked I would flame the Sword of Truth and knight them. I was proud to honor their request. It was definitely one of those times in life when I was shown clearly that its best to not judge a book by its cover. It further solidified my understanding that in life that it doesn't matter what one looks like, what one's beliefs are, or even how one lives their life, what matters most is the energy of the heart.

NOTE: Something special did happen that day, because Robby and Cherry are still married twenty-five years later. They never had to use the "divorce" I gave them and claim they never will.

Chapter Twenty-three

The Big One

The last week of June Lady Bonnie received a call requesting The Blue Knight to present the *Good Knight ABCs of Safety* during a Gang Peace Festival in the town of Compton, located in the suburbs of Los Angeles, California. Jim Brown was working with gangs, trying to bring peace to the streets. We were told via his network that our program had been recommended as a way to have neighborhoods work together in the spirit of child protection and empowerment. Linda was still in her wheelchair from the car accident and really didn't want to travel. She also nurtured a lifelong fear that the day she made it to California would be the day they would have the big earthquake.

I said, "Every citizen in America, who is NOT a Californian, thinks the same thing. Don't worry."

I told her that she could stay home, but I that had to go. She hadn't seen Jim Brown in several years and they had a "little thing" together. I will share it because it will give you a little insight on Linda, and about why I have always said she is the best assignment I have ever had. It is also a true testament to the personality of Jim Brown, who is one of the most admirable humans I have ever met. Russell Means was the second. Both angry men on the outside, but righteous warriors on the inside.

Linda's favorite movie is *Gone with the Wind.* One night, several years earlier, Jim had gone out to dinner with us. We were waiting with him at National Airport in Washington, D.C. just before he was to fly back to L.A. and we were talking about the possibility of making the movie about my police investigations.

Jim turned to Linda and said, "So what's your favorite movie Linda?" He opened the door. So, Linda with all her southern charm walked right through. Linda started going on and on about the good old days in the south, how simple the life was and what a wonderful movie *Gone with the Wind* was.

I could see Jim's ears start to pull back when she said, "Jim don't you just love that movie?"

Jim looked at me with an understanding glance and started his, "He, He, He" chuckle. He replied, "No. Miss Linda I can't say it is. There are too many characters I can relate to in *Gone with the Wind*. I'm not a step and fetch it kind of guy."

Linda is a little naïve and colorblind when it comes to people. She, like Martin Luther King, judges people by the content of their character. She didn't see Jim Brown, as a "black" man. To her, he was just a handsome guy who's nice to talk to, a movie star, and a friend.

I said, "For me the most admirable guy in the whole story was Big Sam. Even after being treated like crap by southern society Big Sam was Scarlett O'Hara's knight in shining armor. Just like you would be 'Big Jim' if push came to shove."

Raising my wine glass for a toast I continued, "I see you helping kids in the future after you've given up on adults. You're my hero and not because you played football or acted in movies. It's because deep down inside where you don't let anyone see, you are a protector of the innocent. And Big Jim, they don't get much more innocent than Miss Linda here."

He winked, smiled and nodded his head in agreement.

After reminding her about that last time she saw Jim, it didn't take much more prodding to get her to agree go on an adventure to California. I just made her promise not to bring up *Gone with the Wind* again, if we got a chance to hook up with Mr. Brown.

On June 26th Lady Bonnie, Lady "Black-Eyed" Susan (the nickname we gave her after the accident because of the black bruises around her eye from hitting the back of Linda's seat), Linda in her wheelchair and I, flew out to Los Angeles to seek our fame and fortune. I figured if Linda had more people with us she would feel more comfortable knowing the earthquake would not happen. There is safety in numbers, right?

After checking into the Marriott Hotel, Lady Susan took us out to Malibu to meet her cousin, Berry, a screenplay writer. He was going to look at *A Good Knight Story* in hopes of adapting it for the stage or a feature film.

Berry was an odd bird. It appeared that he was more interested in jumping Lady Bonnie's bones than adapting the fairytale.

He came right out and said, "I don't give a shit about child safety and how your story saves lives, show me the money." He wanted to be paid just to read the fairytale. He said, "Do you know how many people want me to read their crap? I don't do anything for free."

Lady Susan was so embarrassed; she didn't know what to do. I thanked Berry for his input and said, "We are a struggling charity and don't have a budget for the project."

He quipped back, "Come back when you do."

I replied, "Right," while biting my lip and thinking, *don't hold your breath*.

The next morning, we all suited up for the show in Compton. We gave one of our best performances ever to great applause from the public. There had to be ten thousand people at the festival. I met with the leaders of several of the gangs in the area. We talked about the one thing that could cross gang lines was the mission to provide child protection from sexual predators.

I said, "There are child sexual predators who move through the shadows, that rape and rob your children of their innocence. But if you give your children the knowledge of the ten tricks predators use, the predators will seek out less aware victims."

I could tell the gang leaders were more interested in safe-guarding their turf and criminal enterprises than they were about child safety, but they agreed to distribute the Good Knight materials to families in Compton. It wasn't a slam dunk win, but certainly a step in the right direction.

We received a grant from Los Angeles County and it covered the giveaway of one thousand books, videos and Good Knight T-shirts. The kids loved them. We knighted several thousand kids and adults and our arms got tired of holding the swords. There was a line that wrapped around the stage for autographed books, that Linda organized from her wheelchair. We were happy and could see that we were making a difference in people's lives. Parents came up with tears in their eyes, thanking us.

By the end of the day we were exhausted. All we wanted to do was eat and then go to sleep. The next day we had a much-anticipated tour of Hollywood planned. Linda was so excited. She was determined to get a photo while stepping on Marilyn Monroe's footprints on the Walk of Fame in front of Grauman's Chinese Theater. She was so excited that she had a hard time falling asleep,. Linda told me later that as soon as I said good night to her I was snoring like a buzz saw.

From a very deep state of sleep, around 4:30 a.m., Linda and I woke to the sounds of springs jingling and the room shaking. There was a deep grinding noise that felt as if we were in a movie theater with surround sound. It felt like the sound was vibrating through us. She screamed, "I told you when I came out here the big one was going to hit!"

I ran to the balcony and looked out over the parking lot. The asphalt wasn't breaking up, but looked like someone just threw a rock in a pond and now the asphalt was full of ripples. As the vibration moved along the ground to the street lights I could see the vibration run up the poles to the sodium vapor lights that simultaneously exploded into thousands of sparks all over the lot.

The Marriott Hotel was swaying and Linda was screaming!

For me I thought, "Wow, what a ride." It seemed like it lasted for minutes, but I know it was all over in seconds. Alarms were going off everywhere. I turned on the TV and the news was already covering the earthquake.

Linda pulled herself into the wheelchair and started packing her suitcase. She wanted to go home right there and then. I said, "Take is easy girl. It's all over now. But, I for one could do that ride again."

Shooting me her "don't mess me with right now look" she retorted, "No thank you. That was enough to last me a lifetime. I want to go home."

I shifted her focus to the lady knights along with us on this journey, who were in another room on our floor. "We need to make sure they are okay. Why don't you call them?"

Of course, she snapped out of it right away as her concern for others was activated. She called and found out they were fine. I then turned off the TV and we tried to go back to sleep. After lying there for a while, we both realized trying to sleep was useless. Linda still wanted to pack up and go home. I helped to get her in the shower then went out to make some coffee.

A few minutes later the sound of the springs shaking and the grinding noise started again. We were getting hit with a second earthquake or perhaps aftershock. When I ran into the bathroom Linda was clinging to the handicap railing in the shower screaming, "Get me out of here! You said this would never happen."

I thought, "Never say never."

Linda had just enough time in the shower to put shampoo in her hair before the cold water cut off. Her screams now were from the hot water turned on full blast, that was scalding her.

It was all I could do to pull her out of there as quickly as I could. With tears streaming down her face I tried to lighten things up and asked, "Why is it that I just keep rescuing you?"

Contrary to thought to diffuse things, my comments did not help the situation.

I wrapped her in a towel and carried her to the bed. I gave her another towel for her soapy hair and took off down the hall hoping to get ice from the machine to put on her burns. Once she was feeling a bit better I helped her back into the bathroom and used some of the ice to cool down a pitcher of the hot water coming from the faucet so we could rinse the soap out of her hair. She got dressed and we had a cup of coffee to try to settle into some normalcy.

I called the other girls to come down so we could have a pow-wow. All three were adamant. They wanted to go home on the next available flight out. I said, "What are the chances of another…"

They all interrupted me, "Shut up Sir Edward don't say it!"

Lady Bonnie checked the flights and booked tickets for us all on a flight leaving in five hours.

Because of damage done to the kitchens in the hotel, all food services had stopped. We were all getting hungry. I suggested we should go out for a drive and find a place for breakfast. As we drove there were signs of earthquake damage everywhere. Restaurants along the parkway were closed; even fast food chains. Then I saw a guy go into a Mexican restaurant. I stopped to ask if he was open. I told him that I had a car full of frightened gringo women who were in bad need of a pitcher of margaritas and some eggs.

He laughed a huge bellow. After checking the restaurant for damage, he said, "Bring them in."

A couple of hours and three pitchers of margaritas later, the girls had forgotten all about the two earthquakes. Of course, they were still ready to fly home though. On the drive to the airport I was a bit disappointed, we never got to see Jim Brown to thank him for the invitation to be part of the Gang Peace celebration. I was sure he was having his own problems after the earthquake, so trying to see him may not have happened even if we had chosen to stay.

Chapter Twenty-four

Book of Light and Shadows

Lesson Forty-Eight:

Seven of Diamonds, received July 8th, 1992 Book of Wisdom, channeled from Hierophant:

In this lesson, the Hierophant covered the powers of observation. As a police investigator, I already felt my powers of observation were very keen. However, there was a lot I learned from the experiment he gave me to conduct. He also began preparing me to document the events to be included in my Book of Light and Shadows.

SEE APPENDIX FOR ENTIRE LESSON

When the First Wednesday Club gathering practiced after reviewing the lesson, everyone was shocked to see how much detail they missed. But with just one evening of practice with the group, they all improved.

In preparation for writing the Book of Light and Shadows that the Hierophant described in the last lesson, I began to keep an even more detailed running time line of things that happened in my life I thought were specifically related to Michael's Divine Quest. I talked to my father and mother about things that happened in their lives that had impacted mine, and it helped clear up some misconceptions for me.

What was most interesting was my father's relationship to Archangel Michael. I had never heard all the stories about Michael in my dad's life because I was removed from his care at such a young age. His stories helped me see a different perspective and find new language and ways to describe the interactions I was having. When listening to Dad, I had an image come to mind of the gospels written by the disciples. Each one wrote an account of the same events, but sounded totally different due to the unique perspective of the writer. Up until then I had no idea how I was going to relay most of the stuff I'd been through in my life, particularly my communication method with Michael and the Hierophant. A diary of notes was one thing, but trying to explain this stuff to someone else was completely different.

To help Michael and I gauge whether what I was saying was being understood the way it was intended, he had me ask the Good Knights and First Wednesday Club Members to take a cue from the disciples and start writing, what he called, "Gospels of an Angel-Knight." It not only allowed us to see if the knights were understanding what I was saying but also to become aware of what they were involved in. Likewise, these gospels would help each of them in the future, if and when they decided to write their own Book of Shadows life stories.

It was an extra hot summer so I was glad I was inside working on East Wing Castle. Being a bit of a perfectionist, I was constantly redesigning the exhibits. I planned on moving a lot of the scenes to the RenFest if we were invited back. We all really liked the RenFest, but it was a lot of hours of hard work, weekend after weekend.

Sir Edward creating exhibits at East wing Castle

While waiting for word from the festival committee, the Child Help Gala came up quickly. The organizers of the Gala came to tour the castle and had lunch with us. They fell in love with our organization even more than before.

I mean who wouldn't? The energy of the space had been programmed with love and protection.

They asked me to be a spokesperson for Child Help's Abduction Protection Initiative, during an upcoming seminar at a White House Press Conference. It was an incredible opportunity to get Michael's message of protection out to the world. Of course, I said yes!

Along with the offer of being a spokesperson, the two actresses who started Child Help U.S.A. wanted to hire Two Eagles International to conduct a top-secret investigation into a problem they were having at their Los Angeles headquarters. I called McCarthy to extend an invitation for him to join me at the White House Press Conference and "For the Love of a Child Gala Ball." I was hoping it would be the perfect way for him to find his way back to the charity. Unfortunately, Denny never returned my phone calls.

The Child Help Gala was an event right out of a Hollywood movie. There were over three hundred people dressed to the nines, from captains of industry, U.S. Senators and television celebrities to Hollywood movie stars. I was truly honored during the dinner when I was introduced and received the "For the Love of a Child" award for my work to empower youth. As I walked away from the podium I felt a pang in my heart wishing Denny would have been here to see that we had made a difference.

Later that month when I flew out to Los Angeles, all I could think about was Denny, and how much fun he would have had with the Child Help staff. They were truly the most hospitable people I have ever met. The investigation was very interesting but very hush hush. Denny would have been such an asset. The findings are private, so I can't share details, but I could certainly understand why they wanted to bring in investigators from east coast, who were detached from any known affiliates in the west.

While I was in LA, the RenFest committee called with our answer. We were in! And furthermore, we were asked to become a permanent attraction! Management was carving out a new path through the woods to expand their footprint and they gave us a half an acre to build our Good Knight Castle Complex. We were so pumped by this news. I knew that angels Michael and Metatron wanted us to learn everything we could from the festival and management, because they wanted us build our own outdoor facility one day. I paid close attention to all the details and spoke to the original family who created the festival grounds about how they began; from concept to completion. They were a wealth of information. The main thing I learned was to give a name to everything, much like the Hierophant said to do in the lesson on creating a sacred place.

Michael agreed, "When you name it, you give it character. When something has character, it takes on a spirit of its own."

Michael again did what he normally does when we start a creative project together; he gave me a vision of what everything would look like in the future and a sense of what we would be doing. He doesn't always provide the ease needed to get things done, but at least his vision is like a blueprint to follow.

This time he showed me in the center of the land there would be two large ponds taking up half the property. The top pond spilled over into the larger bottom pond and there was a strong pump to recycle the water to the top pond so that it could spill down again. There were large goldfish, frogs, turtles and lily pads in each pond.

During July and August, festival management would allow vendors to work on their exhibits while their actors were rehearsing their rolls. Lady Judah-Anael went to work seeking donations of lumber, while Sir Gregory-Metatron attracted volunteers who wanted to become Good Knights to help in the construction

When we arrived in late July at the RenFest grounds, the manager walked us over to our new spot. This section of the property was wooded with a lot of downed trees, thorn bushes, poison ivy, snakes and yellow jackets. The land was on a slight incline too, which made it hard to negotiate.

We would have our work cut out for us. Glad to be there and to have the opportunity, we went right to work laying out the new Blue Knight's encampment. The first thing we did was cut up the downed trees and then arranged the logs in such a way as to create a two-foot wall to support the lower end of the pond. It took us three days working 'round the clock with volunteers taking shifts to clear the area and level it enough to start the building. Once that was done, we moved like lightening to build out the area like in the vision Michael gave me. First, we built shorter walls for the top pond, which staggered as you went up the hill. We covered the insides of the pond area with large rubber sheets of roofing material; filled the ponds with water and added three hundred donated feeder goldfish, carp, frogs, turtles and plants. It all worked and looked just like the vision Michael gave me.

During the process, I hurt my back dragging trees out of the way and was laid up for almost a week. That was bad because when I wasn't there nothing got done. Although I always try to be mindful of my old injury, my willfulness sometime gets the best of me.

Linda got angry at me saying, "You are going to seriously re-injure your back one day and won't be of use to anyone." But time was running out and opening day was just around the corner.

Watching how other vendors constructed and painted their exhibits was imperative. It brought us back to the Hierophant's lesson on the powers of observation. We weren't just seeing, we all had developed photographic memories that were able to capture details. We used the same method as other vendors to create our Good Knight Castle Gift Shop, which fit right in with the shops that had cost tens of thousands to create.

One day when Lady Leah-Israfel and I were working alone together building the castle gift shop, it brought back visions of me building that first plywood castle in the woods with my childhood friend Frankie. She was proportionally about his size, with a similar complexion and temperament. This castle, however, was already shaping up to be far better than that one Frankie and I created so many years earlier.

Around the outside of the gift shop, scattered along the pathways, were small scenes that included fairy houses, villages, animals and bench seats for guests to sit on along their journey through the magical kingdom. Everywhere you looked there was something to see. Under logs were fairies hiding. In the hollows of trees were life-like animals. At the foot of the hill we made an entrance path to the Good Knight Camp that had two options. You could enter the walking path or the gift shop. The shop's purpose was to display ceramics, wooden swords, shields, fairy wands and sparkly fairy ring halos for kids. Linda had supplied some beautiful ceramic angels, knights, dragons, castles, and other medieval pieces. And all the proceeds of the shop's sales went to our outreach fund to do safety programs.

Across from the gift shop we created a large Angelic Knighting Circle, enclosed by thick rope strung between waist high posts. It was my favorite part of the camp. Hanging on each rope was a wooden sign with an angel name: Michael, Uriel, Raphael, Gabriel, Sachiel, Metatron and Anael. We used all-natural wood tree limbs for the posts that held the ropes. Inside of the circle were nine 30-inch circular tree trunk "pods" that the children could stand on while being knighted. The surrounding area was covered with a thick bed of cedar chips and pine bark mulch. It smelled absolutely heavenly. The Good Knight Kingdom was definitely a sight to be seen and experienced. We had truly manifested Michael's vision into our physical world.

After the work was complete we all gathered at the front of the parcel of land to admire our creations. It was hard work, but we were all really impressed, and maybe just a little bit in awe, having accomplished the feat.

About two hours later, when we were packing up the tools and hauling the extra building materials away, we got a visit from another vendor and his wife. "Just want you all to know we voted against you being allowed into the festival again for just that reason," the man grumbled while pointing at the gift shop. "You didn't pay for your space and we paid premium. We sell much better wooden swords and ceramics and the stupid patrons will come by your cheap rip-offs instead of ours."

Despite their rude and insulting demeanor, I tried to defuse the situation. They came trying to pick a fight and I was determined not to let them get their way. Bullies normally never get caught, it's the defenders and retaliators who are seen. The last thing I wanted was for the management to hear we had caused trouble. Michael told me that after last year's RenFest run, word of the Blue Knight had spread like wildfire, so the number of children we could potentially reach this year should triple! Plus, we just finished a kick-ass campsite.

I put my "nice-nice" face on and said, "I know it doesn't appear fair, but we are all volunteers who don't get paid and we are primarily here to knight children and empower families with our Good Knight ABC's of Safety Program. It helps save lives and trauma."

The woman replied, "I don't give a shit what it does. We just came by to let you know that you and your kind are not welcome here." And with that they flipped us off and started to walk away. It reminded me of the phrase "Don't go away mad, just go away."

Have you ever just stood in stun mode after someone says something like that and wonder? I mean really, it's mind blowing that people like that exist in a so-called civilized society. These people were of the same mindset as the gang that tied Frankie and me to those trees and destroyed what we were trying to build. I couldn't believe my ears. At that moment, all I knew was that I wasn't a little kid anymore and I certainly wasn't going to be bullied by anyone.

Before they had completely turned their backs to us I said, "Hey! Exactly what kind of people are we? You don't know a thing about us, but I know who you are." At this, they turned around. Once I had them locked eye to eye again I finished, "You better watch out before someone drops a house on you."

They grumbled and walked away.

All the volunteers who were still there witnessed the conversation. I told them all not to play into the negativity, greed and politics of the festival. We were there to simply be a positive influence and serve the little ones.

When I got home I drafted a letter to be copied and sent out to all the volunteers saying the same thing. Normally I would have had Sir Gregory just call everyone, but he had a flare for the dramatic and loved spreading bad news. Even though he was quite tapped in, and evolving with the lessons, he still slipped back into the dark place of gossip and unimpeccable speech.

In preparation for opening weekend, Linda was busy everyday painting one of a kind ceramic pieces and making golden fairy ring halos. It was a perfect way for her to pass the time since she was still in a wheelchair from the accident. Her ankle wasn't healing as quickly as the doctors had hoped. We cleared an entire back room of the house to serve as our art and craft area. When I would come home in the evenings after working all day to build the campsite, I would create our signature trademark wooden "Swords of Tenacity." The difference between our swords and swords sold by the other vendors at the festival was that ours were lightweight and made for *knighting*, not *fighting*. Parents loved them because of their purpose. The Good Knighs were all about creating "Peaceful Warriors" who protected children, not harming or bullying them.

Chapter Twenty-five

Hercules, the Pied Piping Horse

Lesson Forty-Nine:

Six of Diamonds, received August 8th, 1992 Book of Wisdom, channeled from Hierophant:

In this lesson, the Hierophant gave me a list of thirty-one "Heed these Seeds to Succeed" tips. I was to read one each day to remind me of why I was on the Path of the Magi.

SEE APPENDIX FOR ENTIRE LESSON

After Lesson Forty-nine, I felt ashamed of myself for telling that negative woman to "watch out before someone dropped a house on her." The hierophant was right. It was going to be a long road ahead for me. I was also reminded that one of the reasons I wear the armor is because I'm too thin skinned. However, the good thing was, I didn't always say what I wanted to anymore. I had begun to learn temperance, so there had been some improvement. So, I began to implement a new personal mantra, "shut your mouth and live to fight another day."

When the Renaissance Festival began, our exhibit was mobbed from the opening at 10 a.m. until closing at 7 p.m. Many families visited us several times during the eight-week season - every weekend from the end of August through the middle of October. They told us their kids kept reminding them about how much fun they'd had while visiting the Good Knight Castle and walking through the fairy paths and gardens. It truly was a child's paradise. Just so the adventure would change a bit, we always added something new during the week. The kids who came back actually thought the fairies were moving their houses from week to week!

Midway through that second year I finished the horse stable area next to the knighting circle. Sir Gregory had a friend who owned a brown

Morgan gelding named Hercules. The horse had arthritis in his hindquarters and needed to be ridden. His friend brought him over every Saturday morning and he stayed overnight until closing on Sunday. Hercules was a big hit with the kids. We had him clad in Blue and Gold armor to match mine. He was gentle and loved for the children to pet him. As Michael and I rode Hercules through the festival's twenty-five-acre Revel Grove Village, we were functioned much like the piped piper. A trail of children would always follow us back to the castle grounds to be knighted. I can honestly say those were some of the happiest days in my life thus far.

Sir Edward and Hercules in Full Regalia

Chapter Twenty-six

The Blessed Mary

Lesson Fifty:

Five of Diamonds, received September 8th, 1992 Book of Wisdom, channeled from Hierophant:

In this lesson, the Hierophant revealed why each lesson is earmarked with a playing card. He gave me instructions on how to deal out a deck of cards to find out what lesson I will need to study to overcome a problem that awaits in my future. He also covered the use of gemstones to draw in great energy, while also giving me instructions on how to create Astral Crystal Beacons.

SEE APPENDIX FOR ENTIRE LESSON

During the third week at the Renaissance Festival that year Michael's energy felt very excited. He said, "She's coming, my Mary is coming." I didn't know what he was talking about. I asked Sir Gregory if we had any new volunteers coming that day because Michael was excited.

He said, "Yes a friend of Barbara's. A young girl by the name of Mary. She volunteered to fill out Certificates of Knighthood.

A short time later, Michael told me to get some copper wire and small beads from Lady Linda's craft kits. I put them in small bag in my pouch as I had Sir James Gray, our Good Knight biker dude, help me strap on the armor. When we finished, Michael entered my body and said, "Sir James you have been claimed. Are you ready to receive the angel?" Like a bullet, he made his way into the knighting circle.

Sir James had been wanting to knight the children for well over a year, but that privilege was reserved for Angel-Knights alone. As Michael entered the knighting circle, Sir James dropped to one knee and bowed his head as all his fellow knights gathered outside the sacred circle. Before I leveled the sword, my attention was abruptly drawn to the large wooden structure on the hill that over looked our camp. There was a brown-haired bearded man all dressed in white, wearing a beret with a long white feather sticking out the side. He had a certain look and radiant aura that I had only seen around two other people before, Jim Brown and Russell Means. He was staring at me intently. I could tell he saw *something* that most could not see.

Glancing back down at Sir James, Michael went right to work. He called down his angels and three white orbs began rotating around Sir James' head. Sir Thomas-Sachiel was very proud of his friend. Everybody had grown to love Sir James. His heart had opened and he was no longer full of hate and distrust. I knew he held great shame because his past was full of gang related activity. Our mission to protect children was where he was going to find his redemption.

Archangel Michael said, "Cup your hands."

One of the orbs of light moved down and into his waiting hands as the other two orbs disappeared. Michael pierced the orb with his short boot sword then touched the glowing sword to Sir James' head. Michael said some sacred words in Latin then proclaimed, "I dub thee an Angel-Knight Sir James-Sandalphon, my Silver Knight. Rise Sir Knight."

Once again, my gaze went to the hill and the bearded man in white. I thoughts his eyes were going to fall out of his head. He couldn't stop staring. When he noticed me looking at him, he moved out of my line of sight. *Who was this man?* The Knowing came over me that somehow, he would play an important role in the future of the quest.

The sound of giggling drew me back to Sir James. Everyone was still congratulating him . It was a really big deal to become an Angel Knight. A few of the lady knights, Bonnie and June, were becoming very interested in Sir James. They were gifting him items from their tunics. Bonnie gave him a red feather pin and Lady June gave him a coin pin. I was hoping nothing romantic would come of this interaction, because that could become a recipe for disaster.

Normally I stood at the entrance of our castle complex to greet the new arrivals, but this day Michael wanted us to stand on a huge tree stump that stood about four-foot-high just outside of the stable where Hercules was eating some hay. I saw a group of people coming down the path toward our camp. One of them was a blond with a golden light that seemed to surround her body. I thought it was just something between Michael and me until Sir James came running over to me saying, "Excuse me Sir Edward, what does it mean when you see a golden light around someone?"

Michael said, "It means you are looking at a soul mate."

Sir James smiled a devilish smile and I felt there was going be trouble. I knew it was the "Mary" that Michael had been waiting for. Sir Gregory showed her around the castle complex and introduced her to everyone, except me. It was like Mary didn't see me or thought I was a statue on exhibit. Sir James was love struck. He couldn't keep his eyes off of her. Michael and I stood on that tree stump for well over an hour watching the knights and new volunteers prepare for the opening and the many visitors that we would be receiving that day.

Lady Linda was busy setting up the gift shop when I noticed a sinister looking woman dressed as a Bawdy Wench walk up to Linda and ask, "So what is this all about? What are you Christians or Pagans?"

Linda said, "What do you mean?"

Without answering, the woman walked off in a grumbling huff.

Michael said to me, "Now it begins."

We looked down at Mary, and then he had me reach into my leather pouch and pull out the wire. He started twisting, wrapping and bending. Then we added the three beads and twisted some more until he had created a most incredibly beautiful ring. Michael jumped off the tree stump and when he hit the ground all the chains and metal plates on his blue armor made an unmistakable sound.

That's one thing about Michael that I will always remember the most. He loved to jump off of high places, particularly stages when we were doing safety programs. I knew my human knee joints would pay for those jumps one day, but for him each time was like landing on earth for the first time.

As we walked over to the new female volunteer with the gleaming gold aura I felt like we had met before. There was a motherly quality about her that was very comforting. Then it hit me where I had seen that glow before; it was all around the Constant Walker when she saved me from drowning as a child. Mary had just turned twenty-one and was working as an aid to a congresswoman on Capitol Hill.

Michael said, "Lady Mary, this ring will help cure your headache. We don't want you to leave over a silly headache, because if you leave you will never come back. If you accept this ring, you will never leave." Michael didn't have anything further to say to her that day. I could tell he was afraid he would scare her if he continued. His presence could be overwhelming at times, the price of which I was left holding the bag for on many occasions.

About an hour later after Michael left me in the armor alone, I told Mary that the ring would grant three wishes and she should make the first one to relieve her headache.

She said, "How did you know I have a migraine?"

I replied, "Do you believe in angels?"

She said, "Yes, but I never saw one."

I said, "Well one saw you today and he told me to make you that ring." I told her that I had to start knighting children and if she wanted to talk we could later.

To my left, I felt Mary watching my every move. I could only imagine how strange all this was for her. I wouldn't have been surprised if she had left.

At the same time Mary was watching me, I also felt the gaze once again of the bearded man in white. He was sitting atop his lofty perch. As I was talking to the kids standing in the knighting circle throughout the day, every time I'd look up he was watching my every move. It was kind of creepy. I asked Sir James and his friend Sir Thomas to discreetly go up to the bearded man's shop and find out who he was and what he did.

An hour and a half later, my two spies still hadn't returned. Michael said that the bearded man was keeping them entertained, and that the man was waiting to test me directly.

In a vision, Michael showed me a large gold and silver sword with a beautiful crystal in its pommel. I remember seeing that same sword in visions of the past. It was firmly etched in my memory. I had seen none like it anywhere.

Michael said, "Take Lady Mary with you." I asked Mary if she wanted to take a walk so we could talk. She smiled the most loving smile and nodded, yes. Her presence was truly angelic.

As we approached the shop I could see the walls were lined with swords of all different shapes and sizes. Sir James and Sir Thomas were standing at the counter talking with the bearded man.

He said, "Sir Edward the Blue Knight, it's so good of you to finally come for a visit. I thought I would have to hold your two knights hostage all day."

I smiled and bowed my head.

Fearing that I would screw things up I let Michael do all the taking. "It's been a long time my brother. Good to see you again," he began. We hugged and for some strange reason I felt like I knew this man from another place and time.

He was Master Swordsmith Daniel Watson, owner of the Angel Sword Forge in Austin, Texas. Sir James realized how long he and Thomas had been gone and apologized.

I asked, "Would you and Sir Thomas mind taking Lady Mary for a tour of the festival? My brother and I have some catching up to do."

You would have thought I gave Sir James a million dollars. I could see poor Mary didn't know what was going on, but she went along with it.

Brother Daniel told me that he has been waiting for over ten years for me to walk into his forge. He went on to say that he had to tour the country in the hopes that we would come together one day. I saw he had a statue of Archangel Michael mounted over top of his flaming forge. He asked me if I could stay for a few moments because he was just about to give a demonstration to a few patrons on swordsmithing.

"It would be an honor, Brother," Michael replied.

Brother Daniel then began to speak, telling a brief history of swordsmithing through the ages. He explained how he uses an ancient form of mind over matter to polarize the molecules within the steel that would normally flow outward to the edges of the blade. He told the crowd that with focused concentration he is able to turn the molecules inward as he beats and folds the metal many times to form the blade and tang. Master Watson pumped the bellows several times then pulled a white-hot chunk of metal out of the forge. Laying it on the anvil he started striking the steel with a heavy hammer. I could see that Daniel went into a trance, deeper and deeper with every strike of his mighty hammer. He was amazing. Within five minutes he had beaten the metal into the beginnings of a sword blade. As the blade cooled, he then told his audience a story of a mighty vision quest that he had taken ten years earlier, that changed his life forever. While treasure hunting in Mexico he stopped to pray at the Church of the Blessed Virgin Mary Magdalene. When he turned to leave, he became paralyzed and saw an apparition of Archangel Michael who told him to create a special sword of a specific weight and mass. Michael told him he would travel for ten years trying to sell the sword, but that no one would feel worthy enough to claim it. Then on the tenth year, the one who would safeguard this Sword of Swords would be revealed.

He took the cooled blade and handed it to a patron to pass around for all to see.

The Master went on, "Today marks the last day of that ten-year quest and I believe it was not by chance that on this, the last day of my quest, I would find myself next to the Good Knight's Camp. I believe Sir Edward the Blue Knight is the man that Archangel Michael commissioned that mighty sword for, so that he might safeguard it on his Divine Quest to save the Children of Tomorrow. Now the true test will be to see if the Blue Knight can pick out that special sword from all the other swords that line my walls."

Wow, now I was really wondering who this guy standing before me was. He used the words "Children of Tomorrow" and Michael was the only one I've ever heard use those terms.

Sir James and Lady Mary had just returned in time to hear the Master's challenge. I received a round of applause and a few cheers from the onlookers as I shook Master Daniel's hand and stepped behind the counter.

He said, "Take your time. You only get one chance and one choice. Any sword you pick is yours to keep." He gave me a mischievous grin, as he peeked out over his glasses.

I smiled and said, "No pressure there!"

I knew exactly what the sword looked like. Michael had etched its image into my brain. I went quickly through all fifty-two swords he had on display. I couldn't believe the prices he had on those swords. They were priced from as low as $150.00 and all the way up in the thousands. Three swords had a crystal in the pommel, but none of them was the sword Michael showed me. I then started to take swords down to feel the different energy the Master had put into each one.

Brother Daniel was making a game of this and I played along. More and more people were gathering. I could see this was half challenge and half good publicity for him. He was there to sell swords and his challenge to me was drawing crowds into his shop to watch. He was truly an artist, both in craftsmanship and sales.

While feeling my way through the wall of swords I said, "My dear brother you wouldn't be trying to fool the old Blue Knight, would you?"

"What do you mean dear brother? He replied.

I said, "I cannot find the Sword of Swords from the Lord of Lords if 'IT' is not present!"

The crowd looked surprised. They wanted to see this mighty sword that the angel wanted the Blue Knight to have.

I said, "We can finish this noble contest when you actually have the Sword with the Stone present. Until then, I must get back to the knighting circle, for there are children who await me there."

Master Watson smiled. I could see he knew, I that knew what I was doing.

As I walked Lady Mary back to camp I told her, "Twice now as I stood next to you I saw a vision of people crawling on an old cobble stone street with bloody hands and knees. When I asked Michael just now what it all means he told me "Ask Mary, she knows.""

"You must have been seeing my birth in Messina, Sicily, twenty-one years ago. I was born four weeks premature and back then a baby born that underdeveloped always died," she said. "My mother was broken hearted after being told that her baby wouldn't live through the night. The grandmother of a girlfriend told my mom that she should crawl on her hands and knees from her house to the church of Santo Michaelo several miles away, while praying to the Blessed Virgin Mary to save her baby. All I heard from neighbors while growing up was how my mother and many of her friends crawled on my behalf for weeks. They would come home bloody every night, but every time they did, I apparently got stronger. My mom felt I was spared from death for a reason. When I was released from the hospital she took me to the priest and named me Maria Angela in honor of the two saints."

I said, "Well that sure explains why Archangel Michael was so excited when you found your way to his encampment today and why he had me make that special ring to welcome you."

I told Mary my Michael story and how it fit in to my father's war story. I also told her that my father talked about heavy fighting against the Germans during the war when his unit helped drive the Nazi's out of Messina. It made us wonder if that cleared the way for Mary's mother to grow up to give birth to her. Everything seems so very interconnected.

Michael showed me in a vision how Mary now stood at a crossroad. Her Jewish boyfriend had asked her to marry him and she hadn't made up her mind. If she married him it would only last four years before she filed for divorce.

Michael said, "She needs to be honored and protected. Not used and abused." I felt a big brother or fatherly kinship to Mary. She was about the same age as my step-daughter Dawn and I didn't want her to fall prey to a bad marriage like Dawn had.

I realized how late it was and said, "I must get back to knighting, but we should talk again."

She said, "Yes of course, I know you are busy and maybe we could talk next week since I'm not scheduled to volunteer again until then."

I told her, "You will have a lot to process between now and then, since Archangel Michael is sending a special angel to comfort and ease your pain. You are at a turning point in your life and the decisions you make in the next few weeks will affect the rest of your life."

A bewildered yet knowing look came over her as we said goodbye.

The following day was Sunday. The weather forecasters said it was going to be a killer hot and humid day. Lady Judah, who was always looking ahead to plan effectively, was afraid that I was going to pass out from heat stroke since I was in the armor all day. To prevent this from happening she went to a costume shop and bought a freezer vest for me to wear under the breastplate; similar to those the Disney characters wear under their costumes. Thank goodness, she got it! Between the outside temperature and my core temperature rising when Michael came into the body, I felt like I was going to burst into flames. The freezer vest was a dream come true in helping me to conquer the heat. The only problem was, that with the humidity in the air, the breastplate would frost up. I kind of looked like a big blue popsicle! I always try to make the most fun of a situation though, so I let kids leave their handprints on the armor. As soon as one faded away, frost would form again! They thought it was some kind of magic trick.

The Good Knights were loved by all young and old. Well, maybe not quite all. There was this one group of zealots who didn't like anyone who didn't agree with their belief systems. They targeted the Blue Knight as a heretic that needed to be burned at the stake. This was coming from the same people dressed in medieval garb, walking around eating turkey legs, and selling fake "witch craft potion." It was a festival and almost every vendor was also a period actor as well. It's entertainment, right? For some reason though, they viewed the Good Knighthood as a Pagan cult. I knew they didn't mess with any of the others in costume, so I asked Michael what was up?

"They are sensitive enough to feel that there is more to you than a fairytale for kids. They also can't marry in their feeble little minds the strength of persona with the fact that you are a child advocate," he said.

One woman hissed at me and said, "That armor you are wearing isn't Christian."

I said, "Maybe not, but it certainly is Godly! But is it any less Christian than a Templar tunic?"

Since Michael's armor was covered in ornate gold leaf talismans and ancient symbols she wanted to know what each one meant. As I told her she hissed again, "You can't wear those symbols. You are a heretic!"

Deciding this was one of those times that discretion was the better part of valor, I said "They are just pretty designs to make the armor authentic to the period."

"Bullshit!" she growled as she stomped away.

I just shook my head. We had vendors selling new age things, witches with candles, magicians, jesters, pagans, and all sorts of ne'er-do-wells at the RenFest, but this chick chose to pick on me.

When the word spread that the Good Knights were Pagans, the Pagan people who worked at the Renaissance Festival started taunting me. They decided that we were Christians. So now we I had the Christians calling us

Pagans and the Pagans calling us Christians - what an odd place to be - between a rock and a hard place.

From that point on when we were confronted, I told both sides, "I believe in everything that you believe in and more. But my religion is the same as the Creator's. I believe in children and that's who I am here to serve."

Neither side liked that answer.

John, one of the younger volunteers said, "For the life of me I can't figure out why certain people just have an inbred problem with the Good Knights when others have a natural love and affection for the movement. It's mind boggling."

Michael answered back, "If someone has a problem with what the Good Knights do, it is normally because that person feels threatened and is casting their dark shadow on us. So goes the way of the Sons of Darkness. Just send them love."

Seeming a little flustered, John replied, "Well that is a little hard when they are all up in our faces."

I added, "I do send them love, but it's also nice that I have a Private Detective license *and* an unrestricted gun carry permit. I've seen the faces of crazy and I've had to draw down on more than one person in my life that was hell bent on putting me on the other side of the dirt. I've seen too many good people lose their lives to some crazy zealot thug. As a cop I always believed, that it's better to be judged by twelve than carried by six. I believe in the power of God, the Sword of Truth, and my Colt Python that I carry in the middle of my back."

Just then, Sir James-Sandalphon came riding into camp on his motorcycle, a blue 1948 Harley-Davison Pan Head. He was wearing his Pagan's leather jacket over top of his Angel-Knight tunic. We suddenly got a new name. Outlaws.

"Seriously man you're killing me. You know they don't allow bikes in here. Do you want to get us kicked out?" I blasted.

"Yesterday my bike was vandalized in the lot. I thought I could just park it behind the castle," he explained.

"No, you can't. Get it out of here. NOW!" Michael boomed.

And so it goes, I thought.

"Just the price of doing business," Michael whispered in my ear.

Chapter Twenty-seven

The Sword of Swords

Lesson Fifty-One:

Four of Diamonds, received October 8th, 1992 Book of Wisdom, channeled from Hierophant:

As the lessons neared their end, the Hierophant again taught about the importance of working with crystals. He was still preparing me to create the Philosopher's Stone that would be needed to attract the millions of dollars necessary to fund Michael's effort to reach the children. He also expressed how important the Stone would be if I ever received the gift of the Sword from Master Daniel Watson.

SEE APPENDIX FOR ENTIRE LESSON

I knew now that it was more important than ever that I pass Master Daniel's test. I got the feeling that he wanted to hold on to the "Sword of Swords," and that was why it wasn't included in the collection hanging on the wall when he first tested me. Daniel had been watching me, observing my energy and moves. He knew exactly who walked in the armor. He was a gifted energy worker. I wondered why he would have hidden the sword from view, other than the possibility of him wanting me to choose the wrong sword? Then I thought, I see what he has done! Not having the real sword displayed in the collection was the greatest test of all.

Lady Mary hadn't been back to volunteer for a while. When she showed up at the Good Knight encampment this month, Archangel Michael gave her a wrapped present as a gift from the Good Knighthood. She was happy and glad to see everybody. It seemed like she had come home. "The week after I saw you last, I had a revelation about my life. I had a dream that an angel wearing a blue tunic and red robe told me that my destiny would be revealed if I walked the Path of Righteousness with

Saint Michael. And, that it was my birthright if I chose to accept it," she said. "It hit me pretty hard though. I hate making decisions. I had migraine after migraine just thinking about it. I felt torn between my family, Mark (her boyfriend) and following this vision that I have no idea where it will take me."

I asked her to open the gift and to her amazement the box contained a blue Good Knight tunic, gold chain belt and blood red cape. She slipped it on over top of the tee shirt and shorts that she was wearing and completely transformed into someone else. Her eyes were bluer, her hair was more golden, and she glowed. Oh, how she glowed.

Michael asked Lady Barbara-Raphael to drape and saddle Hercules. Lady Mary helped me strap on Michael's Armor. Once in the armor Michael hoisted Mary up into the saddle and he started walking alongside her while they talked. The walk looped around one half of the festival grounds. Many patrons stopped to take photographs of St. Mary and St. Michael together again. They didn't consciously know that was what was happening, but they could sense that a special moment in time was being captured.

The walk lasted about an hour; I don't know what they talked about. It was obviously personal, but along the way I saw her laugh and cry. All I remember was Michael saying that, "On this path you will find love and commitment like nowhere else and from that love you will give birth to a very special girl child who will help to shape a new consciousness for the new world that is to come."

When we returned to the Good Knight Castle camp, Mary was glowing brighter than before and all the knights could see it. Master Watson gave a wave from his shop on top of the hill and Michael waved for him to come down. After positioning Hercules in the center of the Angelic Knighting Circle, with Mary still in the saddle, Michael called for all the knights to gather around the outside of the circle. Michael had hand carved twelve special wooden swords for each Angel-Knight to use in ceremonies and during the knighting of children. Every sword was made especially for the individual knight. Depending on their energy it was either painted silver, gold, black or white and had unique symbols, gems stones, crystals and sacred angelic names on the blades.

When Master Daniel arrived carrying a long cloth bag Michael said, "Brother are you ready?"

Daniel smiled and nodded, "Why yes, I am."

Michael knelt down on one knee before the Master and said, "Then make me worthy."

The Master reached into the bag and produced out a huge broad sword still in its black leather sheath. He ceremonially, slid the blade out of the covering. The sun's rays struck the blade, reflected and pierced my left eye.

Step one, I thought.

Everyone gasped at the sight of the sword. There was an undefinable magical energy to it. It seemed to be alive. The hilt was made of layered, highly polished, sacred hardwoods from around the world. In its pommel was a stone of brilliant magnificence. It was a large clear quartz crystal with rainbow facets that had been mounted in highly polish brass.

Michael bowed his head to the Master as Daniel spoke a verse in Spanish, that no one, but Lady Mary understood. Then the Master drew up the sword. This time it's highly-polished, silver-etched blade caught the sunlight and radiated it back on Lady Mary and Hercules the horse.

Awestruck faces watched on as the scene unfolded. The Master then leveled the sword to my armor and tapped both shoulders saying, "Michael, Excalibur, the Sword of Truth and the Stone of Light have risen from the darkness of the abyss as one, in this your final mission."

Watson handed the sword to Michael as he brought me to my feet.

Michael said to all in witness, "Behold, I give you Lady Mary-Uriel, our Blue Princess. Serve her in all the ways and keep her strong so that one day she may become Cinderella, Queen of the Angel-Knights."

All of the Angel-Knights raised their swords to the sky and we felt a great power flowing around us. Seven white orbs appeared over the Blue Princess' head and began rotating as if to form a crown of white light. Her body radiated a bright blue glow. It was truly an amazing experience.

After the ceremony, Master Daniel asked to examine the wooden swords each knight was carrying. He was shocked to feel that dead wood could hold such energy. Michael spoke through me to the master saying, "A sword is not known by its metal, but by its master's deeds."

Daniel vowed, "To support your quest Blue Knight, I will supply you with a sword for each Angel-Knight who becomes deserving. But, if one knight should disrespect the meaning of the Angel Swords, the gifts will end.

"That is quite a generous offer, Sword Master. You see, there are to be 144 Angel-Knights that walk alongside me," Michael said.

Daniel just smiled.

At sunset we walked to the hill and I formally retired Tenacity, the sword I carried, and began carrying Excalibur.

Master Daniel Watson and Sir Edward with Excalibur

After walking back down the hill, I could see the crush Sir James had on Lady Mary now jumped up a level. He was in awe of the Blue Princess' splendor. He said to me later, "She looks just like Cinderella surrounded by her adoring knights."

I said, "Your physic sight is right on target. She is the fairy Cinderella incarnate and it's up to us to keep her in her position through respect. We can't let her become Lady Guinevere, weakened by the charms of some would-be-prince, so don't let anyone weaken her with a selfish kiss. She can't belong to just one. The Blue Princess must focus her love on the whole world in order to help our mission succeed." The warning was generic and aimed at all of the male knights, but it certainly put Sir James on notice to back off. That was no human glow he was seeing around her. Stretching my hand out to him as noble brothers in arms I continued, "I am counting on you to help me keep the skirt sniffing dogs at bay."

Sir James gave me a hug and agreed to protect our princess for as long as he lived. When he said that, I got a ping in my heart.

I said, "Sir James just make sure that when I call you come and all will be right with the world."

Lady Mary-Uriel was a changed woman. I could tell that there was a bond that had re-formed, which many would try to break, but by the grace of God it shall never be broken.

When the Renaissance Festival was over that year we were all exhausted. It was tough saying good-bye to Brother Daniel Watson who was traveling back home to Texas. We had grown very close. During the weekdays when I came down to work on the campsite he and I would sip

tequila, play chess and talk. He truly felt like my long-lost brother. On the spirit level, he actually was. Synchronistically, he also had twelve student apprentices that he called his "Angel-Knights." Master Watson was teaching Tai-Chi, the powers of meditation and swordsmithing. We were able to meet them all at varying times during the festival. Some would be there one weekend while others stayed at the forge in Texas. They were a great bunch of very humble guys.

Our Good Knight Angel-Knights held a special feast and ceremony for Master Daniel and his Angel-Sword Staff at the East Wing Castle the night before they left Maryland that year. After working hard packing up his vendor wares and the Angel Sword inventory, they all deserved a break.

The evening was quite special and held a surprise for both Master Watson and the Blue Knight. The Angel-Knights had decided to honor us in a very unique way. They had purchased two sets of spurs; one set for each of us. Mine was to commemorate the first year the Blue Knight rode a horse during a Good Knight event. The only difference between the two sets of spurs was the shape of the silver inlays. On mine the inlays were round and Daniel's they were square. The reason for the gift to Daniel was due to a warning I had given him a month earlier.

After getting to know Daniel from weekend to weekend, I began to see that he was a very mysterious man with many passions. One of his greatest passions was treasure hunting. He would search the southwest investigating sites where gold and silver hordes were rumored to be hidden. The people who buried these treasure hordes had since died and the treasures were never re-claimed. One treasure he had been searching for was the "Lost Dutchmen's Gold Mine." It was reportedly somewhere the Superstition Mountain range east of Phoenix, Arizona.

During one of our RenFest weekday tequila afternoons, when we were sharing "little known" facts about ourselves I told Brother Daniel I did card readings. We had already drunk the better half of a bottle of Mescal when he said, "Read my cards. Please? Maybe you can reveal the clues I need on my quest for the Dutchman's Gold. You know, I was following up on leads to the gold when I stumbled into the church where Archangel Michael asked me to forge the Sword of Swords."

How could I not read his cards after that revelation?

I laid the cards out. A great feathered winged serpent appeared in my mind's eye. Michael whispered, "It guides Daniel as I guide you."

I also saw that there were times when he and the Serpent were one and in the same, similar to the times when Michael and I are in the armor together.

The cards said the spirit's name was Quetzalcoatl. I was shown that the winged serpent was the driving force behind Daniel's search to reclaim the treasure that was stolen from its beloved people many years in the past.

"You were within a few yards of what you were searching for when you stood near the town of Durango," I relayed.

Hi mouth dropped open, "Damn! I knew it! I could *feel* it!"

"I'm also hearing there is a horde of gold and silver buried in place called the Zone of Silence next to a place called Turtle Rock." I told him a few other incidental things and then the cards were done talking.

At the end of the reading Master Daniel said, "Well my good brother, when do we leave for Mexico?"

"My quest is not for gold, that is yours. And seriously though, you have met Linda. There was no way in hell she would put up with me running around Mexico looking for lost treasure. It's hard enough on her with me being gone a few days a month doing out of town gigs for the Good Knight programs." I sighed for some reason and then continued, "Make no mistake, I am on a treasure hunt and I find gold every time I level the sword to a child's shoulder."

"But before you pack your bags, I need to tell you one more thing. There was a warning for you in the cards. I saw you walking by a pile of rocks and cactus. The sun was at your back and you were alone. You were looking over to the left at a rock formation and unknowingly startled a rattlesnake on your right. It struck out and bit you near the groin. I saw the fang puncture an artery, the venom spread fast and then there was darkness. The cards also told me you have been very lucky in the past with near misses," I told him.

"That is very true. So much so I care not think about them," he shared.

"You need to wear your spurs to announce your presence to the creatures of the desert. And of course, the jingling of the spurs will be like church bells bringing spiritual help to your Divine Quest to find the lost treasure of the Winged Serpent," I said.

"I don't have spurs," he told me.

I replied, "Well I say it's about time you get a set because the final message in the cards for you was, when you are searching and you can't hear your spur jingling, you are within feet of what you seek!"

Daniel and I accepted our tokens of honor. We both thanked the Angel-Knights in unison. Then I turned to Daniel and said, "Brother Daniel we never know when there is a snake out and about, and they are worse when they cross our path in human form. I certainly like them to hear me coming. We both need to announce ourselves to snakes; mine

walk on two feet and yours slither and curl. Take my right spur and I'll take yours. That way when your right foot hits the ground it's me and when my right foot hits the ground it's you. When we are together we are a part and when we are apart we are together."

He smiled, scratched his head trying to figure that one out, and said, "Deal! Be safe brother."

Chapter Twenty-eight

Hate

Lesson Fifty-Two:

Three of Diamonds, received November 8ᵗʰ, 1992 Book of Wisdom, channeled from Hierophant:

In this lesson, the Hierophant covered the history of hatred and how humans use it to justify committing unspeakable crimes against humanity. I remembered that Michael had said said years ago that I would once again stand before Russell Means and a host of American Indians to ask for the forgiveness necessary to release the trapped earth-bound spirits of Crazy Horse and our ancestors.

By far this was the shortest lesson of all so far, but at the same time it was the longest. The hierophant wanted me to use everything I had learned from all the lessons and write my own lesson on "Hate" for the next First Wednesday Club gathering. Where do I start I wondered? I created a 5-D gateway and asked for guidance. This is what came through.

SEE APPENDIX FOR ENTIRE LESSON

I created a handout of the lesson and gave each student a copy. I called my stab at instruction:

"Lesson Fifty-Two Plus The black/white Joker"
Book of Wisdom November 9, 1992
from the Sir Edward-The Hermit

Dear First Wednesday Club Members:

For my practicum, the Hierophant has assigned me the task of designing a lesson for you surrounding the question, "What is hate?" The first thing I want you to do as part of this lesson is to write down your definition of hate. Your answers will become part of the new Book of Wisdom that I will be adding to my Book of Light and Shadow. It is important for the Children of Tomorrow to have the benefit of different perspectives on hate since understanding anything comes from the lives we have led and how we have been affected along the way.

Some of you are victims of hate and/or producers of hate. So take the time and do a little reflection or go into a meditation to answer the question, "What is hate to you?"

Thank you,

The Hermit

Reviewing the definition of hate made us look at our own past actions. I found it very interesting how each of the members expressed their personal views on hate. Everybody had a different take on what hate really was. Most of the members felt that people confused hate, which is a very strong emotion, with dislike.

Michael told the gathering, "There are people who give others good reason to dislike them. They fear disapproval. So in trying to dominate and control the way others view them, they purposely do things that make them undesirable to others."

I could understand that completely. My brother Damian's wife Jinx was one of those people. I call them "toxic personalities" - the type that are better left alone. Life is too short to put up with all their twisted drama when all they want to do is put others down in order to lift themselves up. One of the knights asked Michael, "What is in it for them to be so toxic?"

He simply stated, "Dopamine. It is the pleasure chemical behind most of humanity's sinful behavior and secret cravings. When they cause pain, they receive a dopamine rush from tormenting someone. The rush causes pleasure just as a joyous moment would." The class was really beginning to understand human behavior and motivation. It was rewarding to see everyone's minds expanding, along with an ability to understand new perspectives.

With Linda still in a wheel chair, I was pretty much sidetracked from going in to the castle for a while. Michael had me go for long walks up to Cove Point Lighthouse and back. On one of the walks, he showed me a vision of our ABC's of Safety program. The demand was about to become so great that I wouldn't physically be able to do all the programs. I saw the Angel-Knights must start spreading the message and become presenters as well. In order to do that Michael wanted to maintain quality control over the core information that was going out to the children.

I called a meeting of the charity board. Linda didn't want to go because it was such an ordeal getting the wheelchair in and out of our small car. I had Dawn come sit with her mother while I went in to the castle.

I met with key staff, Lady Bonnie, Sir Gregory, Lady Judah and Lady Mary, telling them that Michael said it was time for others to start spreading the message of safety for children. I relayed what Michael showed me. We hashed around a few ideas like just reading the storybook showing the video of the Blue Knight's stage presentations. Michael came through with a resounding "no" on all of those ideas. He then showed me sitting with a writer and creating a script.

"We need to act out the *ABC's of Safety* from the child's perspective to show them the different scenarios that could take place. Michael just flashed a concept to me. We've discussed a video format before but it is time we move forward completely. It will be done in a candid camera style," I finished. It was decided we should create a video presentation of the *ABC's of Safety*. Lady Bonnie and I could train teachers and Good Knight volunteers how to present the program. This way anyone could present the program by merely segueing in and out of the film.

We started working on a script for the video production while Lady Bonnie went to work lining up a professional film crew. We had a psychologist and a few therapists in our volunteer pool; one of which contacted Lady Bonnie after she heard about the film concept. She told Judah that she and a few colleagues were working with a support group and healing circle for local families whose kids had fallen prey to pedophiles. After talking about our project, the therapists felt the best way to help these kids heal was for them to help others. The idea of volunteer kids acting out the trick that they fell for in order to save another child from harm, was psychological genius. Lady Bonnie stepped up to take on the task of getting the parents and child volunteers signed up for the video taping of the children acting out the ten tricks.

Michael wanted it to be a live action/animation mix so we decided to create a contest for kids to draw MacAroni Mouse from the book. We scripted him as the narrator, so we wanted him to pop in to announce each of the ten tricks. Michael also said we needed a Good Knight theme song and music video. I found that Angel Anael was already working in that direction and had guided Lady Judah to a meeting with Arthur Leasy, the music writer and composer for the Cosby Show at the time.

The speed at which everything was coming together was surreal. I was assured there was a Divine plan here and we were just all surrendering to the process and being guided. Another win for the Book of Wisdom's Lessons!

Chapter Twenty-nine

Trouble within the Knighthood

With the addition of Lady Mary and the Angel Uriel, Michael was able to pull together the cosmic ingredients of the Angels of the Four Directions on Earth within the knighthood. He said it would form a strong foundation for the mission and allow the Good Knights to expand. One purpose for activating the angels of the Four Directions was to safeguard the Blue Princess from negative influences and to help Lady Mary-Uriel acquire the "Knowing" she would need to pass down to her special daughter one day - if she claimed her birthright. The responsibility of training Lady Mary fell upon Sir Gregory. Michael gave him express permission to give her a crash course on the lessons in the Book of Wisdom to help her catch up. She didn't have to know the lessons; she just needed to know about them in their most basic form.

Lady Bonnie-Gabriel suggested that the four get a house together to save money and pool their resources. Lady Mary worked on Capitol Hill not far from the other three, so it seemed to be the perfect match, plus it would be good to have a man, Sir Gregory-Metatron, in the house to again keep the sniffing dogs at bay.

After several weeks of looking, the four found the perfect little white house with a swimming pool in a quiet subdivision in Bowie, Maryland. The house was just a few miles from East Wing Castle. I was happy for them. Living together would give them support and more spendable income. However, whether or not these dominant personalities could get along was the question.

And that was the real test.

It would have been perfect if we were only dealing with angels and not humans. Because with humans come hormones, and with hormones comes mood swings and with mood swing come PMS (ooops did I just say PMS?) No, I am not a chauvinist, far from it as a matter of fact. I am a realist - and baby it doesn't get more real than the drama that ensued.

It wasn't long before the Four Directions got on each other's nerves and they became the "Bitches of East Wing." I never knew a guy could suffer from PMS, but it happened right before my very eyes. Sir Gregory wound up being the biggest bitch of them all.

It was a miracle we ever got anything accomplished. Sir Gregory and Lady Bonnie were always arguing and nobody wanted to work with Lady Judah because of the way she went about doing business. Judah was always in everybody else's business trying to micro manage things she was not even supposed to be working on. Michael had brought together four very strong personalities. All I could think about was poor Lady Mary - what have we done to her? I was putting out fires every other day between them.

It was exhausting.

"Before coming together," I reminded them, "it was with the understanding that you were going to be helping to keep Mary strong and courageous. Quite the opposite is taking place."

I asked Michael what could I do for Mary and he said, "Mary must find her own inner strength if she wants to inherit her birthright. If her body and mind are weakened by all of the stimuli, then that is on her. She is allowing it to happen and right now is enjoying the attention and feeding into the drama that she allows to be around her. We can only wait and see what comes of it. Remember this group is a microcosm, an experiment in human interaction. If you can't live with your own people, how can you ever hope to live with the star people?"

I let that sink in and released the need to intervene.

With my newfound detached state of being Lady Mary's guardian, I saw all of the dynamics of human behavior playing out. The problem was each of the housemates wanted to be in charge of the others in the house and the organization, and all that Michael wanted was for them to just work together. I wasn't even in charge. Once the Blue Princess arrived, I backed out of the charity organization all together. I was in command of the order of Angel-Knights, but no longer in charge of the charity.

The way Michael structured it was that Lady Mary-Uriel, the Good Knight Princess, and her Board of Directors would dictate the direction of the charity and her fellow captains would handle their areas of responsibility. Lady Bonnie was in charge of media, books and film productions; Sir Gregory was in charge of scheduling safety programs, coordinating the Master Studies Programs for adults, and organizing the mail order requests for lessons; and Lady Judah was in charge of the finances; taxes and writing grants to support the charity's outreach programs and materials.

As far as the Order of Good Knights, the Four Directions were all captains of equal rank, including Mary. Each Captain was in charge of a legion of twelve Angel-Knights, Good Knights and/or volunteers. The legions: red, blue, green and yellow, were responsible for support, helping to present safety programs, coming up with new and innovative ways of helping the community and fundraising. Snap-aroo simple, right?

Wrong!

Did you ever meet "those kind of kids" who just don't play well with others? Well that kind of kid made up our upper echelon staff.

I'd shake my head at times and think, "Well, Michael wanted misfits and he got them." Incredulously, you would think that after forty-three years of having Michael's consciousness in and around me I would stop making statements as if he couldn't hear me.

He quipped back with his pat answer, "But look at all the passion and emotion that they are generating. Humans tend to create drama in their lives so that they have something to criticize. Criticism hurts feelings which leads to a further negative response. If the knights stayed focused on the mission at hand, keeping children from being sexually abused, bullied and murdered, they might eventfully solve the problem. But for now, they were just getting in each other's way. Have patience and just remain an observer. No interfering."

"I can't just let them continue to deceive each other. They jockey for position all the time. The hardest thing for me is I hear their thoughts and I know they are lying to me," I replied.

Michael responded, "Are they still walking the 'Path of the Magi' Are they applying the lessons they've learned to their lives every day? Have they found the 'Knowing?' If not, why not? Yes, they lie to you and what's worse is they lie to themselves. That's the biggest sin of all."

I asked him what was I to do to bring them all together. He said, "You can lead a horse to water, but you can't make him drink. You can lead a human to knowledge, but you can't make him think. They have taken everything for granted that has been given to them. Take everything away by sending them home. Banish them from the castle for thirty days and those who come back were never gone, and those who don't were never here."

This was also the day "Rule One" was carved in stone for the knighthood. Once you became an Angel-Knight, there are two types of gatherings. "Attendance Performances" which meant you made an appearance at a program or meditation ceremony if you could make it. Then there were "Command Performances" which meant being on your deathbed was the only thing that could keep you from being at the performance.

Michael had me explain the need for the two types of performances and he explained the differences between the two. "You should all take to heart the work of the Order and know the importance of each program. The impact you make on the children will ripple out into the human consciousness. Michael sees that mankind has a hard time believing the un-seeable. If you can't feel the impact and draw to give he can't care, but if feel it you won't just have to trust me. The need for the various types of Angel Knight programs is to help you make a conscious choice when trying to decide to attend a function or not. Mark and remember my words: Everyone has a predestined time of birth and time of death, with specifics on the place of each as well. The time of your death cannot change, but the place can. Therefore, when Michael calls a "command performance" its purpose is to remove one of us from their place of death. With that variable removed from the equation, the life will be spared until a new time of death is recalibrated. There is a lot more to it, but that's the easiest translation I can offer to you. The choice to attend either performance is obviously still up to you individually. But take my advice, when he calls a Command Performance, I would personally show up anywhere and be there when he told me to be."

This subject never came up before with the group. I knew Michael was working at a more intrinsic level with each member as he had with me, but all the same, I had a feeling Michael could see something on the horizon that I did not.

My suspicions were correct. Archangel Michael called for a "Command Performance" on December 9th during the fifty-third and final gathering of the First Wednesday Club. I had received the last lesson from the Hierophant just the day before. To my great surprise, it was not the Hierophant who delivered the final message, but his teacher, Master ERU.

When the channel opened, The Master seemed disappointed to see that our students were not staying as positive as was expected. Despite his ability to always see a positive way to look at the problem, he said, "Always remember no matter how old humans get they will always be like children! And never forget, this is an experiment. Whatever happens, during an experiment is important data. There is no good or bad. This last lesson could very well help bind all the Angel-Knights back together again."

Chapter Thirty

Master ERU's Lesson

Lesson Fifty-Three:

Two of Diamonds, received December 8th, 1992 Book of Wisdom, channeled from Master ERU:

In Master ERU's lesson he explained the importance of reaching the 144,000 Light Bearers. I learned about the three Energy Grids, Crystalline, Light and Solar, that Atlantis erected to help hold the earth in balance and stop the poles from shifting during the great wobble every twenty thousand years. He discussed the purpose for the positive and negative forces in the universe and the creation of Solar Reflector Shields used to disrupt negative energy and people. I was guided in the use of the Angelic Gateway and Fifth Dimensional Gateway. He ended the lesson explaining the importance of re-creating Pandora's box - a 5-D Prism Cell that would trap and contain all the past evil and negativity created by humanity.

SEE APPENDIX FOR ENTIRE LESSON

After I channeled the final lesson to complete the Book of Wisdom, the story of Atlantis all made sense to me now. The nameless child that I saw in Michael's arms in the cavern, when I drowned, was Queen Sophia's unborn child. It was she to whom Michael was to deliver the Sword of Truth. That is why he was seeking her on earth now. I prayed that Lady Mary, our Blue Princess, could be worthy someday of attracting the Universal Queen and bringing Michael's Victory forth before our time ran out. Her bittersweet nature and the weaknesses she gave into, held little promise, but still I remained hopeful.

It was now December 1992. After channeling directly from Master ERU I had several visions. They were like puzzle pieces to be sorted out. From what I could piece together, we had until 2015 to rebuild a microcosm of Atlantis, elevate fifty-two volunteers to the level of Angel-

Knight, reach ten million Good Knight children with Michael's message of Safety, trap seven Arch-Demons in a Fifth Dimensional Prism Cell, and bring forth the birth of the last heir of Atlantis.

Any normal person would take one look at that list of Herculean tasks, coupled with the reality of the crew of in-fighters I had to work with, and they would head for the hills. "No problem," I thought. "Where do I start?" Michael had always told me that he was sent to fail. So I figured that because he had set the bar so low, I couldn't possibly screw this up. What did I have to lose?

After coming to that conclusion, Michael reminded me, "Twenty-three years is not much time. The fourth-dimensional clock is counting down. We need to get to work.

Prior to the First Wednesday Gathering and the last class to include Lesson Fifty-three, I sent out a letter to all members. Michael and I challenged the members to join the Great Crystal debate Master ERU suggested in Lesson Fifty-three. Each member was to research crystals and their uses. An experiment had to be included with one or more crystals to see if science or the new age belief in the ever-increasing use of crystals was correct. The assignment was to serve as the "final exam" in this course of study, and was to be completed and turned in prior to the last class date.

I went into a meditation about the topic after doing my research but prior to doing my experiment. This was the report I submitted to the class as per the assignment:

The Great Debate
The Power of Crystals

What it comes down to in the war between "New Age" concepts and "Old Age" thinking is, open vs closed minds. New Age thinkers were those who believed in endless possibilities. The Old Age thinkers take the posture that if you can't measure the claims scientifically, then the claims are false.

The truth of the matter is, humans believe what they want to believe, even when the truth is staring them in the face. All science "fact" started off as science fiction. We know through science that it took four billion years to create all that we have on earth, but there are still millions of people who think it was all built in seven days, four thousand years ago by God. Are they right? Of course they are, if that is what they choose to believe. Just as those that believe it has taken us four billion years to get here. Truth, like beauty in art, is in the mind of the beholder.

In the case of crystals. Science dissects them into tiny mineral components and "proves" how they were formed. Native American indigenous people believe their ancestors are present in the rocks and crystals. "New Age" practitioners believe crystals have power and that thought can be programmed into the matrix of the stone.

As far as programing objects is concerned, I have found that I can program just about anything to create a desired effect. It does not have to be a crystal. Whether people want to claim it is a placebo effect or not, it is still my desired effect.

The Hermit's Conclusion:

What we have with this study is the fact that crystals, whether quartz or plastic, still created the desired effect when combined with thought through the power of the fifth dimensional mind. The mind, not the brain, cannot be weighed, photographed or measured by science. What science can measure is what separates the human mind from all other species on the planet: self-awareness. In the beginning with the Creator's first cosmic thought of, "We…" self-awareness was born.

The mind and its power to manifest is the key factor. There are also those who claim that the use of crystals is evil and they're tools of the Devil. Let us be reminded that the Creator placed protein crystals inside each of our ear canals to help us maintain our balance. If those crystals are dislodged you will suffer from dizziness and vertigo. Can science measure the power of those crystals? Yes, and plastic implants would not work. Furthermore, up to 60% of an adult human body is made up of water. Water molecules are a crystalline structure.

There are two fundamental types of crystals in our four-dimensional world. The crystals that most people are familiar with are solid minerals like diamonds, rubies, quartz and even sugar and salt. The second kind of crystal has a more fluid structure even though its molecules maintain an organized pattern. Familiar examples of liquid crystals include digital watch faces and laptop computer screens.

Our body contains numerous crystalline structures that are fundamental to the working of our organism. We stand up straight because our body has a skeleton made up of calcium phosphate crystals. We keep our balance thanks to calcite crystals that are found in the inner ear, and we chew with teeth made with apatite microcrystals. We, like the planet we live on, are filled with different types of crystals. In fact, science has determined that the human body is a liquid crystal full of smaller crystals.

The Placebo Effect:

What is a placebo in the first place? Angel Michael showed me that it is giving someone the psychological means to activate one's own healing powers. When Jesus told the Roman Centurion, "Your faith has cured your servant" His words were the placebo effect that allowed the power of belief in the solider to affect the cure. Belief is everything. Skeptics lack that belief so they cancel out any positive outcome.

I also highly recommend that you plan a trip to a mine or dig your own crystal treasures, it is much more fulfilling.

Just remember the power comes from you not the stones, but some stones can amplify your powers better than others. I have found that real diamonds are the strongest amplifier of thought and echo that thought the longest. That may be partly why we put our love in the diamond ring when we propose marriage to our beloved.

Because it was a "Command Performance" all fifty-three students, volunteers, Good Knights and Angel-Knights showed up at East Wing Castle for Lesson Fifty-three, "The Final." It was graduation, a time for cerebration and a grand party. It was also a fitting farewell and act of gratitude to my great teacher, the Hierophant. The night was a combination of closure to the lessons and festive atmosphere of "making it to the end."

We went over our lesson and some of the student's papers. The lesson also gave more of an understanding to the amazing story of Atlantis and the Sons of Light. One student remarked that she didn't know whether it was her understanding that had elevated or that the story in Lesson Fifty-three was clearer, but she said that she finally grasped the Atlantean legend much better.

We had a potluck so everyone brought a dish or something to drink. We danced, sang, played games and had one heavenly good time. I noticed Lady Mary was really enjoying the company of Sir James, but true to his oath, he was never going to let it be anything more than a knight in service to his Blue Princess. I was so proud of him; proud of all of them.

With the completion of fifty-three months of instruction, I knew there would be a few in the group we would never see again and some who would remain Good Knight volunteers. Obviously, the Angel Knight level Good Knights had already taken vows within the Order so they would continue on, but before I could let that happen I had to clear the air around the infighting that was taking place. Everyone loved the magical meditation ceremonies and parties, but when it came to the day-to-day labors, well that was another thing. They just could not seem to get along no matter what rules I implemented.

At the end of the party the volunteers and students cleaned up while I called for the Angel-Knights to move into my office for a private meeting with Michael and me.

Walking down the hall the entrance of my office loomed large. It was all done in castle rock and looked like its own castle within a castle. It had 8' high stone towers on either side of the door. The arched windows that ran along the two walls surrounding the office were covered in stained glass scenes from *"A Good Knight Story."* Children from a local elementary school had painted them as a gift for me. The door to my office was a spiked wooden gate that slid into one of the stone towers. Over the entrance was 2' mechanical angel in armor holding a sword and her wings were flapping.

The walls that held my diplomas, military and police certificates, plaques, awards, pictures and paintings had a sky-blue background. In the corner was a large walnut desk, with a high back brown leather swivel chair and a corner cabinet that held my computer. The shelves were lined with resource and legal books. It was a very large room with a powerful energetic presence.

I reached my office first and propped myself up against the edge of my desk. The Angel-Knights filed in one by one. Michael invited everyone to take a seat on the floor in a meditative yoga posture while we held our meeting.

Michael and I aired our views on the infighting amongst the Angel-Knights and they aired their views as well. Most of points were petty and didn't hold up under close examination. What it came down to was that certain personalities were frustrating to others. Some people were deemed lazy, while others were exposed for claiming credit for doing things that others did, just to win favor in my eyes.

I shared a little-known secret with them, "Very little escapes Michael. You cannot lie to him."

"Why did you think Greg got the donation of the plywood, when it was actually me?" Asked Judah.

"What makes you think I *thought* anything?" I asked.

"He told you that!" she screamed through her tears. Every time Judah got frustrated or caught in a lie, she cried. Normally I was a sucker for a crying woman, but her ploy was a sad one and just that, a ploy.

"Remember this," I told her and the rest, "I am here as a chess piece like you all. When you tell me something, I am to listen and for the most part not intervene. Especially with this petty stuff. I knew who got the plywood. And what you don't realize is, you are humanly taking credit for something the angel working with you did. Without Anael, you would not be as successful at getting donations. We are a team and team Angel Knight is collectively gathering energy and items to make the mission a success, not to further your personal goals. We are all like lab rats in a maze, creating our own emotional responses to the stimuli we present to each other. We must all start to see through our shadow sides and go into the light. Letting go of who we were, is crucial to creating the person we want to be. The bottom line is, just be the best you, you can be. Stop trying to be someone else in the group. You can't. And by putting someone else down,

I see right through it, even though you think I am stupid. I do not like any one of you more than I like another."

The crying, fighting and finger pointing continued for another 30 minutes. After the explanation I just gave them, I expected more. So did Michael.

A strong diaphragm bellow of "Enough!" came out of me. I am banishing everyone from East Wing Castle for the entire month of January 1993. After the volunteer party on the Epiphany that Lady Linda is throwing for you all, you will not show your faces here again until February. Now that First Wednesday classes are over you have no pressing reason to be here until you can work out your differences. This is my command to you all with the exception of Lady Mary. Because of the position she holds, she cannot be banished." Turning to look directly into Lady Mary's eyes, Michael said, "You will soon know what an empty castle feels like. Hopefully you will learn to appreciate your knights more and realize that squabbling, to a certain degree, is just the cost of doing business. Anything over that 'degree,' you need to assert your command to dispel it."

I reminded everyone that we were just raw data in Michael's experiment, and that we should start applying the lessons it took us fifty-three months to acquire.

"My January is going to be dedicated to healing Linda and focused upon manifesting a larger parcel of land where we can build the real Good Knight Kingdom and microcosm of Atlantis. During January, we are all also to reflect on how lucky we are to be in each other's lives. Michael said most of your in-fighting stems from unfinished business and problems you had with parents and siblings. Unfortunately, those problems have been transferred to your fellow knights.

Michael reminded everyone, "If you can't return in February as a more focused, positive individual then you should let your journey end here. You have to be truly committed to the Path of the Magi from this point forward. Anything short of that will be unacceptable."

"So, you are leaving the choice up to us?" Barbara asked.

"Yes, I cannot make you leave unless you commit a crime. Once you have been aligned with an Angel, the choice to remain is yours and yours alone," I said.

Michael told me in the beginning when Dr. Gregory Peterson and Attorney Judah Weinstein first stepped forward, that I could not terminate or dismiss any Angel-Knight unless they committed a crime. They would have to leave on their own accord. Truly though, Michael wanted them to leave if they couldn't be counted on, but it would take an act of God to release someone if their human ego held tight. My authority over the knighthood only left me with the power of temporary banishment from the Order for conduct unbecoming an Angel Knight.

Michael told me that the Angel-Knights were like chess pieces. All we could hope for, is that they are in the right places and have a good temperament, when it's time for me to reach out to make the next move on the boards. He also said this entire group of fifty-three are the cards I've been dealt. He reminded me, "You only need five or seven to be holding a winning hand."

As the Angel-Knights bid me adieu, I asked Lady June to stay behind. Michael wanted to talked to her about a contact she had.

Earlier in the evening Michael told me in July of 1973, when actor Bruce Lee died, that something happened that should not have happened. When I asked for more information he gave me a riddle to solve - about six of the seven brothers that I was to seek out. "The brothers are all priests of nothing, but together they can reveal to the world everything. One is red. One is black, while one was black. One is brown, one was yellow and of the white ones, one will deliver the child to the Holy See."

He said, "Bruce Lee was the yellow brother, but a Son of Darkness murdered him. His light has now passed to his son, Brandon Bruce Lee, born February 1st, 1965 and when he becomes a man seek him out to be part of a great festival of the spirit. It is important that all seven brothers be present during the request for redemption. Have Lady June contact Brandon Lee about what the Good Knight Network is doing to keep children safe and ask if he would make an appearance at a festival we were planning within the next year."

"Lady June, Sir Gregory has told me that through your acting career, you have a connection to Brandon Lee, Bruce Lee's son," I said.

"Yes, I do," she replied. "A dear friend knows him very well."

"I need you to contact him about what the Good Knights do to keep kids safe. Soon we will be holding a festival of spirit and we would like him to make an appearance," I told her.

"What does us keeping kids safe and a festival of spirits have to do with Brandon Lee?" she asked.

"It's a long story, but for now just trust me and contact him. He will either feel the draw or not. Keep it simple and straight forward!" I put emphasis on simple and straight forward because Lady June tended to let her imagination run wild and get elaborate in her discussions. I finished my instructions to her and gave her a hug good-bye.

Chapter Thirty-one

Path of the Magi

On January 6th, 1993, all the Angel-Knights gathered at our Cove Point beach house for the second annual Epiphany or "Little Christmas" party. We were celebrating the completion of four-years of lessons from the Book of Wisdom course of study, a successful RenFest season and multiple awards for the charity. We added to the tradition that the men should wear tuxedos and the ladies would wear nice evening gowns. My wife, Lady Linda, had been cooking for several days and the feast was exquisite. I am so lucky to have married such a great cook, although it didn't help with my "battle of the bulge."

"Food fit for a King," was the champagne toast Dr. Peterson made.

East Wing Castle had only been off limits to the knights for a week, but I could all ready see it was having a positive effect on the knights. Lady Bonnie, Sir Gregory and Lady Judah had been with the charity, almost since its inception, and this was the first time their authority had dropped to zero. The temporary banishment leveled the playing field and left Lady Mary in charge of everyone. If we were going to be successful, everyone would have to surrender to loving one another and set aside their inflated egos. Of course, only time would tell if the experiment would take hold. If nothing else, it would definitely reveal each individual's true intentions for being part of the organization. It was nice seeing everyone dressed up and getting along for once.

It was a beautiful moonlit evening, so Sir Thomas and Sir James went down to the beach to build a bonfire at the water's edge. We all joined them a short time later to toast good fortune for the knights and the charity in the New Year. The bonfire was roaring, the night was chilly and the moon was beautiful. Everyone but Lady Linda saw shooting stars that night. She was always looking down when she should've been looking up.

As we all stood around the fire, Michael told us, "Enjoy East Wing Castle while you still have it. Soon you will have to move."

I couldn't believe my ears. I had just finished filling and decorating the space with exhibits and it was time to move? I turned to Lady Judah and said, "I think that means you and Angel Anael need to start looking for a new location, preferably with some outside acreage around it."

"I'm not allowed to be there right now remember?" she snipped back.

Hmmmm, she is holding onto some animosity about the banishment I thought. Guess some lessons take longer to learn than others.

With resolve, and a stern fatherly look in my eyes, I said, "I think you can pick up a phone to make some calls from any location. Right?"

I turned back to the rest of the knights gathered around the fire and said, "Let's all now take a deep breath and come together energetically in a meditation under this beautiful moon. With every breath we take collectivity, focus all your love and energy to the upcoming Presidential Inauguration of William Jefferson Clinton. It is on the horizon. News of his campaign staff looking for entertainment for the event has hit the streets. They are planning daylong festivities for families and need child related entertainment and program services. Lady Bonnie-Gabriel made calls two weeks ago offering our safety programs and knighting ceremonies. Michael told me that President Clinton is going to be very important in helping us to spread our message of safety to the masses. Our focus with this meditation is to be accepted as part of the inauguration festivities so that a connection is made with President Clinton."

When I finished prepping them for the focus we all closed our eyes, held hands and sent energy around the circle. While we stood as one, Michael showed me in a vision of why we had to move our headquarters.

I saw all the work I had done with the exhibits shooting up through the roof of East Wing Castle like rocketing fireworks. It wasn't ominous, it actually was festive like the 4th of July. One exhibit after another landed on a pie-shaped piece of property. As each one hit, it exploded open, in even larger form than it was inside East Wing. He said, "You created miniature, I am creating "big-ature." I saw room for expansion on the land. Then there were more colorful blasts and out came more castle structures, waterfalls, a lake, a labyrinth and so much more. "Your imagination will be your only limitation," he assured me. He projected me onto a hill overlooking the property. I saw a beautiful brown-haired little girl in a super girl costume run past the lake and into the arms of Snow White. My heart swelled with that same love I felt when looking at the sleeping babe in Michael's arms years ago in the cave. I knew that if that's what Michael was moving us toward, I was more than ready to let go of East Wing.

With a smile on my face and my heart beating rapidly with joy I squeezed the hand of Lady Mary on my right side and had her squeeze the person next to her and so on. Unbeknownst to them, we sent the love that filled my heart with the sight of that little girl, into the hearts of all the knights. This firmly planted the vision of the future within the knighthood.

We ended the party with hugs and sent everyone home with plates full of leftovers!

A few days later we got the call from the White House. The Good Knight Network had been accepted to perform during President Clinton's Inauguration cerebration. Bam! That was a quick return on a meditation. And love was the Key.

Lady Mary had to choose twelve Good Knights to accompany her to the January 19th Fleetwood Mac Inaugural event. She and I programed quartz crystals that we hoped would help draw the Clinton administration to recognize the Good Knight Network as a viable resource in the President's Child Empowerment Initiative. Michael said that the Blue Knight should not make an appearance at the event because there was still a chance of some rouge cops or special agents being there, who were still harboring a grudge about the illegal bodyguard investigation that I had conducted ten years earlier. I didn't feel that there would be a problem, but Michael sees things I cannot. I couldn't believe that there were still people out there that could be that petty, but Master ERU did warn me of an attack from the dark side. I heeded the warning and did not go with them.

Lady Mary led the charge and everything went off like clockwork. They presented four programs that day and knighted about a thousand children and adults. Lady Eleanor had put her crystal on a silver chain and was even able to pass it on to the President's daughter, Chelsea, as a gift from the Good Knights. They reported back to me that it was a most magical day and that the President's advisors loved our program.

It sounded amazing. I wished we all could have been there. Linda and I loved Fleetwood Mac. Stevie Nicks always reminds me of the Constant Walker. But I understood that my presence there could have led to disaster. I thought back to the time when I was undercover on the National Mall after the anti-war demonstration, when the black motorcycle Park Police Officer kicked me into the fire. I spent that night in jail and I didn't want to tempt fate again. Everything was as it should be.

January ended on a high note and February brought the knights back to East Wing. I sent out an invitation for all to gather on February 1st to see if we had resolved the issues that were tearing the knighthood apart. Of the fifty-four total members, we lost about six volunteers and two Good Knights. It was unfortunate, but if they were having problems that they couldn't get over, it was time for them to move on anyway. For the most part everyone came back with renewed energy and a mindset to get along for the sake of the mission.

No sooner than we were finished our first meeting, a call came in from the local school system with a request for us to present Good Knight Safety programs to six elementary schools in the county. Dr. Arlene Forbes with Prince George's County Schools was in charge of a grant to bring empowerment programs into the schools at the elementary and intermediate levels. Dr. Forbes headed the county's psychological services division. She immediately recognized that the ABC's of Safety Program not only kept children safe and empowered them, but it was really teaching the dynamics of human psychological behavior to youth. She asked the charity to be part of a study to determine our program's retention rate for students. It would mean we would be under contract for the next two years doing programs in over half the elementary and middle schools in Prince Georges County Maryland. I knew Michael was behind the maneuver. It was a great breakthrough for the mission.

To prepare for the missions and days ahead, Michael had me design an official Good Knight T-Shirt with the emblem on the front to match Michael's breastplate. On the back was a large Egyptian Ankh, also known as the Key of Life. I surrounded the Ankh with line drawings of the seven archangels for guidance and four special talismans for love, protection, good health and prosperity. We put the design on purple, blue, red, green, and yellow T-shirts. The Ankh reminded me of the day I stood before the Creator in the Temple of Wisdom. It was that very feeling of love I experienced there that I was trying to put into the T-shirts.

Through Lady Judah's efforts, several local companies sponsored the free give away of the Good Knight T-Shirts for kids who attended the programs. We printed extra shirts to sell in the gift shop at the East Wing Castle. I also had a couple dozen extra breastplate emblems printed on black felt so that the Good Knight volunteers and the Angel-Knights could cut them out and sew them on their tunics. Now when we went into battle against ignorance we were starting to look like a force to be reckoned with. The knights seem very proud to wear the symbol of the earth draped with the wings of their angel.

Meanwhile, Lady June-ZigZagael, who had been selected by Michael to contact Bruce Lee's son Brandon, called Sir Gregory to tell me she had news to share. Originally from the Philippines, June was an actress who had strong ties to the Asian community. When I took the call, she told me, "Brandon Lee is currently working a movie called *The Crow* that will be wrapping up by the end of August. I talked to him today and he said he is interested in meeting with you later this year. He said that as soon as I told him your name and what we do, he had chills go up his arms and he saw a blue orb in the window of the hotel room."

I was beyond thrilled. Thanks Michael!

Better yet, Michael told me that Brandon Lee was to become a film producer in the future and that one of his film projects could be to bring *A Good Knight Story* to the screen.

As fate would have it, a month after Lady June's conversation with him, on March 31st, Brandon Lee was shot to death under suspicious circumstances on the movie set.

The Announcment was released-

With Brandon Bruce Lee's career on an upswing, Lee signed on to play Eric Draven in "The Crow" based on the comic books written by James O' Barr. In the film, his character is a murdered rock musician who comes back from the dead to take his revenge on the gang that killed him and his girlfriend.

Unfortunately, there were a series of mishaps during the course of shooting, starting with the first day when a crew member was almost electrocuted. Toward the end of production, Lee was performing his death scene for the film when a bullet that had been lodged in the prop gun, that was only supposed to be a blank, struck him. The bullet pierced through his abdomen and ended up near his spine. Lee was taken to the hospital where surgeons tried to stop the bleeding and repair the damage, but they were unsuccessful. He died on March 31, 1993, from his injuries.

There were definitely dark forces at work that didn't want the Yellow Brother to contact the Good Knight Network. For months, stories swirled around about whether or not the shooting was intentional. There was an investigation, which determined that his death was the result of the prop gun accidentally not being properly checked between uses. *The Crow* was released the next year after additional scenes were added to complete the film. Audiences turned out in droves to see Lee's haunting final film.

Archangel Michael said that the real truth was the forces of darkness had Brandon killed for a number of reasons. The official report appeared to be a cover up. The man who fired the gun at Brandon Lee was actor Michael Massee. Mr. Massee wasn't supposed to handle the gun that day, but at the last minute the director changed the script. In an interview following Lee's death, Massee contradicts the official report by stating he fired the gun twice in the scene where Brandon Lee was actually shot. If that was indeed the case, the first round was the blank, but the second bullet was real, which means there couldn't have been a bullet lodged in the barrel of the pistol. Once again, we will probably never know the truth.

Everyone was devastated over his death, especially Lady June. She wanted to contact Brandon Lee's sister, Shannon Emery Lee, who was also an actress. I told her she could try, but Michael had told me that the spirit line had been broken forever.

Michael also said that the dark forces were now coming to silence me.

Chapter Thirty-two

A Good Knight's Crucifixion

After the devastating news of Bruce Lee's death, the remainder of spring was energetically quiet. We were busy doing Good Knight Programs in schools and had little time for anything else. The staff was working like a well-oiled machine which was music to my ears. Everything was going well.

Until May 25th that is.

Lady Bonnie received a phone call from a resident of Brentwood, Maryland, about fifteen miles away from the East Wing Castle. The woman, Mrs. Stevens, stated that a ten-year-old little boy, Theo Stevenski, hadn't returned home from school the day before. His bike was found on the sidewalk at a street corner just two blocks from his home.

She said, "It was like the boy just vanished into thin air." Mrs. Stevens went on to say, "My three kids go to the same school as Theo. All the children in the community are frightened." Mrs. Stevens had been to East Wing Castle with her kids for a program several months earlier and was very impressed. She immediately thought about us when the incident happened and wanted to know how much it would cost for the charity to do a program at Brentwood Elementary School. She said that two known pedophiles in the neighborhood were suspects in the boy's disappearance. She wanted everyone to be aware. Lady Bonnie told her that she would talk to the charity's board of directors about doing a free program that coming weekend.

Later that same day, Lady Judah received a call from Dr. Forbes. She also wanted to know if the Blue Knight would bring his child safety program to Brentwood Elementary. She told Judah that it would fall under the grant since this was a county elementary school. She also stated that many of the children there were fearful they be abducted next. We called an emergency meeting and it was agreed we would co-host in-service training programs in every classroom at Brentwood during the week and a community at-large event on Saturday night at 7:00 o'clock.

The day of the in-service training for kids started with Angel-Knights Lady Bonnie, and Sir Gregory going to each classroom to read, *A Good*

Knight Story, to the children, the same way they did at Birdneck Elementary School, after the murders in Virginia Beach. After each class heard the story, I arrived as the Blue Knight, going from classroom to classroom to bring the fairytale to life right before their eyes. I also answered any questions the children might have.

Halfway through the day, Michael told me a storm was brewing and that the dark forces were gathering to destroy the Blue Knight once and for all.

He said, "They can't crucify your body. This time it will be the crucifixion of your name and integrity." I couldn't believe anyone would have the nerve to attack a charity and a man that was trying to help the community in their time of need.

"What would motivate anyone to do that?" I thought.

Michael said, "You threaten to expose the deceivers and their plan of attack is to deceive. It's what they do. That's the bullshit the armor protects you from. Remember you are a walking talisman. You are in their face and they hate you for it."

I spoke with the principal to see if he had heard of any concerns about our safety program coming to his school. He said that the only objection he heard was that one of his teachers didn't like the use of an angel in the story. The teacher said angels were religious characters and had no place in public school. I told him that angels belong to mythology, not theology. I went on to say that I used the angel in the story as a metaphor for listening to the voice from another dimension speaking to my mind. I also said, "I have a talking white mouse in the story as well. They should have a problem with that because mice can't really talk." He agreed and told me not to worry about it because the teacher was one of "those people" who has a problem with everything.

About an hour later a female reporter from a local CBS news affiliate came to the school to get some film footage of the Good Knights working with the kids in the classrooms and to interview me. The reporter started asking some very odd questions - about why the charity was upsetting parents and police in the community. She said, "There is one police official in particular who is set to arrest you for interring with the investigation if he gets the chance."

I said, "That's crazy. Who is it?"

She refused to say who the police official was.

I told her about what had happened ten years earlier when I was a D.C. Police investigating off duty law enforcement officers working illegally in the District of Columbia, "My investigation uncovered an unlicensed Virginia detective agency supplying armed bodyguard services to foreign dignitaries at the Watergate Hotel. It was even illegal for off duty out of state police officers to carry their firearms in the District of Columbia. I could have charged them all with a felony, but used discretion and just wrote tickets for being unlicensed security officers. I am beyond shocked that due to that investigation I am still labeled a "Rat" within the police community ten years later.

"Look, I'm new to this station and love what you are doing to empower youth. Off the record though, all I know is that there is one police officer and a veteran reporter at my station who are bent on painting a negative picture of the 'Blue Knight' (doing air quotes with her fingers) and your charity during the Saturday evening program," she revealed.

"Thanks for the heads up," I said.

That evening I called a meeting of all the Angel-Knights to brief them about the potential of an attack on our creditability. Everyone felt that we should cancel the program. They didn't want to take the chance of having me arrested on some trumped-up charges, feeling it would destroy the credibility of the charity. Lady Mary seemed to think that if we canceled the event, it would eliminate fuel for their vengeance and protect me from harm. It was sweet that the staff cared so much, but I'm not one to be bullied.

I had the knights go into a meditation to ask their angels what should be done. What came back loud and clear was, "The darkness is coming to snuff out the light." I felt that if I didn't do the program Saturday night as requested by the grieving community, I would be giving in to fear and intimidation.

Lady Mary said, "Okay, but I'm afraid for your safety. Have the Angel-Knights do the program for you."

"That's crazy. You are stopping me before I even have a chance to get started," I told them. "Michael has me wearing armor just for this reason. We are at war with ignorance and I need to flush out the ignorant police official if I can. I have seen malfeasance first hand on the force. It has to be stopped whenever we see it. And I'm not some sandal-foot prophet of old who can be pushed around. This time Michael has a well-educated ex-cop and armed private investigator who knows his rights and just how far the police can go. Don't worry. Your fears will attract negativity and that's a tool of the darkness. You get scared, and they win. I just need to have witnesses around who can testify to what happens. So, clear your energy and get your heads straight."

I've seen so many cops lie on the stand and make up information from confidential informants over the years. I knew I needed everyone to be present and calm. However, I also wasn't going to go down without a fight.

I told the knights that I was going to do the program and briefed them about their rights as a citizen. "Every American citizen has the constitutional right to make a 'Citizens Arrest' for a felony committed in their presence. That does not exclude police officers from being arrested by a citizen if the officer commits a felony in your presence. However, any attempt to arrest a cop could lead to one of his colleagues arresting you for interfering with or obstructing a police officer on duty. So, I will need to have plenty of witnesses, police and civilians, around me at all times. I am never to be alone. We are going to do the program, but I want two knights assigned to me as witnesses at all times. Understood?"

When we arrived at the school I was so proud. Every single knight and all our volunteers decided to come to the event dressed proudly in support of the community and their charity. The evening was very hot with temperatures in the high nineties. Despite the heat, they all were dressed in full regalia.

Sir Gregory and Lady Bonnie helped bring in my props and the large black suitcase that contained Michael's armor. As they did I noticed a police captain and corporal follow them behind the stage. I was standing off to one side in the shadows and no one saw me. After the two knights left my gear behind the stage curtain they returned to our van for the remainder. I noticed the corporal bend over and start to unzip my suitcase. He then flipped open the lid and started searching through the contents of the suitcase.

I stepped out from the shadows and with my foot I flipped the lid closed again. "Can I help you gentleman?" I asked. "Back stage is off limits to audience members." Being startled by me appearing out of nowhere, the corporal scrambled to his feet.

I stuck out my hand to greet the captain and said, "I'm Ed Jagen."

The Captain just stood there with his arms crossed tight around his chest. He replied. "I know who you are Jagen and I hear you've come to embarrass the police tonight."

Puzzled, I asked, "Who told you that? I am a retired D.C. police officer and I have utmost respect for the badge."

Cross armed, the Captain remained in place, stone-faced. No response. Sir Gregory and Lady Bonnie returned with more props and listened from a distance to the tense encounter.

I continued, "It looks like it's me who is under attack with your corporal here illegally searching my personal belongs like I'm some sort of criminal."

The corporal spoke up and said, "We have information that has led us to believe you are here to embarrass the police during your performance tonight. So, you won't mind if we take a little look at what you are hiding in here."

The corporal dropped back to his knees as if he was going to attempt another illegal search of my belongings. I put my foot on top of the suitcase lid blocking him from opening the case again. I could tell this corporal had his nose so far up this captain's butt, no light could reach his brain. Captain Black glared at the Corporal and clenched his teeth like he had just let the cat out of the bag.

He looked back at me and asked, "Does it haunt you when you sleep at night that you hurt the very families you claim to be helping? You hamper the investigations of police who are trying to find these poor children."

I shook my head in disbelief at their perception of me. Frustrated and at a loss for words at them not being able to see the truth with their own eyes, I replied, "Captain, what haunts me is that I didn't get this message to a kid like Theo Stevinski before someone grabbed him. I'm here tonight to teach the community how to recognize the tricks pedophiles use to gain control over their intended victims. You should be more concerned with who took him than with harassing me."

The corporal moved to another bag in an attempt to impress his captain with his commitment to expose me as hiding some kind of evidence in the suitcases.

I picked up the bag and said, "Who exactly in your department is so suspicious of me? Who has been spreading lies about me? I never had a problem with the Prince George's County Police in all the years I was a D.C. Detective. I'm not the enemy here."

Captain Black just continued to shoot daggers at me as the corporal moved back to the first large suitcase which contained Michael's armor.

I said, "Captain as you know search and seizure without a warrant is a felony and your corporal has committed this crime in our presence. He has no warrant yet he keeps trying to impress you with his tenacity. Have you ordered him to take this illegal action against me? You know I'm not the only witness to his illegal actions, right?" I motioned for my two knights to step forward as I continued, "I wouldn't dare use my Congressional citizen's right to arrest him for a felony committed in my presence, but I am reporting his criminal actions to you. What are you going to do?"

Both police officials just stared at me like zombies not knowing what to do next. Tired of all the bullshit I said, "Gentlemen I have a program to do. You have nothing to worry about. I didn't come here tonight to embarrass anyone."

I flipped open my suitcase and pulled out the breastplate. Both men's eyes darted through the contents of the large case like they thought I had the missing boy's body inside. It was weird.

Captain Black said, "This isn't over Jagen, we're going to expose you for what you really are."

Michael had enough of these two yahoos. They were obviously trying to bait me into an altercation of some sort. He said, "Watch what you say tonight captain, it will come back to haunt you and could cost you your badge."

They left without another word. Sir Gregory helped me put on Michael's armor. He couldn't believe the aggressive behavior of the police toward me for no reason. I told him, "The weak minded never need a reason when they are under the influence of a demon. Master ERU warned that the attacks were going to start against me. Like it or not, I am ready."

Since the video presentation of the *ABC's of Safety* was now finished, I had Lady Mary prepared to show it during the program. It would be the debut of the film. The small elementary auditorium was packed with about two hundred and fifty people. It was standing room only.

Michael wanted me to light a candle for the missing boy and his family before we started the program.

When I took the stage, there was a round of applause from all the children in the audience who we had met a few days earlier. I put the candle on a small chair in front of the microphone and lit it while saying, "I light this candle for Prince Theo Melvin Stevinski, known to everyone as "JT," and for his beloved family who is awaiting his return. We stand here tonight in Prince George's County to honor JT's spirit in the hopes that our little angel is found by police professionals and brought home to us unharmed." Just then the electricity went off throughout the building. All lights and air conditioning, gone.

The only light in the auditorium was coming from JT's chair on the stage.

I asked everyone to remain seated while the problem was resolved. About five minutes later the lights came back on, but the air conditioning did not. Within just a few minutes the temperature in the auditorium started to become very uncomfortable. But, I continued to talk about the importance of teaching our children the *ABC's of Safety*, and the tricks that predators use to abduct adults as well as children. I announced that we had a short video presentation that would shed some light on how these tricks are used. I signaled Lady Mary to turn on the video projector.

I noticed some scuffling going on around the Captain and then the Corporal left the room. The film ran for about two minutes before the lights and the projector went off again.

Sir Gregory stepped onto the stage and said "Sir Edward, ladies and gentlemen, excuse us we are going to see what is happening with the electricity tonight. Give us a few moments. We are investigating the situation." He then sent Sir James and Sir Thomas to see what was going on with the lights. When they returned, Sir James called me over to the side of the stage, "I spoke with a janitor who told me that the police were controlling the lights and air conditioning. He went on to say that it looked like the cops wanted the event to end." I was shocked at the length they would go to sabotage the Good Knight presentation. It was apparent that the captain wanted me to give up and go home, but I stood my ground.

I walked back to center stage and continued to talk to the audience, never skipping a beat from that point forward. I started going through the ABC's one at a time, just as I had back in the beginning several years earlier. Police officers started moving through the crowd telling people that they had to leave the building for their own safety, but they were ignored. Every eye was fixed on Michael's armor and what slid down the sword and out of "our" mouth. Archangel Michael made a pledge that night, "I will build a real Good Knight Castle and Family Museum in Prince George's County to honor JT and all the missing and abused children of the world. You will all be welcome."

I pointed to the candle on the stage, "Look how brightly Prince Theo's light is shining amidst all the darkness that is surrounding it. Let's call in all of the goodness we can from our hearts. Focus your heart light on the 'Sword of Tenacity'." I raised the sword and every eye in the room followed the flame as it traveled up the blade to the tip. Members of the audience who came up to me after the program said that when the sword burst into flames, the armor looked like it was electrified and orbs of white light were flying all around.

Lady Mary told me that the armor stayed illuminated throughout the entire program, even though the red emergency exit lights were the only lights on in the room, except that one single white candle for JT sitting on the stage. When I looked for the captain to ask why he had the lights turned off he was nowhere to be found.

That evening the local CBS news ran a negative smear campaign against me and the charity. They claimed that we upset the police by hampering their investigation into the kidnapping of Theo Stevinski, and that we disrupted his family and the community. There was not one word about the positive impact we had at the Brentwood Elementary School that evening or earlier in the week. The reporter said a lot of negative one-sided things about me, but didn't seem to have any facts to back them up. He ended his yellow journalistic report with an interview with my old partner, Dennis V.N. McCarthy. It was obvious Denny had been drinking before the interview. He was swaying and his eyes looked like he couldn't focus. The reporter was trying to put words in his mouth. I felt so sorry for Denny, he had fallen so far and my heart was breaking for him.

The reporter asked, "Well if Jagen isn't doing it for money what's driving him?"

Denny looked down. I was hoping he would say that it was my passion to get to the kids before the bad guys did, or I had seen too many kids fall victim to predators, or even that I was crazy as a loon thinking the Archangel Michael was guiding me to protect children, but he didn't. McCarthy said, "You know, I don't know I guess it's just his ego!"

Michael was right. A year earlier he told me that the next time I saw Denny he would wear the face of betrayal. Before that could happen, I was hoping to run into him again to apologize for not being able help fill the hole he had inside. He once loved and believed in me, but something happened to turn that love to hate. Maybe that's why the Hierophant had me write the lesson on hate, to prepare me for McCarthy's farewell betrayal. His demons had set out to crucify me but Denny was left holding the hammer. My heart was broken.

We all have our demons and Denny took his to the grave with him. He died shortly after that. For me, Dennis McCarthy will always be the man who flew through the air landing on John Hinckley Jr. He broke the "Curse of Chief Tecumseh" and saved the life of President Reagan. Denny is a true American hero and will always be my beloved friend.

A few days after the presentation at the elementary school I received a call from the female reporter who interviewed me at the school. She told me about the storm that was brewing. She said that the police captain was reassigned for making negative comments about the Stevinski family.

I told her about my confrontation with the captain and that I suspected the police were responsible for turning off the lights and air conditioning that night in the hope of stopping our program. She wanted to know if I would go on camera with my allegation.

I said, "Sorry to hear about Captain Black, but he was told that night he needed to watch what he says because it would come back to haunt him. His karma has run full circle and for me the matter is now closed." I could tell that she just wanted to keep stirring the pot of negativity and I just wanted peace. It was old news and nothing news for that matter.

Chapter Thirty-three

Return of Lancelot

With the addition of Sword of Truth to our Museum, Michael wanted me to create a scene befitting its splendor. Since it also represented, to the public, the legendary sword Excalibur of King Arthur fame, I decided to build a "Sword in the Stone" display.

I took a battery-operated electro-magnet device, and hid it in a metal sleeve that would act as a sheath for the sword's blade. I bonded the sleeve into a large Styrofoam block that was carved to look like a rock and covered the rock with steel mesh and concrete. I painted the concrete gray then dry brushed it with brown and white to pick up the rough surface areas. To secure it, I bolted the rock to a wooden platform so it wouldn't move when someone tried to pull the sword.

I placed the exhibit in the woodland scene next to the Knighting Circle at Eastwing Castle so Michael could pull the sword when it was needed. I must say, the sword looked magnificent. Michael had me mount a small spotlight in the ceiling shining directly down into the large rainbow quartz crystal in the sword's pommel. In the darkened room with the light passing through the crystal, it cast out rays of red, blue, green and yellow light throughout the scene. It was truly a sight to behold. I think it was Sword Master Watson's greatest accomplishment.

The purpose of the electro-magnets inside the sheath was to lock the blade in place. As I finished a few trial runs to see if it would work, I realized that using electro-magnetic power truly did make it the God Sword. With the remote-control device that I wore on my belt I could press a button without anyone seeing and send the magnetic locking energy through the blade to control who could pull the sword from the stone and who could not. I flashed forward to how cool it would be to do this during programs and festivals. I mean what fun could be had locking the sword down tight for a father or big brother, just to have a little child be able to pull the sword free from the stone? It would make me more Wizard Merlin than the Blue Knight.

I had just finished the Sword in the Stone exhibit when Sir Gregory, the "good doctor" as he is now known, asked if he could show Excalibur to a client.

Dr. Peterson, who was getting to be a very well-known psychic throughout the country, would have clients come visit the castle when they were in passing through the Baltimore/Washington area. One of those clients was a very wealthy woman by the name of Rose Marie from Detroit, Michigan. Rose and her twenty-two-year-old son Bobby, who loved the Arthurian legend, would be stopping in on Saturday. I agreed, but warned him not to let anyone touch the sword.

I explained, "The sword is at rest. It is to be seen, not touched and not drawn out unless I am here. Understand?"

Just as a precaution, before I left the castle for the weekend Michael had me paint a sign and lean it against the base of the stone. It read, **"LOOK, BUT DO NOT TOUCH."**

When I returned the following Monday, and walked through the Great Hall I saw that the sword was missing from the stone and my sign was gone as well. Someone had removed the sword and laid it on the center pod of the knighting circle.

When Sir Gregory came in I asked, "Who tampered with Excalibur?"

He replied, "It was Bobby, Rose's son." He went on to say, "During the tour of the castle complex, Bobby had to use the restroom. He told us as he passed by the sword display he felt drawn in to test his strength. Then he couldn't get it back in. Afterward he came to get us and everyone tried to slide the sword blade back into the stone. However, the sword refused to reenter the stone even through the opening on the top was perfectly clear."

I thought, "That's strange."

I walked back down to the knighting circle, picked up the sword and slid it easily back in place. I turned to look at the good doctor while shrugging my shoulders and shaking my head.

Sir Gregory looked at me dumbfounded saying, "I swear, we all tried. I even came back over last night and tried to put it back but it still wouldn't fit. It was like the hole closed up."

Michael flashed a series of visions through my mind that made me happy and very sad at the same time. One vision was the broken heart King Arthur had after discovering the betrayal of Sir Lancelot, his first and most trusted knight. My first thoughts after were of Bobby and how I would never dare touch such an object in such a surreal setting. Then I saw Sir Lancelot who was charged with the protection of Queen Guinevere taking her from her Divine Status for himself.

I knew it was a warning.

My heart was hurting for some reason beyond this sword incident. I couldn't grasp why. What I did know was the last thing I wanted was to be in the presence of such an impetuous individual as Bobby. I had never met the lad, but already knew I couldn't trust him.

Michael, on the other hand had other ideas for Bobby and me… as usual. He told me that the spirit of Lancelot was sending a message through Bobby that kingdoms can be destroyed out of love and rebuilt out of love as well. Since I now was to start building a real castle to secure the Blue Princess, I needed to utilize the help from the past, here in the present.

Michael said, "Trust me. I have a plan."

"When have I heard that before?" I shot back. "There's usually a lot of turmoil from start to end when you say that."

That afternoon I channeled a message from Michael for Bobby, telling him of his misdeed and comparing it to the impetuous nature of Sir Lancelot. Michael said it was that nature which helped destroy the Kingdom of Camelot long ago. In the letter, Michael was offering Bobby to help the spirit of Lancelot reclaim his honor by helping the Blue Knight rebuild the Kingdom again for Lady Mary, our Blue Princess. Michael wrote, "Strength is not measured in pulling the sword from the stone, it is in having the 'Knowing' of how to put it back." He invited Bobby to come out and volunteer at the Maryland Renaissance Festival that August.

Lady Bonnie and I spent the summer working on editing the remaining pieces we needed for the *ABC's of Safety* VHS tape. I learned to have a more respect for movies, films and actors during those five months. We had the ten tricks portion of the film completed but we wanted to make a different impact so we decided to add animation to the live action. Arthur Leasey wrote us a beautiful theme song and found us a couple of professional singers to record it. We used raw film footage from the school assemblies, the Renaissance Festival and the kids in the *ABC's of Safety* video, for the music video portion. It ended up being a bit long for a video, but it did its job of spreading the child safety message.

Once production of the VHS was complete, it made our presentations much easier and fit within standard assembly format times. It also allowed for volunteers other than our core group to go into the schools to present the lessons in their own personal way.

The Angel-Knights loved it too. Each knight was averaging four or five programs a month and the number of Good Knight children was climbing. Many of the kids wanted to do what Macaroni, the magical wishing mouse, asked them to do in the video, "Teach what they had learned to other children."

Lady Judah-Anael and Lady Mary-Uriel went to businesses seeking sponsors for our public-school library fund. We wanted to place five *Good Knight Story* book/video sets in each school library where we had already presented the programs, so that kids who wanted to mentor others would have access to the materials.

Everything was working out beautifully all around. The charity was receiving grants to take the program into other public-school systems so the mission was reaching kids who were learning, as well as caring about others. The Angel-Knights were applying the Hierophant's Book of Wisdom, to their lives and it showed. Linda was happy because Dawn and Spencer seemed to be getting along after I made Spencer a special talisman to carry with him all the time. Life was sweet and everything was progressing in a positive direction.

But smooth seas rarely stay smooth.

Michael reminded me that our time was running out at East Wing Castle so he had me call a mandatory "Command Performance" gathering of the Angel-Knights for a meditation.

Michael said, "We have to build a microcosm world where we can draw in and do battle with the arch-demons. Too many demons have been left to roam the earth since the removal of Atlantis. They must be contained or they will continue to exponentially infect the consciousness."

In a guided visualization, Michael showed all the Angel-Knights the same visions he had shown me for years. It was triangular piece of property with a large castle structure in the middle surrounded by beautiful gardens, statuary, waterfalls, ponds, a labyrinth, swimming pond, and small exhibit buildings spread out all across the property.

After the visualization was over, Lady Mary, our Blue Princess, summed it up perfectly, "It looks like the land of milk and honey. It's the Garden of Eden and the Angels of the Four Direction have opened the gates again to us all."

It was now a dream in all our minds and our job was to manifest it in the physical world as the Hierophant taught us in the lessons.

Michael reminded everyone, "The main component necessary to achieve all of this it to remain positive." He then took a long 3/8" silver chain off of his armor and cut it into short lengths making rings for each Angel-Knight. He had me circle all the knights together so I could show them the Fugio Cent I had received from John Kennedy as a child.

I explained the wisdom Benjamin Franklin put into the coin, "See here on the front. The sun is shining down on the sundial with Ben's words of power, 'Mind your business.' Michael says the words mean, Time is flying, get busy.' For me it is a reminder that we only have until 2015 to complete this mission. On the back of the coin is a chain containing thirteen links encircling the motto, 'We are one'."

Michael said, "A chain is as strong as its weakest link, just like your sacred circle is only as strong as your weakest brother or sister Angel Knight. Wear these rings; they will bond you all together as one. If the ring should break, fall off or disappear it's a reminder to you all that you are falling short of the mark. You are your brother's keeper. So, keep each other strong and all that you need will be provided."

I couldn't believe the difference that came over the Angel-Knights when Michael held the special ring ceremony where he put a ring on each knight's finger and then kissed them on the third eye. They all seemed to gain an enormous amount of mental fortitude.

Over the years many chain link rings broke, fell off and disappeared, but as long as the knights were working on bettering themselves Michael restored the rings. However, if the knight chose to leave the order, the ring had to be surrendered.

When the time for the Renaissance Festival came around that year we added the Sword and the Stone exhibit. Brother Daniel loved how we displayed the sword he'd crafted, but what he liked most was watching from his vantage point across the dirt road. He loved to see the kids in the knighting circle.

Other than the knighting circle, one of the main attractions at the Good Knight Camp was our fairy-wishing pond where people could only toss silver coins because copper pennies would kill the gold fish. With our sign, "Make Your Donation Match the Value of Your Wish" and the knights explaining, "Don't expect a big wish to be granted for a dime," most of the coins we recovered every Monday were quarters and half dollars. The charity would collect about sixty dollars in coin donations every weekend just from the fairy-wishing pond. One Monday, Lady June-ZigZagal found an old collector silver dollar in the pond and gave it to me for luck.

Michael immediately said, "Polish it and make it shine brighter than the sun."

I asked, "Why?"

No answer.

"Come on!" I responded. "Why can't you answer me all the time and not just when you feel like?"

"All will be known when your waiting is full. Just do it," Michael commanded.

I started to shrug it off and walk into the lunch room, but an overwhelming compulsion to go get the rag and silver polish from the supply cabinet came over me. There was a bit of a struggle with my thoughts, but I then relented and said, "Okay, okay, I'm going!"

Across from our encampment that year, a new vendor moved in. It appeared to be a dark spirited exhibit. The shop looked like a rundown, haunted shack. Over top of it there was a sign written in red blood-like paint that had the words, "The Ken Show, a Museum of Un-Natural History."

Kenneth Repper, the owner of the haunted exhibit, was a longhaired, thin, hippy-looking fellow who dressed in black Grim Reaper style clothing. All the Angel-Knights viewed him as a satanic Son of the Darkness. Ken would sit at his ticket booth and growl at patrons who scurried by; too afraid to go into his showroom. His exhibit was some sort of haunted attraction, but it was so scary looking on the outside that few people wanted to see what was on the inside.

Whenever I would pass by Ken would say, "There he is, our "St. Michael. I always love to see a man in drag." Or "Lovely outfit baby sister." He was taunting me, but not in a bad way. Where others felt negative vibes from him, I felt kindness. I could tell this man was here in my life for a reason and I was to learn a lot from him. One good thing was he did take away some of the fire directed at my camp from the born-again zealots. They were now focused on having poor Ken kicked out of the festival. They were convinced he was a devil worshiper.

Once when I passed Ken, he asked in a low raspy voice, "Hay dragster what's your secret on getting all those wretched people to visit your camp?" I smiled and walked over to talk. The more we talked the more I liked this troubled soul. I got to know him quite well, but felt there was more to him than he said. I knew Ken was a good man, pretending to be dark. He told me that since people liked to dump their darkness on him, he had no problem wearing it well. During the first few weeks of the season I heard scuttlebutt from people around the festival that Ken was a recovering addict from New York City and was now dying from a rare blood disease. I also found out he lived out of his van and the only money he had come from setting up his "Museum of Un-Natural History" exhibit at various renaissance festivals around the country. His story was a sad one and touched my heart. He was one of those books you couldn't judge by its cover.

One day Ken asked me a strange question, "What slogan do you have for the world?"

The first thing that came to mind were the words on Michael's banner hanging over the knighting circle. So, I pointed at it and said, "Love thy Children." Then I said, "And, I tell the children to love their parents as well."

"I agreed with the first one, but as far as that goes I tell children they should kill their parents," he said chuckling. He wasn't joking, but I knew he had a deeper meaning in mind.

I asked, "What slogan would you have for the world?"

Without hesitation he growled, "Be Nice."

I realized he was showing me his true essence. Michael said that at the renaissance festival we all represented a microcosm of a time when things went wrong. Christianity was falling apart because of poor choices made by Popes and Kings. "The Ken Show" and "The Good Knight Camp" were where the Darkness met the Light and the people walking down the center of the street had a choice of which side to visit.

Ken then invited me to see his exhibit for free instead of charging me the customary one-dollar fee. It was incredibly creative and strange at the same time. The building was a maze that zigzagged through macabre scary scenes of realistic looking skulls, bones, rats, snakes and window displays of all kinds of strange stuff in large jars. There were things like, cut up baby doll body parts, rubber eyeballs, fingers and Gremlins that move in some sort of mechanical way. One large jar was broken open and the window glass was busted where the creature had escaped leaving bloody footprints leading down the hall. I could hear the sound of the creature breathing on the other side of the wall. The sound system he used was great and the music was very creepy. I loved "The Ken Show's" twisted creativity and with the "Ed Show" across the street it truly did feel like where the Darkness met the Light.

As I left the exhibit I had the pressing feeling Michael wanted to help him. I couldn't understand why since Ken represented the darkness. Despite my lack of understanding, I told Ken, "If you want to know my secret it will cost you some silver." Michael then had me reach into my black leather pouch attached to the armor and pull out the silver dollar that Lady June gave me. As I pulled it out the sun gleaned off the surface like a laser. I admired the shine for a moment and silently patted myself on the back for the highly skilled polishing job.

I heard Michael laugh. Then he handed it to Ken saying, "This 1887-O Morgan Silver Dollar is worth over one hundred dollars on the rare coin market, but it's also a magic coin that can reveal a secret if you can find a nearby pond to cast your lot. You can keep the coin for luck, cash it in for the money or toss it in the pond. The choice is yours to make. If you toss it in the pond, within two weeks you will have people lining up at your door to enter the 'Museum of Un-Natural History'." Ken took the coin, examined it, grumbled, then put it in the small black bag he had swinging from his belt.

"That went well," I thought as I returned to my camp.

The weekend ended at 7pm on Sunday. Ken never tossed the coin. As we closed up shop, Brother Daniel told me he thought that Ken would probably cash it in because he needed the money to pay the Festival for the monthly rental of his exhibit space. Daniel also shared something I had no idea about. "Management also gets half of his gate and if he doesn't start making them some money they will kick him out and give his booth to someone that will," he said.

I suddenly saw why Michael wanted to help Ken. He needed to keep us all in place and on the chessboard. The key to humanity's survival wasn't getting rid of the darkness or the light, it was keeping it in balance. If we indeed represented the two sides of the equation then removing Ken from the festival would throw everything out of balance. *Now* I understood!

The following Wednesday Lady June came to East Wing Castle after helping to clean up our camp at the festival grounds. She said she found another silver dollar in the pond.

"Another one? I asked.

"Yes, it is the exact same year and circulation as the one I gave you before, except this one is highly polished," she answered. "What are the odds of that happening?" When she showed it to me, I recognized it on the spot. It was the same one Michael gave to Ken.

Michael told me, "Ken sleeps in his van behind his exhibit building every night. He went to our camp at midnight on Sunday. He made his wish saying, 'I wish that the fools and wretched people who come to this festival would throw their money my way,' and then he threw the coin in."

I took the coin from June and meditated in the center of the knighting circle in the Great Hall asking for a vision of what would get people to throw money Ken's way. I owed him a secret now since he followed the directions. But I didn't have the foggiest idea what to tell him. As I looked into the waterfall next to the Constant Walker Angel mannequin, a vision of our camp's waterfall of light was transformed into a waterfall of darkness. Instead of blue water flowing over white rocks with a sign that read, "Wishing Well" I saw red blood flowing over skulls into a dark pit with a sign that read, "Cursing Pond."

On Thursday when I was taking several boxes of Lady Linda's ceramics down to our camp at the festival, I stopped by the Un-Natural Museum. Ken was on the roof of his building putting up a huge red dragon with a 20' wingspan. It was incredible. I yelled up to see if he needed help. He nodded his head and up the ladder I went. After I helped him lock the dragon down together we went over to clean up the area for my horse.

Seeing us in the stable with Hercules, Brother Daniel came down as well with a bottle of tequila, three glasses, salt and limes, as it was always his quest to get us drunk. From my days undercover drinking in bars all day and night, I had built up a strong tolerance to alcohol so it took quite a bit to get me visually drunk. Master Watson was hell bent on getting me to cross that line. Nevertheless, we three newly formed amigos spent the afternoon drinking and telling old war stories.

Brother Daniel shared that good luck had found him earlier that year when he was on expedition searching for buried treasure. He was walking through an area of thick tumbleweeds, and as he approached a pile of rocks he remembered the reading I gave him. He stopped, stomped his feet letting the spurs sound, and he heard a nest of rattlesnakes in the surrounding bushes. He thanked me for the spurs and we toasted to his lucky day even though he didn't find any treasure.

I looked at Ken and said, "I had a dream that you threw the silver dollar at me yelling, 'I wish that the fools and wretched people that come to the festival would throw their money my way'." Ken looked quizzically at me with squinting eyes. He knew those were the same words he spoke that night under the midnight sky, but he didn't say a word so I went on. "In the dream you built an opposite type of pond from mine. Yours was a "Cursing Pond" with a waterfall of blood that spilled over skulls resting in a smoky dark pond of red bloody water. You had people buy special cursing tokens for $1, $5 or $10 dollars depending on the strength of the curse they wished to make. The tokens were large silver washers with magical symbols painted on them in black."

Master Watson said, "Wow, that will definitely draw in customers and the 'born agains' with a rope to lynch you."

I said, "Like the Good Knights have a fairy wishing pond across the street, you should have a dark Cursing Pond outside of your exhibit. It's only fair. We balance each other."

After describing what I saw in the vision I could see Ken's creative wheels were turning. He tossed back another shot of tequila then said, "Brothers, I've got to go to Home Depot." And off he went.

When the weekend came, I couldn't wait to see what Ken had created. Michael led on that I would not be disappointed. I stopped by Ken's place on the way to our camp. He had constructed the same skull mountain waterfall with bloody water spilling into a dark pit in the ground exactly as I had seen in the vision. He added red strobe lights and a fog machine that pumped fog underground which allowed smoke to come out of the dark hole. The red flashes of light made the smoke look like it was on fire. Then he put an iron gate with an old padlock holding it in place. It truly looked like the Gates of Hell. The scene was sitting back in a shadowed area that made it even spookier.

Ken poked his head out of the museum and I gave him a thumb's up. He walked down to meet me and gave me the low-down on his plan. "I'm going to charge people five dollars to write a curse on a special piece of parchment paper with these symbols around the edges. Then they will roll the paper up, stick it through the center of the token and toss the curse in the pond." I could tell Ken knew what he was doing and was guided by something. What he actually made was a blank talisman and it was the customer's job to finish it. He was so proud of his new Dark Creation.

I returned to my camp feeling torn. I had a problem with the real cursing that was going to be taking place across the street. After seeing the effects of the Indian curse on the presidency, I knew too well that curses could harm and kill. I felt like I had conspired with the Devil to hurt people innocent or not.

As I was suited up in the armor Michael said, "The passion must be real. Remember it's an experiment. I will take the stinger out of the curses so no one gets hurt." Suddenly I felt a pinch on my finger and realized that one of the thick wire threads holding the chains on the breastplate stabbed me in the finger. Blood was running everywhere. Michael quickly pulled out the Morgan Silver Dollar and used the blood dripping from my finger to paint Master ERU's Jupiter symbol on the face of the coin.

Just before the festival opened for the day, Michael and I mounted Hercules then rode back over to the Ken Show. Michael said, "Ken I just want to wish you Bad-Luck." He pulled the coin out of my black leather pouch, held it up so Ken could see the symbol and continued, "Since the idea for your cursing pond came from across the street, you know I can't let anyone get hurt in all of this cursing that's getting ready to happen. Right? Do you mind if I'm the first one to toss a curse in your pond?"

Ken growled once again and replied, "Sure curse away my blue brother."

Michael leaned forward in the saddle and speaking directly into the smoky pit he said, "I curse anyone with peace who has the nerve to cast a negative curse into this pond. Let them find peace by allowing the negativity from within to be released into the waters. I ask that it be replaced with positivity, letting no harm befall anyone in this exchange." Then looking at Ken, Michael said, "You okay with that?"

He nodded yes. Michael tossed the coin into the hole as Ken growled again saying, "Killjoy."

Then as we rode through the festival that day we told everyone that when they stopped by the Good Knight Camp they should also check out the haunted house across the street from us saying, "The kids would love it." My goal was for everyone to see it as folly and fun and not take it seriously. I rated it PG-9 for the parents. Everything started coming together for Ken. Our word of mouth was priceless advertising because everyone, except the born-again zealots that is, loved us so they tried it out. By the end of the first day, Ken had a long line waiting to get into see his Museum of Un-Natural History. He was so busy by the third week of the festival he had to hire two assistants to handle the crowd.

Midway through the festival that year the impetuous sword snatcher, Bobby, showed up with his best friend Johnny Kidd. They were a dynamic duo reminding me of Batman and his side kick, Robin. Bobby was a good-looking blond, over 6' tall with a muscular build. Johnny was dark-haired, dark-skinned, very good looking, fit and shorter. As Sir Gregory was introducing them to the lady knights the flirting immediately commenced. I noticed Sir James having a problem with it at the same time a feeling of dread came over me.

When the boys from Detroit arrived, they were dressed identically; wearing puffy sleeved white shirts with 6" black leather straps crisscrossing their chest. They had the Good Knight logo created on a round patch and mounted in the center of the X. They were both wearing long broad swords. It was funny, they looked like targets to me running around wearing the X's.

I asked to meet with both men across from our camp at Chapel of St. George. I remember Michael saying to Bobby when they were introduced "Is that Bobby with one 'O' or two?"

"Booby" didn't get it, but I knew it was the start of a major tug-o-war between us. I talked to them about what we do to empower children and if, by the end of the weekend, they wanted to become part of the Good Knight staff they must swear an oath to protect Lady Mary our beloved Blue Princess.

They wanted to know why it was important to protect Mary. Looking Bobby in the eyes Michael said, "We must protect her from those of us who would diminish her position. Like Lancelot did to Lady Guinevere long ago."

I stressed the fact that they are not here to chase skirts like dogs in heat and that this was a noble order of knighthood not some renaissance festival fantasy game. Both boys already knew my connection to Archangel Michael from Dr. Peterson, so I let them know that Michael said this festival was a spiritual gateway linking the past to the present. In the mid 1500's, during the reign of King Henry the VIII, things went wrong and we were here in the present trying to set things right. We were also here to educate children about the deception and lies people use, dub them Good Knights, and send them out on the quest to teach and protect others.

Both men agreed to the terms so Michael granted them permission to join us as weekend prospects. Michael changed Bobby's name to Robert because he seemed to take things more seriously as soon as he was called Robert. I now had hope for the young impetuous man. On the other hand, Johnny smiled in agreement at me, but at the same time his eyes followed the next good-looking girl that passed us by.

We walked back over to camp and I had Sir Gregory put the prospects to work. They both seemed to fit right in with the other knights. Their duties were to take families on the tour through the fairy gardens around the great ponds.

By the end of that second day Sir James came to me. He had a problem with both prospects flirting with women, in particular Robert. He said that Robert had become infatuated with Lady Mary. I could see James was jealous. I told Sir James that I too had noticed the flirting and reminded him little escapes Angel Michael. He went on to advise me that Sir Gregory had arranged for the boys to stay at the White House, with the Four Directions, while they were in town. With that statement alarm bells were going off in my head. He told me that after the festival the day before, all the Angel-Knights gathered at the White House for a party. During the party, Sir James felt Robert was getting way to friendly with Lady Mary and he was going to intervene, but felt it wasn't his place.

Standing there hearing all of this, I felt sorry for Sir James, I knew he fell in love with Lady Mary the moment he saw her, but his honor and oath to Archangel Michael kept him from acting on it. Now he sees some young kid come in off the street trying to romance his beloved Blue Princess within twenty-four hours of meeting her.

That pit in my stomach came flooding back over me.

I wasn't surprised when Sir James said that Lady Bonnie was pushing for Mary to hook-up with Robert. Earlier that same day, Lady Bonnie came to me and reported that her chain ring had broken. She asked me to fix it. Rings break when vows break. I now connected the pit in my stomach with

Sir James words. "Lady Bonnie has her sights set on Johnny. She was pushing Mary and Robert together the whole night."

I knew Lady Bonnie was jealous of Lady Mary's position and she was the root of stirring up most of the trouble at the White House, but it was a problem the Four-Directions had to work out between themselves with no interference from me.

I told Sir James, "There are things working through all of us. All I can do is hand out the rope. Each knight has to choose to climb or hang." I didn't dare tell Sir James that Michael had already shown me in a vision how Robert did steal a kiss from the Blue Princess that night, but that it seemed she felt sorry for him and was flattered by his affections. If Sir James knew how far Robert had really gone, the outlaw biker in him would come out and somebody could wind up in the hospital or the morgue. I couldn't let that happen. Michael said this was not only a test for Robert, it was for Lady Mary as well. A test she would have to pass if she was ever to take her place as Queen of the Good Knights and give birth to the nameless child.

I saw this was setting up as some ultimate testing grounds. Michael was bringing together all the elements of a Big Bang. What else could you have when the Darkness meets the Light?

As an observer, I knew Sir James would have been the perfect match for Mary's personality. He wouldn't be afraid of losing her, which would keep her on her toes and in the place that St. Michael put her. Robert on the other hand, would feed her weaknesses, which was the last thing she needed at this stage on the path. As the watcher, all I could do was see the pieces moving on the chess boards.

Any time I felt drawn to step in, Michael would always remind me that the Angel-Knights were a control group and this was a psychological experiment. When he reminded me, I reminded the Angel-Knights. Unfortunately, it was all words to them. They were young and hormones controlled their lives. The odd man out here was Robert who didn't have the foggiest idea what he just walked into. He and Johnny found themselves surrounded by hot chicks and they were just living out the fairy tale of knights looking for romance.

It took less than a day and Robert was love struck stupid. I had to tell him several times to focus on the kids and not on Lady Mary. I finally had to put Lady Mary-Uriel back in the saddle and walk with her around the festival. I told her that Michael was not going to knight the boys this year because they couldn't honor his simple request not to be Dog Knights chasing skirts. They lacked the honor and integrity for this path. I asked for her feeling on the subject.

She said, "I think you are right. Both boys were too immature to become knights at this stage in their life, plus they live in Michigan. They can't be at First Wednesday Club meetings."

I responded, "They could become mail order knights if they truly wish to obtain the 'Knowing.' Only time will tell."

By the end of that Sunday both boys came to me and said they wanted to become part of the Good Knight staff. I said, "Then meet me in the Knighting Circle." All the knights gathered around as I drew the Sword of Truth out of the stone and walked into the circle.

I could feel the excitement in both boys as Archangel Michael said, "We gather here today daring to stand in the Shadow of the Spirit of Truth. We are here to cast our vote on these two prospects for knighthood and admittance into the sacred Order of Righteousness. Yesterday in front of the Chapel of St. George they promised that they would uphold the values of our order and Lady Mary, our Blue Princess. If you feel they are truthful and possess the divine qualities for you to call them brother, stay facing them and witness the mighty Sword of Truth dub them Sir Knights."

Sir James turned his back to the knighting circle. The Lady Knights stayed facing. Johnny stood tall on the knighting pod with his handsome smile beaming, but Robert walked out of the circle with his head hung low.

Michael said, "Since you came as a pair you must leave a pair. There will be no knighting this evening."

I then walked over to Robert who was feeling really low and said, "Leaving the knighting circle was the most honest thing you have done since you arrived here. It showed us all you still have a chance." I hugged Robert while saying, "Thank you. Now return to Michigan and think long and hard about the oath you took. I can bring any man in to weaken Lady Mary, but what she needs is to find a true knight that can help strengthen her to become the queen she was meant to be. I will talk with Michael and the Angel-Knights. We may invite you back next year."

Chapter Thirty-four

The Big Move

Late fall brought a scurry of activity for the Network. We were receiving bulk orders of our new Good Knight *ABC's of Safety* video. It was a huge hit. Lady Judah was working with the Clinton administration on a plan to draft a law to submit to the U.S. Congress mandating that the *ABC's of Safety* be taught in elementary schools around the country under the U.S. Department of Health and Human Services. Dr. Forbes' study had proven the video's effectiveness in reducing vulnerability to child abuse, crime and violence amongst children.

A woman that produced and performed in stage plays at the Kennedy Center, in Washington D.C. approached me. She wanted to adapt *A Good Knight Story* into a stage play. Her non-profit theater group had a government grant to perform in schools and she loved our message. I agreed to her request and after several weeks of collaboration we had a script. Then by spring of 1994, the Knight Time Players debuted *The Good Knights Quest* at the National Theater just a block away from the White House.

The play was a light-hearted little tongue-in-cheek adventure that was more of a comedy than my original fairytale, but I left it in the hands of the professionals. The non-profit theater company used the play to raise money for their efforts touring the public school and national festival circuit. It was great exposure for our real safety message. The main thing was that children loved the play.

The Knight Time Players wanted the charity to pursue grants so they could give away *A Good Knight Story* books after each performance. The original book was too costly to print so Lady Bonnie and I designed a cheaper activity book with an abridged version of the original story, plus games, puzzles, mazes and a test for youth with questions that when answered, would let parents know if their child had been approached by any possible predators. *The Quest of the Good Knight* Activity Book was a big hit with Dr. Forbes and the Maryland Public School System. She began using the activity book as a key tool in her study. She loved that the new book also gave children the means to teach what they had learned to other children. Dr. Forbes wanted to premier the study by bringing selected classes from twelve Maryland schools to a huge assembly at Montgomery College. Maryland's Governor Schaefer agreed to be the Master of Ceremonies for the day's event. Lady Bonnie's public relations company represented actor Ted Danson and his non-profit American Oceans Campaign, so she invited Mr. Danson to join the Blue Knight on stage to talk about saving the oceans. It was a project he was working on with his children. I felt it was an important issue as well.

It was an incredible event and during the introduction, the Governor officially dubbed me "Sir Edward, The Blue Knight of Maryland, Protector of Children." Standing on the stage with the governor and Ted Danson was very powerful. The energy was at a high pitch and everyone in the audience could feel it. When it came time to flame the Sword of Truth I thought Ted Danson's eyes were going to pop out of his head.

Afterward I saw him examining the sword to see how it was done, but he didn't have a clue. When he asked me a little later how the blade caught fire I said, "I don't know. Its powered by the children in the audience. Sometimes the flame is brighter than others, but today's flame was the brightest I've ever seen. Thank you for helping the light today." At the end of the program, while I was knighting the children, the governor came to me and said, "If I can ever help Sir Edward, just give me a call." I thanked him for all his support over the years and told him I would stay in touch.

A few weeks after that event, time had run out for the charity at East Wing Castle. The office complex had been sold and we had to move. We had until November to relocate. Michael wanted to do one last grand gathering at the castle before the move. He had been showing me a vision of a Woodstock style music concert festival with a Native American Powwow twist that he wanted the Good Knights to sponsor. He also wanted me to reconnect with Russell Means to finish what he set in motion twenty years earlier.

It was still very important that I apologize to the spirit of Crazy Horse, through Russell Means, for all the mistreatment of the native people. He was also trying to form a unity of the spirit for the protection of America's children. Unfortunately for me, Russell Means had gone on to become a respected author and actor, and had just stared in the blockbuster action film, *Last of the Mohicans,* with Daniel Day Lewis. Means portrayed Chingachgook in the title role. I was sure due to his notoriety, there was no possible chance of meeting with Means again. I considered myself doubly lucky for having met him the first time and quadruply lucky to have made it out of the BIA building alive.

Despite the bleak outlook of getting Means to attend, Michael said forge on with the festival planning.

While Lady Mary-Uriel was researching craft festivals, she found an opportunity to reserve the Anne Arundel County Fairgrounds for our event. It was a huge venue and very accessible to the residents from the Baltimore/ Washington Corridor. Sir Gregory-Metatron made quick work of lining up bands and craft vendors. Sixteen different groups signed on and 48 different vendors. Lady Bonnie-Gabriel worked on the Native American drummers and dancers while Lady Judah-Anael arranged for all the licenses, permits and refreshments.

The festival was taking shape but time was running out as the days clicked off toward our move…to nowhere. We still hadn't found a replacement office setting. We needed a miracle. The Charity needed a new home and I needed to find a contact that could get a message to Russell Means. Maybe it was actually two miracles we needed.

My thoughts drifted to the offer Governor Schaeffer had made when he knighted me, saying, "Jagen, if there is ever anything I can do for the organization, please contact my office."

I was hoping it was real and not just the thing someone says to be cordial. Taking the bull by the horns, I dug out his card and picked up the phone to make the call myself. The receptionist at the Statehouse answered. I went through my whole story and she said, "Please hold and I will forward you to the appropriate office."

"Governor Schaeffer's Office," said a sweet little voice on the other end.

I then went through my whole story and was once again asked to "Please hold so I can forward your call."

Argggg! I hate when that happens.

"Tim Kitchens, Governor's scheduler, may I help you?" the next voice answered.

Ahhhh! "Yes, please. Did the lady I was just speaking to tell you my information or do I need to repeat it?" I asked.

"Actually Mr. Jagen she gave me an overview so you do not need to repeat it. The Governor has a 15-minute slot Tuesday of next week at 2pm. Can you make that?"

In shock, I responded, "Absolutely! Thank you!"

With empowered energy surging through me I then decided to tackle a letter to Russel Means. Michael said, "Whoa boy. Take a breath and let me help you."

Letter to Crazy Horse

Michael had me leave East Wing Castle and go for a drive downtown past the BIA building. I couldn't' figure out why, but that wasn't the first time I didn't know the reason something needed to be done. I just did it and released any attachment to the "need to know" thing. I had faith it would all become clear to me, when and if it was necessary.

After driving full circle around the block where the building was, Michael said, "Okay, let's go home."

"Home?" I asked.

"Yes, to the beach. We have a letter to write," he said.

Trying to check my ego at this moment was a wee bit hard. I said "I mean really? If we had just gone straight home to write the letter, we would be there by now. Not only are we 45 minutes away in the opposite direction of home, we are also now in the second wave of government employee rush hour traffic. In the position we are in, I feel every moment counts. I got the appointment with the Governor quickly, but now we are behind again."

"Who do you think got you that appointment with the governor?" was Michael's response.

"So you are not even going to tell me why we circled the building?" I barked.

Silence.

Shaking my head, I took a deep breath and remembered to utilize all my tools in the lessons to bring my ego under control. I recognized that's what this was, which is a victory of sorts. Now the challenge was to chill. I wondered if I could do progressive relaxation while driving?

When I arrived home Linda was making dinner. She had a cocktail ready for me. I informed her, "I'm going out on the beach to write a letter. I'll take the drink with me."

"I've been here all day by myself and now you are going out to drink on the beach without me?" she blasted.

"Yes, actually I am. I'm sorry if this doesn't fit with your plan. But we have been married long enough for you to realize this is my mission and to that I made my first vows," I explained.

More silence. Story of my life. And with that I picked up my drink and headed to the beach with pen and paper.

The letter I channeled was from Archangel Michael for the spirit of Crazy Horse and the human he guided, Russell Means. The letter revealed that I was the undercover police detective who brought the food to the BIA building years earlier in an attempt to prevent a clash between the

Native Americans and government troops. I told him that I was there when he took the gun from the cop in the parking lot behind the building and I yelled, "It's a better day to live." I went on to say that it was my information that kept a confrontation from occuring that day, when so many were destined to die. I could only hope that he would remember the incident.

In the letter, I detailed events after I left the force, such as the creation of a charity that teaches children not to fall victim to the deceptions people use to lure them down the negative paths in life. I also revealed that I drowned when I was a child, and that ever since that time I have been guided with visions of what needs to be done to help humanity. Some of those visions helped keep the peace at the B.I.A. building that fateful day and now there were other visions which were guiding me to ask him to co-host a new event called Spirit Fest '94.

Michael guided me to include, "It's a Festival to awaken the Great Spirit in us all. We will bring all our religions and people together on the twenty-fifth anniversary of Woodstock - the original festival of Peace and Love." He also had me write about how important it was to work toward peace, by bringing together the music of the current day with the sacred drums, singing and dancing of a Native American Powwow. Trying to jog Means' memory some more I included, "You once compared me to and old Texas Ranger by the name of Charlie Goodnight and dared me to find out why. I accepted your dare and followed the Goodnight-Loving trail all the way to the Pine Ridge Reservation. I learned that, like me, Goodnight risked his life to feed your people after the buffalo were all slaughtered. I risked my life to feed and protect the people of Crazy Horse at the Bureau of Indian Affairs that day."

Michael ended the letter stating, "Since I met you, I was guided to meet an old Hopi medicine man who gave me a rawhide buffalo skin from which I was to fashion a suit of blue armor. The medicine man said it would protect me from all the 'bullshit in the world' as I traveled to empower the children. If you join me again in the great battle of the spirit, I would be honored, but to do so you must dare to accept my offer."

We signed the letter, "Sir Edward Michael Jagen, Founder, Good-Knight Child Empowerment Network." Michael had me attach the Washington Post article showing me in the blue armor, which also did a great job of explaining our quest.

When I met with Governor Schaefer the following week I showed him the letter and asked if he knew how I could get it the letter to Russell Means. After he read the letter he said, "Sir Edward you're crazier than I am."

"I take that as a complement, because you're crazy like a fox," I answered.

We talked about some of the investigations I conducted on the police department that now drive my passion to empower youth and keep them safe from crime and violence. I could see something come over him. He felt my passion and he opened up. He told me, "I have a very good friend on a local reservation that will get the letter to Russell's people, but there is no guarantee that he will answer you of course." He then said, "How else can I help you? I really like what you and your volunteers are doing in our schools."

I paused for a moment before responding because I knew that whatever I said would set in motion the physical manifestation what the Angel-Knights were attempting to will into being.

Clear of mind I replied, "For the past four years the charity has been using a donated space in an office park in Landover, but the complex has been sold and we must relocate. The charity needs to find a small school or building in Prince George's County, with two to five acres of ground around it. It would best serve the students and communities if we could create a Good Knight Castle and Family Museum with outdoor exhibits. Field trips for schools and family outings could be a once in a lifetime adventure for some of these kids.

The governor took notes while I was talking. He looked up at me and said, "Let me see what my old friend Parris Glendenning, your County Executive, has available."

"Thank you, sir. Parris Glendenning has been to several of our safety programs at his children's school in Laurel, Maryland, so he is familiar with our work," I said, as we shook hands and ended the meeting.

With the move deadline looming, Lady Judah and her Angel Anael were working diligently with a commercial real estate developer to locate new office space. Oddly enough, or not, the company's name was the 'Michael Company.' It felt like just another reminder that the Archangel was always looking out for us. The company's representative wanted us to look at several office spaces in the area that could be donated as temporary offices for the charity.

When we visited them, it was obvious most of office spaces were in dangerous sections of the county that I felt were too unsafe to even have the lady volunteers drive through, let alone work in. But one space was perfect! It was an empty forty thousand square foot computer technology research center that had gone out of business and the building was in foreclosure with the bank. The Michael Company was securing the property with the hope of developing it, but the representative said he felt it would be tied up in court for a couple of years. He also said that due to it being vacant, the building had been broken into and vandalized several times. The company owners liked the fact that a number of our volunteers were retired police officers who could help secure the entire building. The building was in Beltsville, Maryland about a fifteen-minute drive from East Wing Castle. Michael said that the space was a golden opportunity for us to expand our Good Knight Museum concept. A meeting was called with all the charity members and we voted to take the offer.

A week after we accepted the offer of the Beltsville office space, I got a call from an official at the County Executive's Office. He said that Mr. Glendenning had been talking with the Governor and learned that we were interested in a surplus property in the county to create a Castle and Family Safety Museum. He gave me the name of a lawyer, Mr. Hoyer, who was in charge of a trust which had a three-acre property that was a former YMCA daycare center. The property was zoned only for non-profit use in Beltsville. It was like celebratory fireworks were going off. I hadn't felt Michael this excited since Lady Mary showed up at the renaissance festival two years earlier.

When we were given the address of the property we realized it was only three blocks from the office complex we had decided to move into. Everyone sensed that there was definitely a higher power at work here guiding our way. What were the chances of acquiring two properties so close in proximity to one another which both fit to a tee what the Angel-Knights were trying to make manifest through the meditations we had learned from the Book of Wisdom? Lady Judah called Mr. Hoyer and made an appointment for us to walk the property.

It was love at first step for me! But it was nowhere near the vision that Michael gave the other knights during the meditations. We handed Mr. Hoyer the paperwork on the charity that he requested. He looked it over and handed us a set of keys. I was in shock! I couldn't believe it! One minute we were homeless and the very next, the charity had been given a property valued at over a million dollars and a free space down the street to use as an interim museum and office space as well.

I wanted to say, "pinch me to see if I'm dreaming!" but quickly changed my mind to, "No, never mind, don't! This dream is too good to wake up from!"

That Saturday we convened a meeting of the Angel-Knights at the new property to assess how much work we had to do. While we were there, a county ordinance inspector pulled up and asked if we were the owners of the property. Sir Gregory responded, "Yes, our charity just received the title to the property two days ago, but we have not taken up occupancy yet.

As a matter of fact, we are in process of moving our headquarters from Lanham to three blocks down from here in the Powder Mill office park.

Looking as if she didn't hear a word Sir Gregory said, the inspector handed Sir Gregory some paperwork. Then she said, "We have received numerous complaints that the grass is over grown and that there are trash heaps and abandoned vehicles on the property. The property has been deemed to be unsafe eye sore. You are hereby given thirty days to clean it up or the country will do it for you and send the bill."

All I could think was, "Welcome to Beltsville!"

I had Lady Judah get Hoyer on the phone to get some more information. We learned that the property had been abandoned for five years and a nearby church group wanted the property for a community center. They had approached him to get the trust to deed the property over to the church, but Mr. Hoyer didn't like their threatening manner they took when asking for it, so a war ensued. The local community leaders knew how to use the system and manipulate the local county council representatives.   The church had gotten every parishioner to file complaints about something wrong with the property. With seventy-six outstanding complaints and the property being vacant, they were hoping the county would condemn the property so they could claim it.

Wow! I felt like we had been dropped into a nest of vipers.

After hearing this news, we agreed to not let it faze us. We continued on with a tour of the property trying to visualize the images that Michael had given me. As I walked Lady Mary around, I could tell all she wanted to do was bulldoze everything down and start over. She's a "posh condo" kind of girl. The sensation became stronger with every step we took through the forested area, which was thick with brambles, beer cans and whiskey bottles. She tip-toed over them like they were snakes going to strike at her. I have to admit, the area looked like a germ-infested local hangout for teens. There were six abandoned vehicles, washing machines, stoves and bags of trash scattered all over the grounds. Then there was the building.

When we went into the first floor we stepped into an inch of water. It was flooded from a broken pipe and the drop ceiling was caving in. Wait…it gets better. On the second floor, there had to be two inches of dead flies, roaches and wasps on the floor. At this point we all wanted to go back downstairs into the inch of water! Boy did we have our work cut out for us! I saw the others looking out of the upstairs window at the waist-high weeds. I heard their thoughts, "The charity doesn't even own a lawn mower. Now we have acres of grass to cut every week or our lovely neighbors will complain and we'll just get more tickets and fines."

They were thinking twice about taking responsibility for the property.

I had to bring them out of their downward spin of negative thoughts. I shook out my arms, clapped my hands together and started my pep talk, "Hey! You are forgetting who you are! Who WE are! Remember, we built the pyramids! We can certainly maintain a few acres of land. Plus, now the angels have a home. This is what you wanted. Now we have a blank slate to create and make it ours."

Blank stares were all I got in return. Well, not all I got. There were two who dug their heels in stating their stance against taking the property. Lady Bonnie and Lady Judah were indoor kind of girls and not much for yard work. They saw the work load piling up and wanted nothing to do with it.

"I think we should just be happy that we have that space down the street to move into," Lady Bonnie said.

"Yes, that is a god-send. We will move in there and make it our home base while we ready this property. It's a win on both ends of the spectrum," I replied.

I tried to reassure them all that everything Michael showed us would come to pass if they just trusted me. I continued our walk with the whole crew outside and up to the top of the hill overlooking the property.

Pointing at the sloping hill Michael spoke, "Here we will build the Star-Gate that the Hierophant and Master ERU told me about. All that dirt and sand below will be dug out to create a magical pond. The sand will then be placed over enormous concrete tubes that will make up the equilateral cross passageways inside the Star-Gate." Motioning to the right he said, "At the western point of the property we will build a great living labyrinth with an open-air castle filled with white doves, surrounded by beautiful flower gardens. It will represent the Light that we bring to the world." Michael pointed toward the forest on his east side, "And in the Forbidden Forest we will build four small Castles of Darkness all surrounded by nightmarish things that go bump in the night. It will be one of the most thrilling adventures humans have ever seen and it will represent the Darkness in the World." Pointing to the north he said, "And at our front gate we will build the Castle of Zeus. It will house Pandora's box, a mirrored containment chamber that will imprison the seven demons, or urges, that man can't control. It will be home to the scene of a great battle between angels and demons for the souls of humankind." Then pointing to the south, he said, "And at our southern gates we will build the Seven Celestial Sisters waterfall, a sacred pool of water and two small castles in which we will display scenes, in miniature, of the great clash between the

Sons of Light and Sons of Darkness. This sanctuary will become a spiritual microcosm of all that has happened during the human experiment, to bring us to the End of Days."

"End of days?" Lady June-ZigZagael spoke up, "But Michael, then what happens? Do we all die?"

Michael smiled and looked into the eyes of the overwhelmed knights standing next to us on that hill and said, "Then what happens? We start anew, but much wiser this time for you will have located the 144,000 Light-Bearers. With their help, humanity will reach critical mass; and the tipping point of human consciousness will shift. It will be a time when mankind will let go of the old man-made superstitions and fairytales. The wise will embrace the message and release the messengers."

I must say Michael painted a pretty picture for those of us with the eyes to see it. Now all we need to do was put forth the brawn to achieve it. One thing was obvious; it would take an enormous amount of work to manifest it all in the physical world.

While turning around in a three-hundred-and-sixty-degree circle, with arms open wide, Michael shared "And we will wrap the entire property with a tall castle wall to keep our sacred gardens safe and pure for a special child with the initials M.V. This will be her home. This will be her school and playground, where Angel-Knights will teach her all that they have learned. This will be the place where she will leave her legacy for the world." He turned to Lady Mary and said, "But only if we can stay strong and elevate enough to receive such a Divine gift." Mary smiled and bowed her head.

Later that week, Lady Judah and Lady Mary went right to work contacting the neighbors, letting them know about the charity and our mission to empower youth. They were also invited them to volunteer days we had scheduled to clean up of the property.

Lady Eleanor-Haniel, a high-ranking government official with the Department of Justice, co-signed for the charity to have a credit card with $25,000 limit. This gave us the freedom to buy building supplies and the equipment needed to clean up the property.

On our first scheduled cleanup day, I was shocked at the outpouring of support that came forward. Two neighbors that had been having a ten-year blood feud came together and agreed to cut the grass. I just smiled and thought how wonderful it was that the energy of the angels was already radiating out into the neighborhood and spreading love.

Day after day, neighborhood volunteers would come and help. They loaded debris into large metal trash containers that were taken away and brought back weekly. The old cars were hauled away, and sixty-three large bags full of glass bottles, cans, and litter was collected. The place was rapidly cleaning up. I was reminded by Michael that "Many hands make light work." The energy on the property was uplifting and peaceful.

However, as with everything in the universe, energy always seeks a balance. It's the age-old swirling of light and dark as represented by the Yin Yang symbol. On earth though, when the darkness rears its head it is does so through the egos of mankind and balance isn't its objective; winning and snuffing out the light is the darkness' aim. In our case, on the heels of such tremendous forward movement for good, it didn't take long before the darkness made itself known.

One Saturday, volunteers told us about a local church group that was spreading negative rumors about the charity. Charlie and Susan Kraft owned a house which bordered our property. Charlie confided, "They are trying to turn the neighborhood against you. They don't want this place cleaned up. They are literally going door to door. It's crazy."

All the Angel-Knights started to worry about the ramifications of this gossip. I reminded them, "If you let this scare you, they win. Don't give it any energy. What you think, you draw to you. Haven't you learned anything through your lessons? Let it go." I had to stop this downward spiral in its tracks. I saw in their eyes that most of them shifted immediately with the reminder of who they were and what they were doing by being afraid. There were a few in the group though that couldn't control their thoughts as well. They still held seeds of doubt and fear. Either way, I couldn't focus on the negativity. They were all welcome to carry whatever beliefs they wanted to. I had work to do.

I spent every day that I could with a chainsaw cutting up broken trees and cutting out thick brush. Michael gave me the vision and I was the one who had to pave the way. Others helped out enormously by carrying the debris away that I was leaving in my wake. The more brush and thicket that was cleared away, the more trash was exposed. During the years that the property lay unused, people had used it as a dumping ground for anything they no longer wanted. Astonishingly, an additional 168 bags of trash were removed from the land.

Even though cleanup was ongoing, we finally made it to a place where we could almost feel the grounds breathe a sigh of relief from the weight lifted with the removal of all that debris. I stood outside with Lady Judah as I sketched the outline of the wall we would erect. She reminded me, "We've been warned by the neighborhood volunteers that the church group will fight us on everything we want to do. This permit isn't going to be easy to come by."

"And by saying those words, you've just programmed our fate. Remember to think positive and ignore ignorance." I reminded her.

The fear of the volunteers and the knights who couldn't let it go was just enough to tip the scales in the darkness' direction. True to form, the first block came when we applied for a building permit to construct a ten-foot security wall around the castle complex. The church group was against the wall because it would block neighbors from seeing what was happening on the property. They had already spread lies in the neighborhood that the charity was a halfway house for criminals and drug addicts.

Really, I wondered? Why do intelligent people believe this type of rumor without at least investigating on their own?

On the night of the County's Park and Planning Commission hearing for our wall permit, the church group's spokesperson presented their case. "We feel that a 6' chain link fence would be more than sufficient to secure their property. And we want to keep an eye on what they are doing on the property. A wall would keep that from happening."

I wish I would've had a camera to take a photo of the Madam Chairwoman's face. You could tell that she was incredulous someone would admit so freely that they were nosey and wanted to spy on us.

When it was our turn, I testified, "First of all, a chain link fence is inconsistent with the castle motif we are creating. Second of all, we are about keeping children and families who visit, safe in a wonderland were certain people with a creepy Peeping-Tom persona won't be able to stalk them. The Beltsville area is peppered with pedophiles who have been released from jail and others who have never been caught doing the deed." I went on to add, "Most of our neighbors are volunteers at the castle already and they know what we were doing there. And as for those who aren't working with us, the charity had Good-Knight volunteers go door to door before the hearing. They gathered five hundred names and addresses in support of the construction of the wall." I motioned to Lady Mary to present the petition to the board.

I went on to point out, "The Good Knight Castle Museum Complex will house many priceless exhibits, such as a sword valued at over $75,000." I then took the Excalibur sword out of it sheath and laid it on the table for all to see. I closed with, "Another simple but extremely important fact is that the castle is located on Rhode Island Avenue, one of the busiest roads in the county. Not only does the museum need the solid high wall for security, but the wall will also act as a sound barrier, shielding visitors from the traffic noise."

After a short deliberation, the board asked us to compromise on two points; lowering our request from a ten-foot wall to eight feet and to create six-foot setbacks from the property line. We agreed and the board granted our permit. A commotion broke out when the Chairwoman announced her decree. The church group was furious. One woman brazenly yelled, "I vow to make your lives a living Hell!"

A burst of laughter came out of me that I couldn't contain. Michael said he made me do it - the best way to diffuse a demon. Once I composed myself I apologized. "I'm sorry. I don't know where that came from. Maybe I thought you were joking, because what you said didn't sound very Christian of you. Why do you feel the need to act like that? What is so wrong in your life that you feel the need to make others live in the hell you create?" The group just marched out of the hearing room glaring at us all the way.

Permit in hand, we were ready to roll!

I phoned Admiral Zumwalt to ask him to contact the Army Corps of Engineers and Navy Seabees, seeking volunteers to help us excavate the land and to build the wall. There was a lot of work to do and many hands would make the load lighter.

To energetically set up the property, I followed what Master ERU had taught me in lesson fifty-three. In the bottom of every hole which was drilled to accept one of the 4' x 4' posts, I dropped an Astral Projection Crystal Beacon. As each post was set I could feel the property aligning with the three grids that surround the Earth. There were 8' x 8' openings between each post. Each section between posts was closed with 4 pieces of 4' x 8' plywood. Two stacked, one on top the other, to form an inner and outer wall. Even with a host of volunteers and military engineers, it took us two months to complete the project.

Once the property was completely enclosed the energy started to build. I didn't understand at first why it became so intense, simultaneously with the last section being screwed in place. Then Michael gave me a vision of a swirling cloud, "You just enclosed in the energy of a vortex. Most vortexes are free to spread outward. You just gave this one a border. It will channel upward and serve as the ear of God."

What a sensation! Now that it felt amazing and powerful, we had to make it look just as good. The entire perimeter wall had to be painted inside and outside to look like castle blocks. I taught the volunteers the method I learned when I was a kid from the window designers at the Burdine's department store - the same method I used to decorate the castle Frankie and I built. As I told everyone the story of how I learned this technique, Frankie came to mind. No coincidence, Lady Leah was standing beside me again when his name came up. Every time she was around, I felt his spirit. I still often wondered about Frankie. I said a little prayer for him, winked at Lady Leah and moved on with the instruction. Once everyone had grasped the concept, we broke up into inside the wall teams and outside the wall teams. We began by spraying heavy coats of blue-gray paint on both sides of the wall as a basecoat. We would start at one gate and by the time we got to where we had started, the paint was dry enough to do another application. We did a total of three coats on each side of the wall. It took all day using two sprayers. We used a LOT of paint, but finally the entire wall was gray, with no bare wood showing anywhere. It was shaping up nicely!

The next time we gathered I gave the volunteers a training session on how to use sea sponges to create the stone look. This was a tricky aspect of the work because it took just the right pressure to make it look real. Too little paint and it didn't give the wood a stone look. Too much paint and it looked fake. The sea sponge layer required a lot of patience and the right touch with its application. It also had to be done twice all over the walls both inside and outside. The first layer was brown and then a white layer had to be dabbed over top. The brown had to dry completely before the white could be done. If we tried to apply the white paint too soon, the colors would run together.

After trial and much error, and a few messy sections, everyone got the hang of it. We were off to the races! The process took many hours over the course of many days to get the entire hand done layers complete. When it was finished, the walls looked like granite slabs. We took black flat paint and cut in mortar lines so that when we were finished the walls looked like stacked castle stone blocks. The neighbors were very impressed with our creativity. People would even stop their cars on Rhode Island Avenue to take pictures of us painting.

Then there was the church group. True to their threats, they called in a complaint about us. They were livid about the colors we painted on the wall. They said we needed to have approval from the "homeowner's association." I know that phrase is one we are all very familiar within suburban gated communities, but if you saw Beltsville, that statement would make you laugh. It is the biggest hodgepodge of house colors, styles etc. Really? A homeowner's association needed to approve our wall colors? We accepted the complaint, checked in with the county and found out that we didn't need approval from a non-existent association. Beltsville had a community civic association, but that was was just a bunch of nosey neighbors who had nothing better to do with their lives except to spy on others. It was so sad that people needed to be so petty. I almost want to say "Check! We're good. Next complaint…" But I bit my lip. Why invite that sort of trouble in!

Chapter Thirty-five

East Wing Good-bye

Before we took down the East Wing Castle exhibits and packed them up for the big move to the Powder Mill office space, the Angel-Knights wanted to have one last hurrah to honor all the work we accomplished at the site. They also wanted to do something nice to acknowledge all of the hours Lady Linda and I had put into the charity. They asked if they could host a family reunion for our two families, the Jagens and the Fortes, since neither family had had a chance to visit the Castle. Linda and I were honored and agreed to the event. I have to admit though, I had reservations about it since my brother Damian's wife Jinx, was one of those people who resented me breathing the same air that she did. That fact had been confirmed time and time again, up to and including the call I made to my sister about the reunion event.

Kathy told me, "Eddie, the last time Damian and Jinx came to visit me in West Virginia, Jinx was talking trash about you." She told Kathy that she heard I was fired from the police department because I was really a member of the Mafia, and that's how I could afford a big boat, a house and a beach cottage. As I was listening to my baby sister on the phone, I just shook my head and thought how it seemed Detective Sharkey's paranoia and rumors had spread even to my family. I decide to let it go and to not feed into any of the drama.

Despite my prior reservations, the party was wonderful. The Angel-Knights were so kind to our families. My mother truly enjoyed seeing all the creations, decorations and exhibits I had designed. I loved watching her face light up at every turn. Michael told me that my mother only had another month to live, so I did everything in my power to make sure she was having a good time and understood the meaning behind all the exhibits.

Billy and his wife Betty didn't come, but Damian and Jinx did. Jinx was in rare form that evening, looking for some way to put what I was doing down. My mother had asked me years ago to try to stay close to my brothers and sisters as long as she lived. I honored her wish but that was easier said than done. I could tolerate Damian, but in a word, Jinx was a killjoy. She was even worse now because they had become born again zealots and she was the self-proclaimed Jesus police. When she examined the upside-down Christmas tree exhibit at East Wing Castle she said, "That is sacrilegious."

"It is a Christmas tree from Heaven. I hung the tree upside down because once a little girl told me she never got to see the top of the Christmas tree," I said. "When she told me that I got to thinking she was right. Little kids never can see the top of the tree at home. But they can here."

Jinx didn't buy it. She was convinced that I had a more sinister motive. She was even more convinced when her witch hunt moved in to the next room where I had created scenes depicting the eight modern religions of the world, including their texts and some sacred objects which had been donated to the museum.

"I want every man, woman and child who visits our Castle and museum to feel at home, no matter what their religious beliefs are." Continuing I said, "As long as they are positive and of the light they will find a piece of themselves here."

The first faith exhibit was Kwanzaa. I asked Lady Eleanor-Haniel to explain the exhibit to our guest since it came from her culture.

She said, "The colors of Kwanzaa are black, red and green; black for the people, red for their struggle, and green for the future and hope that comes from their struggle. Therefore, there is one black candle, three red and three green candles. They are the Mishumaa Saba, the seven candles, and they represent the seven principles. She pointed to a plaque I had hand lettered with *The Seven Principles of Kwanzaa*. I felt that Lady Eleanor did a nice job of explaining, but Jinx had her own interpretation. She started telling people, "Black candles were *only* used in Voodoo and the worship of Satan."

I tried to tell her again what the candles represented, but she was convinced that the scene was Satanic in nature. She looked right past me while I was speaking as if I wasn't there. I could see that Jinx was spoiling for a fight.

When several of the Angel-Knights tried to explain that her view was wrong she said, "He is deceiving you all. What is wrong with you people?"

I went to Damian and said, "Our mother is dying and this party is in her honor. Why is your wife acting like a fool?"

All he would say was, "You disturb her."

"Seriously? That is what you have to say? I replied. "Okay, then she should have stayed home."

I could see that there was something Jinx was dying to say to me even though she didn't want to give me the honor of looking me in the eye. Funny thing with a demon is, once it's up your butt, you can't control yourself and your will no longer belongs to you. The tension was mounting and this debate wouldn't be over until she said it was. So, I gave her a little nudge out the door, so to speak.

I asked, "Jinx, what do you really think of our children's castle and museum?"

Her eyes went as black as the candle. She smiled at me saying, "Only you would create a fantasy world, because you can't face the reality of the real world."

Wow, I thought. That must have felt so good for her to get off her chest. Finally, she said to my face what she had been saying behind my back for so many years. I replied, "What do you know of the real-world Jinx? How many years did you serve your country in the military? How many years did you infiltrate the criminal underbelly of humanity as a police investigator? How many children have you reached with a lifesaving message? That's my world. Your world is based on casting negative lies about everyone outside of your little Jesus cult." I took the black candle from her hand and put it back on the Kwanzaa exhibit, then continued. "You set yourself up to be some sort of authority on life, but you are afraid of the real truth. You are afraid that people will find out you really don't know what you're talking about. That's why you go around lying about me all the time. You don't know me. Everyone sees you as a jealous opinionated fool. Why do you have to be so hateful all the time? I invited everyone here for a happy family reunion, but all you've brought to this party is a zealot's negativity."

Have you ever seen a pressure cooker ready to explode? Well, that night I did. My statements had made Jinx steaming hot. The present moment felt frozen in time, suspended in the air between us. I could see the thoughts in her head and visions of moments in her life which had caused tremendous hurt and pain. That hurt was at the core of her hatred. She was a damaged soul and I felt pity.

As I snapped back in to present moment I could see that she was working hard to find something to counter me with. It felt like forever, waiting for something to spew from her mouth. Damian, embarrassed, walked away from her. Over the years together she had done her best to emasculate him. Now she wasn't going to be happy until she had gnawed my nuts off as well. I was hoping she would follow him and let the matter drop, but that was wishful thinking on my part.

She finally challenged with, "You have an altar where you worship Satan and you call me an opinionated fool?"

"No," I said, "I'm just a mirror and what you don't like about me is your own reflection." I had enough of her. My brother married her I didn't. I also knew there is no getting through to someone blinded by willfulness. But she wouldn't leave it alone. She was fixated on that damn black candle in an African religion exhibit claiming it was "satanic." WTF I thought?

Finally, when Michael had had enough of her, I could feel him enter my consciousness. He said, "Satan cannot be found in a candle. He can only manifest through the negative actions of humans acting out like you are doing now. I am sure the Dark Lord is very proud of you. Since you are so judgmental and so convinced that your view is the only acceptable truth, I will light this black candle in your honor. Now Satan can worship you tonight."

Michael lit the black candle and we walked away. Boom! Slam dunk and the crowd goes wild!

Jinx and Damian left the party without another word. I knew, however, that it wasn't over. Michael reminded me that Jinx was in my life for a reason. I certainly understood that, but I could, at least control how often we'd meet. My poor brother Damian didn't have that choice. I was just glad that my mother and most of the guests had left the party before all of Jinx's negativity came out.

Chapter Thirty-six

Mercy for Mom

For several years the Angel-Knights had been helping me extend my mother's life through energy work, focused meditation and prayer. There's not a doubt in my mind that we kept her comfortable and enjoying her life. Although, even with help, humans have free will, so not everything can be affected. Mom still made food and lifestyle choices which did not benefit her health. She ate sugar like it was going out of style. This obviously did not help her severe diabetes. Out of control sugar levels had led to the removal of several toes, so she was now wheelchair bound and very uncomfortable.

The week after the party I went to visit her. She told me the doctors were now talking about removing her feet. With all that on her plate, she was still happy to see me, but I could see the underlying pain through her smile. One ailment after another was taking a toll on the quality of her life. It was no longer a matter of using the "White Light" to keep her alive. It was beginning to be about helping her leave life on her terms.

A few weeks after my visit, Mom went into the hospital to have her feet removed. Michael said that we had been helping to extend her life for years beyond her given time of death and she was ready to go. My mother made me promise when I was young that I would be by her side holding her hand when she died. Even when I was little I thought it was an odd request to make of a little boy, but I was never frightened of it. It was always something I felt honored to be asked to do. I knew now it was time to keep that promise. She was suffering and we all had to let her go.

To assist her, Michael guided me in the creation of a special "Pillow of White Light" which had crystals and a blessed rosary sewed within. Its purpose was to give energy while honoring her free will. The choice of what to do with that energy would be up to Mom. Combined with desire and will, it could be used to heal her if she chose, or it could be used for an easy passing.

While finishing the pillow I got a call from Mom. Her voice was strained. "Are you okay Mom?" I asked

"Oh yes, I just thought Linda would answer the phone, that's all," she responded.

"Do you want to talk to her? I asked.

"No, no it's okay. I just woke up from a dream where you were walking down the hallway of the hospital carrying something for me so I expected you to not answer," she replied weakly.

"Well Mom, you must be psychic! I am leaving the house soon to come see you and I have something for you," I said.

"Okay Eddie. I love you son…" her voice trailed off.

The phone line went dead. I knew she must be suffering greatly because she didn't even ask what I was bringing her and she didn't say goodbye. Mom always got excited when she knew she was getting a gift. I had an immediate sense of urgency so I grabbed the pillow and off I went.

When I arrived at the hospital Mom was in terrible pain and extremely low energy. The surgeons had removed her feet at the ankle the day before. Not only was she in physical pain, she was very sad.

She said, "Eddie it hurts too much to keep living." I felt a deep pity and heartache for her.

I told her, "I brought you a special pillow that will help ease your pain." I laid the "Pillow of White Light" over her heart and told her to hold on to the rosary cross in the center. I said, "Mom when you are want to, just put the pillow under your head, call the angels in, and fall asleep."

Her faced contorted and she screamed out, "I'm ready Eddie, now. Oh, now! I hurt so bad." Tears were rolling from the corners of her eyes.

In that moment visions and thoughts flooded into my mind. I ran towards the door to get help while saying, "Okay mom, hold on. I'll be right back."

I stepped into the hallway to find the nurse. Instead I bumped into the doctor. He said "She is experiencing phantom pain. She told me this morning that she could feel her feet move even though she knew they had been removed. It's a normal reaction to this type of surgery. Even though the feet are gone the pain is very much real."

My heart was breaking for her. I went back in and stood at her side. I started to cry seeing her in such a helpless condition. I noticed she had already put the pillow under her head. I started to call my brothers and sisters, but Mom grabbed my hand and wouldn't let go. I knew that my mother could only leave in divine time and when she was ready. I prayed my siblings could make it in time. The level of Mom's suffering seemed to make up her mind.

I reached down and took Mom's hand and said, "I am going to call all the angels into the room now, okay?"

She said, "Yes, please."

As the Angels of the Four Directions came to rest at the four corners of her hospital bed, she saw them as her children who had come to visit her bedside one last time. I could see that it brought her peace.

She whispered, "Billy I love you. Kathy, I love you. Maureen, I love you. Michael, I love you…" As she turned her face to me, she squeezed my hand and took her last breath. The heart monitor showed a flat-line. Even though I knew it was coming, I was not ready for the immensity of the moment. I burst into tears. I ran out into the hall, stopped a nurse and said, "I think my mother just died."

I was frantic. My heart was racing.

I thought I had my act together, but nothing could have prepared me for the loss of my mom. For some reason my first thoughts were of Lady Mary, our Blue Princess, and then Jesus hanging on the cross in his last moments of sorrow and pain. He looked down at John and his mother Mary saying, "John, behold your mother." From that moment on I still feel my mother's spirit around our Lady Mary.

I called my brothers and sisters to let them know that mom had died peacefully. Later that day when they came to the hospital, Kathy was her normal loving self, but Maureen was angry with me for being the only one at the hospital when mom passed. I overheard her tell her husband, "That's just like him. He didn't give a crap while I took care of mom, but he's the one with her at the end."

I told them, "Mom saw all five of her children standing at her bedside when she chose to leave."

Kathy was the only one that wanted to hear it. All the rest were too self absorbed to hear.

Chapter Thirty-seven

Last of the Mohicans

In the days following mom's passing I was still feeling low. Then a call came which truly shocked me. "Sir Edward, an agent is on the phone for you," Lady Judah said.

"An agent? What kind of agent?" I asked.

Shrugging her shoulders, and holding her hand over the phone receiver, Lady Judah pushed the phone in my direction.

Shaking my head, I took the phone, "Hello, this is Ed Jagen. May I help you?"

"Yes Mr. Jagen this is Sam Navi. I am Russell Means' assistant. We are in receipt of your request for Russell to co-host a Spirit Fest event honoring Mother Earth and her children next month. I want to confirm the details with you as Russell is pleased to accept your invitation. As fate would have it, he is going to be in Washington D.C. meeting with Native American leaders on other business at the same time."

"That is wonderful news, thank you," I responded.

Sam asked, "Also, Mr. Jagen, Russell wants to know if you want him to put the word out to have other tribal reservations participate in the event as well?

Uh, hello, of course I thought!

I was bursting with excitement inside but held it together long enough to respond, "Yes sir, please tell Mr. Means we would be delighted for him to invite other tribal nations. And tell him thank you for us please. I am going to hand the phone back to one of my staff members to give you all the details."

As soon as I handed Judah the phone, Michael told me, "Now the real work has to begin."

We had a little over a month to work out all the details. Appropriately, we had scheduled the event coincide with Earth Day celebrations. Now that Russell was set to come, we had to revamp the two-day schedule to accommodate him. We also needed to incorporate the other tribes attending, as well as plan a pre-event welcome dinner. There was so much to do and so little time to do it.

When Russell Means came into town, the Angel-Knights held a great feast for our reunion. I couldn't believe that it had been twenty-two years since the BIA take over. When Russell arrived at the castle his energy was very serious and guarded. But during the tour of the museum exhibits he became like a kid again. He could feel the peace and no hassle energy around everything. I think for the first time ever, he felt free to do or say anything he wanted.

I reveled at how the castle was truly a childhood kingdom full of innocence. I loved seeing the transformation visitors went through when they experienced the sweet energy of our space. What Russell appeared to be feeling was the same effect that I noticed happen to a lot of adults over the years, after being exposed to the programing of our exhibits. Michael always said to me, "You must be like a child to be in the presence of the Creator." This was confirmed by verses in the Bible: Matthew chapter 18: 3 said, "Verily I say unto you, except ye be converted, and become as little children, ye shall not enter into the kingdom of heaven.," and Mark chapter 10:15 "Verily I say unto you, Whosoever shall not receive the kingdom of God as a little child, he shall not enter therein."

Russell Means loved the castle. After the feast we convened in the Great Hall. Russell and I sat on the floor in the knighting circle while the Angel-Knights sat on the ground outside of us. We talked about the BIA building take over. He corrected me and called it a "give over" as all the government employees exited the building leaving the Native Americans inside the building on their own.

I told Russell, "That day came close to much blood shed."

He got very defiant and said, "We were ready to take and give blood that day."

I said, "I knew that. That is why the Great Spirit had sent an angel to guide me to stop any further bloodshed. That is the real reason I brought in a car load of food. However, in doing so I was in a position where I would have had to use deadly force to stop you when you took the other undercover cop hostage and placed that pistol to his head. Not knowing what else to do I yelled, 'Russell, it's a good day to live.' Then you put the pistol in your belt and dragged the cop inside. That was the most intense moment of my life. Here I was sent to keep you alive and was put in a situation where I may have been forced to kill you."

Russell said, "And do you know what would have happened to you?"

I responded, "What difference would that have made? You'd be dead and I would have failed my divine mission. We'd both be playing in the happy hunting grounds now, but instead we are going to have a festival on Earth tomorrow honoring the spirit. Let's focus on that."

Russell's demeanor remained very stoic, but his eyes softened. The Great Spirit was showing through. The "Knowing" was kicking in and washing away his anger.

I went on to say, "You know as well as I do we must learn to live together with love and understanding. And if we are going to build a better future, it will only come from empowering the Children of Tomorrow by safeguarding the Children of Today." I reminded him of all the non-Indians that came out to support his people holed up in the BIA that day. "Remember all the people who came out and locked arms in solidarity for your cause? They formed a human barricade to keep the invading government troops out. Those people were of all colors, white included. They felt the spirit and that's the proof it can happen."

Russell said, "Nixon was afraid to attack us. It was too close to the election. He just couldn't afford another Indian massacre that would leave blood on his hands. So Nixon lied to get us out of the building. His people drafted and signed a document of amnesty from prosecution for all of the demonstrators, but as soon as Nixon was re-elected, federal indictments came down on all of us."

He was getting mad again so I ended that part of our conversation by saying, "Well my brother from another mother, I'm just glad we survived all that bullshit the government put us through. You're not the only one that was betrayed by Tricky Dick. He betrayed all of us, but old warriors like us are just lucky to still be this side of the dirt." He smiled, looked down and nodded his head.

His energy diffused! Humor really is the best medicine.

Russell then told us stories about life growing up on the reservation. He said there was a high degree of alcoholism and child abuse that went on there. He hung his head down low saying, "The spirit of my people is broken." Michael spoke through me saying, "The only thing that never changes is the fact that things will always change. All humans must adapt to what change comes along unless they have the power to change it."

Russell scratched his head and asked, "What the hell does that mean?"

Michael said, "We must be the change we want to see in this world. Your thoughts create your reality. Think you are broken, and you are. Know you aren't, and you will be confident and powerful beyond measure. If we are strong and patient enough, change will emanate from us. Your essence in the present moment will affect the children and those who guide them. People are too quick to wage war. We need them to radiate love"

Russell said, "Before the white man came we didn't have the word war in our vocabulary."

"I beg to differ my friend. As I toured the reservations to the east and west of the Lakota territory, your neighbors told me stories of many battles with the Lakota before the whites came. You might not have a word for war, but you must have had a word for battle. Mankind has been battling their brothers and the elements since the beginning of time. Unfortunately, it's human nature. There has always been a group of people who want something another group of people have. Or a culture's belief system which feels uncomfortable unless *everyone* believes as they do. Some will even kill and enslave people that refuse to convert to their beliefs."

I saw the flames of anger rise within him and I knew I had to change the subject fast. I didn't want to get in a pissing match with this brother any more than I did with Jim Brown in the 70's over his issues on race and religion. The way I saw it, I represented the last of the blue people and I told them both that. However, I am sure they just saw me as a crazy white guy with strange views.

I quickly shifted the subject by talking about the Good Knight Network's mission to teach children the *ABC's of Safety* - ten tricks, which negative people use to deceive and take advantage of children. I had Lady June-ZigZagel show him a local news documentary that had just aired on our work in the public school system. He seemed very impressed with our effort.

"I would very much like for the Blue Knight to come to the Pine Ridge Reservation and share the Good-Knight message with my people," he said.

Russell told us a story of the White Buffalo Calf Woman who brought wisdom to his people in the beginning and of Iktomi the trickster god who came to earth to deceive the Lakota people. Russel said, "Interestingly enough, Wakan-Tanka, the Great Spirit, sent a blue warrior as well. His name was Wakinyon. He came with a mighty staff to beat back Iktomi so the Buffalo People could live in peace on the plains."

As Russel recounted the tale I saw similarities to the story Archangel Michael told me about how he and Lucifer battled over the Sword of Truth and Stone of Light.

I told Russell about the old Hopi medicine man, Eagle Hunter, giving me his sacred buffalo rawhide skin. "Eagle Hunter said that the buffalo's spirit would protect me from all the bullshit in the world. About twenty-five years later the angel guided me to cut the rawhide up in order to create the armor of the Blue Knight. I wear the armor when I do the programs for children." We walked over to the stage where the armor was on display. He was surprised to find that it was leather because it looked like blue steel.

He said, "The Hopi say they are descended from the Sky Elders that came from the stars. I dated a Hopi woman once, they are a crazy people, but very gifted."

I said, "I have found that much wisdom can come from things that sound crazy. We call something crazy when we can't yet understand it. Many think I'm crazy for wearing the armor."

In a somber knowing voice, he said, "When we dance, the white man call us crazy, but they just can't hear the music." He took a deep breath and released a peaceful sigh. A powerful energy came over him then said, "Because you wear the skin of Tatanka (buffalo) every step you take in the armor is Wakan (holy)." He put his hand over his heart and bowed his head to me while saying, "I feel you are part of the Great Mystery Sir Edward."

The conversation shifted as the energy that came through Russel lifted. We started talking about the movies he had been in and how much running he had to do during the filming of *Last of the Mohicans.* He cracked a joke saying he felt like he had run across the entire state of North Carolina and the Blue Ridge Mountains by the time it was finished. "Movies only tell part of the story. Books are important," he declared. "I am writing a book, *Where White Men Fear to Tread.* History is written by the ones who print the most books. That's why I want to tell my story of what really happened." Again, something came over him while he was talking. He sat up straight and said, "I have something for your children's museum."

Russel left the building and went out to his car. When he came back in he was carrying a large box that appeared to be quite heavy. He took it right over to the knighting circle and sat down. He then opened the lid and removed a large tan and brown book entitled *Navajo.* He said, "I want you to have these books. They tell the true story about what happened to the Indian people. Share these stories with the children. The books contain the same stories the white man tells about the great Indian Wars, but they written from our perspective."

It was truly one of the greatest gifts we had received for the future generations. "We are truly honored to accept this gift on behalf of the children," I said.

Sir Tray picked up one of the books and began to read. He was clearly moved by what he was saw. Tray's Great Grandfather was a Cherokee medicine man who passed down to him many oral stories from generations long ago. "My Grandfather gave me the gift of the truth and a sacred bear peace pipe. I live his truth and I brought his pipe with me today. I would be honored to share smoke with you from that pipe"

Russel nodded yes and smiled.

While Tray went to his car, I told Russell that everyone who was at the Bureau of Indian Affairs building that day needed to tell their personal story because no two would tell the same tale. I said, "It could have become the worst massacre in the history of the United States. But it didn't. Once I saw that you weren't going to hurt Roger Day, the detective you caught spying, the angel told me to help buy 'Crazy Horse' time to find what you were looking for."

"Well, we found exactly what we were looking for. The documents to prove the government broke the treaties when they took back the Black Hills after discovering gold there," he replied.

I told him about the vision, the angel gave me where he was wearing a buffalo headdress and how important it was that he survived that day. "As you remember, you kept saying, 'It's a good day to die' and I replied back, 'It's a better day to live.' My brother, look at all the wonderful things you have accomplished because you lived. Dying is easy, it's the living that's hard."

"Indeed," he said while looking upward, "indeed." Then something caught his eye. He rose and walked over to an exhibit wall. He picked up the Sun Spear from its resting place.

I explained to Russell how the angel guided me to receive the crystal Sun Spear from another crazy Indian I met.

"You run into a lot of crazy Indians don't you, my brother?" he asked laughing.

"Come to think of it, I suppose I do," I replied. "This one's name was Chief Thomas, from Oklahoma. He was on a pilgrimage to Prophetstown State Park on the Wabash River. It was the original homeland of his people. Coincidentally the angel had me there on a vision quest at the same time as well. The old man's Indian name was, Lalawethika which means, 'He who makes noise.' It was the perfect name for him because the buffalo jerky he was eating had him farting a tune all night long."

Russell laughed and said, "It's healthy to fart."

I continued, "I told Chief Thomas about the angel who guided me to the BIA building in the hope of saving the lives of all the Trail of Broken Treaties Indians. He revealed to me that he too was there that day. Do you remember him?"

"Many tribes from all over came that day. I didn't know most of them," he admitted.

"Well, he knew of you." I continued, "I told Chief Thomas that I was guided to him in hopes of breaking the Indian curse on the Presidency, and that the angel said it was time to bring peace to the ancestors and the land, for the benefit of the children."

Russell just sat there and stared at his feet as if I was doing a terrible thing, then he spoke up, "So what did the chief say to that?"

I said, "Well when I got up to go to sleep that night in my car he said, 'If the Great Spirit tells me to stop you. I will cut your throat in the night and put you out of your misery. If the Great Spirit says I should help you I will give you what we both came here for.'" I took a breath as everyone was listening intently. Then I continued, "The next day when I woke up I found the chief had gone and on the hood of my car was this double terminated crystal wand. The angel called it the Sun Spear."

While examining the spear, Russell asked "And what did you do with this great medicine wand?"

"Two years later the angel told me to take the Sun Spear to the Washington Hilton Hotel and have my friend Dennis McCarthy just hold it for a while."

Russell snapped his head back so fast I thought it was going to pop off. Sternly he asked, "Why would you want to go and do something like that?"

I said, "To help keep our country and her children safe. There are a lot of countries out there wanting to bring our country down and the angel said that with Reagan dead the U.S. would have been plunged into World War III. The United States is not perfect, but we are freer than most countries out there."

He laughed diffusing the tension and said, "Sir Edward you are crazier than most Indians. We get a bad rap. You need to write a book about all this someday."

"I already wrote a book, remember?" I asked. "*A Good Knight Story*. It's my life just spun into a fairy tale. If I went any further with it than a kid's book, people really would think I was crazy."

He said, "Everybody's a little crazy. You are good crazy. That's all that counts."

"Well my life hasn't been all butterflies and roses," I said. We talked about my abduction as a child from my father by my mother, the drowning and the beautiful woman in the tunnel of light who asked me to return to life to help the angel save lives and elevate the collective consciousness of humanity. I said, "You are one of those lives," I could see that he was growing more comfortable with me as I spoke freely.

Russell broke the conversation off as Sir Trey entered the room with the peace pipe, "I must leave soon so let's talk about Spirit Fest."

"Okay, let's all sit in the knighting circle," I directed. Trey handed me the pipe. It was literally a carving of a bear. There was a large hole in the bear's back that served as the bowl. Trey had stuffed the bowl with a special blend of sacred herbs and Indian tobacco. I handed the pipe to Russell to light. I could feel Michael move into my body. Russell lit the pipe. We puffed and passed the pipe around the Angel Knight circle. I didn't know what the herbs were, but the smoke did have a calming effect in a "far out" kind of way.

Michael turned and asked, "And what is it that rustle means?" The angel often used words that sounded the same, but are spelled different in sentences to make a point or tell a joke. I could see that Michael was making a joke, but Russell didn't get it.

Russell straightened up and replied, "Russell means many things. Russell Means freedom for his people."

Michael then lit the pipe and passed it back saying, "It's also the sound the wind makes as it moves through the eagle's wing feathers." Russell smiled and nodded.

Sir Tray was so taken with the ceremony that he donated the sacred Bear Pipe to the Good Knight Museum.

Michael said, "Let me dismiss the knights so they can clean up and we can talk of things that are not for the ears of others." From then on I was blocked from knowing what was being discussed. I could only assume that it had something private to do with the upcoming event and the forgiveness apology I was to deliver.

I came back into awareness as Russell was leaving that night. I invited him to see the property in Beltsville that the charity had just acquired. I told him that I was in the process of building a living labyrinth that Angel Michael called a medicine wheel-healing circle. "Would you by any chance be interested in placing a few of key stones that I need to be laid tomorrow? They will mark the spirit of the four directions."

"I will meet you there tomorrow at noon," and off he went.

The next day I spent the morning leveling the ground around the center tower with a Bobcat. At noon sharp, just as promised, Russell came to the property. Michael did most of the talking while they walked. He gave a detailed explanation of how the property would be laid out, up to and including the sanctuary for fifty-two white doves of peace and the Lakota village in the clearing dedicated to the spirit of Crazy Horse. When they reached the center of the property at its highest point he said, "And here we will build a Star-Gate Castle. It will be a vehicle to reach our cosmic brothers and beyond."

Eventually they made their way back to the labyrinth area where they starting laying out the cinder blocks representing the true directions of North, South, East and West. This inner circle of blocks was laid around a two-story octagonal unpainted plywood tower that rose up out of the ground like a huge monolith. It had no adornments except a ladder leaning on its western side. It was the first thing I built in the clearing to mark the center of the labyrinth. As Russel was setting the ring, Michael asked him to drop a small quartz crystal inside each cinder block that circled around the center tower. I held the crystals and Russel dropped one at a time in as he set the blocks. The inner circle of the Medicine Wheel was laid completely by Russell Means. What a gift in and of itself! When that first ring was complete, Michael asked Russel if he would bless the grounds and the construction of the labyrinth.

I "just happened" to bring the Bear Pipe with me for the blessing ceremony. I passed the pipe to Russell. He took it from me and started to climb the ladder to the top section of the tower. With arms outstretched, he raised the ceremonial pipe to the heavens, lit it, then blew smoke and tossed Indian tobacco to the four directions.

I did not participate in the blessing. I just watched in amazement. I could see the imprint of energy from another man wearing a buffalo headdress guiding Russell in all of his movements. Around the edges of the land that I had leveled that morning, I saw the pale ghostly images of Indians beating drums. Surrounding the tower, I saw the spirits of Indian men, woman and children dancing as if they were making their way through a labyrinth. It was an incredible sight to behold.

When Russell came down from the tower, he was somewhat dazed. "Are you hungry? There is a great Tex-Mex restaurant, the Alamo, not far from us in Riverdale." I said.

He asked, "How are the chile rellenos?"

"They're awesome. Let's go."

The restaurant was all but empty. We sat at the round table in the back room. He asked, "So I understand that at the Spirit Festival event you want to apologize to me for all the wrongs that have been done to the Indian peoples by the white man."

I said, "Not quite. As I understand it, I must apologize to the Great Spirit and to the spirit of Crazy Horse for all the wrongs that have been done to **all** the children born on Turtle Island. Remember, my brother, we were both born here. It doesn't matter when our ancestors got here. What matters is we are here now, born from the spirit of the great turtle." Turtle

Island is one of the names the ancient elders used to refer to North America. I went on to say, "I know you don't have the power or authority to accept such an apology, plus I'm apologizing for the wrongs done from both sides dating back thousands of years."

"What if Crazy Horse doesn't accept your apology?" he asked.

Looking Russell in the eyes I could see he was troubled and torn. He wanted to hate me, but found it hard. He couldn't quite release the thought that I was a former enemy who once spied on him during the takeover of the BIA building. I didn't respond. We ate in silence, not looking up once. I could feel Russell was waiting for me to say something. I knew that whatever came out of my mouth next was going to make or break Spirit Fest '94. Michael was flashing visions from the past through my mind.

I took a breath then opened my mouth and these words came sliding out, "It won't be me asking. It will be the Spirit of the Blue Warrior, Wakinyon, trying to bring peace to the spirits of all those who came before us. I think the angel that guides me, and Wakinyon from the Lakota myths are one in the same entity. I think he has come back to finish what he was sent to do long ago, to shed light upon the tricksters in this world. There is a reason why he saved both of our lives and I believe it was for this special confrontation of truth that will occur at Spirit Fest in the morning."

Russell looked up and said, "If I accept the apology from you, I will be criticized."

I said, "Russell it's not important that you accept the apology and quite frankly I never expected you to. What's important is that the peaceful warrior in blue offers it. The angel has me wearing blue for many reasons. Your personal problem, keeping you from opening up, stems from the fact that you still see me as a spying government agent. If that's all I was, you and most of your raiding party would have died twenty-two years ago inside the Bureau of Indian Affairs. I was a Peace Officer then and I will forever be a Peace Maker. You do what you want at the festival. In fact, you don't even have to show up tomorrow. I will apologize to the spirits of Crazy Horse and Sitting Bull regardless."

Russell looked stunned and said, "Then you will understand if I must decline your request of forgiveness when asked."

I replied, "Russell, you say whatever the spirit of Crazy Horse wants to say at the time. Not what Russell Means thinks. Right now, you are speaking from this dimension of ego. Tomorrow, if it is destined, Crazy Horse will speak from the spirit dimension through the heart. All he wants is to be free from the hatred. That's why the angel asked you last night, 'What does rustle mean?' Just let the breeze blow through the eagle feather that you will be wearing on the back of your head. It's not our hour it's theirs, and it is time for us to seek redemption from our over inflated egos."

Russell looked at me surprised when I mentioned he'd be wearing an eagle feather. "How did you know I had the eagle feather."

I replied, "I saw in a vision that if the Great Spirit accepted the apology, redemption would come in the form of a mighty Eagle Feather that will be placed on the Staff of Wakinyon. Beneath the Eagle Feather will be the twelve feathers of the Angel-Knights who witnessed the moment of redemption."

Russell had to leave the Alamo for other business that afternoon or we would have sat talking for the rest of the day. I could see Russell had a lot to think about. It was a delicate dance of words. With every second, I felt like I was always one step away from putting my foot in my mouth and screwing everything up. In spite of that I truly did enjoy Russell's company. It felt like we were spirit brothers.

When we walked to our cars the last thing Michael said to him was, "By the way, the name Russell is Anglo-Saxon and it means fox. I hope to see you in the morning. If not, I promise we will meet again, until then just 'Remember the Alamo'." He smiled. I think he got the joke.

The Alamo was the scene of another great massacre in American history which also could have been avoided.

Chapter Thirty-eight

The Seven Brothers

Michael said long ago when actor Bruce Lee died, that I was one of seven spirit brothers. We all had the same spirit father, but were born from different mothers. Michael gave me a riddle to solve about the identity of the seven brothers that I was to seek out:

"The brothers are all priests of nothing, but together they can reveal to the world everything. One is red. One is black, while one was black. One is brown, one was yellow and of the two whites, one will deliver the child to the Holy See."

Through visions given to me over the years I realized that Jim Brown, the football legend and actor was the Black Brother. Jim was the first that I met in 1982. He was a wealth of information and guidance. He prepared me for the transition I had to make from the police department to forming a non-profit working on behalf of children. I will be forever in his debt.

The second Black Brother was Michael Jackson who "was black," but then he wasn't anymore. I first contacted Michael in 1990 when *A Good Knight Story* was first published. Archangel Michael and I handcrafted a metal sculpture of a stone right-handed gauntlet holding a sword. We sent the gift and the first seven copies of the fairytale to Michael. I felt the gift never reached him. I made my second contact with Michael Jackson at Never Land Ranch through Child Help USA in 1991, but Jackson's people kept him isolated from all adults that day. I always thought that if he and I had come face to face like I did with Jim Brown we would have been able to help each other. Michael Jackson did have the ability to rally billions of children, but he lacked a true purpose for the children to rally behind. His message was love and peace, but the angel said it needed a direction. It was a tremendous tragedy that Michael Jackson went out having been accused of molesting children. I know the course of events could have been changed if he hadn't been so guarded by gatekeepers.

As far as the brown brother is concerned, I was expecting him to be Hispanic. Turns out it was to be the Dalai Lama. Go figure! He and I met during a reception at the U.S. Capitol in April of 1994. I gave him a special rainbow quartz crystal and he gave me a small polished stone monkey. We talked about keeping children safe from those who would deceive, manipulate and abuse them. I said to him, "Deception is deception no matter the age. It's much like the people who pull the strings for People's Republic of China. It is a people's republic in name only, because the real people living in china have no say so about their future or what happens in their country."

From listening to the Dalai Lama talk I could see that the only thing he really wanted was to return to Tibet and the status that the thirteen Dalai's before him enjoyed. Michael said that the Dalai Lama was truly homeless and should use his time in exile to make the entire Earth his home, and her children, his children. I didn't sense that was something he resonated with though. His heart ached for his home.

Although the Dalai Lama is an extremely impressive individual, I did not feel a brotherhood kinship to him as I did the others.

The Yellow Brother was Bruce Lee. He died on July 20, 1973 at the age of 32 from a brain aneurysm. Archangel Michael told me that he was the victim of foul play as was his son Brandon. The light passed to Brandon Lee, but a month after Angel-Knight June-Zagzagel contacted him, he died from a gunshot wound while filming *The Crow*. Lady June continued to follow the lead and contacted Bruce Lee's daughter Shannon Emery Lee about Spirit Fest '94, but she was working on a project in Hollywood at the time and sent a letter on behalf of her brother to be read during the Spirit Fest ceremony.

The White Brother still eludes me. I have reason to believe it is Sean Connery from the many visions I have received over the years. I have written Mr. Connery three times, but I have no way of knowing if the letters ever got to him. Nevertheless, from looking into Sean Connery's charitable interests his concerns are all about Scottish heritage and education, not the children of the future.

The last part of the riddle still eludes me. I am still confused about the meaning of, "he will deliver the child to the Holy See."

The one thing all the brothers had in common was that they were actors as well as activists for human rights. Although where I am concerned with all the children of the world being empowered, the others seem to be more interested in their personal country and/or ethnic group. There are those who might ask why there was no true representative for the Brown Brother and that the Dalai Lama would be considered yellow.

In my search for the sixth brother my quest lead to Actor Edward James Olmos. He hosted Lady Mary's programs at the inaugural concert for President Clinton, but Michael said I was wrong. I was also following leads that the brown brother might have been Cesar Chavez. I sent several letters in the hope of meeting with him in Yuma, Arizona only to find out that he was sick and dying. Cesar Chavez died on April 23rd, 1993 a year to the day of the opening of Spirit Fest '94.

Now I know that there are some out there that would say the Dalia Lama is an activist but not an actor like the others. Well, I watched him and felt that he was the best actor of them all. Underneath that boyish persona is a calculating man with one agenda - returning to his beloved Tibet. He has to play the hardest role of all, that of Man-God.

Then of course there was me. I am not an actor either. But on the other hand I had to take on many roles during my undercover assignments and if I gave a bad performance there would have been more than rotten tomatoes thrown at me.

Chapter Thirty-nine

Spirit-Fest '94

On April 23rd, 1994 the Angel-Knights gathered early in Annapolis for our festival of the Spirit. Vendors were setting up in the two huge event buildings at the Anne Arundel County Fairgrounds. The smell of food filled the air and musicians were practicing on the two stages. It was truly going to be a once in a lifetime event.

Several Native American tribes from around the country sent dancers and drummers, but one local tribe was given the honor of being "First Drum." I watched as the Powwow dancers came in. They were incredibly powerful. The energy that came from them was electric! Even their regalia was powerful - and oh so beautiful. I couldn't believe my eyes - or ears. I felt like I was caught up in a great dream and I never wanted it to end. "This is how is should be," I said out loud to no one and to everyone at the same time.

I found Lady Barbara-Raphael who had cleaned and saddled Hercules, my horse. With two days of steady rain during the festival, he was a muddy mess. She did a stellar job prepping him though. He looked magnificent. Under his saddle the horse wore a royal blue drape with highly polished gold inlays that cast a fiery glint when the rays of the sun hit them. Hercules was a stunning sight to see even though I had truly enjoyed the last two days of watching Russell Means ride him bareback. One spirit horse and rider running free came to mind.

The boys from Detroit, Bobby and Johnny who had been taking the Masters Studies Program from Dr. Peterson through the mail, walked up to me. They now had a better understanding of what the Angel-Knights were trying to accomplish. They sent letters of apologies asking to be forgiven for the foolish way they had acted the year before, so we invited them to join us for the festival.

I asked them to help me strap on the armor. As they focused on my armor I took the chance to counsel them. "I hope you can both do better this trip than last one. Do your best to focus more on our spiritual intent rather than trying to score with the ladies." Turning to Bobby I said, "I am going to make it easy for you. Our Blue Princess, Lady Mary, is off limits to you. I am her First Knight and I am here to keep her strong and focused. If you can honor that, the day may come that I will trust you with that position of Lady Mary's First Knight. Consider yourself served!"

He said, "I understand and I hope someday I am worthy."

I saw a big change in both boys that day. They were now men. So, after Michael and I set up the sacred Exhibit of the Sword and Stone surrounded by huge quartz crystals, I called them in. Michael dubbed them Angel-Knights. Bobby became Sir Robert-Cassiel and Johnny became Sir Johnny-Rothanael. This did not sit well with Sir James-Sandalphon who was watching nearby.

He told me, "I don't trust Bobby. He's out to have Lady Mary for himself."

I said, "Maybe that's why Michael brought him forward? Mary has free will and that 'will' will be tested."

Sir James was in love and didn't know how to live with it. He said, "Sir Edward I am sorry, I can't stay. I care too much for Lady Mary and I've seen how she acts when he's around. I can't be around that. She diminishes herself." I knew this was Sir James' test. I could only hope that he would find a way to surrender his ego. But it didn't come that day. Sir James left the festival.

Onward!

I stationed Sir Robert and Sir Johnny as sentries at the opening of the knighting circle. As each Angel-Knight entered the knighting circle they were given a special color feather of red, blue, brown, yellow, green, white or black. A lock of hair, representing their scalp or DNA, was clipped from the nape of the neck of each Angel-Knight. The feather and the hair were then handed to Lady Mary who attached both items to a 2" round beaded medallion. In the center of the medallion was a circle and equilateral cross. The medallions were hand-beaded by a shaman from the local tribe that was helping us coordinate the event.

Lady Black-Eyed Susan was asked to bring a six-foot staff to the festival that she carved out of a small cedar tree trunk so that the sacred medallions could be attached to it during the final ceremony on Sunday. That's when Michael planned to put together the Staff of Wakinyon and make his request of forgiveness to Crazy Horse.

In the meantime, Sir Gregory approached me about a female client of his, who was the great, great, great granddaughter of Hernando Cortez the famous Spanish explorer. As history goes, Cortez wore plumbs of bird feathers about his armor. The Aztec King Montezuma saw Cortez as the returning legendary God, Quetzalcoatl, a winged feathered serpent and welcomed him and his soldiers into his palace. Once inside Cortez saw all of the gold and riches the empire had to offer. He staked his claim and massacred the Aztec people. Sir Gregory said that Miss Cortez heard about the apology I was to make, and she too wanted to apologize for the mistreatment of the native people by her ancestors. I was against, it feeling that her apology would take away from the ceremony, but Michael over ruled me and welcomed her participation. I told Sir Gregory to put her on the schedule.

My watch alarm went off. I had it set to 3 minutes before the gate opening time. I drew The Sword from its sheath upon my belt and walked over the Sacred Sword and Stone exhibit. At precisely 10am when the first visitor passed through the gate, Michael slid the sword into its resting place within the stone.

People were coming in by the droves. The festival was underway. As I surveyed the crowd, the "Seven Brothers" riddle Michael gave me to solve in the early seventies, came to mind. I was to match the faiths of the original seven kingdoms of Atlantis with representatives of today by following a spirit line, not a bloodline. Each of the seven brothers represented a prince from each kingdom. Today marked the day I was to have them all here to ask forgiveness from each brother for all the atrocities that occurred within their kingdoms. Seems I failed again. The only one who stepped foot onto the festival grounds was Russell Means.

"I've told you many times, you were sent to fail. Don't give it another thought," Michael said. "Russell represents the kingdom of Turtle Island. The Natives say it is North America when in fact it is Earth. He can accept the apology for all 'native' Earthlings."

Going into the festival we knew that Russell was the only Brother coming, so we had a backup plan. I had Lady Mary invite leaders from the seven major religions of the world and ask them to address the audience about their beliefs and traditions. Each would represent a Hierophant from the seven Kingdoms. Hierophant is the title given to a special person or priest in ancient times who interprets sacred mysteries or esoteric principles. It turned out that she found twelve to invite. I was sure the selections would be an interesting grouping since they all would have a different concept of the same thing; the "Divine Mystery."

Dressed in shadow, I officially opened the festival by welcoming everyone who came. I let them know the two-day event was to honor the human spirit, their beliefs and to ask forgiveness for transgressions against humanity by our ancestors. It would be a grand celebration in words, crafts, music and dance. Russell Means then joined me on stage. When I introduced him, the crowd went wild with cheers and Indian chants. The energy was incredible. I told the audience that we had assembled representatives of religions from all over the world; from Christianity to Satanism. after I said "Satanism" the crowd went silent.

I said, "This is a festival of love and forgiveness. And in all fairness, we must give the devil his due. You be the judge, you be the jury and, in the end, you decide if you are strong enough to accept the forgiveness of the day."

Prior to each "hierophant" stepping forward to give their blessing of faith, I gave a little background on the religion and its spiritual traditions and in some cases had an open discussion with the representative of the faith. I wanted give the audience a chance to see the common threads.

Although we originally only wanted seven representatives to speak on their religion, Angel Michael invited all twelve religions Lady Mary found. This was actual perfect on so many levels, because of the similarities of the faith. Sadly, the video recording of the Seven Hierophants speaking that day was lost to time.

As I sat to the side of the stage listening to each representative Michael told me to take notes. "You know how slow I write, right?" I asked.

"Okay, ask each hierophant for a copy of their speech for historical documentation," Michael responded.

"That I can do!" I replied.

Miraculously, the audience embraced each representative with open minds. I saw heads nodding and I saw their thoughts connecting the dots with the realization that all these religions shared a common core belief and practices. They were not so different after all. They also saw the common element of power, ego and control threaded through most of the religions.

While the last speaker, the satanist, was addressing the crowd, I went back stage to remove the shadow clothing I was wearing and change into Michael's full armor. As I listened, I thought about how much the words sounded like the same words spoken by the other holy men in attendance that day. The only difference was that the Satanists seemed to be honest, admitting that they lead a selfish self-serving materialistic life style. I've seen most of the people from all the other religions in America living that same life style, they just don't admit to it. He was also the only speaker that thanked the audience for inviting him to speak about his beliefs. I found him to be an honest man and did not sense one ounce of evil in him.

The presentations of religions were over. We scheduled a 30-minute break for lunch, when a Pow Wow dance group would take the stage. As fate would have it, Michael had a different plan.

Chapter Forty

Center Stage

The native dancers started up the stairs to the stage, but in unison and as if choreographed, they all stopped dead in their tracks. The reason for their sudden halt?

Archangel Michael was standing in full armor like a statue mid stage. The crowd went silent. He pushed a microphone stand aside and pointed past the crowd at the Sword of Truth in the center of the exhibit some 50 yards away. In a bellowing voice he said, "Somewhere between me and the crystal in the pommel of that sword, lies the truth. You have been exposed to the religious truth of others and now you know that the difference between good and evil can be found within the intent of man's actions. There are many claiming to be positive who hide a dark heart and there are many who claim to be negative that possess a heart of Light. Good and evil are not found in words, only actions. But be careful: Judge no man, for you shall be judged by your judgment."

Walking to the edge of the stage Michael looked down and said, "Where did the one we call Satan the great Adversary come from? Most claim he is Lucifer a fallen angel. Some say he corrupted man, yet others claim man corrupted Lucifer. What is the difference between a righteous man and a self-righteous man? Gladly it is the perception of those around the man. For a self-righteous man feels he is righteous while a true righteous man is selfless."

A ray of sunshine broke through the cloudy sky. Looking upward and spreading his arms to embrace the light, Michael continued, "We have chosen to eat the forbidden fruit of the Sacred Tree and we gained the knowledge of good and evil. There are those who cannot control their urges, live the lie, and blame Satan for their devilish misdeeds. There are those who will claim evil was done here today because a Son of Darkness was allowed to speak. The reason Jesus said, 'Love and embrace your enemy' is so you would seek a greater understanding of those you persecute. I tell you this because it is my dream that the day will come when mankind breaks its hold on Archangel Lucifer so he can return to the loving embrace of our Father in Heaven. Then whom will mankind blame for their sins against Humanity? There are those who see all the evil and wickedness in this world and ask, 'How can a loving God let this happen?' I look at the free will that was given to humans and ask, how can *humanity* let this happen?'"

Looking back out toward the Sword of Truth, Angel Michael modified Ephesians 6:11-12 by saying, "Put on the whole armor of God, it will protect you from all the bullshit in this world, so that you might be able to stand against the wiles of your own personal demons. We do not wrestle against flesh and blood, but against our own minds, against our powers, against our own dark rulers of this age, against the spiritual host of our own wickedness in this heavenly place we call earth."

He pointed at the Sword once again and closed with, "We fight against our own inconsistencies and fearful nature. However, the residue of our ancestors' wickedness still haunts us all today. When we die our spirit leaves this third-dimension existence and enters the fourth or fifth dimensions based on how much understanding we gained in life. Unfortunately, many dark selfish spirits resist the Light and remain trapped on Earth, caught between dimensions. It is these dark troubled spirits influencing man that are the demons. They surround us all and influence the ego and weak-minded to do all forms of mischief and evil. Since these dark spirits are man-made they have no leader. However, when they clump together like flies on a dead rotting carcass we call that collective dark energy force the Devil or Satan, the Great Adversary. Since their energy is that of selfishness and hatred, and it opposes the forces of selflessness, our body, mind and spirit become the devil's chessboard. We are here today to send all the dark spirits that surround us into the rays of Light being cast from the crystal in the pommel of the Sword of Truth. I want you all to now focus your thoughts and send any darkness that might be haunting you right into the crystal of that sword."

A hush fell over the crowd as everyone turned to look at the sword in the middle of the field. Michael left me and moved to the Sword and Stone.

It was amazing to watch. I could see dark orbs lifting up from the people in the crowd. It was like a swarm of black flies and hornets flying around trying to escape a tractor beam force field radiating from the sword. They were all being pulled into the beam of White Light being cast out from the crystal. Within seconds the dark orbs were gone. Everyone started smiling and laughing. I thought to myself, "Wow if we could just do that for the whole world?"

I immediately heard Michael say, "It will happen once the 144,000 Light Bearers of legend I seek awaken. There will be no place on earth for the dark spirits to hide. Only then will Archangel Lucifer be free from man's grip and humanity will start with a clean slate."

I pulled the microphone stand back in front of me and announced, "Please welcome the Pow Wow Dancers."

I took a lunch break, while the audience enjoyed the entertainment. The percussion of the drums and the rhythmic beat of feet pounding on stage began transforming the energy. How perfect was it that after the dancers finished their performance I was scheduled to walk on stage and introduce Russel Means?

As I finished lunch, Russel arrived at the back of the stage. I looked across at him and in my mind, I asked, "Are you ready for this?" He nodded his head in affirmation. Out loud I then said, "Then let's do this!"

I took the stage to introduce our co-host of Spirit Fest '94. I welcomed Russell Means to the stage by saying, "Ho-Ka-Hey! Some say, it's a good day to die, but let us hope that day is long in coming. Twelve years ago, I met a man that changed my life forever. He found himself in a situation where he and many others that followed him decided it was a good day to die. But the Great Spirit had a different idea. The man had to survive so he could be with us today. He is here to take us back to our spiritual roots. Back to a time before we made things so complicated. I am proud to introduce my good friend and brother from another mother, Russell Means."

The crowd erupted into great cheers and Indian yelps as Russell took the stage.

Russel then delivered a Native prayer for peace

"O Great Spirit of our Ancestors, we raise the pipe to you, to your messengers the four winds, and to Mother Earth who provides for your children. Give us the wisdom to teach our children to love, to respect, to be kind to each other so that they may grow with peace in mind. Let us learn to share all the good things that you provide for us on this Earth. We pray O Great Spirit that you help us to eradicate all the misery in the world, that understanding triumph over ignorance, that generosity triumph over contempt, and that truth triumph over falsehood."

Holding a drum in one had he said, "There was a time when life was simple. The Native People of Turtle Island were one with Mother Earth and Father Sky. The People did not believe that they could own the land or the animals that roamed it. Then white visitors from a distant land came to

Turtle Island, they brought with them lies and wicked ways. The white visitors claimed that they discovered Turtle Island, therefore it belonged to them.

When the Native People resisted the white visitors decide they wanted to buy the land, but our ancestors said, 'One does not sell the earth upon which the people walk.' So the visitors took the land they wanted and gave the parts they didn't want to the Native People. But in time the visitors needed more land and took back all the land they had given. They finally gave the Native People the wastelands. In many treaties they promised, 'In the future, these lands will never be taken from you. You will always have these lands. As long as the earth exists and nature grows. This land will be yours and you can live and never be restricted.' But the visitors were greedy and dishonest. Within a few years they took back the lands.

One of our wise leaders said, 'I am a red man. If the Great Spirit wanted me to be a white man he would have made white at birth. We each were gifted with different thoughts and paths and gifts. We are different but the same, like birds. Eagles can't be songbirds. We may habve nothing but we are free. No white man controls our fate. If we must die, we will die defending our rights'."

He paused and stared into the mesmerized faces in the audience then continued, "The white man's army and Christian settlers took away our simple ways and told us that we had to live like them, speak like them and pray like them. They took away our way of life and forbid our sacred dance. We told them that land is sacred. This is our belief. The land is our mother, our source. If you take it way we will die.' When we resisted they murdered our men, women and children with bullets, swords and disease. Chief Crazy Horse said, 'HokaHe! It is a good time to die!' When the blue soldiers battled the Native People and won, it was called a great victory, but when they lost it was called a great massacre by heathens. The white man would not stop until our great hoop of life itself was broken."

Russell ended with a quote from Crazy Horse, "Upon suffering beyond suffering the Red Nation shall rise again and it shall be a blessing for a sick world. A world filled with broken promises, selfishness and separations, a world longing for light again. I see a time of Seven Generations when all the colors of mankind will gather under the Sacred Tree of Life and the whole Earth will become one circle again."

Russell, filled with the spirit of Crazy Horse, began slowly beating his drum. He said there once was a time when the rhythm of the people matched the heartbeat of Mother Earth and that now it was time to get our hearts right again. As the sound reverberated through the crowd, we all became one heart beating strong. Russell then put down his drum and said,

"We will make a great medicine wheel to signify the coming together of the Seven generations Crazy Horse spoke of."

While he created the great hoop of life, a Native American Buffalo Princess dressed in white buckskin walked on stage. She described what the Great Medicine Wheel represents, "The Medicine Wheel symbolizes great spiritual significance for the Sioux. The belief is that the shape of the wheel represents the circle of life and death, which is considered never ending and most importantly represents the unity in the Great Spirit or Grandfather. The Medicine Wheel was only to be used by a Holy or Medicine Man. Within the circle is an equilateral cross shape that symbolizes the four directions and each direction is signified with a color or feather and meaning.

North – Red feather is wisdom and the place where the ancient ones passed over
South – White feather -youth and friendships
East – Yellow feather -new beginnings and family

West – Black feather-solitude, adulthood

Once complete Russell Means presented Lady Mary, the Good Knights' Blue Princess, with the sacred Medicine Wheel, she was instructed to mount it inside the tower at the center of the Medicine Wheel Healing Labyrinth Russell helped lay out the day before. Next the Indian Princess held up a Lakota Dream Catcher and told the story of how in their tradition Satan was seen as a trickster sent by the Great Spirit to challenge the buffalo people.

Legend of the Dream Catcher

The Buffalo Princess said, "Iktomi, who is told to be the great trickster and teacher of wisdom, manifested to an elder. It was as a spider he appeared. He spun web and told our elder to help our people use it to make their dreams come true. He also said if our people listen to the Great Spirit, the web will catch the good dreams and ideas while letting the bad ones pass through. The elder shared the event with our people and until this day we still hang dreamcatchers over our beds."

Now finished with her tale, the beautiful, raven-haired Indian Princess then passed the Dream Catcher to Russell Means. He blessed it and presented it to me saying, "Dream the great dream for the safety and protection of the children of the seventh generation, the Children of Tomorrow."

Hokatha, an elder from another tribe stepped up to the mic to describe the Sun Dance:

The Outlawed Sun Dance

"The Sun Dance was a ritual of the Native American Tribes of the Great Plains There was much preparation involved, not just the dance," Hokatha said.

"The Government outlawed the Sun Dance in 1880. They were threatened by our beliefs and traditions. It was an important ceremony for the Sioux and it was taken away. The ceremony was held in the summer and brave warriors were pierced in the chest with a bone as a rite of passage. Then dancers would be tethered to the tree or they would dance with many skulls dangling off of them. If the warrior broke free he would be called most courageous. The dance lasted for many days. We still do this ceremony to this day but it has more symbolism and less pain," Hokatha finished.

At this point Russell Means had the "First Drum" of the lead tribe take the stage. As he drummed, twelve Native American males in full feathered regalia danced and sang. It was one of the most beautiful things to watch. It was as if they were being carried by the wind while their feet kept time with the drums. At one point a young child joined the dance. With arms outstretched, he looked like an eagle with wings spread. At times it appeared his feet lifted from the ground and he was soaring through the air.

After about ten minutes, the dance was over and the Buffalo Princess spoke again telling the legend of the White Buffalo. She told how this legend was passed down from age to age.

"The White Buffalo Calf Woman was sent to us by the Great Spirit to teach us how to use the sacred pipe. The Great Spirit gave her seven sacred ceremonies for us to have harmony and peace as we stay in balance with Gaia.
She told us of a prophecy of four ages and in the fourth age she would return to earth to bring back spirituality and peace. We believe this is the fourth age."

When the singing, drumming and dancing was over Russell Means was handed the ceremonial pipe. He held it out to the four directions and blessed the gathering. I thought he was going to light it and pass it around the stage, but he said that he must take it to the native village that the tribes had set up on the festival grounds and smoke with the elders.

Then out of the blue, someone in the audience yelled out, "What religion does the Blue Knight belong to?"

It hit me like a lightning bolt. The holy representatives of all the faiths looked at me wondering which one of them I was going to pick. Russell handed me the microphone and smiled saying, "You've been called brother. I am certain you will find the words."

Turning to the crowd I said, "As a baby I was baptized Catholic and found it was a good start on my journey to spiritual enlightenment. I was taught that Satan was the "root of all evil." Then, as a young boy, I found myself being repeatedly tortured and sexually abused for several years by a wicked Bible thumping woman masquerading as a "Good Christian." At about that same time I had a near death drowning experience that changed my perspective of life forever. I learned two things at an early age, all life is precious and adults will lie. I believe that everyone has divine guidance, whether you call it intuition, spirits or angels. I was guided into the U.S. Army then through a career as a police investigator and now into the non-profit realm of the Good Knight Child Empowerment Network. I have learned so many truths over the years and much great wisdom, to include all that I heard on this stage today."

The crowd broke into a round of clapping, cheers and wolf whistles.

I continued, "I believe and support all these great religions of the world, but I believe in that sword out there." I paused pointing to the sword in the middle of the field. "Long ago in channeled visions, I was once given the Ancient Wisdom Books of Atlantis to study. I received one lesson each month for fifty-three months. The lessons gave me all the truth I needed to know to bring me to the point of sharing this day in peace, unconditional love and acceptance with you today.

Then someone else in the crowd yelled out, "What about Satan, do you believe in the devil?

I replied, "I believe in the power of humans to manifest acts of duality, good and evil. In doing so they create positive and negative energy that travels up and down their bodies through their vortex centers called chakras. Since we call evil acts satanic, yes, I believe in Satan, when the human takes on that evil form. I've been asked, which of the religions do I practice and whom do I worship? Long ago in a meditation, I asked God to reveal *His* faith to me, when asking how I could serve the Divine. What I heard loud and clear was, "My faith is in the Children. Serve and protect them and you serve your Creator."

Yet another from the audience yelled out, "Do you believe in demons?"

Michael walked off the stage and behind me Sir Gregory went to the mic and announced the Q&A period was over and that we must clear the stage for music so those who want to know the answer to that question will have to go inside the story telling exhibit hall for the next presentation.

I went to check in with Linda to see how the vendors were doing and by the time I got to the story telling exhibit about thirty people were waiting. They didn't want a story told they wanted more information. They wanted their questions answered; everything from near death experiences, spirit guides, angels, demons and my views of the afterlife.

I started by telling them about the afterlife and demons saying, "As a police officer I have had some very close encounters with demons in the flesh and in the form of negative dark spirits that influence people. I learned that when Jesus said, 'In my Father's house there are many mansions,' he was referring to the different levels of Heaven. What he didn't explain was that you only have access to the levels you can comprehend. For example, we're told when we die and go to Heaven all of a sudden, we know everything and we live forever on a brilliant cloud in a castle of light overlooking the sky-blue ocean of Eternity. That's a nice fairytale of rainbows and unicorns, but it's just not true. When we die, we are no wiser than we were in life. The understanding we gained in life, is what we carry with us when we cross over. If we haven't tried to gain the Greater Understanding while on Earth, when we get to the afterlife, we find we must reside in a gloomy shack on a dismal swamp forever reviewing the life we lived. Then upon seeing this, the first thing we want to do is return to life, to find a deeper understanding and become a less selfish person. Unfortunately, the Laws of Reincarnation were broken over 2,000 years ago when Jesus died for our sins and now we only get one time to live in a body. Some are given a chance to return to this dimension as Spirit Guides to assist the angelic guidance while they help us negotiate life. As the human gains a better understanding, the spirit guide also elevates. However, if the human turns wicked, corrupted by their own selfish urges, or by the influence of other dark human spirits who are trapped between this dimension and the next, when the human dies both are trapped there as well.

Michael came through me to explain that God created Angels out of unconditional love in order to serve all creation. "Angels were given the will to serve but when God created humans He gave them free will and the power to co-create. Humans had a choice to create or destroy with their power. The divine spirit with the human, could become full of light the more selfless a life the human led. If the human became overly selfish or evil, the spirit would turn dark and demonic in nature. If that happened the demons would find no place in heaven and be forced to roam the earth without a body." Michael then spoke of a Demonic Agenda, "Misery loves company and dark spirits attach themselves to weak-willed people to join their energy in the hope that humanity is driven to extinction. The only failsafe is that every 500 years a Heavenly Legion of 144,000 Warrior Angels are sent to Earth to merge with humans who have attained the "Knowing" in order to trap and contain the dark spirits until they can be transported to the Great Red Spot on the planet Jupiter." With that Michael stood up and said, "But that's a story that will have to wait to be told another day."

"For now, know that calling the current great religions of the world together at Spirit Fest was intended to let everyone learn how similar all the faiths are to one another. And to shed light on those that are just interested in elevating their numbers for mind control purposes. It is said that so many wars have been fought over religion, but that's not true. Those wars were fought over wealth, land, control and domination of our fellow man. Large and small groups of people do not feel secure unless everyone around them thinks and believes the same way they do. I have learned much from humankind. There is one simple truth about people, whatever they believe is true is true, even if it's a lie, and people will kill one another to preserve the lie. Every religion presently on earth has borrowed some of their beliefs from other beliefs, myths and legends. I suggest that you do the same. It is said that humans are spiritual beings having a physical experience. However, far too many of you are lazy and quick to believe second hand truth. As I see it you are all artists in life, gifted with all the colors of Divine thought so that you can paint a portrait of your own personal belief. Now go and paint a masterpiece!" Michael finished as I wiped the sweat from my brow.

The music that first day was insane. We had everything from Elvis, Dean Martin and Cher impersonators to Jazz, Blues, Rock and Heavy metal bands. It was good to see people having fun. I mostly enjoyed riding Hercules down to watch the Native American Powwow. The power in the singing and dancing was incredible. When we shut down for the night I gathered all the Angel-Knights and thanked them for all their hard work, that it had not gone unnoticed. Russell Means thanked them as well and said what a peaceful day it was. He was surprised that no one caused any disruptions over the calling together of so many religions with such different viewpoints.

I said, "Thank God that's behind us. Tomorrow comes the hard ceremony, making peace with the ancestors."

Russell just smiled and nodded his head.

During one of the many times Russell Means spoke on stage to the crowd he reminded us that rain was Wankan, and that it was the Great Spirit's way of blessing us all. Being an accomplished drummer, he led all in attendance who brought hand drums in the Great Heartbeat of Mother Earth drumming ceremony. The percussion was astounding and the vibrations coursed right through us. We could all feel our hearts switch to the beat of his drum as the hearts in the crowd began beating as one. Rain clouds darkened in the sky as if it were night. The only light around came from the crystals encircling the Sword and the Stone in the middle of the knighting circle. like a glimmer in the night. We had set up spotlights around the exhibit and now the beams were shooting through the crystals and outward to the crowd. Magical doesn't even half describe the way it felt.

When the drumming stopped and the ceremony was over there was a palpable difference in the air. The crowd disbursed. Something had shifted. It was similar to the sensation after a heavy downpour. The air was ionized, charged with love and the vibration of Oneness.

Many of the people who came to the festival were spiritual in nature and could feel what a powerful crystal grid Archangel Michael had created in the heart of the main event area. Even those who didn't give crystals a second thought were drawn to the grid - walking over to look at the exhibit. From the stage where I stood, it appeared to me like a scene from Woodstock. I saw a sea of humanity surrounding the Sword and Stone. There was a break in the clouds and the sun came out. The crystal in the sword's pommel was gleaming. It shot sunlit rainbow rays of hope to all who watched on. Amazingly, no one attempted to touch the sword or any of the crystals that surrounded it. Michael had ceremoniously placed the sword in the stone when the first festival guest walked through the entrance of the gate and he wouldn't retrieve it until the closing ceremony when the primary purpose of the festival was revealed.

It truly was a miracle that the Angel-Knights were able to come together and coordinate such a unified presentation. I was so proud of them. It was their finest moment when they, the humans, stepped aside and let their angels do what they were sent to do. The "Knowing" they had attained beamed all around them. Sir Robert and Sir Johnny volunteered to be security for the night at the fairgrounds to make sure that no one tampered with the Sword of Truth and the crystal grid that surrounded it. Sir James and Sir Thomas were originally assigned the task, but all that changed when James had a problem with Sir Robert being around Lady Mary. I was sorry he didn't stay, of all the knights he needed to be at SpiritFest the most.

Chapter Forty-one

Apology Accepted

The next day started off with a bang -literally! A rock and roll band shot off a cannon on stage to the delight of the crowd, launching a full day of multicultural music, singing, dancing and fine art displays. We had Irish Cloggers, Islamic Whirling Dervishes from Turkey, and Mariachi Bands doing the Mexican Hat dance. You name it, and Spirit Fest had it.

The guests who came the second day were serious shoppers. All the vendors were happy about that and Lady Linda all but sold out of her inventory. It was so nice looking out over the crowd seeing women wearing Linda's golden fairy rings in their hair.

The gathering was peaceful, much like the Woodstock Festival. Some say the Woodstock gathering of half a million people for peace and love on August 15th, 1969 was the beginning of the hippie movement, but it was really the end. The movement had actually begun elsewhere around the world before it came to the U.S. in the 1960's. By 1967 the free love movement and use of recreational drugs, coupled with unsanitary conditions, left the Haight Ashbury area trashed and youth scrambling home penniless, and sometimes ill. It was a sign of things to come.

I remembered back to another counter culture event where tragedy struck. It happened in 1970 at the Altamont Music Festival. A teenager was killed by Hells Angels who were the security for the festival. This sad turn of events occurred while the Rolling Stones were on stage. With all of the love and peace being projected, it was unfortunate that the media focused their reports on the death. And that in turn became the focal point for society. Hippies = drugs + destruction + death.

With that historical outcome in mind, I was worried about our second day. Day one was a little *too* peaceful. Russel walked by and I said, "Well brother, day one was pure love and peace. Here's to day two!" He looked at me with a "knowing" smile, nodded his head, and continued walking.

I looked at my watch and saw that it was time to suit up for the "Ceremony of Forgiveness." I then left to put on Michael's armor.

About twenty minutes later, while saddling Hercules for the ceremony, I found myself surrounded by twelve guys looking to pick a fight. They were a racially mixed group, all in their early twenties. The gang's leader, Chris Hawkins, was dressed all in white.

He demanded to know, "Why the hell are you promoting Satanism and hosting a satanic festival in our own backyard? It's criminal you blasphemer."

I asked, "Were you here at the festival yesterday? What exactly do you feel is blasphemy?"

Chris admitted, "No we were not here yesterday, but I heard you spoke against, Jesus Christ, the Son of God."

I said, "We brought in all the beliefs to speak on their views of God and…"

"Isn't it a little early to be dressed for Halloween? You look like a faggot or birdman with all those feathers. Satanists are criminals. Don't you know that?" one of the guys in the group interrupted.

I'm sorry, I had to laugh at the birdman comment. I then said, "Boys the last thing I would promote is a criminal organization," while pointing to the badge on the lower right side of the breastplate. "And I'm wearing this armor for two reasons. One, because it was once written, 'Put on the full armor of the Lord', and secondly to remind me not to be thin skinned."

Chris then demanded to know what all the 'satanic golden symbols' were all over the armor. The twelve began moving closer in to me and Hercules. They were getting very aggressive and obviously looking for an argument; *or more*. Time was ticking and the ceremony was about to begin. Off in the distance, I could see Miss Cortes being escorted to the stage by Sir Gregory.

The last thing I wanted was a confrontation. I knew whatever I said at this point would just piss these guys off more. I turned to mount my horse but when I went to hoist myself up into the saddle my sword strap broke and the sword hit the ground. One of the guys quickly grabbed the sword and handed it to Chris. I thought, "Holy crap, what do I do now?" As I slid back to the ground I could feel Michael's consciousness moving into my mind. "Yes! Michael will set these guys straight!"

Chris stood there defiantly and asked, "What we want to know is Jesus Christ your Lord and Savior?"

Michael said, "I pray that he is! And as for the markings on my armor they tell a story. The gold lines are lightning bolts sent to cover my body with the Lord's protection. The blue color with the silver specks represents the universe the Lord created. The two crosses on my knees are in memory of the two men who were crucified with Jesus. And that's what the cross in the center of my chest represents. The symbols on each shoulder are really one cut in half. When the symbols are brought together they form a sacred heart that has been ripped apart resting on the same two crosses from my knees. The feathers in my black fur cape represent the thousands of children that I've knighted, as protectors of one another, with that sword you hold in your hand. You see I've been sent to deliver a message of love and protection to all God's children."

The twelve were spell bound. They didn't know what to say as the clouds let loose a fine mist drizzle. I could see Chris was embarrassed for his aggressive behavior, but he was too prideful to apologize in front of his buddies. Michael let me know that Chris had a Christ complex. When Chris reached out to return the sword to me, Michael put up my hand and said, "Chris, I know you are just one letter short of the Christ." Chris smiled at that observation. Michael continued, "That missing 't' in your first name is also represented in the form of the cross in the center of my chest."

Taking the sword from Chris' hand and pointing to the Sword of Truth in the center of the field Michael said, "I know who you are my brother. I must go now, but by the time I leave that stage, if you feel I am false; you may go and pull the Sword of Truth from the Stone and take it home with you. My quest will end here. You will decide if I should continue."

I couldn't believe what was coming out of my own mouth. Michael was leaving our fate in the understanding and hands of one man. We climbed into the saddle and rode toward the stage.

Looking back I know the great angel has taught me many things, but that day Archangel Michael taught me a lot about humility and forgiveness.

The time had finally come for the "Ceremony of Forgiveness" request. Miss Cortes went first. She was a stunning presence as she walked across the stage, her long black hair draped down across her shoulders and cascaded around her as the wind blew. Looking Russell Means in the eyes she read a beautifully prepared apology on behalf of her, her people and her ancestor, Cortes. She brought tears to the eyes of many in the audience. I could see why Archangel Michael wanted her to speak. It was very moving and inspirational. I later wished I had asked her for a copy of what she wrote. She covered the invasion of the Americas by her ancestor, his greed for gold and lust for power, but mostly she asked forgiveness for the murder of countless Native American Indians.

All eyes then moved to Russell Means who looked so regal and proud dressed all in black with a long black eagle feather trailing down the back of his head next to his long braids. The rain began to come down harder, but the audience was steadfast. They welcomed the confrontation. Everyone knew that Russell was very out spoken and aggressive. Instead of answering her immediately he pointed up to the sky, "Wakan," he said. "This is Holy."

Silence then followed for few minutes. Then he turned to Miss Cortes, "Although your words were well crafted, I find they were not from the heart since the heart must speak now in this present moment in time and giving to the spirit of all the things around us today. Great Spirit does not want what was happening around you when you wrote your beautiful request down. I do not think you have either the right or the authority to speak for your ancestor, or your people here today. Nor do I have the authority to speak for mine. I cannot accept your apology."

A bolt of energy shot through the crowd. All who spoke of it afterwards said they felt a disc-like object cut through their heart chakra. The Native Americans in the crowd let out a supportive yelp for Russell's reply. Miss Cortes was devastated. She left the stage weeping.

Although I realize you can't go into an apology expecting forgiveness, because that would be manipulation, my heart was breaking for her nonetheless. I could see the wisdom in brother Russell's words but wondered, was that actually Crazy Horse speaking?

I was up next. I slowly rode Hercules forward to the stage, slid out of the saddle and climbed the steps wondering, now what? What I was going to say? I felt that Russell had truly connected deeply with the spirit of the moment and that he wasn't about to accept my request either. Many were waiting to hear what was going to come out of my mouth, myself included. As I took the microphone I looked out into the crowd and saw Chris and his followers standing next to the Sword in the Stone. In that moment I was at a loss. I felt like I was going to make an ass of myself by asking forgiveness from a man that seemingly deserved to be holding hostility against the invaders of his people's land. Colonists were responsible for murdering more people than Hitler.

As these thoughts raced through my head in a split second, I was also faced with the image of the group of born-again zealots who were going to walk off with the Sword of Truth. Not in my wildest dreams could I have imagined getting myself into this type of predicament, but there I was. Looking up at the drizzle falling from the sky I was reminded of an argument I had witnessed the day before. I opened my mouth and said.

"Yesterday I saw four small children standing in the Arts and Crafts building arguing over the weather. Let's call them Billy, Barbara, Mary and Sophia. They were the cutest little angels with brown, red, blond and black hair accordingly. Billy said, 'My mommy told me I had to stay inside because it's *sprinkling*!' Barbara said quickly pointing her finger at Billy's face, 'My momma says it's *raining*!' Billy then replied, 'No, my mommy told me it *sprinkling*, not *raining*!' The two bickered back and forth over whether or not it was raining or sprinkling until, in her zeal, Barbara, who kept pointing a finger at Billy, accidentally poked him in the eye. Billy cried out, 'Ouch, Barbara you poked my eye and it hurts.' Barbara continued to argue that it was raining not sprinkling.

While listening to the banter and seeing Billy get poked in the eye Mary said to Barbara, 'Now you say sorry to Billy, Barbara that's not good.' Barbara became embarrassed, as an outraged Billy yelled, No, my mommy said it's sprinkling not raining. You're not real, I'm real.'

Mary, stepping in as a peacemaker then said, 'Okay let's go outside and see if it's sprinkling or raining.'

Billy replied in a loud voice, 'No, the rain is just sprinkling outside I know that because my mommy said so.'

Barbara interrupted saying, 'Rain, you just said rain, it's raining so I am right.'

Billy yelled back, 'No I said the rain is sprinkling and you say it's raining. It's not raining it's sprinkling outside.'

Sophia, who had been quietly watching, and as the voice of reason, stepped up and said, "You are both saying the same thing. What difference does it make? It's watering the ground."

Billy and Barbara both looked at her like she was stupid and said, 'The rain can't be watering, only sprinkling or raining on the ground."

I tell you this story because I feel I owe you all an apology. It has been brought to my attention that my calling all the great Religions of the world together to explain their belief systems, has offended some people. If you are offended and think that my actions are blasphemy or satanic, I am truly sorry. I, like little Sophia, just think we are all saying the same thing in different ways. We confuse nouns with verbs all the time in our zeal to be right. I'm sorry; whether it's sprinkling, raining or drizzling it's water - and we all need sacred water to survive.

I turned to Russell. He smiled and started once again drumming the heartbeat of Mother Earth.

He spoke softly giving a special greeting speaking in native Lakota. In English he spoke to the gathering about the importance of preserving nature and stopping the pollution of Mother Earth. He then told a tale his mother often told, "If you take all of the green things from the Earth, then nothing would live. If you take all of the winds from the Earth, then nothing would live. But if you take all of the people from the Earth, everything would flourish."

I mounted Hercules and went riding out into the main field. The people parted as I approached the sacred circle that contained the Sword of Truth and Light. I was told later, that even though it was drizzling rain at the time, Michael's Armor was a blaze with blue and gold light. The Angel-Knights had taken away the rope and joined hands, facing outward, around the Sword and Stone. Lady Susan handed me the staff she had carved and Michael raised it high over our head to signal to Russell that we were coming. I took the white feather talisman from my hair and clipped it onto the bottom of the sacred staff and then gave it back to Lady Susan.

Legend of the Lakota Cou Stick or Staff

Sioux warriors like other native tribes received standing through their bravery and actions in war. One way this was achieved is known as "counting cou." This happened when warriors got close to their enemy and touched them without them knowing or harm coming to the brave. This was considered a great honor. The more cou one had, the more honorable they were.

Lady Susan then walked to each of the Angel-Knights, around the circle, having them clip their feather and hair talisman to the staff. She then brought it back to me. Again, I raised the stick high above my head to show Russell. This time it was filled on both sides with feathers of many colors that contained our DNA. It was our "Coup Stick" that represented what we each had confronted with our demons in order to get there. We had also confronted the personal demons of everyone present at SpiritFest and emerged victorious. As I raised the staff high, I was asked the spirits of the ancestors that had assembled around us, to release their hostilities and count coup against the Trickster God Iktomi. I asked that they let go of their negative feelings and find the peace that the afterlife held in store for them.

As I lowered the staff to the saddle, I looked towards the stage. I could see in a vision, the Great Indian leader Crazy Horse, wearing his black buffalo headdress, standing behind Russell drumming. All around us in the ceremonial field I could see the ancestors' spirits dancing. Crazy Horse then stepped forward into Russell and they were one. Now in the vision Russell was wearing a white buffalo headdress. He stood there like a pillar of might.

Russell stopped drumming and let out a blood curtailing battle yelp that echoed throughout the field. The Natives Americans in the crowd let out a yelp in response, and then everything went silent again. The Great

Spirit had touched everyone by that point. You would have had to be dead not to feel it.

Angel Michael told me to look up. When I did the clouds had parted and seven eagles from the nearby nature preserve had taken to the air. They were now circling above us. I pointed the staff toward the sky and said, "Look the Great Spirit has sent his eagles to witness this sacred moment when his children have banded together in the true meaning of life. Turning back to Russell, Michael went on to say, "That's what 'Russell' Means, it's a good day to live my brother."

I rode Hercules toward the stage. I dismounted and walked up the stairs clearing my mind; not searching for what I was going to say when I stood toe to toe with Crazy Horse. When I reached him, I could see from the look in his eyes Russell Means was gone.

I said to Crazy Horse, "I hold the spirit of Wakinyon the blue warrior and this is our coup stick. I have defeated the Great Trickster Iktomi and count many coups on his followers both living and dead. I would be honored to present this staff of the peaceful warrior to the spirit of Crazy Horse. In doing so, as the spirit of the Good Knight, I take on to me all the misdeeds of the world done by white, black, yellow and red man. I now personally bear full responsibility for the human actions that caused the sins of our fathers. Since I alone am responsible for all the pain, suffering and death that has ever been afflicted on humankind…"

Dropping to one knee, but continuing to hold the staff of Wakinyon out to Crazy Horse, Michael continued. "I ask that you accept my deepest heartfelt apology. I ask forgiveness for all the wrongs that have ever been done to you and your ancestors, and to all those spirits who have ever suffered at the hands of another."

I could now see clearly what Michael had done thru SpiritFest. He brought together the great religions from around the world to be viewed by the shaman who represented the first belief, the nature religions.

The piercing eyes of Crazy Horse looked down at me with sadness. I could tell that he wanted to be angry, but Michael had given him a chance to finally be free. Was he going to hang on to the dark anger of the past or look to the light of the future?

Taking the black eagle feather talisman from his hair, Means attached it to the head of Wakinyon Staff. Then Russell-Crazy Horse said, "I will forgive you…" He paused as a cold hush came over the gathering. Then hesmiled saying, "…but we must never forget."

Sir Edward-Michael and Russell Means -Apology Accepted

Taking the Staff of Wakinyon from my hand he raised it up high for everyone in the crowd to see. I stood up and hugged my brother saying, "I hope nobody forgets and we all learn how to forgive. Holding onto anger and hate is truly like shooting yourself in the head and waiting for the other guy to die."

Russell then said, "How do you want to end this thing."

I took the microphone and said to the crowd, "My brother Russell wants to know how we should end SpiritFest '94? I say we honor the ancestors with the forbidden Ghost Dance." Russell smiled and let out his traditional Indian yelp, and we danced and danced.

During the dance I glanced through the crowd. It warmed my heart to see Chris and his followers in the circle shuffling their feet and whirling about around the Sword of Truth. I walked over to him. Michael said, "Well Sir, if I let you down the Sword is yours to keep."

Chris replied, "No, too much responsibility comes with such a blade. I have been humbled. Thank you."

When the dancing stopped I invited everyone to select one quartz crystal from around the Sword and hold it in sacred remembrance of what we had accomplished at SpiritFest '94.

Everybody left the festival happy, content and illuminated.

Upon leaving that night Russell and I had sat down and talked one last time. I asked if he understood what we had achieved over the past two days. Shaking his head, no, he responded, "Can mere mortals understand what is above their understanding? I do feel it was good though."

I said, "Then you know the all. When you think you know you don't, and when you know you don't you do! What I saw however, was amazing. While we were doing the Ceremony of Forgiveness I saw the spirit of Crazy Horse merge with you and when it happened, his black buffalo headdress turned white. Then during the Ghost Dance, I saw our ancestors letting go of the negativity that was holding their spirits earth bound and they were ascending into the sky, through the eagles, on beams of light. I also had a vision while dancing of a white buffalo calf being born near the Black Hills. Then I saw a huge herd of black, red and cream-colored buffalo on the move that turned into human beings walking across North America. They journeyed from the Atlantic Ocean to the Pacific. It was led by the living and the spirits of the dead were following. As the living would pass by old battlefields, cities and towns, more spirits would rise up to join them. I saw white, black, Asian and Indian people wearing all sorts of dress. Many were in uniforms like those worn by civil war soldiers. When the walkers arrived at a great yellow circle within a golden triangle all the spirits let go of their anger. Then they were lifted up to heaven in a beam of white light. The living then continued their march toward the sea. However, the walkers also attracted something they did not want. I kept hearing, 'Tom-Tom will divide the tribe and infect the march with pride, anger, greed, envy, sloth, gluttony and lust'."

After I finished, Russell just sat there a while and looked at me. I must have sounded crazy to him. He laughed and said, "White people can't have visions, Sir Edward."

To which I replied, "Then it's a good thing that I'm the last of the blue people."

He laughed, "Right! I forgot."

We just sat there in silence. I could tell he didn't know how to take me. But again, what else was there to say?

He stood up and said, "We need to get together again."

I replied, "Yes maybe in another twenty years."

He shook his head, took a breath and sighed. With a frown on his face he said, "No it will be sooner than that."

But I knew our work together was done and that I'd never smoke the pipe of peace with my red brother again.

One of Russell's people came to him and said that a reporter wanted to interview him about the festival so I started helping the Angel-Knights dismantle the sound equipment on the stage. I noticed that as soon as Means started the interview he returned to being the hardhearted wounded warrior I met at the Bureau of Indian Affairs so long ago. The reporter wanted to know how Russell got involved with the Good Knight Network, so he told the story of how I was an undercover cop that infiltrated the BIA building during the takeover in 1972 and how I had reported on the conditions inside. I was hoping Russell would mention the angel that was guiding me and that same angel was responsible for bringing us together to host the Spirit Fest event, but he didn't. He just talked about how the event brought him face to face with a former enemy. When the reporter asked him how that made him feel he simply said that he doesn't hold grudges and he could never forget what the Wasichu did to his people.

I could see then that Russell Means could never see me as anything more than an untrustworthy white man. Wasichu is the Lakota word for white man and it means "Greedy person who steals the fat." Michael finally learned what Russell Means. It saddens me to this very day. I had failed to free my human red brother's heart and spirit, but what could I expect? The history between the U.S. Government and the Native People is long, bloody and full of lies. Dressed in blue and gold I was the symbol of everything the Indians hated.

On December 29th, 1890, when the U.S. Army's, blue pony soldiers from the, 7th Cavalry rode into the Wounded Knee village to stop the forbidden Ghost Dance, they left an hour later after massacring over one hundred and fifty men, women and children. Sitting Bull had been killed at a Ghost Dance two weeks earlier. It was believed that the soldiers were deliberately taking revenge for their regiment's defeat at the Little Big Horn, which left Custer and all the men that rode with him dead. The Wounded Knee Creek massacre ended the Ghost Dance Movement in America. I was sure that was why Michael ended Spirit Fest '94 with the Ghost Dance. It was a new beginning for us all.

I could only imagine how the Indians felt about seeing me riding my horse around the festival dressed in blue from head to toe. Michael told me that was all part of the plan of forgiveness and despite what Russell Means told the reporter he still put his eagle feather at the top of the Cou Stick. Michael said, "You did not fail your brother. You honored him and his great Buffalo People."

After the interview, as I walked Russell to his car he told me that there was a Sun Bow Walk of Native Americans planned for the spring and summer of 1995. He recommended that I hurry and finish our medicine wheel-healing labyrinth saying, "If you paint it yellow, like the sun, they might bless the medicine wheel for us." I was shocked that he said, "...for us."

I said, "How do I get them there."

Russell replied, "The same way you got me here, dare Great Grandfather not to come and he'll come!"

Chapter Forty-two

Good Knight Museum

After Spirit Fest '94 the Angel-Knights and I focused on moving everything out of East Wing Castle and into the charity's temporary museum headquarters which was just around the corner from the property we were gifted. The building was a maze of hallways and rooms and there was no great room where I could set up the stage for programs. Michael felt that the building should be used for offices and museum tours. I had my work cut out for me. I used everything I had learned at the renaissance festival to paint the walls in all the display rooms to look like stone block walls inside a castle.

Michael showed me a vision of how I could transform one large computer room to look like we were on the surface of the moon. We called it the "Room with a View." The walls were all painted black, like the void of deep space, with dots of white phosphorescent paint. That created the illusion of our Milky Way Galaxy when the black lights were turned on.

In the middle of the back wall was a forty-eight-inch photograph of the Earth from NASA. I cut it out from a photo I ordered and mounted the earth in the center of the wall so the viewers were looking at the blue, white and green earth coming up over the horizon.

I moved the Tree of Life, Constant Walker angel mannequin, the flower fairy gardens, Sword and Stone and angelic knighting circle into the back half of the room. I then suspended one hundred and forty-four Swarovski Crystal stars from the ceiling with black thread at different levels within the scene, while scattering six hundred white mini lights that slowly pulsated in the garden area beneath them. The crystals twinkled like real stars when the room was activated. Michael said the Room with a View would serve as a gateway to the dimensions where the Seven Celestial Sisters dwell, and that if Lady Mary and the Angel-Knights were going to succeed, they would need the sisters' support to do so.

Creating Pandora's box

In a second room Michael created "The Void and Pandora's Box."

Everything the Hierophant had taught us was coming together and being used. We painted the 12' x 12' room's walls and ceiling black as well. Then I peppered the walls, carpet and ceiling with white phosphorescent paint giving the illusion of being in deep space.

Michael gave Sir Gregory the dimensions to create a 24" x 48" six-sided hexagonal shaped box made from maple wood. The box had to be lined inside and out with mirrors covering all the wood surfaces except for the viewing port door that had to house a two-way glass mirror, where we could see in, but what was trapped inside could not see out and escape.

What Michael was asking us to create was what he called, "a negativity containment chamber."

Michael had the Angel-Knights help us program sixteen special quartz crystals from SpiritFest '94. On the first eight crystals he wrote Pride, Envy, Sloth, Greed, Gluttony, Pride, Lust, Wrath and Injustice; the vices of selfishness. He asked that any of the dark negative energy traits that haunt us, go into the crystals during the programing.

On the second eight crystals he wrote Humility, Kindness, Diligence, Generosity, Abstinence, Purity, Patience and Justice, the Virtues of Selflessness. He asked that any of these benevolent traits that we might have go into the crystals.

I then crushed the vice and a virtue crystals into dust and put the dust into eight corresponding, Vice and Virtue jars. I filled the eight jars with ceramic clay slip then stirred the Vice and Virtue mixture together. I then poured the contents of those eight jars into eight ceramic skull molds. I built up about a quarter of an inch of clay slip mixture on the inside walls of the molds and marked each mold with the names of the vice-virtue that it contained. The clay set in the molds for 24 hours. When Michael said it was time to take the skulls out of the molds, one by one I cleaned the greenware and carved the name of the Vice and Virtue into the forehead of the skull along with carving four angelic talisman on the sides and back. When all eight were cleaned and carved they were left to dry for eight days, and were fired in a ceramic kiln.

Michael programed eight additional crystals with a cloaking prayer for each skull and mixed the dust from them into eight jars of clear ceramic glaze. Once the eight skulls came out of the kiln and cooled, I painted the corresponding clear glaze onto the skulls, let them dry, then put them back in the kiln to fuse the crystal-glass coating on the skulls inside and out. I then coated each skull with an additional phosphorescent clear paint wash so they would glow in the dark. Once complete, the eight were called the Skulls of the Heroes, to represent all the innocents who have been victimized by individuals whose selfish vices are out of control and who lack the virtues.

I then cut out special drawings of human faces to fit the name of the vice and coated it with a clear yellowish wash of phosphorescent transparent paint. After drying I carefully mounted the face inside the skull so you could see the faces if you looked into the skulls eye sockets. When the mirror-covered box was complete we placed it in the back of room named the "Great Void." I drilled a small hole in one corner of the box just large enough for an electrical wire so I could light the interior of the box.

To further enhance the impact of the exhibit, Michael chose a Halloween mask to represent Seth-Belial, the commander of the Sons of Darkness. It had a black hood, red bullish face, and horns. It was very scary and looked life-like. I stuffed the head with cotton fiber and put a slow-moving rotisserie grill motor inside the head to make the cheeks and mouth move. Fake flame fire pots were placed on either side of the head to bring the interior of the box alive with a fiery presence. With the mirrored inside walls of the box angled to reflect one another the viewer would see the face of ultimate "Evil" and an endless pit of fire. It was comforting to know that you could see the head of the "Evil One," but that it couldn't see you.

I then illuminated the room with a black light, suspended the eight Skulls of the Heroes on black wires from the ceiling so as the viewer walked the marked path through the room toward "Pandora's Box" they would pass the skulls. The black lights brought the skulls and stars on the walls alive giving you the sense that you were walking through space while being watched by the negative forces in the universe. If you looked into the skulls, you would see the human faces of the vice hiding within. The purpose of the exhibit for adults was to allow the individual to cast their negativity into the box and never let those demons haunt them again. For kids it was just an outer space haunted house exhibit - an amazing dual purpose.

Michael programed the box with positive energy to purge everyone who came in contact with it from his or her own personal darkness. He said that negativity is attracted to the positive, so the box acted like a vacuum cleaner and once the negative energy enters the box it can't find its way back out. He reminded me that the darkness hates mirrors and that this was all an experiment with collecting human darkness and then moving it to the "Red Spot" on planet Jupiter; or at least that was the plan. He said, "There are many factors that play into the outcome. The most important part is keeping the Angel-Knights positive and bringing forth the child with the initials M.V.

Chapter Forty-three

The Swords of Power

That year for the renaissance festival we were the talk of the grounds because so many of the people had been to our Spirit Fest '94 celebration. Everyone asked us if we were going to do it again, but we told them it was so expensive and a lot of work which gave us a new appreciation for the people who manage festivals we attended. To give our visitors hope we informed everyone we had acquired three acres in Beltsville and were in the process of building a Good Knight Castle Museum complex. Our visitors couldn't wait for us to open.

Our theme that year at the Ren-Fest was, "The Quest for the Holy Grail." Michael said, "No one finds the Grail, the Grail must find you," so I built a large white gazebo, carved a huge Styrofoam blocks into a rocky waterfall that spilled into a pond in the back of the gazebo. We called it the Chapel of the Holy Grail. I then crafted a blue and gold ceramic cup with an Angel of the Four Directions on each side. Mounting the false grail on top of the waterfall, the Angel-Knights and I waited for the real Grail to find us. It was a good year for the festival; not too hot in the beginning and not too cold by its end. Good things were coming.

Master Daniel Watson of Angel Sword Forge came to our RenFest camp as soon as he arrived in town. He informed me it was time to make good on his promise. "I have vowed to deliver seven swords to Michael's Armory this year, and that I intend to do."

I invited brother Ken and brother Daniel to a feast at our new headquarters building to help participate in the honoring ceremony of the Seven Celestial Sisters.

Both men loved the "Room with a View" but brother Ken really loved the Void and Pandora's box exhibits. He came out physically shaken and sweating profusely telling me, "You took some shit away from me in there that I wanted to keep."

To which I replied, "Sorry Ken, the box only attracts shit that is drawn to it. Once it's in the box it gone, but I'm sure you can create more my friend." He flashed me a smirky smile and walked away.

During the meditation in the "Room with a View," Michael had Lady Mary-Uriel stand on the center pod within the Knighting Circle of Light, as it had become known. It actually looked like the transporter room on the starship enterprise. After about ten minutes seven orbs of white light descended down from the ceiling and hovered around her head like a crown or halo. One orb moved to her crown chakra and the other orbs moved and hovered over the outside pods. Our honoring ceremony was successful. The celestial sisters had manifested.

Michael had all the Angel-Knights take turns moving through the remaining six sisters' energies as if they were being tested for purity. At that time none but Mary, made the grade. As happy as I was that one sister merged, a heavy sigh came over me. I could only hope we could keep Mary in a state of grace since Sir Robert was sitting there looking love struck with an "I must make her mine look on his face."

Michael likes to invite high-spirited emotion into the mix. I wondered how he expected me to keep everyone positive with a dog-knight sniffing around. I shook my head and moved on thinking that this was going to be a huge test for me.

With the honoring of the sisters completed, a tribute was in order. It was time for the "Gifting Ceremony." Brother Ken asked to go first. He produced two leather bags one red and one blue from under his cloak. He asked me to examine the bags. I saw that they were both empty. He asked me to hold out my hands and I did. Then he put an empty bag in each hand and said, "In your right hand do you want gold or silver?"

I said, "Silver," thinking he would expect me to say gold.

He said "Pour the contents onto the floor." When I turned the empty red bag over thirty silver dollars fell out. Master Ken said, "And in the blue bag, do you want silver or gold?"

I said, "Gold." When I turned the blue bag over thirty Spanish gold coins fell onto the floor.

Brother Daniel's mouth flew open in disbelief.

I said, "Daniel you have walked across half of Mexico looking for lost gold treasure. I just sat here and the gold and silver found us." He laughed with wide eyes glaring.

Master Ken said that the coins were payment for the kindness the Angel-Knights and I had showed him when everyone else shunned him.

Master Watson was up next. He had his apprentice and First Knight Benedicto bring in a long narrow wooden crate with runes carved on its lid.

As he unlocked the crate Daniel said, "I have agreed to forge the one hundred and forty-four Angel Knight Swords you seek and will continue to do so so long as your knights respect the meaning of the sword entrusted to their safe keeping. If one knight amongst you dishonors the sword, or the sacred position they hold, that sword must be returned to me and that knight will be responsible to complete the collection. Is that understood?"

I had each knight stand, joining me by placing their hands crossed over their heart. We took the pledge together, "We understand and accept the terms."

Master Daniel then reached into the create and passed me the first blade it was the "Sword of Raphael the Healer." He had made the sword as a short twenty-eight-inch silver and gold duplicate of Excalibur with one exception it had brass crescent moons on each side of the hilt. I presented the Healer Sword to Lady Barbara-Raphael for all of her hard work coordinating SpiritFest that year. Lady Barbara was a young, tall, slender, horsewoman with long straight auburn hair. She was half Algonquin Indian and half Irish. I knew she would honor the sword

The second sword was the "Shekinah, or the Flaming Heart of the Virgin." It was a twenty-two-inch silver sword. The flame shaped blade had seventeen points that radiated from its razor-sharp edges. I presented that sword to Lady Mary-Uriel. Master Daniel made it special for her because, as he put it, "It is rare to find a twenty-three-year-old, beautiful virgin in the world these days outside of a monastery." When you held the sword you could feel the flames flowing up and out from its blade. I knew that Lady Mary would honor the sword.

The third sword was called the "Bright Knight" a thirty-three-inch blue steel broad sword. It was sleek and wise. It held all the virtue and honor that I saw in Sir Thomas-Sachiel. He was shocked when I presented it to him. He did not feel worthy. Sir Thomas had fallen in love with Lady Barbara, which put a monkey wrench into their lives, but they were trying to maintain balance between their families and the Path of the Magi. It was hard since Lady Barbara's family was mostly Born-Again Christians. They had disowned her for not following their belief system.

The fifth sword was "Prince Ali" an Arabian Scimitar with a wide Saracen blade. It was right out of Ali Baba and the Forty Thieves. It was short, charming and swift. When Brother Daniel pulled it from the sheath I could see Sir Johnny- Rothanael's eyes light up.

Sir Johnny had settled his libido down and was driving with Sir Robert-Cassiel back and forth from Michigan every couple of months. They had been diligently studying the lessons from the Hierophant and showed a definite commitment to the Path of the Magi.

I was against presenting the sword to Sir Johnny, but Angel Michael said, "Johnny has what it takes to become one of the greatest knights within the Order of Angel-Knights. He will come through for you when you least expect it." He then to presented Prince Ali to Sir Johnny-Rothanael.

The sixth sword was "The Clan Macgregor" a Scottish Claymore broadsword with thirty-inch silver double-edged blade and highly polished brass basket that safeguarded the hand at the hilt. There was only one within our ranks that could wield a sword like that, Sir Gregory-Metatron. From being with me from the start, he had more than earned the Clan Sword for helping keep the knights banded together for one common cause and for teaching the lessons from the Book of Wisdom to all newcomers. When I presented the sword to Sir Gregory, he informed me that earlier in the evening Chris, the Born-Again Christian from SpiritFest, and six of his followers had signed up to take the Master Studies Course from him! That news touched my heart deeply. Minds which are open, often lead to infinite possibilities.

The seventh sword was the "Spirit of Buddha" it was the smallest, but most powerful sword of them all. It measured sixteen inches from tip to pommel. With a three quarter of an inch silver double edged blade and highly polished stone handle. The Spirit of Buddha could go to only one person, Lady Eleanor-Haniel our sweet beloved Buddhist. Lady Eleanor had become the calm, cool-headed matriarch of the knighthood, always first to recite the wisdom of the Buddha when times were hard. She also arranged the large lines of credit for the charity so that we could afford to create new exhibits and pay the mortgage when times were hard.

The eighth Sword was "Dragon's Tongue" a thirty-two inch highly polished silver sword with a fine double-edged blade shaped like a long flat tongue. The sword had an intricate etched pattern running down the center of the blade. The Dragon's Tongue was an incredible sword and it had Sir James-Sandalphon's energy all over it. Unfortunately, he was not present to accept it. Coming from the outlaw biker community you have to know when to hold your tongue. The same held true for him and the way he held his tongue about his feelings for Lady Mary. He started pulling away from the gatherings, but as an electrician he would work with me on the weekends running electrical wires and cables throughout the grounds of the Good Knight Castle complex. Because Sir Robert was coming back more often, the other knights didn't see as much of Sir James. I decided to hold on to the Dragon Tongue Sword for him, in case he ever came back to claim it.

Sir Robert-Cassiel and Sir Johnny asked if they could make a presentation of swords and armament to Michael's Armory in repentance for any disrespect they may have shown in the past. As avid sword collectors they each presented a matched set of Knights Templar, two handed broadswords, with thirty-six-inch blades. Michael named the swords, "Batman and Robin." Sir Johnny also presented a Norman helmet with a sword dent in it from a blow to the head he had received from Sir Robert the year before.

Sir Robert then presented a thirty-inch short sword that he had forged called the "Sword of Adam," along with a silver battle-axe he named "Hardhead" - named appropriately after himself. He asked if I would wear it on my belt while dressed in Michael's Armor. A bold request, if I may say so myself.

Once the presentation ceremony was complete, it was time for some "labors." Time to serve the energies and honor the process. Together we moved our large glass showcase into one of the new rooms. Everyone chipped in and grabbed a paint brush to help make the walls look like castle block. The new exhibit came to life quickly. We decreed that the new space was to become Michael's Armory. We now had the first twelve Angel-Knight Swords for the wall mounts. It looked stunning, but most of all the space felt powerful. The energies of the angels had aligned with those swords.

Afterwards we all moved into the large conference room where we dined on Chinese food and warm sake. It felt good when Brother Ken stood up to make a toast to the knights, for accepting him as family. He said that most people treated him like he was the enemy.

I said, "Most of our enemies should be our friends and most of our friends are really our enemies. That's why we should trust no one and love everyone."

The following weekend, we returned to our camp at the renaissance festival and the weather was unseasonably cold. I could feel that something was getting ready to happen.

The morning started with a demand that Hercules, my horse, be taken back to his owner because there were complaints from jealous vendors that it wasn't fair I got to ride around the festival in order to draw people to the Good Knight camp, and away from their booths. Seriously? Just wait, it gets better…

My uneasy feeling was correct. Within the first hour after Herc left, vendors showed up at our camp with the management, complaining that we were selling things cheaper than they were, and they didn't like it.

It wasn't cheap for a family to attend the festival and buy items for their kids. All the girly girls wanted the beautiful dried flowered crowns for their hair. However, twenty to forty dollars a piece was a lot to spend on one kid, not to mention the cost if you had two. So, Lady Linda's silver and gold Fairy Ring crowns with colorful ribbons flowing down the back of the head, selling for $2-$5 dollars was a great buy. And she couldn't make the fairy rings fast enough to keep up with the demand.

I tried to reason with management by pointing out the vendors' complaints were based on personal greed and that everything the charity was making was accepted as a donation. Not wanting to look like the greedy asses they were, the vendors changed their complaint to the fact that the materials used in our fairy crowns was not something that would have been used in the fifteenth century. Again, seriously, I thought?

I pleaded our case as best that I could, but in the end, we were told we could no longer sell the fairy crowns. This decision opened the door for all the vendors at the festival to pick apart our inventory! Next the ceramics fell prey to the complaints, followed closely afterward by my hand-made wooden swords.

"Wait a minute!" I interjected to the owner of the festival. "Remember, our original arrangement was to help draw families to the festival, and then the charity would use this as a fundraiser to help us with our outreach programs. If we can't raise money at the festival, then what's in it for us?"

The vendors countered saying that passing on the child safety message and being allowed to knight the children should be reward enough for the charity and it's volunteers. The vendors reminded the festival owner that everyone who comes through the front gates intends to spend a certain amount of money, and that every dollar that's given to the Good Knights is one less dollar they have a chance to receive.

I couldn't believe my ears. The energy swirled and felt like wolves pulling apart a dead carcass.

The owner said., "Look I had an agreement, and to that I stand. As long I am in charge, the Good Knights can vend everything they are currently offering."

Score one for the good guys!

The compromise was that I would not ride my horse Hercules around the festival anymore, but he could be stabled at our camp since the children loved him so. I told Sir Gregory to get on the phone and have Herc brought back.

The day was winding down and what a day it was. Michael asked me to go stand on top of the hill above the Chapel. "The Grail is coming you, should be ready to pass the test to receive it," he said. "Remember what I told you about the Grail."

I replied, "No, what?"

All I heard in response was, "It's a test remember"?

Crap, I thought! Of all the stuff he tells me and on this I was drawing a blank.

Right after closing time, Hercules' owner pulled back through the gates. Walking in right behind him was Sir James Gray, along with his new-found lady love. Her name was Angel and she had an eight-year-old daughter named Autumn. They were sweet together, but I could see that Sir James still had feelings for Lady Mary. He glared at Sir Robert but then glanced away quickly.

Sir James told me that more of his biker buddies were interested in having me marry them. "I have a whole list with telephone numbers of people who want to schedule with you," he said. This led to us booking weddings in the Grail Chapel at the festival. It was a very sacred setting to get married and each wedding drew a crowd to our camp. To make the marriage ceremony Divinely sacred, Michael had me create a blessed juice concoction he named the Golden Elixir. With all those visitors making their way to us, word quickly spread that the Grail could be found at the Good Knight's Camp.

One afternoon at the RenFest while I was finishing a wedding ceremony for a couple of Sir James' friends in the Grail Chapel, Michael poured about two ounces of the Golden Elixir into the blue Grail Cup and dropped in two red grapes. He then passed the cup to the couple saying, "As you drink for the first and last time from this holy cup I bind you as one asking that you be wrapped together in a life of good health, happiness and prosperity as long as you maintain and your hearts remain pure. Remember, you both must work each day on your relationship because there are dark forces out there that will try to pull you apart. So honor one another and keep the fires of love burning strong all the days of your life."

After the couple drank the Golden Elixir Michael took the red sash from around our waist and tied one of each of their hands together. Michael then had them each take a red grape from the cup as he said, "These special red grapes symbolize your love for one another and are filled with the positive energy from the Sun. In their centers are the seeds of your future. When you swallow the grapes and seeds, you are one in the eyes of your Creator. May the happiness that you seek, grow from the seeds inside you forever and for always! Now place the grape in your hand on the tongue of your love."

As the couple placed the grapes in one another's mouth, Michael said, "By the powers vested in me by your Creator and the Great State of Maryland I pronounce you husband and wife. What has been joined together this day let no one put asunder."

As soon as the vibration of the last word was out of my mouth, Michael immediately left my consciousness. I thought that odd and looked around to see what was going on.

My attention was drawn to a man with a bright golden aura that had appeared, seemingly out of nowhere. He was standing in the crowd that had assembled to watch the wedding ceremony. The clean-shaven man, with long brown hair, was dressed in brown leather barbarian clothing and had a long red cape hinged at his shoulders by two bright golden medallions bearing the face of Zeus. He had a huge wooden hammer slung over his shoulder. I could tell that the heavy hammer had to weigh at least fifty pounds, but he was holding it as though it only weighed five.

When the crowd drifted away from the Grail Chapel the man stepped forward and knelt before the waterfall inside the Grail Chapel staring at the blue cup. He then spoke with his back to me, "Sir Edward-Michael I have not come to marry. I came seeking the Holy Grail. Is this the cup I seek?"

I thought, what do you say to that? Do I lie to this man? So, I said the first thing that came, "I can only feel that our Father Zeus has sent you, Thor, on a fool's mission. I am afraid I have failed you my brother and our Father. The Grail Cup that you kneel before is false, but even a false cup has the power to bond lovers together as you can see."

Thor stood up and faced me with a stern look in his eyes. Brother Daniel's and Brother Ken's timing was impeccable. They both showed up to see and experience my humiliation. I could tell there was a special reason for this man's visit that transcended his mortal presence. He was obviously guided by a celestial spirit and was on a Divine Quest.

He asked, "Brother why haven't you found the Grail by now? I have traveled to Hades and back in search of your camp. Has my journey been a in vain?"

Saddened that this special fellow had traveled far just to find a false grail cup, I called to Sir Gregory-Metatron to bring me the Golden Elixir decanter. Lady Bonnie-Gabriel knew that was her cue to wash out the blue cup and bring it to me. Just then I remembered what Michael had told me long ago, so I said, "Brother in my search for the cup I learned from a mighty angel in blue armor that 'No one finds the Grail. The Grail must find those who are worthy. I hope to be so blessed one day."

Lady Bonnie tried to pass me the blue cup, but Thor said to her, "That won't be necessary Lady Red Knight." Lady Bonnie was flattered that Thor noticed her red hair, red tunic and red cape which matched his cape. He took the blue cup and reached back grabbing his red cape covering the cup. Twisting it into a ball then unraveled it. Out of nowhere he produced a large perfectly formed wooden cup. The inside bowl of the cup was solid gold. Thor said, "Yes you have solved the riddle and the Holy Grail has found a worthy home with you Blue Knight. Now you must make ready for the coming of the Grail Queen. She will need to fill this Cup with the Golden Sands of Time during the End of Days."

Once Thor presented me with the Grail I asked my three brothers to join me in the chapel. We called on the Powers of the Four Directions to surround us as I filled the Holy Grail with the Golden Elixir. We drank to the coming of the Child of Victory, and the Grail Queen. Brother Daniel and I told Ken and Thor what had happened at Spirit Fest. I told them all about my vision of the white buffalo calf being born.

Brother Thor said, "It happened in August, several weeks ago."

The following week I invited my three brothers Daniel, Ken and Thor to a First Wednesday Club gathering at the new castle property in Beltsville. We were having a special meditation and ceremony while continuing construction of the medicine wheel-healing labyrinth. I told the gathering that we needed to attract the Sun Bow Walkers that Russell Means told me about, because Michael wanted to help release the earth-bound spirits of the ancestors that would be following them. Thor then produced an article that was written about the birth of the White Buffalo Calf in August. Its name was Miracle.

Chapter Forty-four

Birth of Miracle

Staying in a state of awe when confirmation about channeled information is given from above is the best way to manage ego. It happens time and time again to practitioners of the healing and spiritual arts. The opportunity exists for them to think they are the power, or to see it as having surrendered well enough, to allow the power to flow through them. For me, when amazing things happen or when what I have heard from Michael comes into this dimension of reality, I get giddy like a little kid; definitely never patting myself on the back for "knowing" anything, except for the fact that I don't know a thing. So, I was happy to see that when confirmation of my vision of the white buffalo calf being born came true, that everyone understood the message had not come from "me." It was indeed a miracle.

The article Thor showed us left everyone stunned and filled with hope. Indeed, a female white buffalo calf named Miracle was being called the Sacred White Female Buffalo Calf. She was born on the Heider farm near Janesville, Wisconsin on August 20, 1994. A veterinarian examined it and confirmed it was authentically white, not an albino.

The birth of a white buffalo calf had been foretold and was seen as a significant sign by the Native American community. Many believed it is the most sacred living thing one can encounter. "The arrival of the white buffalo is like the second coming of Christ," says Floyd, Hand-Looks-For - Buffalo, an Oglala Medicine Man from Pine Ridge, South Dakota. "It will bring about purity of mind, body, and spirit and help to unify all nations black, red, yellow, and white."

Thor said he saw the birth of a white calf as an omen, because they happen in the most unexpected places and often among the poorest people in the nation. The birth of the sacred white buffalo provides those within the Native American community with a sense of hope and an indication that good times are coming. Many see the birth of the white buffalo calf as sign to gather under the banner of the Sun Bow, a complete circular rainbow in the sky around the sun caused by water vapor in the air. Due to the birth of the white calf, hundreds of people from all races planned to join Native Americans in a planned walk across America, in fulfillment of the ancient prophecy of Earth's renewal.

The Angel-Knights and I spent the remainder of 1994 finishing the construction of exhibits at our new headquarters. We had to make it suitable for a guided tour museum experience and a distribution center for our programs and materials. A new nook area was created to serve as the medieval gift shop, just like the one at East Wing, so we could sell our ceramics and safety materials. We updated the old exhibits and created new ones as well.

While the others were reassembling exhibits, Michael took me to a room he chose for displaying his armor and the veils of the Seven Celestial Sisters. He told me, "Since each sister represents a universe, we will call this room, "Multiverse," because it will be a microcosm of the six universes that surround our own. The universe earth rotates in is one of seven that are about 10 billion light years in diameter and together they contain 144 billion galaxies. Earth's sun is one of 144 billion stars in what is called the Milky Way Galaxy and is located in an outer spiral arm of the Milky Way called Orion's Spur.

With the size of our universe that he described, I asked, "How do you get around?"

He reminded me of something Master ERU spoke about in one of the lessons, "The fastest speed in 3D, the third dimension in which humans dwell, is the speed of light. The fastest speed in the other dimensions is the speed of thought. With that you can travel from one end of the universe to the other in less than the blink of an eye."

From all this information he was sharing with me, I could tell that this new exhibit was going to be a doozy.

He reminded me, *again*, "My armor can only be worn for seven years so you need an exhibit area suitable enough to display it in a scene that represents all that I must safeguard."

The room Michael chose was 12' x 12'. I painted the walls and ceiling black. With white, yellow and blue phosphorescent paint I speckled the void with several thousands of stars and galaxies. Again, I created an illusion to the viewer which made the room look like one was peering into outer space 360 degrees around.

The room was an old office computer room which had a raised floor made of 3' x 3' wooden tiles and a Halon Fire suppression system below. After finishing the painting of stars, I put Michael's Armor on a life size mannequin and stood the armor in the back of the room. I then pulled up all of the flooring around the armor revealing the 36" drop to the concrete floor below. I scattered 1,000 blue and 1,000 white slow motion pulsating mini lights on the concrete floor, along with a fog machine. Then I covered it all with white fluffy cotton fiber batting. It looked like heavenly clouds filled with energy.

Michael said we couldn't finish the "Multiverse" until we attracted the energy of the Seven Celestial Sisters on eight specially crafted sheer veils.

"Eight?" I asked. "I thought it was seven."

No response.

We had been trying to draw the Seven Sisters energy down to align with the Angel-Knights, but I could not find the right combination and the knights were having problems balancing their positive and negative energy. It's a hard job to be human. We are so emotional and our egos kick in at the most inopportune times. It was my understanding that if we attracted sisters' energy and held it in the veils, we might also be able to attract their Mother, "Wisdom," and in time the spirit of Kei Pistis Sophia, the Queen of Atlantis. All these goals had to be achieved if we had any hope of finding the child with the initials M.V.

I was just taking everything one day at a time.

The Seven Celestial Sisters
Experiment of 1994

During the December 7th, First Wednesday Club gathering we meditated around the Knighting Circle of Light in the Room with a View. Eight of the twelve Angel-Knights were chosen to represent a Celestial Sister and hold one of the sacred veils while standing on the pods inside the circle. Since Lady Mary was the only one that had attracted the Constant Walker, she stood on the center pod representing Mother Earth. As we all focused on our Blue Princess eight white orbs came down from the ceiling and began orbiting around her head once again. One by one the orbs would break away and sit on top of a veil being held by a knight. When all eight came to rest, the knights were instructed to fold the sheer cloth over the orb, then sit the veil on the pod and leave the circle.

We sat around the outside of the circle of stones as the room filled with a pleasant heavenly energy and light that we had not felt before. It was so peaceful. It reminded me of how I felt when I drowned and met the Constant Walker for the first time. Michael explained how each sister represents the intelligent life forms from each of the universes the sisters created.

Michael said that what holds each universe together is the dark matter of the Void. That's why there are seven sisters of Light Matter, but there are eight daughters of the Creators when you include the Dark Matter of the Void. Michael told me that it was a hard thing to explain in earthly terms, and that the psychodrama we had just enacted was the best explanation for our elementary level minds and human intelligence. We felt like we were pawns being moved around on great chessboards.

To help you better understand who played what role, here is a list of the Angel/Knights and the Celestial Sister they represented:

1. Lady Judah/Anael: The sister Urania of the Fish People, living in light matter.

2. Sir Gregory/Metatron: The sister Odessa of the Bird People, living in light matter.

3. Lady Eleanor/Haniel: The sister Tabatha of the Feline or Cat People, living in light matter.

4. Lady Barbara/Raphael: The sister Sabuca of the Canine or Dog People, living in light matter.

5. Lady Bonnie/Gabriel: The sister Scheherazade of the Reptile People, living in light matter.

6. Lady Leah/Israphael: The sister Salamanda of the Amphibian People, living in light matter.

7. Lady Mary/Uriel: The sister Constant Walker of the Primate People, living in light matter.

8. Lady June/Zigael: The sister Lilith of the Void in which all light matter is suspended.

The intelligence of each Celestial Sister guided their Angel-Knight representative to help program the sheer veil fabric and sacred power colors. Lilith had the largest veil measuring 10' x 10'. Lady June was guided to attach 144 cut crystals onto the black lace veil. The other veils were white, red, yellow, blue, green, orange and violet. The veils measured 24" x 48". The knights sewed special sequins and crystals in different patterns on their veils.

245

When they were finished Michael hung the large black veil on the ceiling in the center of the "Multiverse" and the veils of the Seven Sisters were hung creating an arc around the sides and back of Michael's blue armor. It was very striking and the feeling that came over you when you entered the room was indescribable. The setting created offered viewers one of those, "We're not in Kansas anymore," moments.

Chapter Forty-five

No Fireworks Here

Lady Linda and I held our traditional formal attire "Feast of the Magi/Little Christmas" gathering for the Angel-Knights on January 6th, 1995. It was held at our beach house, the Sandcastle. The intention of the gathering was to celebrate all the achievements we had made during the previous year. Again, I was so proud of the knights and their dedication. As they arrived one by one, I was impressed by how elegant they looked in their long gowns and tuxedos. We chose to honor elegance, traditions and standards, at a time when others were letting their standards slip away. Michael said that the day would come when the Good Knight Network would receive presidential honors, and that we must look the part if we were going to visit the White House. I remember thinking this was great, because practice makes perfect! As always, the food that Lady Linda prepared for the feast was delicious.

We ended the evening with a fun meditation around a large bonfire on the beach where we served glasses of champagne. After the meditation, Lady June-ZigZagael asked Lady Linda an odd question that came out of nowhere. "If you ever sell the Sandcastle will you give me the first chance to buy it? The Sandcastle is sacred to us and should be preserved." She went on to say that she had had a dream that Linda was going to move in the coming year.

Lady June, an Engineer and part-time actress, was the runner-up for Miss Philippines contest in the mid-sixties. She always looked like a million bucks, and at times could be very tapped into her angel, ZigZagael. I knew immediately that the words to Lady Linda were coming from ZigZagel. Along with that, I could tell there was something going on between all our angels that night. Something felt like it shifted after SpiritFest and the creation of the "Multiverse."

We had been living at the beach house for seven years and the Hierophant had said that if I hit all the marks, whatever they were, after seven years there would be big change.

When I asked Michael what was going on, he made a statement to the knights, "This year will be our last bonfire. Next year we will have fireworks." Linda quickly retorted, "We can't have fireworks at Cove Point."

Michael threw a big log on the fire and a huge plume of sparks went skyward as he replied to Linda, "Who said you are going to be living at Cove Point next year?"

We spent those early cold winter months working on the exhibits at the headquarters-museum and doing safety programs for Dr. Forbes in the public schools. Sir James and Sir Thomas helped me all spring working on the Medicine Wheel Healing Labyrinth and building the two exhibit buildings on either side of the back gate.

Michael named the building on the left Orion's Castle and the one on the right Sachiel's Lab. We used them for the storage of lumber at first, but Michael had already shown me the amazing exhibits that he intended to create inside. We painted all the walls inside and out to look like a continuation of the castle blue stone blocks which had become our trademark style. One day Sir Gregory parked his car too close to the wall and I accidentally sponged and blocked the dented bumper as well. He didn't see the humor in it, though I thought it was hysterical.

Whenever I worked on the exhibits, grounds and gardens, it was a meditative process in of itself. I was transported into the work with such present moment awareness that I transcended many dimensions at once. Michael, ERU and most of the angels would show me visions or give me thoughts while I was doing the most mundane (at least mundane to society) tasks. One time when I was using a leaf blower to clean debris, Michael gave me a warning.

At the next opportunity I put out an alert, to remind all knights of a statement I made long ago. "If I call a command performance, it would be advisable that all take heed and attend. Michael warned me that the knighthood would lose two knights this year; one to family and one to death."

Not too long after uttering those words, Michael was proven correct again. In early March, Lady Judah-Anael had to leave the knighthood and fly home to Los Angeles to take care of her father and his business. She said that she would return, but I knew her time on the path had come to an end. We all missed Lady Judah greatly, but we had to move on. I knew that rescuing her from that "den of thieves" in Germany had served a higher purpose for Michael and the path of elevation he was leading us all on. Her father's company began making yearly donations to the charity's outreach programs. So a loss in one respect, gave us a much needed benefit.

Michael was always anticipating everything. It seemed like he stayed seven steps ahead of us. He always had someone waiting in the wings, no pun intended, ready to take on the angel that was assigned to another knight if and when they left. It was a truly amazing experiment we were involved in. Michael said "All of them can be replaced with statues or mannequins if the need arises."

I reminded him, "Well, you and your angels have spent the ages as statues in churches or on someone's bookshelf."

He quipped back, "It is refreshing to have warm-blooded vessels that move around so they can enjoy interacting with people. I just wish the knights didn't argue so much."

"I kinda' feel the angels enjoy our emotions," I said, "but I agree, a little less arguing would be nice."

We didn't have to wait long for Lady Judah's replacement. Sir Gregory had another charity volunteer and seeker of the "Knowing" in his Master Studies Class. She was also a lawyer and she ready to become an Angel-Knight. Her name was Justine. She had all the same attributes of Judah, but was a little harder to get along with. When you tried to tell her something she would smile and still do things her way. If I said it was raining she would say it was snowing. I'm not joking!

However, I could see why Michael added her to the mix. It was for contrast - Michael made sure that I didn't surround myself with a bunch of "yes" men and women. Archangel Anael bonded with Justine immediately and I knew in time the Celestial Sister Urania would as well. Lady Justine moved into the white house in Bowie to support Lady Mary.

I could see that there was layer upon layer of psychological experimentation working at the same time around us all. And Michael was always monitoring our moods and motives for doing things.

Lady Mary played the role of Cinderella living in a house with a grumpy stepfather, Sir Gregory and two jealous stepsisters, Ladies Bonnie and Justine. However, in this story Cinderella was our Blue Princess and she was in charge. What was she going to do - continue to be the indecisive character in the original fairy tale, or a strong-willed woman who refused to be dominated by the forces around her? At the same time, would she pick a prince like Sir James who would selflessly give her up rather than see her fall short of her destiny? If James was given the go ahead he would support her leadership role. Sir Robert, on the other hand, as Lancelot would play to Mary's weaknesses because he was afraid he would lose her affection.

Only time would tell, as the social experiments continued.

During April's First Wednesday Club gathering I took Russell Means' advice and had all the knights paint the labyrinth and center Tower of Wisdom yellow and then sponge white on top of the yellow. When the sun hit the tower and walls a brilliant white light gleamed off of the surface. Then we painted black mortar lines that gave the blocks a 3D effect. Michael wanted us to host an Easter party for all of the volunteers and their families that year, so the labyrinth had to be complete.

On April 15th we opened for our first official event on the grounds of the Good Knight Angelic Kingdom. It was great seeing all the kids from the neighborhood dressed up. Lady Linda sewed together a Macaroni Mouse costume, the character from *A Good Knight Story*, and Lady Susan dressed the part for the children. She had fun reading the story before releasing them into the labyrinth area to search for the several hundred plastic Easter eggs, filled with prizes we had hidden there. I could see that this was to be the first of many great events we would host.

Chapter Forty-six

The F.B.I. Informant

In May of 1995 I received a call, out of the blue, from my old partner Detective Bender. He had retired from the D.C. Police Department and had become the sheriff of a small Massachusetts township just outside of Boston. "Ed, remember the IRA gunning case that we worked on in the mid-seventies? For years I could not understand how the feds screwed the case up when it crossed into New York City, but now I might have the answer! Did a fellow by the name of James "Whitey" Bulger ever come up as one of Belfast Harry's contacts in Boston?"

"Well Billy O'Shea, Harry's cousin, once mentioned Whitey Bulger's name as the I.R.A. sympathizer who helped raise a lot of money in Boston bars for the effort, and he also told me Bulger's gang ran the docks. That was also why after the bust he and Harry wanted me to drive them to Boston. They felt Bulger would help smuggle them out of the country."

I advised Sheriff Bender that Billy O'Shea told me he and Belfast Harry needed to get to Boston on that last day because they had an in with the mob there. "I passed the information on Bulger to Detective Sharkey and he passed it on to the F.B.I. taskforce."

Sheriff Bender said "Bulger was an F.B.I. informant for years and Bulger's control agent for the bureau was Special Agent John Connolly." That name didn't ring any bells with me. He said "There was an ongoing investigation, but it looks like Connolly was protecting his source for the past twelve years from criminal investigations like ours. Connolly grew up in the south side projects in Boston with Bulger and may have been a criminal plant within the bureau."

It was starting to make sense. If the federal agent was protecting his friend, taking that truckload of weapons down in New York City before it reached the Boston Harbor was a must because Whitey Bulger would have been implicated if the weapons had reached the docks.

Bender said "The investigation has found Whitey Bulger was linked to other IRA weapons shipments in the mid 1980's and an Irish fishing vessel, Valhalla. It would dock in Boston's Gloucester harbor to pick up guns and transport IRA members to and from Ireland.

The call brought up memories and I couldn't help but wonder, "Why now?" What link did this information have in my life at this point?

Michael said, "Closure. By the time the world reads about this part of your life, Whitey Bulger's story will come to an end."

Icey shivers went up my spine as I see a vision of a reporter announcing Bulger's death while a dark-haired woman who is typing about my life looks up from her work to watch the newscast.

Chapter Forty-seven

The Sun Bow Walkers

That June the Good Knight Angelic Kingdom opened to the public for its first summer festival. In *A Good Knight Story,* the fairy tale I wrote in 1989, the King and Queen of Eagleton held four seasonal festivals every year to honor the children in their kingdom who were born within the same season. Michael wanted the Good Knight Kingdom to do the same as part of bringing the fairytale to life. We held the event on June 23rd and 24th making it a Midsummer's Eve Festival.

I had spoken to Russell Means and he told me that the "Sun Bow Five" Native Americans were starting their walk across America on June 23rd. He told me that the walk was to be led by a very powerful spiritual leader, Grandfather William Commanda. Our plan was to draw the sacred pilgrimage to Michael's energy vortex, the Medicine Wheel Healing Labyrinth, on my birthday July 22nd. It was our hope that Grandfather Commanda would bless the labyrinth. He carried two very powerful medicine belts with him. One was an ancient record of his people and the other one symbolized the fulfillment of the End of Days prophecy. Michael knew that the angry and grieving earth-bound spirits of the Native American ancestors would be drawn to journey with the living. He wanted to see if those spirits would let go and move on to the Creator or continue to hold on to the negative thoughts which were trapping them on Earth, left to wander forever in the third dimension of life.

It was really important to the angels to help the wandering spirits still on the Earth find peace, because they were responsible for influencing the living with negative thoughts. The Angel-Knights and I were going to do everything in our power to make it happen. Unfortunately, it seemed all but impossible to do. Michael asked us to conduct a special meditation calling on the ancestors to guide Grandfather Commanda to the Medicine Wheel Labyrinth. It was important that it be on my birthday for some reason. It had something to do with the Great Red Spot of the planet Jupiter and

Earth's alignment to it.

For the Mid-Summer Festival, the Angel-Knights dressed in their brightly colored tunics. They offered food, drink and carnival games for the visiting families. There were also Labyrinth walks provided under the guidance of Sir Gregory and Lady Barbara, while I taught the *ABC's of Safety Program* and knighted those who wanted to be into the Order of Good Knights. About three hundred local families came and enjoyed themselves over the two days.

It was a command performance so all knights were in attendance. Even Sir Robert and Sir Johnny drove in from Michigan for the event. I was trying to have Sir James work out any hard feelings he still had being around Sir Robert so I assigned them to work together as security and parking safety. The only negative thing that occurred was a ruckus from a group of born-again zealots who confronted the two knights in the parking lot. The group was walking around the neighborhood telling people that the Good Knights were a cult and not Christian. "We demand to see your leader," they told Sir James.

James dispatched Sir Robert to find me. I was at the end of a program knighting 5-year old. When Sir Robert told me what was happening my thought was to blow it off. Instead Michael said, "This is a learning event." So off I went.

My I popped through the gate in full regalia it looked as if their eyes bulged out enough to leave their sockets. I knew what they saw was not the "leader" they expected. Nevertheless, I said, "I hear you wanted to speak to 'the leader.'

"You are the craziest looking cult leader I have ever seen," the tall WWF looking dude said.

"The Good Knight Network is not a cult, we are not Jewish or Buddhists either. Nor are we a religious organization. We are a non-profit volunteer organization that empowers youth to recognize negative individuals by their words and behavior."

Two of them spoke back at once, "Is Jesus Christ your lord and savior?"

I replied, "I certainly hope so!"

After shaking their heads and delivering a deadly glare they turned and left…very angry.

I do not know why the Angel-Knights are magnets for crazies, but we often are. I, for one, would be embarrassed to force my beliefs on other people. While watching these folks walk away I had a stray thought, wondering what a field day people like these would have if I ever published the diaries I'm writing.

Hearing my thought, Michael said, "Most of the zealots are under the mental influence of dark spirits trapped on earth. They prey on the zealots' insecurities about their religion. They will only feel secure when everyone believes as they do. Your book will send shockwaves through the world order as it ought to."

"So, when am I to publish my diaries? I don't think I am ready to have a world full of those guys coming at us," I said.

"When your waiting is full and the right person comes along who will be able to understand you and everyone else in your life, so she can make sense of what you wrote," he responded.

"She? And what do you mean 'make sense'? I think I make sense now," I retorted.

In the midst of my banter with Michael, Sir Robert fell ill. Sir James and I discussed that the festival was winding down for the day, so I had him take Robert to the First Aid station on the second floor of the castle to lie down.

After the last visitor left for the day I went upstairs to remove the armor. On the same floor was the first aid area so I went in to check on Sir Robert. As I poked my head in the door, I interrupted several of the female volunteers, who were also Master Studies students of Sir Gregory, while they were setting up to do a calling down of the "White Light" for Robert. It was obvious the four ladies had a crush on him. They were trying to impress him with their caring ways and newly learned powers. Not to mention some other things they wanted to impress him with.

I said, "Ladies, would you have such an interest if the sick knight was a short fat old bald guy? Have you forgotten the 'White Light' can only be used on a person once during their lifetime? Don't you think we should save it for when Sir Robert is on his death bed?"

They scurried out, full of embarrassment. Sir James and I turned to each other and laughed at how much Sir Robert was enjoying the attention.

Michael let me know that the main reason why Sir Robert got sick was because Lady Mary had been avoiding him all day. Mary was tired of being pulled in so many directions and decided to focus on her spiritual direction. He also said that Sir Robert was experiencing a nervous breakdown from his feelings of rejection. I felt so sorry for Robert as I felt a fatherly responsibility towards him. Being young and in love with someone you have sworn to safeguard as a knight is the hardest of emotions to conquer.

However, this was an experiment in human emotions all around and I could see why Michael was letting Robert do all this stuff to himself. If he could conquer this demon, both he and the spirit of Lancelot would be free, and in the end, he would get the girl of his dreams. In this case the girl of his dreams was holding a position where Michael had placed her in the knighthood as Good Knight Queen in waiting. We all loved Lady Mary, what wasn't there not to love about her? She was the most beautiful of all the current knights and as Michael reminded her often, "almost perfect in every way." No one wanted to be responsible for her not achieving her Divine Destiny but ultimately it was up to her to determine if that would ever happen.

Sir Robert was sweating profusely so I took his temperature; it was a hundred and three. I asked, "How do you feel."

He said, "Boss, I feel like my stomach is tied in knots and someone is beating me in the head with a sledgehammer."

Michael spoke through me saying, "Son, I will show you the power of the Blue Princess. Remember how you feel right now when you meet me in the labyrinth in five minutes."

Robert replied, "I can't get up and walk."

Michael said, "You will feel better soon. All that ails you will be gone."

I asked Sir James to help me unstrap Michael's blue breastplate and set it in the corner of the room. Leaving Sir James with Robert in the room I walked outside. Lady Mary-Uriel was cleaning up the main gate ticket booth as I approached. Michael said to her, "Hold out your hands, palms up Mary." Michael rubbed my hands together very fast until they were very hot from the friction. He placed my hands on top of hers and said, "Go seek out our beloved Sir Robert and place one of your hands on his forehead and the other on his stomach. Then command him to rise and walk with you to meet me in the labyrinth. Okay?"

She smiled and walked toward the castle.

I moved to the labyrinth tower and lit a candle for the spirit of Lancelot. My concentration was interrupted by the roar of a motorcycle engine and muffler driving off from the parking lot on Rhode Island Avenue. A few minutes later Sir Robert and Lady Mary walked into the labyrinth.

Michael and I looked at the two. I could see that they were bound to marry one day. Michael gave me a vision of all the knights in tuxedos and gowns standing with raised crossed swords as the two walked under them towards an altar. Then I was standing at a baptismal pool as they passed me with their beautiful baby girl. "Was this the child with the initials M.V?" I thought, as my heart raced. My mind snapped back to what I was doing. Sir Robert had a lot of maturing to do before that one could happen.

Michael asked, "How did you feel five minutes ago good sir?"

Sir Robert answered, "Like death warmed over Master Hermit."

"And how do you feel now?" I asked.

Sir Robert was obviously healed and good health had returned to him when he answered, "I feel like a fool."

Michael replied, "Then you are in good company. It has been said that I am the Prince of Fools and I have more than one foolish knight within my legion. Problem solved. You are well."

As we walked out of the labyrinth Lady Bonnie-Gabriel ran to me and said, "Sir James jumped on his motorcycle and left without a word. He was very angry."

That's how it was back then, putting out one bonfire of emotions just to have another explosion ignite somewhere else. If indeed God created humans to feel our emotions He was getting his fill that day.

As I went to the Tower of Wisdom to blow out the candle, I had a vision of Sir James riding down the road distracted thinking of Mary. I then saw a tractor-trailer making a wide turn and James and his motorcycle being crushed beneath the wheels of the trailer. I broke out in a cold sweat and had to sit down in one of the tower chairs trying to get the horrid scene out of my mind. I called on Michael to explain the vision, but he didn't come into my consciousness. He must have been elsewhere.

Days later when I was able to ask, all he would say was, "We can only keep them safe from death if they are not present when the Angel of Death comes for them. Before there is the possibility of a knight falling, you will have a warning from me to call for a command performance. If they are here, death cannot find them. I promise."

Chapter Forty-eight

Grandfather's Blessing

Even though the formal lessons from the Hierophant had ended months ago, Michael had us maintain the tradition of the First Wednesday Club. However, it was held exclusively as a gathering of already merged Angel-Knights, with no new students. Michael would host most of the meeting if there were new insights and lessons coming to the Earth that he wanted the knights to learn.

Each First Wednesday gathering there was always a time for giving service to the land when we would do "labors," such as planting, painting, sprucing etc. When finished, we would dress in our tunics for a meditation and sacred labyrinth walk, and then perhaps a feast. During the July First Wednesday Club gathering Archangel Michael never made his presence known. He was watching to see what we were going to do. Without formal instruction from him, I decided to do what I had seen in a past vision I had of the grounds.

After SpiritFest '94 one of the tribes donated a Native American teepee to the charity. I told the gathering the goal for the day was to clear a space of land in the Forbidden Forest to set up an authentic Oglala Lakota Sioux encampment to honor our Native American ancestors and the spirit of Crazy Horse. I say our ancestors, because Michael told me that since we were born in North America, "Turtle Island" they are the ancestors of anyone born here. The only Angel-Knight who did not qualify as a descendant of Crazy Horse was Lady Mary, as she was born in Messina, Italy.

After our labors, we had a powerful labyrinth walk with the intention to send the ancestors strength in order to influence Grandfather Commanda in finding his way here for the blessing of the Medicine Wheel. Once the walk was finished we took our places around the labyrinth's outer wall and held a group mediation where we sent positive energy to the Sun Bow Walkers. In the meditation our energy and request were purely in service to the walkers no matter what the decision was, to include us or not. We asked the Creator and Mother Earth to send energy to the effort and its participants; knowing that it was no easy undertaking to walk from Cape Cod, Massachusetts, across the states of Connecticut, New York, New Jersey, Pennsylvania, Maryland, Washington, D.C., Virginia, North Carolina, Tennessee, Arkansas, Oklahoma, Texas, New Mexico, Arizona, and finally ending in, the city of angels - Los Angeles, California.

Whether it was our selfless meditation to send them energy or Michael's intervention, we found out on the morning of July 22nd the Sun Bow Walkers were camping about five miles away from the Good Knight Castle in Greenbelt Park. Michael composed a special letter to the spirits of the ancestors around Grandfather Commanda. The letter invited him and the walkers to the Good Knight Network's Children Museum for a feast in honor of the heroic pilgrimage they had undertaken. He also asked Grandfather if he would consider blessing the Medicine Wheel Healing Labyrinth as Russell Means suggested at Spirit Fest '94. Michael closed with the words, "Come only if you dare!"

In anticipation for a positive response, Michael called for a command performance that day. I wanted Sir James-Sandalphon most of all to be there since he had missed most of Spirit Fest. However, once the call went out via telephone tree, Sir James told Sir Gregory he had a job interview that day and couldn't make the ceremony. Gregory told him this was a command performance and reminded him of Michael's warning surrounding command performances. It fell upon deaf ears.

In the meantime, Michael sent Sir Thomas-Sachiel and Lady Barbara-Raphael with the letter to Grandfather. They were told to wait for a response. It was a hot day and the Angel-Knights outdid themselves making the kingdom shine. We made haste to put the finishing touches on projects all over the grounds that we had in varying degrees of completion.

We turned the castle's first floor into a medieval café with tables, chairs and a buffet table fit for a king. On the second floor of the castle, in the center of the Great Room, I finished the knighting circle by hanging overhead a life-size female angel with long black hair and diamond-encrusted crown. The angel represented the Mother Goddess Pistis Sophia's Divine Energy. Michael said that this was the room where we would call in Sophia to manifest in form. The room measured 40' x 40' with a cathedral ceiling. Three of the outside walls were lined with 6'x10' windows, 3' off the floor. In the corners and along the walls I created nature scenes with small waterfalls, rocks, leaves, trees and real stuffed birds, squirrels, a fox, a deer and other small animals, that I had taken to a taxidermist a few years back. In the center of the right wall I built 8' x 12' floor to ceiling birdcage. Coincidentally (or not) as we were working that day a young college student volunteer came in with three small cages filled with 12 white doves. She said her uncle asked her to take these to the SPCA but before she did so she had a thought "for some reason" that we would want them.

"Uh, yes mam!" I motioned to the huge birdcage I just finished and told her I built it just for them. She looked at me weird, like how would I know she was bringing them? She set the cages down, then turned and walked outside to help the others.

What can I say? I have the tendency to freak people out at times.

I still had a massive amount of work ahead of me so feeling the pressure of a timeline looming, I asked another volunteer to release the doves into their cage and make sure they had food and water. Then I went back to work. In the large stairwell connecting the two floors I placed an exhibit from East Wing Castle called the "Eight Great Religions of the World" and the 10' upside down chandelier called the "Christmas tree from Heaven." The tree was full of rotating ornaments, icicles, red and gold ribbon, mini white lights and a motion activated 18" Christmas Tree with eye balls and a mouth. The small tree was set into the branches blending into the big tree. and was programmable to say whatever I wanted. The tree welcomed all our guests who climbed the staircase.

It was a long day of constant work, hanging decorations and re-setting our old exhibits that were in storage. Just as I plugged the Christmas Tree from Heaven" into a socket. Michael said, "That's it, you are done."

I said, "No we have so many more exhibits still in storage we have to set."

"I gave you until the knights returned with an answer from the Grandfather to complete your work. No more can be done now," he replied.

"Well they are not back yet!" I snapped back at him.

As soon as the last word spilled of out my mouth Sir Thomas-Sachiel walked into the stairwell. "Grandfather Commanda accepted our invitation and the walkers will be arriving within the next two-hours!" Thomas exclaimed, hardly able to contain his excitement.

Dang it Michael, I thought! When will I learn that you knows more than I do?

I sent the word throughout the building and grounds to all the knights and volunteers that we needed to halt progress, clean up and have a brief meeting.

At the meeting Lady Barbara told us that she heard in the "Odyssey of the Eighth Fire" legend that the pilgrimage would reach a fork in the trail and the walkers would divide walking in two different directions, but wind up in the same place.

I said, "It will be interesting to see from which direction they approach the kingdom, because they will hit that divide you speak about if they chose to come down Rhode Island Avenue via Route 1.

Time was ticking so we broke the meeting and I told everyone to suit up. Sir Robert helped me strap on Michael's Armor. I then took up Michael's position atop the Tower of Wisdom in the center of the labyrinth and waited. From that vantage point I could see a mile down Rhode Island Avenue in both directions east and west. I could also see up Sellman Road and down St. Mary's street if they came in from the South.

We did not have to wait long to see what they chose. Off in the western distance I saw the group trekking down Rhode Island Avenue. This path would indeed take them to the divide. The legend was about to be fulfilled. As they approached, I could hear them beating their drums to the heartbeat of Mother Earth. All the Angel-Knights were getting excited and I thought what a wonderful birthday gift I was receiving.

With nothing but the ancestors guiding them, when the walkers reached the fork in the road, I could see from my vantage point on the tower, one half of the group split to their right walking down Sellman Road which brought them in the back gate. The other half chose the fork to the left taking them into our Rhode Island Avenue top gate. How amazing! It was a beautiful sight to see. There must have been a hundred and fifty of them, men, women and children. I noticed that the group was made up of all the races, which was refreshing to see.

As I watched them converge along the inside of our wall, the two groups meeting again on the property between the labyrinth and the castle building, a cold chill shot through me. I released my gaze on the walkers and I looked off into the east toward Laurel where the sounds of emergency vehicles and sirens were getting louder and louder. Sir James' smiling face flashed before my eyes. My heart grew sad. Something had happened I could feel there was a deep disturbance in the God Force that surrounded me. However, I was snapped back to the scene before me. I had to focus on the people and spirits who had gathered before me.

I climbed down from the tower to greet Grandfather William Commanda. He was the 83-year-old patriarch and respected elder of the Algonquin Indian Nation. I learned that he was the keeper of both the Primstaven and Seven Fires Wampum Belt.

Grandfather's aura was golden and the power radiating from this man was incredible. Grandfather introduced me to Ned Gray Eagle, a Sun Bow Medicine Man, and Thomas Crow one of the coordinators of the sacred pilgrimage. The shaman, Gray Eagle, was joyful and very wise, but my read on Tom Crow showed me a man full of self-admiration and false pride. He gave me the feeling that he didn't want to have "his walkers" come to the castle. I also met a very wise man named Steven McFadden, who, too, had a pure golden aura. Steve was a writer whom grandfather had chosen to document the Sun Bow Fire Prayer Walk. With Grandfather's arrival it signified that day was sacred and that their visit to the Good Knight Kingdom was part of the Seven Fires Prophecy of the Anishnabe People, and officially part of the process of reconciliation.

I took the leaders inside the castle to present the dinner buffet of fried chicken, ham, fish, and potato salad, corn pudding, fruit and desserts galore. I was sure our new Native American friends were thirsty and hungry. "Please accept this banquet in your honor," I said.

Grandfather replied, "We are starving but yesterday Tom decided that we should all begin a four-day hunger fast in support of the walk."

I asked, "Is that wise? Don't your people need to keep up their strength if they are going to succeed?"

Tom spoke up in a harsh voice saying, "Don't presume to tell us what to do."

"Wow" I thought. This is starting off on the wrong foot. I asked, "Can we at least offer you all some water?"

They accepted.

When we came out of the building all of the Sun Bow Walkers were scattered around the hillside in front of the labyrinth and the Angel-Knights were passing out bottles of water. I spoke to the crowd thanking them for coming to bless our Medicine Wheel Healing Labyrinth and I also formally apologized for putting out a food buffet the day after they started a hunger fast. "It was done as a thank you and tribute. I did not mean to tempt you. Had we known ahead of time we would not have had it prepared. Please forgive us."

As I looked around I saw the food was indeed a great temptation. Not all of the walkers had taken on the hunger fast. Some had gone inside the castle and brought out plates of food. That didn't sit well with Tom. He had some obvious control issues and every time I turned around I was rubbing him the wrong way.

It was weird for me. If one chose to do so, I could be seen as a Satan tempting these good people from their mission. I was beginning to understand what Michael meant at Spirit Fest '94, about the role Archangel Lucifer was forced to play with humanity.

I continued to address the crowd as I watched the energetic movements of people. I told the crowd what the Good Knight Network did to help protect children from child sexual predators by empowering families with the "ABC's of Safety" Program video we created, and that it will be playing in the Great Hall on the second floor of the castle. We also let everyone know that I would be available to officially knight anyone that wanted to take on the quest to protect and empower the children on their reservations or in their neighborhoods.

To tie in my connection with the Native Americans, I told them about the old Hopi Indian Medicine Man who had a vision of my future and who gave me the buffalo rawhide that became the blue armor that I was wearing. I went on to say that the armor made me a walking talisman of protection that signified I was a peaceful warrior standing in the shadow of the Spirit of Truth against injustice.

A few of the Native women came to me later that day saying that the armor was very powerful and it must be inspiring for the youth. They particularly liked the spurs that jingled when I walked. It was nice to talk to people with an open understanding of spirituality that was not caught up in old biblical references. It was apparent that most of the walkers were accepting of all beliefs.

At this point in the day, Sir Gregory brought me the bucket of rainbow quartz crystals from SpiritFest. I told the gathering about Spirit Fest '94 and that Russell Means co-hosted the event where we brought all the religions of the world together to talk about their beliefs, and combined it with a music and Native American Powwow. I placed the bucket of crystals on a Styrofoam bolder in the center of the field.

"Crazy Horse's spirit came through Russell Means at SpiritFest and he blessed these crystals. I invite anyone who wants to take a crystal with you on your journey to the Pacific Ocean to please take one."

My attention was brought back to Tom. He didn't look happy. My heart hurt for him and I thought, how sad it was that even people within "good" movements cannot set aside their controlling agendas for the mission. I sent Tom love and put him in the back of my mind.

It was time to offer the walkers an opportunity to explore the Oglala Lakota Sioux Indian Campsite exhibit that we dedicated to Crazy Horse and our fellow Good Knight, Russell Means. I told them that in the forest there was a 20' teepee that housed the sacred Staff of Wakinyon that we created at the end of the SpiritFest event. I pointed out that at the top of the staff was Russell's eagle feather.

Great Grandfather said, "A staff containing an eagle feather represents a divine journey is afoot." A woman with the walkers held up the Sun Bow Eagle Feather Staff and nodded. Her bright smile touched my heart.

One of the walkers asked, "Exactly how did Russell Means become affiliated with the Good Knights?"

I told them a brief story of the BIA incident, Russell saying, "It's a good day to die" and me saying, "It's a better day to live." I also told them how he dared me to solve the Charlie Goodnight riddle, which lead to me writing *A Good Knight Story*, which lead to Spirit Fest, which lead to Russell and I laying the first blocks in the Medicine Wheel Labyrinth a year ago, and which ultimately led to Russell telling me that I should try to get Grandfather here to bless the labyrinth on my birthday.

I then shared, "Today is my birthday. Thank you all for celebrating it with me. Your presence is the best present I could ever receive." I knew they soon had to get back to their campsite in Greenbelt Park so I said, "We can all meet back here in an hour for the blessing ceremony. Go now and please enjoy the kingdom."

It gave me a wonderful feeling inside watching the Native people roaming the grounds, enjoying the food (much to Tom's chagrin), the forest and the exhibits. There were many children and mothers who watched the "ABC's of Safety" film in the Great Hall. Angel-Knights then gave the families activity books and videos.

When it came time for the blessing of the Medicine Wheel, Michael had me bring out the Sun Spear crystal wand that helped in the breaking of the Chief Tecumseh Death Curse on the Office of the President. I raised it up and told the crowd, "I was sent on a Vision Quest to help our Native American ancestors find peace and at the same time I was told it was important that President Reagan survive the assassination attempt against him. This Sun Spear was gifted to me to intervene and bring healing to the wound between white men and the native peoples. I was given a vision that if Reagan had been assassinated the United Stated would have been plunged into World War III." With that, I could see that my words were not sitting well with a small group of Indians standing around Tom. I didn't want their darkness to grow and infect the others so I turned to Grandfather and asked if we could begin the blessing ceremony.

Grandfather Commanda gathered the Sun Bow Walkers and the Angel-Knights around the Medicine Wheel Labyrinth. Reaching into his medicine pouch he pulled out the sacred belt of the Seven Fires Prophecy.

I thought how interesting! They are camped in Green*belt* and Grandfather brings the *belt* that represents the ancestors and the End of Days prophecy to our sacred labyrinth which was created as a direct gateway to Heaven from *Belts*ville or Village of the *Belts*. It felt like I was living some kind of Divine Dream. However, I had no idea what a "Pandora's box" was about to be opened.

Michael told me that the real reason that he wanted Grandfather to come to the Medicine Wheel was to increase his life by fifteen years. He went on to say that if Grandfather was to perish on the walk, it would pass the belt that he safeguards to the wrong man; but if he lives by taking on the energy of the Great Grandmother, by the time he dies he will find the perfect person to carry on his people's legacy.

As this great spiritual patriarch held out the Seven Fires Wampum Belt, a hush fell over the gathering. Everyone could sense something otherworldly was about to occur.

The Belt of Power was primarily made up of dark purple "wampum" beads, with a pattern of seven white diamonds. Commanda said "Each diamond represents a "sacred fire,' or epoch - a period of time in history that marks a notable event. This double diamond represents the final middle fire and indicates the promise of an Eighth Fire, if humanity heeds the lessons of love, honesty, caring, sharing, and respect. Legend states that if humanity does not heed the lessons there will be much death and destruction."

It was both surreal and reassuring to hear Grandfather relay the same thing Master ERU told me about the End of Days and the 144,000 Light-Bearers. My mind drifted momentarily to an overview of the past several years. I could see that there were many people on earth working to make the jump in consciousness, but if the people didn't gain the "Knowing" their willpower would not be strong enough to light the beacon within.

I was brought back to present moment when I heard Grandfather, who was standing at the opening of the labyrinth, begin to deliver the same message to this gathering that he gave at the United Nations fifteen days earlier on Friday, July 7, 1995…

"We are in the time of the Seventh Fire now. That's the reason for this Sunbow walk. We need to maintain our honesty, and to bring things into keeping with the way the Creator intended. That way we can bring the double diamond at the center of the belt together, to make one diamond representing the lighting of an Eighth Fire. That fire does not have to burn or destroy, but can illuminate this world that we are part of. It's up to us, which way it burns. We have the choice now, and can use our will as we want. It's up to the people."

"The first key in this healing, is forgiveness: to forgive those people, and nations, and races that we feel have done us harm. We may not forget, but we have to forgive. That will begin to heal the hurt. We have to forgive ourselves too, for the harm we have done to ourselves and to others. It's very difficult. It's not easy. But that's what's required. Those are the teachings that have been handed down to me. That's part of what the wampum belt is about, and that's what I have to share."

"If all the races will come together and stop doing what they are doing, it can begin. Forgiveness, peace, love, and respect, those are the four important things. With all

of that, then the waters can again be pure, the air can be clean, the Earth can be healed, and the children can live. Whether it will happen or not, we don't know. The people have the choice. The time to choose is now. We pray for the good things. That's why the walk."

His words reminded me of the words of forgiveness I spoke to Crazy Horse during the SpiritFest Ceremony of Forgiveness. I realized that the Eighth Fire represented the Light Bearers illuminating the world.

After Grandfather's speech, I climbed the ladder back to the top of the Tower of Wisdom and as Grandfather began his labyrinth walk, I turned on the cassette recorder which was set to repeat the song, "Return to Innocence" by the group Enigma. As Grandfather walked he carried an eagle feather while sprinkling Indian tobacco and grains of corn along the seven maze-like rings of the labyrinth.

Just as he had turned a corner to finish the third quarter he stumbled and fell against the wall. It appeared his left knee gave out. Michael was like a shot jumping from the tower to the ground to help Grandfather. The Archangel placed the Sun Spear on Grandfather's heart and said, "You have walked as far as you can as the Grandfather. If you want to finish the walk you must walk the rest of the way with the Spirit of Great Grandmother."

The great Chief, William Commanda, then rose to his feet with renewed strength. I left his side and although he was limping, he finished the last quarter of the Medicine Wheel without incident. He finally met me at the tower doors, we entered, and shut the doors behind us.

Once inside the Tower of Wisdom, he could see that the room had eight walls, which were painted to look like stone blocks. There were twin arched entrance doors on the north wall and arched exit doors on the south wall. When the doors closed the doorways disappeared. On the west wall was a five-foot high cascading stone waterfall. The waters were spilling down over rainbow quartz crystals; atop the waterfall were ceramic pieces that Lady Linda had created, of an Indian elder telling a story to little children of all the races. I told Grandfather it was statue of him taking to the "Children of Tomorrow." He smiled.

On each wall hung an 18" x 36" mirror that reflected each of the other mirrors, creating the feeling of being surrounded by infinite space and time. The walls met at corner beams that were outlined with mini-multi colored pulsating lights covered with green variegated ivy. The ivy continued up and across the ceiling, then down the other side of the walls. The floor was made up of special gray cobblestone pavers. Against the east wall was a table with two golden high back throne chairs with arms. On the table was the Grail Cup with a lit votive candle in its golden bowl. Also on the table, was our Native American ceremonial pipe in two pieces. The bowl was stone and shaped like a bear. The stem was reddish brown cedarwood, wrapped in a band of colorful beads, fur and feathers. I told Grandfather that during Russell's visit we smoked the pipe together and I would like to smoke with him. He reached inside his pouch and placed a very strong-smelling tobacco into the bowl, screwed the stem into the bowl and then he handed it to me to light.

We passed the pipe back and forth as Michael told Grandfather the importance of his survival during the Sun Bow Five Walk saying, "If you fall ill, you may pass the Belt of Power to the unworthy, but given time, you would see certain people for who they really are and not who they pretend to be."

Grandfather puffed on the pipe again not responding to anything that was said. I could tell he was taking it all in, but his only comment was, "This may sound crazy Blue Knight, but sometimes the pipe talks to me."

Michael said, "That's not crazy at all, if the Creator can speak to Moses through a burning bush, why can't the Creator speak to Grandfather through a sacred pipe? What's important is the message you hear. Do you hear what is being said today Grandfather?"

He shook his head yes.

Michael ended by saying, "When the walkers turn west, egos will flare. The beat of the 'Tom-Tom' will blame the Blue Knight for bringing negativity to the pilgrimage. The walkers will start to leave. There will be a problem on the trail that no one will want to face. That is why you were guided to bring the walkers to the kingdom to learn about the deceptions and child sexual predators." The last thing Michael said in the Tower of Wisdom was, "You must not be deceived by the sweet words of non-violence spoken. The truth will come from the beat of the Tom-Tom's actions that create drama, tension, and conflict throughout the walk."

Still nothing was coming from Grandfather. It was obvious that whoever the troublemakers were within the group Grandfather was just going to let it all play itself out. He was taking on the Taoist approach. Michael showed me a vision of the ugliness infighting that was going to threaten the purity of their Divine Prayer Walk, but at the same time, like the Angel-Knights, the walkers represented a microcosm of humanity. All I could do was wish them well.

Grandfather had that "eyes glazed over" look that Michael and I sometimes get from people.

It was time to stop talking.

I think he was overwhelmed, or just thought I was plain crazy. There really was nothing else to say. We stood, shook hands and I said, "Do you have any questions of me before we leave?"

He looked me in the eyes as if he was trying to see my soul and said, "What are you?"

Finally, a response, I thought. But it wasn't the question Michael was hoping for. I noticed he asked, *what*, not who. So, I replied, "I'm like the Creator, I'm an artist. I create. Look around you. A year ago, none of this existed. This property was literally a garbage dump. Today it's a little slice of Heaven on Earth."

Grandfather smiled and then asked, "Who are you?"

Michael said, "I am the Morning Light that rises in the east and sets in the west."

A slight smile lifted at the right corner of his mouth and Grandfather nodded.

We then walked out through the southern doors. I could tell he didn't know what to think of all this and it was a lot to take in. I just hoped Michael did enough to extend this great man's life. From what I saw it was going to be a rough journey for him, both physically and mentally.

Outside the Sun Bow Walkers had lined up at the entrance to the Medicine Wheel while beating drums and shaking a beaded gourd rattle to a strange ancient rhythm that was hauntingly familiar to me. However, I knew I had never heard it before in this lifetime.

The walker leading the dance spoke out, "Slowly shuffle forward into the Medicine Wheel while the drum is beating, but when it stops and the rattle starts to shake, shuffle your feet backward out of the labyrinth."

The Angel-Knights had planted red, white and blue impatiens, in the tops of the yellow wall block planters of all seven rings. They also filled the walkways between the rings with pea gravel. The sound of their feet in the gravel was beyond description. Now that the ceremony was well underway I had the afterthought to record it. I found myself wishing we had prepared better. Along with the orchestral sounds, it was also an incredible visual to see as everyone moved in rhythm between the blooming flowers. Watching the Angel-Knights in their colorful tunics alongside their Native America brothers and sisters filling the sacred Medicine Wheel Healing Labyrinth was one of the most harmonious images I have ever seen.

The Medicine Wheel was truly brought to life and set in motion by beings of light and love. I knew while watching this event, the words of forgiveness spoken by me to Russell Means the year before at Spirit Fest 94' and the words of forgiveness spoken by Grandfather William Commanda this day would echo throughout eternity and set the stage for humanity to be seen in a better light during the End of Days. Moreover, the words of clemency served to set free the angry, saddened ancestral spirits who had been trapped on this earth plane.

I was in awe watching the scene before me. However, my attention was drawn outside of the labyrinth to a small group of Native walkers who were not participating in the sacred dance. I looked around and I couldn't locate Tom Crow. The group came over to me where I stood at the entrance to the labyrinth. As they approached me I felt a very dark energy.

One stepped forward and said, "White people can't have visions only Indians can."

I said, "I'm sorry. I wish I knew that before I had the visions."

A second fellow said, "We don't like that you tricked Russell Means into his statement forgiving the white man for what they did to our people."

I replied, "I didn't ask grandfather for forgiveness, but he echoed the very same words spoken one year ago. What do you think about grandfather's words of forgiveness?"

The third Indian spoke saying, "We don't like you interfering with our walk. You are trying to put us on a negative path."

I took a deep breath and centered myself in my heart. All I felt was sorrow for these lost souls. They couldn't release their anger and hate. They didn't even know me, but took on the attitude that they resented that I was even breathing the same air they were. All I could say was, "Who are the 'we' you are talking about?" Pointing at the Medicine Wheel I continued, "Are you talking about the men, women and children illuminated by the light of love Grandfather spoke about. Or are you talking about you three wise agents of darkness? My only wish is that Grandfather finish the pilgrimage alive."

They erupted all at once lunging at me with arms by their sides and fists clenched. Then one yelled, "Why is that any of your business?"

I replied, "Grandfather came to my home to meet with me and bless this Medicine Wheel. So, I now owe him the peace that he deserves and to live long enough to see the other end of the trail."

Not liking my answer one of the fellows asked aggressively, "I demand to know what you said to grandfather in the tower?" I walked away from them at that point because I felt they were looking for a physical confrontation. A few minutes later I noticed them talking to Tom.

I focused my attention on the dancers in the labyrinth and the love that was vibrating out. Out of the corner of my eye I could see Tom heading for me so I walked in the opposite direction. But, he followed, of course. Michael told me to stand my ground. He reminded me that there is no talking to a closed-minded person.

When Tom reached me he was fuming. His eyes were black, filled with outrage, but he tried to come off cool and levelheaded. He said, "So you were CIA spying on the Indians at the BIA that day?"

I replied, "No, I was a peace officer trying to stop the massacre from occurring that I was shown in a vision."

He quickly retorted "Whites can't receive visions."

"So I heard," I said; I was really getting so tired of hearing that.

He again said that he was against coming to the castle and then he demanded to know what I said to Grandfather in the tower.

It was hot enough in the suit of armor, but this fool was making my blood boil. Michael told me to laugh. When I did a cool feeling went through my body and allowed me to release the heat that would have otherwise been infused in my words.

I replied to Tom, "I didn't invite you. I only invited Grandfather and the ancestors. Grandfather invited you. You did not have to come. What I said to Grandfather was, 'When the walkers reach the mountains and turn west, egos will flare and people will start to leave the walk. A beating Tom-Tom will blame the negativity on coming to this place and me.' However, you, me and Grandfather know that will be a lie."

He got furious.

I said, "Don't stop me now brother I'm just getting started. Now I will tell you what I didn't tell Grandfather and I will speak in words that you will understand. You say all the right words of peace and humility, but your actions are to the contrary. You will soon show your ass and no one will want to follow your lead. Your actions will make a mockery of the meaning of this prayer walk. However, you can change all that. Leave your ego and the dark spirits that haunt you here. Then leave the kingdom the man you pretend to be."

Tom seemed stunned. An incredulous look came over his face, not believing that I would dare say these things to him.

I continued, "When the Hopi Medicine Man gave me the buffalo leather I'm wearing he said it would protect me from the bullshit. So don't try to bullshit me into thinking you are anything more than a control freak. You are just seeking fame and respect from the true believers on this walk."

I finally hit his button and he exploded. He was yelling something at this point, but I just put up my hand and the energy emitting from it smothered his fire. I closed with, "Beware of the girl from Maryland. She will expose your true nature."

Before Tom could say another word, I turned my back on him and walked away.

Just then the first walkers who had entered the labyrinth were exiting the Medicine Wheel. A mother with her two small sons came up to me. She said that her mother and father were at the BIA building during the Trail of Broken Treaties March on Washington D.C. twenty years earlier. She thanked me for helping to keep the peace, because if her parents had died there that night she and her children would never had a chance at life. Grandfather was behind her when she spoke. He smiled at me and nodded his head.

Grandfather and I then guided the Sun Bow Walkers back up the hill to the Rhode Island Avenue gates. I wanted to end the blessing in a peaceful manner. I wasn't going to give Tom and his three wise guys a chance to spread more discontent on that sacred day.

When the last walker left the kingdom, Grandfather shook my hand and said, "I see Tom is not happy after your little talk."

I replied, "Tom-Tom' is not a happy guy. He needs to be like the eagle and lighten up if he ever expects to fly."

Commanda smiled stating, "You know what made me come here today?"

I said, "Sure do! The ancestors and three little words, if - you - dare…"

He nodded yes and held up his hand in tribute.

I could have spoken more, but Michael said our work was done. I shook his hand one last time and waved good-bye to the Sun Bow Walkers.

After all the walkers were gone, I returned to the labyrinth to meditate on the day's events. All the crystals had been taken from the bucket and not one shard remained. I could feel the spirits of the ancestors still floating high above me. It was a feeling like they finally found peace and could pass on. I felt good, but there was still a dread hanging over me.

Just then Sir Gregory came to me crying. He said that he got a phone message that Sir James had been in an accident with a tractor-trailer several hours earlier on Route #1 in Laurel. He was riding his motorcycle and was killed. My heart sank. The sirens I heard earlier! My thoughts went to the "command performance" decree Michael set up long ago. "If you are here, you can't be were death might find you. Come when told it is a command performance."

I asked Michael if Sir James died as a sacrifice so Grandfather could live. The angel never answered.

The next day Lady June-Zigzagael told me that two amateur astronomers, Alan Hale in New Mexico and Thomas Bopp in Arizona both discovered a new comet in the night sky that would be soon visible to the naked eye it was later named Comet Hale-Bopp. It was once thought that comets were good or bad omens of great importance. We could only pray it would be good. As it goes without saying, I wouldn't have to wait long to find out the answer.

A few days later the Angel-Knights were invited to attend Sir James' funeral in full regalia. James' mother also asked if the Blue Knight would speak since we were such good friends and her son admired me. When we arrived, the room was packed with bikers and family. Michael told me to carve a special wooden sword that resembled the one which was assigned to Sir Johnny. I thought it was odd at the time, but I did as instructed.

When it was my turn to speak at the funeral ceremony, I told everyone what a great guy Sir James was and an inspiration to us all. I talked about the many people he brought forward to get married and how well he protected Lady Mary. I presented the special wooden sword to his mother. She laid the sword on Sir James' chest as the attendants closed the casket.

At the gravesite Angela, James' fiancé, was a mess and Sir Johnny, being a very comforting individual, came to her rescue. Later at the wake, he was still by her side, which I feared was for self-serving reasons. I didn't like where I saw it was going. I told Sir Robert to bring Sir Johnny to me.

I told both Angel-Knights that we must maintain our honor and integrity at all times. I said, "Angela is most vulnerable at this time and I don't want anyone taking advantage of her vulnerability." Looking directly at Sir Johnny I said, "Do you understand me Don Juan?"

He gave me his normal prince charming sparkly-tooth smile saying, "Understood boss."

Johnny was like the horny beagle next door that jumps on your leg whenever you come to visit. We called the male knights, "Dog Knights" to remind them always of their station to honor and protect and not revert to the animal instincts within. We did have our share of Dog Knights who couldn't control their urges when a pretty girl was involved. However, all the knights represent what's good and not so good about humanity, and they have free will. I could say no more and only hope that Johnny would resist self-serving temptation.

An hour later I noticed that both Johnny and Angela were gone. I learned from Sir Robert that Sir Johnny offered to drive her home. I shot Robert a look that he wished he wasn't the recipient of.

Robert knew that his knowledge of Johnny taking Angela home didn't sit well with me so he said, "I'm not my brother's keeper."
I said, "In this case you are since you brought him here. If this doesn't end well you will be responsible for the rift in the fabric of our moral code."

I didn't see the boys again before they left for Michigan. I could only hope that Sir Johnny maintained his dignity.

Well, you know what they say about hope? It can be fleeting. Three days later I got a call from Sir James' mother. She wanted to know why one of my knights screwed her son's fiancé before the casket was covered over with dirt.

She said, "You and your knights are disgusting, you were invited to a funeral not a whorehouse." She slammed the phone down onto the receiver. I was devastated. I wanted to convene a tribunal but Michael said I should just leave it alone.

A few weeks later word came to us that the Sun Bow Prayer Walk to save Mother Earth was in turmoil. Walkers were leaving because of Tom Crow's angry outbursts. Tom was blaming his mood swings on a black magic spell that the Blue Knight put on the prayer walk during their visit to the Good Knight Castle. We were told that Grandfather spoke up saying that the Blue Knight is a good fellow who only wishes us success and he has no power over our prayer walk. Only we control that.

I was glad to hear that Grandfather defended my honor and snuffed out the fear. At the same time, I felt sad that he had entrusted the prayer walk to a man like Tom with such a Jekyll and Hyde personality. However, it was no longer my concern. Michael told me that the spirits of the ancestors are now at rest and the spirits of the people who were alive would have to find their own peace. This was a test for them.

Michael said, "Tom-Tom is only doing what disturbed people do: disturb other people. It's all about the struggle. Within Tom's weakness others will find strength. Steve McFadden believes in the Archangel Michael energy. I will be working through him to shed light on the darkness that is trying to tear Grandfather's dream apart. There are demons at work in the Blue Ridge Mountains and McFadden is going to help light the way." This situation made me realize it was just that simple. We humans really are full of bullshit and spread our crap on everyone else. That's the message the old Hopi Medicine Man was passing onto me so many years ago.

With that awareness I released my connection to the past, the problems of late and the plight of Native Americans. I did my job and accomplished a task I was assigned. It was time to move on. I focused on the future, building the Good Knight Kingdom and the message it was to offer. I was in search of a special little baby girl with the initials M.V. and that was all I could think about.

Chapter Forty-nine

The President's Daughter

That summer we received bad news from the Maryland Renaissance Festival management. They had decided to rent out our castle and fairy village space to new vendors, and they wanted to move us to a new area they were opening up. Sir Gregory and I met with management and toured the new space. It was at the bottom of a hill. I could see that if it rained all the water would run right down into our camp. The area was also similar to the land we cleared two years before. It was full of downed trees, sticker bushes, poison ivy and yellow jackets nests. Such is the plight of those with hand held out. You take what you are given, especially since it was free.

Michael, who had been gone from my consciousness since the Sun Bow Walkers left, said, "I warned you they would do this. Festival management is just using you to clear large areas of land so they can lease it to other vendors in the future. But it is a means to an end. Just take it in stride."

"Hey, glad to have you back!" I said.

"I am holding close watch over the walkers. I will be back and forth when you need counsel," he replied. "All is as it should be."

I was a little defeated but not down and out just yet, and with Michael's words I was reassured. I just thought of all the money and donated supplies we put into the structures. Not to mention the volunteer hours used to create the space. Michael went on to say because of all the vendors were complaining about our sales competing with theirs, management felt it was wise to move our exhibit where no one would find us.

Well, this new location is definitely off the beaten path!

I told management that we no longer had the volunteers to clear the land like we had done before. "Well," George said, "there is another option."

"Where?" I asked.

He walked us over to our old space and pointed to Master Ken's Museum of Un-Natural History.

"Ken's place?"

"No, actually it is the lot right behind it," George replied.

Sir Gregory and I looked at each other with quizzical expressions. I said, "There isn't anything back there. It's the edge of the property, right?"

"No, it is a good size parcel! You can build right up to the fence," George responded while taking a defensive posture. "Take it or leave it, the choice is yours."

They were definitely trying to move us out of the line of visitor traffic and view. I asked George to give me, in writing, an exact outline of our parcel. I told him I needed it to calculate how many of our existing exhibits we could fit inside of it. The real reason I asked was because I was anticipating someone having a problem with what we would do with the space. They could take us out of the visitor's line of sight, but they would never get us out of their hearts. The families loved us! Even putting us behind a pile of horse manure wouldn't stop kids from wanting to visit our camp. Love wins every time.

Even though we *won* and were still in the game, we had a monumental task ahead of us. It was early August and hot as hell. We only had one week to remove all of our stuff from the former site and three weeks to rebuild. It would take a miracle to complete by opening day. We put out a call to all available volunteers to meet at RenFest the next day.

Even though it was mid-week, a Wednesday, we had 24 volunteers show up to help. I was shocked at how quickly we pulled everything out of the old space. The saying, "many hands make light work" sure was true that day. Later in the afternoon Master Ken arrived to start work on upgrading his exhibit. I told him what went down and that we were being moved to the space behind him.

He said in a grave voice, "Welcome to the dark side brother."

We laughed.

A vision of a man chained to a boulder appeared while I was laughing. I thought it odd and then heard, "Remember he aligns with Prometheus."

The year before when Ken was at the castle feast and gave me the gold and silver magic coins, I asked him what mythological character did he feel connected to. He already knew mine was the Archangel Michael and Brother Daniel's was the Quetzalcoatl.

I asked Ken, "Remember last year when I asked you which character you see yourself as and you told me Prometheus? May I ask why? What about him draws you?"

In true Ken form he avoided answering me directly but instead told me the Greek creation tale about Prometheus and his daily torture. He went on for what felt like forever. I think my eyes glazed over.

"I'm sure your answer is in there somewhere," I joked when he finished talking.

"Indeed, it is," Ken replied in a melancholy tone.

I bid our neighbor adieu and started off in the direction of the old camp. So many images and thoughts were swirling in my head now. I could definitely see why things were setting up the way they were. We had to tear down the glorious Fairy Kingdom built just twenty-five yards away, because Michael had upped the ante. We were now going after the root of the problem - the human ego and the things that I saw haunting the Sun Bow Walkers. The things that separated positive Tom, who spoke all the right words of peace, non-violence and understanding from the negative Tom's actions of self-absorbed intolerant fits of rage when he didn't get his way. And it clicked! "Aha! That's why Michael referred to him as Tom-Tom. He is two different personalities!"

"Every human has two different faces," Michael reminded me.

As all the images of the past several weeks flooded into my consciousness, it was like puzzle pieces coming together to reveal the greater picture. I was now certain that Tom was placed on the Sun Bow Prayer Walk as the poster boy of the seven deadly vices, just so Steven McFadden could witness and document everything. The **HOPE** was that McFadden would **H**elp **O**pen **P**eople's **E**yes to the truth Michael intended to show them all. I think that Grandfather's wisdom in the tower that day was to let everything play itself out as the Great Creator intended. Sometimes the best action to take is no action.

I must have been deep in a channel of energy because next thing I knew, we were totally moved out of the old space and everything was piled up at our new location. My body began to feel weary. I had been walking back and forth carrying exhibits pieces while all that "thinking" was going on. Whereas I didn't consciously remember helping with all that moving, my body sure knew it achieved greatness. Time for a rest!

I sat down on a bench in front of Saint George's Chapel next to our new space just taking everything. I asked Archangel Michael, "Where do I start? I feel like all I do is build, build and build some more, just to tear it all down and move it, just to start building it up again."

As I complained Michael said, "When you finally build something on your property you will be the landlord. However, until then build the new Grail Castle to look like it's floating off the ground."

I replied, "I know that I am but a horse and you are the rider. You can ride as long as my back holds out. I am here to serve. Please show me what you mean."

The angel had me walk down to the bottom of St. George's Lane to the first lot where management tried to relocate us and then he had me walk back up the hill.

When I did, Michael showed me a vision of a beautiful white castle complex next to Ken's museum of Darkness. The castle walls looked like they were floating about two feet off the ground over top of a field of brightly colored flowers. The vision took me into the castle complex where I could see that the five foot high walls were built on 4" x 4"s in the ground, but painted green to blend in with the color of the plants and leaves. The stucco-covered plywood that made up the walls began two feet off the ground giving the wall a floating effect. The carved concrete blocks on the walls gave the feeling that all the structures were made of stone.

"Wow!" came out of my mouth as this grand vision unfolded further.

Inside the walls and facing St. George's Lane was to be our newly designed 20' x 20' Castle Gift Shop. It had hinged wooden awnings that when closed, down tight locked to secure our inventory at night, but when opened would act as a rain and sun awning shield, exposing the front and left side of the shops counters for patrons to view our products. There was also shelf space on the inside back walls for additional products. And in the rear of the shop was a 10' x 10' room we could use for storage and costume changing for the Angel-Knights.

In the rear of the property was to be a twenty-five-foot high white "Castle of Zeus" that had a 15' x 25' exhibit room inside where Michael wanted me to place the Pandora's Box exhibit from headquarters. The walls of the room were to be all black. The stars, planets and swirling galaxies would be painted in phosphorescent colors of white, and yellow. As the visitor wound their way down a short passageway, they would enter the main exhibit room. To the right on the back wall would be a wire twenty-foot aviary birdcage. The wire screen would be rolled with black flat paint so that it disappears in black light.

Inside the cage were to be two trees with mini-multicolored pulsating lights, flowers and leaves spaced out along every branch. Between the trees would be a waterfall and a life size white stone statue of a beautiful woman, Pandora, holding a plate filled with birdseed. Flying throughout the cage would be seven pure white doves, representing the seven virtues.

The opposite wall in the center would house the mirrored chamber "Box of Pandora" sitting on an iron lattice gate, covering a glowing red pit with smoke rising out of it. Floating suspended around the box would be the Skulls of the Heroes that housed the names of the seven deadly sins. A sign on a post next to the box was to read:

"If you look through the two-way glass you can see evil, but it can't see you. Return your unwanted negativity to where it once was housed with the HOPE that it will never return to you."

When someone would look into the "Mirrored Box" they would see, the Son of Darkness, the Arch-demon Prince Beliel chewing on the words HOPE.

The Angel-Knight guarding the room will tell visitors of a legend that says, "Once you dare to look into the box you have purged yourself of all negativity.

Continuing on past the "Doves of Virtue" exhibit, visitors will walk down a short hallway and out a hidden secret exit door entering a 15' x 30' magical fairy garden area with a waterfall and pond containing large gold fish and a stable that houses a pure white dwarf pony that stands three-foot-high with a golden horn attached to an armor-plated harness in the center of its forehead. An Angel Knight stands by allowing children to make a wish while petting "Lucky" our magical unicorn. An 8' high wall surrounds the garden.

The face of the "Castle of Zeus" will have five stained glass windows that surround a 10' high brown arched wooden double door façade, covered by the portcullis, a latticed grille or gate made of wood. The real entrance to the exhibit would be a hidden secret door on the right sidewall near the rear of the gift shop.

In the center of the Grail Castle complex would be a 10' x 10' octagonal-shaped white open-sided "Tower of St. Michael" with a 12' high viewing deck. I saw that Michael and I would stand in the tower using the sun's rays reflecting off of the blade of Excalibur and onto people in the crowd, to draw them into the castle as they walk up St. George's Lane. The walls of the tower below would be made of white lattice that let light in, but gives visitors the feeling of being inside of the tower. Special war shields containing powerful symbols would be hung on both sides of the lattice walls.

Inside the lower level of the tower would be the new Angelic Knighting Circle where Michael displays the Sword in the Stone and the Holy Grail on a waterfall that empties in a pond full of large goldfish. The upper walls of the eight-sided tower were to be painted white with eight colorful Shields of Power mounted facing out.

"Wow!" I cried out as the vision ended. And I was standing in nothingness. Seriously, just dust and dirt were beneath my feet. Ah take me back to the vision I thought!

"Nope, time to get to work," Michael said. "I'll be back later." And then he was gone. Again.

It was a beautiful vision that Michael gave me, but now came the hard part. With the old castle complex torn down we had to salvage what building materials we could to be recycled into the new camp. Then we had to find the money to buy the materials needed for the new constructions, unless our new Angel Knight, Lady Justine-Anael, could get some of the materials donated.

I gathered everyone together for a quick meeting and had Sir Gregory take notes as I described the vision of the new camp. Then everyone was given marching orders and tasks to accomplish as soon as possible.

In no time at all we had what we needed. I was shocked! Lady Justine had worked closely with Lady Judah over the years so she was already well versed at asking for donations. We were so lucky or blessed…or both! Between Home Depot, Lowes and Suburban Lumber we received half of the lumber we needed, and we only had to charge $1,800 on Lady Eleanor's line of credit.

As soon as all the supplies arrived onsite, I worked from sun up to sun down building Michael's vision. Sir Gregory, Lady Bonnie, Sir Thomas and Sir Robert, when he was in town, helped when they had time off from work. Even Brother Daniel and his Angel Sword staff came to our aid. By opening day of the Maryland Renaissance Festival 1995 we were ready.

I have to say, The Grail Castle Complex was even more beautiful than what I saw in Michael's vision. Brother Ken was absolutely mesmerized by the Pandora's Box exhibit. So much so that he asked if he could sleep in the room rather than his van at night. I was glad to indulge his request. After all, where else would Prometheus feel secure sleeping?

Lady Linda's ceramics looked so much better in the new gift shop display. They were irresistible. The trouble was, no one could see us because the crowds on St. George's Lane blocked us from view. Then I remembered the vision. I took up a position in the tower where I could ricochet sunrays off the sword and into the faces of patrons a hundred yards away. The Tower of St. Michael became a magical lighthouse. People did come to the light, and we were packed immediately, much to the chagrin of the greedy vendors who wanted us expelled from the festival. Chalk up another minor skirmish as a victory!

Everyone at the festival was talking about what a hit our new exhibits were. We had groups of people lining up trying to solve a new life size Sword and Anvil puzzle I had created. Patrons loved touring through the exhibits.

On the third weekend that year there was a rumor floating around the grounds that Chelsea Clinton, the President's daughter, would be attending the festival. I reminded all the Angel-Knights that Michael told us months back we would have an opportunity to connect with President Clinton and if it really came to fruition, he would be sensitive to the Good Knight effort and help us to reach millions of children.

I told the knights to mentally focus on drawing Chelsea Clinton to the Grail Castle, if in fact she was at the festival. For me she was the "Child of Hope" and it was hope that was left behind in "Pandora's Box." I knew that the only way we would reach the President was through his daughter. I autographed a set of *A Good Knight Story* books and a special one for the President with an angelic talisman symbol that I had learned from the hierophant's lessons.

I sent out several knights to see if the rumor was true. I again took up Michael's position in the lookout tower. I could now understood why he was so emphatic on its placement. About an hour later Lady June came to me. The rumor was true, Chelsea and her girlfriend were at the bottom of the hill working their way up toward our castle. I pulled out Excalibur and attempted to catch a ray of sunlight in hope of attracting Chelsea's attention. Unfortunately, it was a cloudy day with very little sun. I sent Lady June back out to keep us advised.

About thirty minutes later I could see Lady June down by the Mud People Show, which was about forty-five yards away. There wasn't much on our side of the lane to see except for St. George's Chapel. When patrons made their way there it was normally when they were moving to the right side of the lane to where there was food, shopping and entertainment. Then I noticed one of the Secret Service advance men scouting out what Chelsea was walking into.

Michael came to me and said, "Our knights have real swords something that will raise a red flag if you are trying to protect the President's daughter. Right under us in the knighting circle is Sir Johnny with the huge Scimitar sword. You need to lower the risk factor if you want to attract the Child of Hope."

I realized he was right. Real swords would be seen as danger.

I scrambled down from the tower and asked all the Angel-Knights to store their real swords in the gift shop and get out their wooden swords. I put the most endearing knight we had, Lady Eleanor a sixty-two-year-old, gray haired, African-American grandmother, in the knighting circle with the children. When the advance special agent came by our castle everything looked safe and he moved to the other side of the lane. I went back up into the tower and stood watch.

As I watched Chelsea leave the Mud People Show I noticed she did move across the lane with her girlfriend and away from our direction. She was going to miss us completely! I grabbed Excalibur and prayed for the clouds to separate. The girls were now directly across from where our Fairy Kingdom stood the year before. They had their backs to both Ken and us. They were looking at fancy mirrors. Just then, the clouds let a sliver of sunlight peek through. I felt Michael take over. He grabbed Excalibur and caught the ray of sunlight. The light ricocheted off the mirror Chelsea's girlfriend was holding and right into the face of the Child of Hope.

He did it again! Chelsea turned around to see where the light was coming from. Michael hit both girls with light and then waved. They waved back and started to walk over. Noticing we had a gift shop they first stopped to looked at all the art and ceramic figurines. Then the girls noticed our newest interactive exhibit the 4' high metal Sword and Anvil puzzle. I came down from the tower and demonstrated that the sword could be freed from the anvil, but there was a chain through the center of a stone that passed through blade. It's what blocked the sword from being freed. However, while manipulating the slot cut in the middle of the sword's blade over the edges of the anvil the chain and stone could be maneuvered in such a way the sword could be freed. The exhibit was likened to a huge life-sized tavern puzzle. It definitely took some mental power to think it through.

Mesmerized, the girls watched for a good while. Macho men would step forward to give it a try. Each person had only three minutes to solve the puzzle or fail. It was truly funny to watch. Other patrons would stand and watch as someone attempted it, and their brain would think it had the solution. Then when it was that person's time to try they walked away saying, "It can't be done."

Since the line was so long to try to free the sword, the girls moved inside the courtyard to watch the children in the knighting circle. Lady Eleanor told both girls that the Good Knight Child Empowerment Network goes to schools all over the country teaching children the *"ABC's of Safety,"* the tricks predators use to abduct and abuse children. She pointed out that the Blue Knight was a retired D.C. police detective who wrote the fairytale and developed the program.

One of the Secret Service Agents came over to shake my hand telling me that he had been a good friend of Dennis McCarthy and heard of the powerful work our charity was doing. I told him that I really missed Denny and that he was way too young to die. I had Sir Gregory take the group on a tour of the Castle of Zeus and the Fairy Garden to meet our magical unicorn, Lucky. Upon leaving, the girls posed for a few photographs as I presented them with the books I had signed. I pointed out the special one that I was sending to President Clinton. Chelsea said that she would give it to him that night along with a report of what a great job the Good Knight Network was doing in schools.

Michael said that Chelsea Clinton was a very gifted indigo child that would greatly impact the world later in life, if given the chance.

That Saturday after closing we had a gathering in our new camp. All the volunteers attended. It was quite a feast, and it was also nice to have my Lady Linda at a gathering. She was normally home at Cove Point when we had gatherings. She really enjoyed the company of Master Daniel, as did all the lady knights, *ah-hem*. He was quite a dashing figure with a certain mystique.

Midway through the party Brother Ken announced that he had a long day and was going to bed in Castle Zeus. He just loved sleeping next to that creepy box full of negative energy. I had built a long bench in the center of the room. I designed it so that people could sit down to reflect on how the negativity displayed in the skulls impacted their lives, or they could face the other direction looking at the white doves of virtue. Ken started using the bench as his bed. He said that the more people filled the box with their crap the better he slept.

I grabbed Ken's arm and said "Wait a minute brother. Before you retire for the evening it is time for a short ceremony. Master Watson wants to make his annual sword presentation. Everyone, we need to gather in Castle Zeus."

This was a time of new beginnings, so before we could move on there was also the proverbial "elephant in the room" we had to address. I couldn't let the swords enter the armory until I laid bare an open issue.

The previous Friday Sir Johnny came back into town as if nothing had happened at the funeral of Sir James. I knew the old, "A sin not seen, never happened," was his way of thinking. Fortunately, I had more integrity than he did, and a pledge is a pledge.

Once we were all in Castle Zeus between the vices and the virtues Brother Daniel told us the legend behind each of the seven Angel Swords he had created as promised, for Michael's Armory. They were indeed works of art valued at tens of thousands of dollars. Usually I would "assign" a sword to a knight, but this time I didn't pass them on to any of the knights. Instead, I rose and asked Sir Johnny to rise as well. I asked Johnny to unsheathe the Sword of Prince Ali, which was the Angel Sword assigned to Johnny last season. I told him to present his sword to Daniel. When he did I turned to Master Daniel and said, "It saddens me, but Sir Johnny could not control his ego and he suffered a lapse of good judgment. Sir Johnny has dishonored his position as an Angel-Knight. What becomes of the Sword of Prince Ali is now up to you dear brother."

A hush fell over the room. I didn't want to get into the particulars of the issue. I knew it was putting Daniel in a very awkward position. He could forgive the misdeed and continue the arrangement, or reclaim the sword and our purpose together would reach its end.

Master Ken, always a tried and true Satanist, wanted to know more. He knew there was dirt and he wanted to hear all about it so he said in his gravelly voice, "And what dishonor and shameful joy did this very young knight bring upon his order?"

I was hoping that no one would ask, but I knew if a master asked an answer had to be given.

Sir Johnny remained tight lipped and stared straight ahead.

I replied, "In July Sir James, one of the Angel-Knights, was killed in a traffic accident. His mother asked me to speak in armor at his funeral because she knew we were close friends. Sir Johnny felt drawn to overly comfort Sir James' grieving fiancé. He was warned to maintain his honor and integrity because any misdeed will blow back on the order. He assured me that I had nothing to worry about. After the graveside service, Sir Johnny and the girl disappeared from the wake. A few days later I received a call from an outraged grieving mother saying, "You and your people are disgusting. You were invited to a funeral not a whorehouse. She went on to say, 'One of your knights took advantage of my son's fiancé before his casket was even covered with dirt.'" In closing I said to Sir Johnny, "We swore to live by a code and that code defines us. If you feel you dishonored that code offer up Michael's sword." Turning to Master Watson I said, "And if you feel he dishonored our pledge please reclaim it and your commitment is complete."

Ken said jokingly, "Way to go son. You are a proud member of the disgusting human race."

Brother Daniel simply dropped his head and reclaimed the sword.

I was saddened. I knew that this marked a new direction. Ultimately, I was responsible for the misdeed and the mother's disappointment and scourge.

Master Daniel said, "Sir Edward-Michael you once said to me, 'a sword is not known by its metal, but by its master's deeds. The same is true for a knight. This knight is not responsible for the misdeed done to your order, the master is, and I see you are aware of that. You knew the boy's nature, yet you allowed him to remain in your company."

All I could do was nod in agreement.

Brother Ken said, "Now get the f--k out of my bedroom." Making the sign of the cross in the air he said, "Now. Go and sin some more."

We never spoke of that incident again, until now when I am forced to document it as part of the Angel-Knight history. Everyone just went on like nothing happened. Sir Johnny was dating Lady Bonnie now. I also noticed that Sir Robert and Lady Mary had paired up as well. There was nothing more I could do to hold her in position as our Blue Princess. Michael said that none of the knights respected Lady Mary's position and she didn't have the will to fight them anymore. He said I should just let her follow her heart.

I suggested that Sir Robert think about moving down to Maryland because we needed consistent help. With Sir James' death we lost a true knight and needed someone to hold that position. Robert also knew how to run electrical wiring which I did not. He would be a huge asset to the kingdom. I told him that there was a lot of building at the Good Knight Kingdom that needed to be completed, if our hopes to attract a woman powerful enough to house the Spirit of Pistis Sophia came to fruition.

"Johnny and I were just talking about moving down to Maryland," Robert said.

"Sir Johnny was more of a player than a noble knight and that I don't think he has what it takes to elevate above where he was at this point. If you move down, you do so by yourself." I went on to say, "Lady Bonnie is just looking to get married to someone and Sir Johnny is not the marrying kind, if he moves down she would make his life a living hell."

Chapter Fifty

The Black Knight

One of the volunteers who had been helping us now for over two years was a very special police officer and part-time carpenter by the name of Kevin Black. Michael nicknamed him "Irish Kevin." Sir Gregory said that Irish was one of the most gifted students in the Masters Studies Program. What I liked most about Kevin was his smile. No matter how hard things got "Irish Kevin" came out smiling. The weekend after Chelsea Clinton visited us we held a special knighting ceremony where Michael dubbed Kevin the Black Knight and assigned Angel Raziel to him.

The name Raziel means, Secrets of the Lord. Raziel is an archangel within the teachings of Jewish mysticism. In the workings of the Kabbalah it is said that Raziel is "Keeper of Secrets" and the "Angel of Mysteries." Gaining this angel's energy was a very important component to the construction of a tree of life within the Philosopher's Stone. This was something Michael told me was on the horizon. If all the necessary components were in place and construction was done correctly the stone would turn a base substance into gold.

Sir Kevin-Raziel was the first Jewish Irishman I had ever met. When Lady Justine-Anael found out he was Jewish like her, there was an immediate attraction. I was happy to see she was also interested because they both came to the knighthood after being dumped by their significant others. It was time for them to heal.

After his knighting ceremony, Irish Kevin told me that he heard there was a group of investors who were opening a Virginia Renaissance Festival outside of Fredericksburg, and it was going to open in the spring of 1996. He went on to say that the charity should see if we could work out the same arrangement with Virginia as we did with Maryland. Master Ken was standing nearby and heard the conversation. "I hear all the Renfest gossip, and can tell you that it was true, but word has it the Maryland RenFest management doesn't want the competition. Anyone one caught working at the Virginia festival will lose their privileges to work here. I even heard that they are planning to send spotters with cameras to take pictures of the crowds to see if any of their vendors or actors show up over there."

Brother Daniel saw us talking and came over. When he learned what we were talking about he said, "Sir Edward you have a tendency of standing out in a crowd. They won't need a picture to spot little boy blue and his band of renegades."

Ken looked at me and said, "You aren't going, aren't you?"

I replied, "With spurs a-jingling. How can we not? There will be at-risk children there who need our lifesaving message. We will visit as many festivals as will have us."

Brother Daniel just shook his head as Ken replied, "It was nice knowing you brother."

"Come what may. Who would have thought we would make it to the the final week of RenFest without a scuffle, yet here we are," I said.

No sooner were the words out of my mouth and George from management came by for a visit. At first, I thought maybe they had spies listening to our Virginia Festival conversation. But no, it turned out that group of vendors were objecting to the Good Knight gift shop selling the same items they had, and wait for it…they accused us of having a "fake" unicorn. Seriously? I had to laugh at that statement since there are no "real" unicorns. And P.S., if we had real unicorn we wouldn't be working a festival for nickels and dimes. I had to wonder what world these people live in? There was also a complaint by the religious zealots that we housed a "Church of Satan" in our camp, because of the Pandora's box exhibit.

"They say you are devil worshippers," George told us.

Ken laughed out loud, "This is so freaking funny. Not only is the opposite true, here I am with my exhibits of darkness and gore and they never once bother me." Turning to me he continued, "Maybe you should turn to the dark side brother."

George responded to Ken, "Well Ken, the complaints are now about you and your exhibits, Daniel's Angel Sword Forge and the Good Knights. They say you are all guilty by association."

"Wow there just is no getting away from the ignorance, is there?" I asked. Knowing that Ken, Daniel and I were friends brought them into the allegations which was bullshit.

Brother Ken told George, "I don't worship Satan. Satan worships me."

Daniel simply said, "Sir Edward you sure stir people up. That is dangerous you know?"

I replied, "People that have a problem with me, have a problem, but that problem isn't me. They are afraid that 'Pandora's Box' is going to snatch their demons. Their fearful perspective is summed up in the old saying, 'Better the devil I know than the devil I don't.' Evil loves to point the finger at everyone else. Someone, or some energy, is just trying to stop us. They can put up road blocks in front of us, but remember we have wings and can soar right over them." With that all three of us, Ken, Daniel and I walked away from George in unison, as if we rehearsed it. End of conversation. It was time to go about our father's business and attend to the children and families who needed us.

While walking up the tower stairs I reflected on our situation. Here we had the retirement of the creator of the Maryland Renaissance Festival this year, and with all the attacks on us over the years I had my doubts that we would be invited back the next year. It was time to focus on our own property in Beltsville and move on.

At closing on Sunday, I suggested we all go out for some good luck Chinese food and hot Sake for dinner. Since I felt this might be our last year together I invited Ken, Daniel and their crews. In all, we numbered thirty-six people. When we arrived at the Chinese restaurant in Annapolis the place was devoid of customers. It was actually a little creepy but at the same time awesome to have the place to ourselves. The owner was extremely glad to see such a large party; even though we were still in medieval dress. On the way in Linda grabbed one of those homes for sale magazines you see at the entrance of most retail stores and restaurants. She loved to look at all the houses we couldn't afford.

Since we were the only ones in the restaurant, it was like a private banquet. We put all the center tables together so that we could pass food around to get a taste of everything. The feast was amazing. Everyone commented about how it felt like a family reunion of like-minded people. It was so refreshing to talk with people that could follow the topics we were discussing. Most of Daniel's crew had metaphysical knowledge, so it was interesting to hear others' perspectives on the same topics. Most of them thought outside the box. As Ken said that night, "If you can't find the answer inside the box, where else can you look?"

During dinner Linda was looking through the homes magazine and became fixated on a four thousand square foot Georgian Mansion on seventeen acres on Kent Island. It was just on the other side of the Chesapeake Bay Bridge from Annapolis. I had never seen her so excited. Linda was always drawn to the southern style homes and lifestyle she'd seen in movies like *Gone with the Wind*. I always teased her saying, "One day Miss Scarlet you will have your Tara."

Unfortunately, because of the economy, we were living pretty much on her paycheck, since I was only getting a couple of small private investigator jobs a month. We had also been trying to sell the piece of waterfront property we bought after selling our house in Waldorf, but it had been on the market for three years with little interest. Her chance at a house like the one in the magazine was slim to none!

After dinner when it came time for the fortune cookies Sir Gregory asked me to pass them out for good luck, with the understanding that we each had to add the words "in bed" to the end of each fortune. It did put a funny spin on everything. Everyone took turns reading them out loud. We were cracking up. Linda and I were the last to read ours.

My cookie's message read: *You will succeed in all that you do, your waiting is full– in bed.* I said, "Look out Linda it sounds like I have a ticket to 'Nookiesville' tonight."

She rolled her eyes at me and said, "Oh Ed!"

Then Lady Linda read hers, "*You will move into your dream house by year's end – in bed.* Get out! Did you hear that…look…look what it says! My house! I am getting my house!" She had a burst of excitement so big I thought she was going to stroke out.

Lady June piped up, "Picking that magazine up was a good omen."

Then Linda became sullen.

"Where did your excitement go all of a sudden?" I asked

"Well, it's just ridiculous for me to think this could happen. I mean look at all the things that would have to fall into place to make the fortune come true within two months. It's an impossible dream," she said. Linda tended to be pessimistic and to very easily talk herself out of a good thing. The knights chimed in to keep her spirits up.

Lady June remarked, "Remember Lady Linda I want to buy your sandcastle."

Linda said, "June that would still mean me having to sell the beach house *and* the waterfront property, plus having to arrange financing and two settlements."

"Remember what Angel Michael said at the party on the beach in January Lady Linda?" Lady Mary asked. He said, 'This was going to be our last bonfire. Next year a new house and fireworks!'"

Brother Daniel said, "If anyone can make it happen it's you Lady Linda. But don't you think you need to look at that house first?"

It was good to see everyone pumping her up. I was still thinking, it would take a financial miracle to turn it around but Linda was sure that house was for us. By the end of dinner, they had convinced her to at least explore all the options because any dream worth having is one worth pursuing.

Irish Kevin stood up a little wobbly. He said, "You know I can drink Irish whiskey until the cows come home with no effect, but this hot Japanese rice wine has my head a spinning." Holding on with one hand to the top of Sir Johnny's chair next to him, he raised his cup of warm Sake with the other and said, "Let's help Lady Linda get her new house! This is an old Irish toast my great grand pap taught me for good luck. "I-rish you a very nice new place to live, I-rish God's greatest gift to you he'll give. I-rish you health, and wealth, and more-- I-rish to see Linda's smiling face meet us at her new home's door!"

Sir Gregory yelled, "In bed."

We all laughed until tears were flowing! It was a positive close to this leg of our adventure.

I did notice Lady Bonnie cast a flirtatious look at Irish Kevin as he sat down. Lady Justine's facial expression indicated that she did not approve. I could see that when Sir Johnny returned to Michigan there could be trouble. Oh well, what else is new I thought?

I felt that Michael was getting ready to open a new window of opportunity for us all. We said our good-byes in the hopes that we would be reunited the next year.

Chapter Fifty-one

Linda's Dream

Lady Linda had two dreams in life: a big southern plantation house and me all to herself.

The following weekend after Renfest closed, we went to see the house Linda had found in the real estate magazine. It was unbelievable, and very much like a *Gone with the Wind* style plantation. All of the homes in that area of Kent Island were built on at least fifteen acres. This property had horse farms on both sides, which gave the feeling of having horses without the expensive up keep. The back of the house was about thirty yards from Green Creek and two tidal ponds which were fed by Eastern Bay. The left side of the property was a saltwater marsh full of blue crabs. At the back of the house along the shoreline was an 80' wooden deck, bulkhead and boat ramp.

I could tell Linda was in heaven, this was truly her dream home. She was already picturing where she'd put vegetable and flower gardens, patios and a swimming pool. The price was shockingly doable, but we would still have to sell both of our properties to make it happen. While we were sitting on the bench at water's edge Linda said, "If I can make this happen do you want to do it?"

For the past eight years I had been driving 150 miles round trip to the castle six days a week. Moving to Kent Island would knock fifty miles off that trip. I said, "Sure if you can do it, but don't count on it happening by the end of the year."

When I returned to work on Monday, I called a gathering of the Angel-Knights I told them that I was going to put everything the Hierophant had taught me to work for the charity *and* Linda's new home. The charity needed to get a loan from a bank for the construction and renovation of the Good Knight Kingdom. And for Linda's new home, we needed to sell the two properties in order to afford the down payment. Lady Eleanor's line of credit was maxed out at forty thousand dollars because of the high interest rate of nineteen percent being charged monthly so the charity was already in deep debt. Lady Justine had tried for several bank loans, but the charity didn't have any collateral to secure the loans and had been repeatedly turned down.

It was estimated that the charity needed a loan of two hundred and fifty thousand dollars and Linda would need the same amount as profit from the sale of the two properties. Linda's dream was up against the juggling to sell two properties, held by the same bank, and the qualifying for the purchase of a new home - all within a sixty-day period in order to make her financial request go through. The poor charity was in a bit of a bigger pickle. On one hand it had the donated piece of property to use as collateral, which was valued at four hundred thousand dollars. On the other hand it was zoned for non-profit use only, and could not be sold or it would revert back to the trust that had donated it to the charity. In essence it was totally useless to the bank. It was a strange predicament - the charity owned the property, but couldn't sell it or use it as collateral.

I went to work reviewing lessons twenty-four, twenty-five and twenty-six. I made two talismans that took two weeks to prepare because of the waiting periods and planet alignment. The talisman for the charity was under the planet Jupiter and the one for Lady Linda's new house under the planet Saturn. Michael then had me construct a small box to put them in. He said it would help speed up the request for an answer. Michael reminded me that a talisman is just a request for the powers that be to help manifest something to happen. They can't make things happen, but if the right elements are in place, things can be made to happen. It's hard to explain how it works, but it does work.

Now where the talisman comes into play is the human factor. The talisman activates a divine request that stimulates the Godhead, that electro-magnetic stuff we are all made of. It fuels the senses within the human body; primarily the heart and brain. It was the mental mindset of the loan officers which were denying the loans that was holding things back. From the knowledge I gained in the lessons I realized that our focus needed to shift those mindsets. With all of that in mind I concentrated the energy of the talisman on the hearts of the individuals who would make the loan decisions, so that they would look at the good works the charity does for the community and not the bank's traditional bottom line. Better stated, our focus was more like the scene in the movie Star Wars when Obi-Wan-Kenobi says, "These are not the droids you are looking for," which made the storm troopers let the heroes pass.

I had a plan, but the elements would be hard to draw together. With the talismans made, I went to work on creating the transmitter box Michael told me to place them in.

The Crystal Transmitter Box

It was now time to set in motion everything I had learned from the Book of Wisdom. I went to the art supply store and purchased a plain wooden box that measured 2" x 2" x 3 ½." Michael told me the top of the box had to have a copper metal screen on top, so that the interior of the box would draw energy to the talisman. I also bought a quantity of different colored plastic self-sticking gemstones to create colorful patterns on the four sides and top of the box. Michael said the box had to look like it held a celestial request.

If you wish to make a "Transmitter Box" you will need:

1- wooden box with copper screen top 2" x 2" x 3 ½"
2- gold paint marking pens, one with a thick marking head and the other with a fine tip
1- can of black glossy spray paint
2- strong button-sized magnets, the stronger the better

12- water clear quartz crystals (the size should be about half the width your little finger)
Plus, a colorful assortment of plastic self-sticking gemstones

Assembling the Box

1. Spray the copper screen and wooden box inside and out with black glossy spray paint and let dry for four hours (longer if you live in a humid area).
2. With the gold marker, outline all the edges of the box and let dry for one hour. Then with the fine tip gold pen and draw the geometric symbol you created on your talisman inside the bottom of the box and the planet

symbol you made on the talisman on the outside back of the box below the hinges.

3. Hot glue one of the crystals in the center of the bottom on the box, and one in the center of the top of the box so they are over one another but not touching.

4. Hot glue one button magnet on the bottom crystal and reverse the poles of the second button magnet so they push against one another, not attract. This will create an electro-magnetic energy field in the center of the box. This energy field is the perpetual motion that will power your talisman. Make sure there is at least a ¼" to ½" gap between the two magnets.

The inside of the box is now complete.

5. You should run a bar of soap around the top lid of the box where it touches the bottom of the box so the two painted edges won't stick together.

6. Hot glue the remaining ten quartz crystals into an attractive cluster on the top of the box over the copper screen.

7. Meditate and ask for guidance on how to lay out the self-sticking gemstones, and then place them accordingly. Just follow your guidance. "Make the box look celestial" was what I was told.

Put your Transmitter Box in the most sacred space you can find where it won't be disturbed and wait for your answer. You should give it a year, depending on what you have asked for.

With my "Crystal Transmitter Box" complete I taped the two talismans together and put the box on top of the waterfall in the Tower of Wisdom at the center of the Medicine Healing Labyrinth.

In my case Michael also had me program eight amethyst crystals, because we wanted to activate people's sensitive hearts.

With the fine tip gold paint marker, I wrote:
a. "Castle Loan" on two amethyst crystals,
b. "Beach House Sell" on two amethyst crystals
c. "Property Sell" on two amethyst crystals
d. "Linda's Dream" on the last two amethyst crystals.
e. I then gave one of the "Castle Loan" crystals to Lady Justine-Anael since she would be meeting with the loan officers at the bank for the charity.
f. I buried one marked "Beach House" in the sandcastle display in front of the beach house.

g. I buried one marked "Property Sell" next to the for-sale sign at the waterfront property we wanted to sell.

h. I buried the last one marked "Linda's Dream" next to the for-sale sign when we were ready to submit a contract on the property.

j. The last item needed was to get the owners to accept a lot less for the property in order for us to afford the house. So I put the corresponding amethyst crystals next to the Transmitter Box in the Tower of Wisdom.

I walked away and trusted with every cell in my being that God's Will would be DONE!

A week later, we received a cash contract on the waterfront property and the buyers were in a hurry to go to settlement because they wanted to start clearing the land for a prefab home they wanted to drop on the property by spring. That same week Lady Justine told me that the same bank that turned her down six months earlier, approved the loan because of the good work the charity does for the community.

The only hold out was the beach house at Cove Point. It was showing, but we weren't getting any contract offers. Lady June called me on Monday to say she still wanted the house, but she had to sell her house in Montgomery County first. She asked me to add the selling of her house to the talisman, but Michael said that it was too late and the Transmitter Box could not be opened without destroying everything we had set in motion.

Right after I hung up with Lady June, Lady Linda rang to tell me our real estate agent called and said the people who owned the Kent Island property were going to pull the house off the market for the winter and re-list it in the spring for more money. She told Linda, "If you want the house you have to write an offer today." Linda was so upset. I felt so bad for her because I could feel her heart was breaking. I remembered that Michael told me human emotion is what powers the talisman and my wife was pouring out tons of that right now so let it flow and ride the energy.

I had to tell Linda that June couldn't buy the beach house until she sold her other house and I also relayed what June just told she was up against. June had said that couldn't even list her house until she made a lot of repairs on it. Michael told me to have Linda call June because they are both very good at leveraging money and June's emotion to acquire the sandcastle was matched to Linda's emotion to acquire the Kent Island property. Where there was a will there was a way!

After I hung up with her, Linda hopped in the car and went to our real estate agent's office. They got June on a conference call and the three spoke about how to make this work. June agreed to buy the beach house for a fixed opening price, paying a small monthly mortgage with a two-year balloon payment. The owners of the Kent Island property miraculously had lowered the asking price to $395,000 while Linda was in the agent's office. However, the most we could afford was $375.000. Regardless, we were all in and ready to submit the contract to the sellers. All of our collective fingers crossed!

Crossing fingers is a good thing, but I wasn't leaving the outcome to just that superstition. I drove to the Kent Island property and buried the crystal I'd prepared next to the for-sale sign. I then called Linda telling her to wait at the agent's office because I was on my way to sign the contract. Together we put our John Hancocks on the dotted line of the offer! Now all that was left was the waiting to hear back from the sellers.

A week went by and we hadn't heard anything.

Our agent checked and learned that the sellers had not rejected our contract, but that the house had shown several more times and they were waiting to see if they got a better offer. I called some of the Angel-Knights together and asked them to walk the labyrinth and focus on the sellers deciding one way or the other within twenty-four hours.

That evening Linda received a call from our agent. The couple had accepted our offer. Linda was going to get her house! Now the next step was to see was if she could manage to get the all settlement companies to close quickly, so that we would be in the house before the end of the year.

Miracles can and do happen. On October 8, 1995 Linda got the fortune cookie saying she'd be in her new home by the end of the year, and on December 8, 1995 we moved into our new home on Kent Island! And all of the Angel-Knights came together to help us move in. I had never seen them work so hard. Normally there is a separation of the human from the Angel when they are outside of the castle grounds, but on that moving day, both were working overtime for a common cause. The men were working with me to remove everything from the two trucks I rented and the ladies were working with Linda to empty boxes and put stuff away as soon as it came in the house. It was pure teamwork.

That Christmas Eve, Dawn, Spencer and Meghan drove down from Pennsylvania. They were stunned with the house we had purchased and how quickly we had settled in. We had a nice Christmas with them as Spencer was surprisingly on his best behavior. I had a wonderful time with Meghan Victoria but I was sad seeing who, or what, she was becoming. I could see that the tension between Spencer and Dawn was taking its toll on her. It was also becoming more and more obvious why she didn't have a chance of becoming the "M.V." child that Michael was looking for. I felt if something weren't done soon, she would wind up in therapy with anger issues in the future. It's terrible to see what some people do to their children.

Other than the obvious changes in Meghan, the visit was going surprisingly smooth. It was a Christmas miracle for certain! I found myself holding my breath as they were packing to go home. It was as if I was just waiting for the other shoe to drop. Dang it if my gut wasn't right on that count! Five minutes before they left, as Spencer was out packing the car, Dawn told us that they were going to be evicted in January because they were four months behind on their mortgage payments.

We sat her down and talked. Spencer stayed outside taking his good old time packing the car. Dawn confessed that Spencer had made her ask Linda's mother, Hester, for money to pay the mortgage. Hester had given it to them, but good old Spence had used the money to open a comic book store.

"Instead of paying the mortgage he's buying comics and now wants us to bail his family out?" I asked.

Linda was crying, fearing that her daughter and grandchild were going to be homeless.

I bent down and looked Linda in the eye and said, "They will never be homeless as long as we have this big house, but we can't keep getting sucked into Spencer's manipulation of Dawn. Think about it. Do you remember all of the weekends we've spent over the past two years working on their house in Gettysburg? We've wallpapered, painted and bought furniture to make their house nice, but Spencer was always MIA when there was work to be done. His other trick has been, once we loan him money we don't hear from them again until they need more money." Looking at Dawn now I asked, "So, how many more years are you going to let Spencer use You?

"I can't leave him dad! I don't want my daughter to grow up without a father," she snapped at me.

"First of all, I never said leave him, but now that you bring it up, there are some fathers worth growing up without, and Spencer is one of them," I replied.

I felt bad for Linda so I said no more on the subject. I just hugged Dawn and Meghan and said my good-byes. Spencer never came back in the house. This was more than a pattern on his part. It was a habit.

As a side note, Linda did wind up paying the back-mortgage payments for Dawn, just to have the bank foreclose on the house the following year. **Enabling does nothing for nobody.** Sometimes it hurts to see people fail, but failure is great stimulus for the soul.

Chapter Fifty-two

Blizzard of '96

On January 6th, 1996 Linda and I hosted the annual Angel Knight Epiphany Feast of the Magi gathering as planned. As usual, the ladies were all decked out in their long gowns and the gentlemen in their black tuxedos. Sir Robert and Irish Kevin looked like movie stars. I was glad that Archangel Michael was setting this standard and tradition at a time when people were always finding reasons to dress down. Our annual event gave us a reason to dress up. Sir Kevin made a joke of being James Bond, in British Secret Service and Michael replied, "No, you are in Her Majesty's Sacred Service." This brought a smile to the Blue Princess's face. Then Michael continued, "But one day I see you in the U.S. Secret Service."

"How did you know that is one of my dreams?" Irish Kevin asked.

I just winked my eye at him.

The house was so festively decorated. It truly looked like we were living in a mansion. Linda finally had the house she wanted to be able to entertain properly. The dining room was 15' x 17' and had a three-leaf walnut dining table which wold sit ten, with a matching hutch and buffet. Hanging over the center of the table was a crystal chandelier that took me six hours to put together. Every square foot of the table was taken up with her delicious food samplings, from smoked salmon, turkey and ham to candied vegetables and a seven-layer dessert parfait truffle. Linda had cooked like she was feeding an army.

Everyone was amazed at how settled the house was. Lady Mary said it looked like we had been living there for years. The knights all brought house-warming presents. Sir Robert-Cassiel was the best present I could have gotten that year. He was like the son I never had. He had finally decided to move down from Michigan to help me build the Good Knight Kingdom. Lady Eleanor-Haniel let him move into the guesthouse over her garage and I could see that a whole new world was opening up for him.

I was happiest, however, to see the large present Sir Irish Kevin-Raziel had brought me. He had driven to Phantom Fireworks in Pennsylvania and brought back a large assortment of fireworks, rockets and mortars. We closed the party that night by going outside in the brisk winter air so that my dream could come true. For a half an hour I got to tickle the heavens with explosives. I felt like the Wizard Gandalf from the Lord of the Rings, with wiz-poppers and colorful rockets exploding in the air as it began to snow all around us. It was simply a magical evening.

Each Angel Knight was given a Roman candle that shot out twelve fireballs that would explode amongst the snowflakes. When the fireballs exploded they illuminated the white snowflakes, making the entire sky light up. No two candles had the same design pattern or sparkling color combination. It was truly amazing and will be remembered as one the greatest days of my life. Here I was, surround by wonderful friends and a loving wife who was equally as happy…although she was a nervous wreck watching me run around lighting the fireworks.

Michael announced, "As our rockets explode in the winter sky, let us think of the Children of the Four Directions that will be born over the next ten years. The sign will be a golden egg from a pure white dove that will mark the coming of the child with the initials MV. The Kingdom that you build will safeguard her and become the playground from which she will discover the secrets of the universe."

Michael had been right on target with his prediction the year before. Lady Linda now had her dream house and the Angel-Knights had begun the New Year with a big bang over a fresh covering of snow. So now we could look forward to the arrival of the children!

It snowed and snowed all right. As a matter of fact, it snowed for three and a half days straight. Kent Island received five feet of snow and we had eight-foot snowdrifts around the house. When it stopped snowing I went out to try and shovel the driveway. Linda said I was crazy because the driveway was a third of a mile long. I figured it didn't matter how long it was, it wasn't going to shovel itself so if I did a little at a time. I figured it would be done sooner than if I sat on the couch and waited for it to melt. It was pretty funny, because when I would finally get through the snow to the ground with my shoveling, all I would find was grass. I couldn't get my bearings on where the twisting driveway was located because the snow was laying so beautifully around all the tall pines and oak trees we had on the property. I finally gave up after an hour because a ridiculous wind kicked up and just blew all the snow right back into my face.

I called our neighbor Jim who lived next store to see what he did about snow removal.

"We pay a guy when storms like this hit. Cost me around a thousand dollars two years ago when the blizzard hit," he said.

I hung up and told Linda what he had said.

She replied, "Well we just had a party and have plenty of food and wine left over. It looks like we are stuck here until the spring thaw."

I said, "I can't do that. I've got a castle to build."

Ten days later we were still snowed in. Sir Gregory called and wanted to know if the Angel-Knights could come down to shovel us out. I laughed and reminded him how long the driveway was.

He said, "Let us try Boss."

"Okay, that would be wonderful," I responded. Linda told me to ask him if they could pick up some food and wine because we were running low. They were more than glad to help out in any way they could.

In the meantime, I walked up to the road with the intention of shoveling two spaces for them to park. I was exhausted by the time I got there from moving forward in waist high snow. Two hours later I was just finishing the spaces when two carloads of knights pulled up. What timing! They all dug right in with their shovels. I rested a bit and then joined them. It was a funny sight watching their battle against the snow. It looked like a military movement.

As they worked Sir Robert noticed that one large area of snow was peppered with holes and wanted to know what caused it. I was new to the Eastern Shore so I didn't have a clue.

It was so peaceful, even more so than normal, as we shoveled. All we could hear was the beautiful sound of the wildlife that surrounded us off in the distance. A short time later four white-tailed deer came out of the thicket running towards us then cut to the right, leaping high in the deep snow. Then huge flock of Canadian Geese, some ducks and white Trumpeter Swans were spooked off the surface waters of Eastern Bay by a dog running to the shore. There were so many waterfowl in the air at one time that they blocked the sun as they flew overhead. We had to run to the cover of the nearby pine trees as the birds answered Sir Robert's question. It was birds raining down poop as they flew overhead, that had caused the holes in the snow.

There's your answer Sir!" I exclaimed

The work we were doing was backbreaking, we were cold, and the birds weren't the only things pooping out on me.

Two hours later we had only cleared about thirty yards and gave up. We walked back to the house and ate all the food and drank all the wine our rescuers had brought.

While we feasted and the wine was flowing, Sir Gregory filled me in on the happenings I had missed. He told me that tension began escalating at the White House as soon as Sir Johnny left for Michigan, because Lady Bonnie had made her moves on Irish Kevin. That had made Lady Justine furious. Gregory went on to say that this was why the girls were not helping with the snow removal.

Since the rescue party had only cleared a portion of the driveway, it looked like we would be socked in for a while longer. Then Lady Mary had an idea.

She said, "Let's manifest that the snow in the driveway disappears." She was so naïve. I told everyone that it didn't work like that, but Mary wasn't going to accept my pronouncement.

She said, "As we walk back to the cars let's cut a path down the drive with our feet and legs so that the sun can melt that area faster." It was a long and tiring gesture that they completed on their way out, but I couldn't see it working. It would take a miracle to get rid of that much snow.

The next morning Linda and I were awakened by the sound of a loud truck engine. It was our neighbor Steve driving a yellow bulldozer with a huge plow blade on the front. He was cutting through the high snowdrifts with the machine, like a knife through butter. I went out to greet our rescuer.

Steve owned a construction company that had heavy equipment so he had one of his men bring over a large bulldozer. He said that it was a good thing we had tramped down the snow to mark the driveway or he wouldn't have known where to plow. He said that from now on I should get some five-foot yellow fiberglass marking sticks to mark the driveway edges and he would plow our driveway when he did his.

Now that's a great neighbor! Steve and his wife Rita were from New Hampshire and had moved into the neighborhood two years before us. She was a horsewoman and owned several thoroughbreds. They traveled a lot, so we repaid their kindness by keeping an eye on their property when they were gone and caring for their cats.

Lady Mary had done well. It was nice to see that the knights had developed the mindsets to put to work the visualization techniques the Hierophant had taught them in the lessons - to solve someone else's problems. She didn't see the exact outcome in her visualization, but she had gotten the message of what to do for it to be accomplished. Listening is the first step, following through is the second. The knights taught me a lesson during that storm. In fact, they taught me many lessons over the years. Their dedication gave me hope for the future.

Linda's dream home, blizzard 1996

Chapter Fifty-three

Grandfather's Nightmare

During February's First Wednesday Club gathering I spoke to the Angel-Knights about the importance of documenting their journey through life. I suggested that they should keep notes or a diary journal, because the time would come for them to write their personal Book of Shadows too. I reminded them that Master ERU's lesson of journaling was extremely important and then gave the example of Steve McFadden's "Odyssey of the Eighth Fire" which documented the Sun Bow Walkers on their journey. I asked for volunteers who had attended the Sun Bow blessing of the labyrinth to raise their hand and tell everyone what happened the year before. Only a few spoke and I was quite shocked at how little they understood and/or remembered. They must have been too busy socializing, playing a fantasy role, or trying to impress the opposite sex to really see what was going on. So, I shared with them what they missed.

"As you are all aware, I have several sources who have kept me up to date on the progress of the Sun Bow Walkers. The walk has just ended so I would like to give you an overview of their journey since they left us. They became like family to me so I have sent "White Light" to them every day when I walk the labyrinth. I learned that when the walkers left the Good Knight Castle on July 22nd 1995 it took them three weeks to walk down through Virginia and North Carolina. When they turned west to cross the Great Smokey Mountains, trouble began. Half the walkers refused to continue with Tom Crow in charge. Some of you may remember me telling you that Tom tried to convince grandfather and the other elders that the Blue Knight used black magic to turn the walkers against him when they visited the Good Knight Kingdom. It was Grandfather who put a lid on that energy by telling them that the Blue Knight had no power over the walk and that he just shared his vision of what could happen if they did not forgive and keep their hearts pure," I said. "Furthermore, do you remember Michael predicting that a girl from Maryland would expose the deceiver during the journey?' I asked. "Over the next one hundred-fifty days, Tom stirred up more and more trouble for the group and finally he was accused of attempting to molest a seventeen-year-old female walker. Instead of helping the girl, most of the men said the girl was at fault and she should have known better than to be alone with Tom. The girl was from Maryland. Disgraced, she left the walk."

Heads shook in disgust and disbelief and an audible groan came from the group.

"I can't believe after all of them hearing our message, that they wouldn't support that girl!" Sir Robert yelled out.

"It wasn't in the cards. Ego intervened. And Michael told us this would happen. Do you also remember he said grandfather would fall, then rise and finish the walk under the energy of the Great Grandmother, just as we saw him do in the labyrinth? Well, it was reported to me that by the fourth quarter of the walk Grandfather had a mild heart attack, or stroke - they do not know which for sure. Although he fell and damaged his left knee, he rose again stronger than ever to finish the walk. Michael also told us that Tom would have to set aside his ego and lead his people like Moses or he would become the poster boy for the Seven Deadly Sins. When Tom left the kingdom Michael asked him, 'Will you walk the path of vice or virtue?' Which path do you all think he chose?"

"Michael's prediction of Tom not finishing the Sun Bow walk with his people came true. Tom chose to drive away from the walk in its last quarter. Michael also said that the Sun Bow pilgrims would never reach the Western Gate. It was recorded that the Sun Bow walkers reached East Beach on the shores of Pacific Ocean at Santa Barbara on February 2nd, 1996, it was day 225 and Grandfather said the walk would end there. In the spirit of peace and forgiveness Grandfather invited Tom and his small group of followers to re-join the walkers for the closing ceremony of the Sun Bow, but Tom refused to come. With the Sun Bow Ceremony complete, Grandfather said, "We are unable to ride off into the sunset. We have journeyed as far west as we might go. Now, at the end, we turn east and journey off in the direction of the Morning Light.""

"Remember when Grandfather asked me, 'What are you?' in the tower during the blessing of the labyrinth Michael answered, 'I am the Morning Light'."

*(**Steven McFadden wrote in his diary of Grandfather's choice to end the prayer walk in Santa Barbara. I invite you to look it up on the web)*

I told the Angel-Knights, "I realize more and more each day as I record my journey through life, it is you who need to know what you are a part of. It has also become apparent to me, that what we do is not for the living, it is for those who have lived and for those who have yet to be born."

As I think on it now, Tom Crow was one of the most important characters on the Sun Bow pilgrimage. Tom was like the tortured Gollum/Sméagol character in Lord of the Rings and Grandfather was like the wise wizard Gandalf. He knew that for good or ill, Tom had a significant role to play in the great pilgrimage. Tom was like a mirror being held up in the faces of all of us as a reminder that there are all kinds of role models in this world - and that we must learn from them all.

Chapter Fifty-four

Hawaii

Interactions among the Angel-Knights were getting a little out of control for my taste. It was late winter and our outside activities were few and far between, so perhaps they were all getting a little bit bored. I had to remind the Angel-Knights again that this was a Divine Order, not a cult or singles club, and that our gatherings were for a positive purpose, so I called them all in for a brief meeting.

I said, "There are reasons why you're not supposed to date a co-worker or fellow knight. Sir Robert is chasing after our Blue Princess, Sir Thomas is chasing after Lady Barbara and Lady Bonnie-Gabriel was chasing after Sir Johnny. But now with Johnny back home in Michigan, I can see she now wants Irish Kevin, who is chasing after Lady Justine. I almost need a racing form to keep up with you guys. If you don't get yourselves under control this isn't going to end well."

I again reminded everyone that this was a human social experiment that Michael was conducting. They would come to me with their problems and try to make me their father or friend, but I couldn't let that happen. I was put in place as their mentor and director. It was my responsibility to maintain order despite all the chaos. None of the knights had been in the military, so they had never learned true discipline. They actually reminded me of the first test group I began with at Marriott security. Those folks were all ex-military and had a whole different set of problems. Each person had his or her own personal agenda and I tried to respect those while still getting the job done. I guess every group just has its own dynamic as well as its pros and cons.

After the meeting, I went to work outside with Sir Robert on some of the structures. It was interesting working with him. Robert had a loving heart when you got to know him, but he always remained on guard. After moving to Maryland, he had landed a job with an electrical contractor and was going to school for Massage Therapy at night. Robert was a natural healer, but I felt that he should have become a police officer. He was working with me at the castle two days a week now and I was trying to help him with his anger issues.

Robert grew up with a dominant mother and older sister who always made him think that he couldn't do anything right. I told him that in time, with the Angel Cassiel's help, he would learn that he can't do anything wrong. He couldn't understand that yet, and I could see that his childhood programing was going to be hard to break.

It's terrible what we do to our children.

Michael said that Robert's father was a gifted carpenter and he wanted to bring that out in him. We spent most of that spring running electrical cables to the locations around the property where Michael wanted us to construct special exhibit buildings. Robert's carpentry skills were blossoming, just as Michael wanted.

In March Sir Gregory called the Virginia Renaissance Festival management about the possibility of setting up an exhibit area during their eight-week run in the spring. "They knew all about the Good Knight Network and want us to set up a permanent campsite like the one we had at the Maryland Festival. They want us to include Pandora's box, the Unicorn and all our exhibit features. They also want to showcase the Good Knights on their schedule as holding hourly knighting ceremonies for children on all eight weekends," Gregory said.

"There is no way we can do the whole season. We don't have the building materials or the manpower to construct the buildings, plus I can't drive four hours every day to do the build. Linda will freaking kill me! Tell them this year all we can do is one weekend with a small crew, to check things out, and we will see if we can squeeze in more, depending upon the crowd and distance we have to travel," I told him.

For some time, Michael had been showing me that it was important to plan a trip to Hawaii. Apparently, we had reached peaceful settlement with the ancient spirits of North America, but we also needed to connect with the ancient volcano spirits of America's furthest western lands in the Hawaiian Island chain. I thought there was no way in hell I could make it happen, since we had a new mortgage and any extra money was flowing out to fix up the house. Of course, I have learned that when Michael says something has to happen, the Universe conspires to make it so…

It just so happened that Linda's mother, Hester had remarried a very nice fellow, Bill Ladson, and they honeymooned in Maui. She fell in love with the island and wanted to give us the gift of a trip to Maui. BINGO!

Michael started flooding me with visions as soon as the plans were set. He showed me a castle built of skulls with no windows or doors. He said,

"You must be in spirit to enter. He also said the Castle of Skulls is hidden somewhere on the island of Oahu."

Somewhere on the island of Oahu? "Can you narrow that down a bit?" I asked. No answer. That's typical.

"All will be known when your waiting is full…" came a response.

"Okay, so we're winging it! I got it!" I quipped back.

The visual instructions continued and focused in on the Castle of Skulls. I was shown that inside there was a Purple Orb that had to be released by the Goddess Pele. In order to do this, the spirit energies of Maui and Pele would need humans to be in the right places at the right time. There was also a very short window of time for me to locate the skull castle and present a special fertility pouch to the ancestors. Michael said that it had to be delivered by midnight, Easter Sunday, April 7th or I would have to wait another seven years before I could make another attempt.

With the deadline I was given I told Linda that since this was going to be a very busy year for the charity, that if we were going to Hawaii it had to be by the end of March. I learned long ago, that the less spiritual information I gave her, the better off I was.

Michael then showed me that I had to go to the highest point of land on the Island of Maui to make an offering to attract the spirit energy of the Goddess Pele. He said that while on Maui I should also try to meet with Sergeant Ki-Ki from my Army days in Augsburg, Germany. Sgt. Ki-Ki was the son of a Kahuna Nui, a blood-line of Hawaiian medicine men. Michael said that he might have some information that could help me locate the Castle of Skulls on Oahu. Then we would have to fly to the Island of Oahu to find the castle and search for a hidden gateway where I could leave the fertility pouch.

"Ha! Easy-peasy lemon squeezy," I thought. "I've got this!"

Linda planned a two-week vacation for us. While she packed and prepped, Michael showed me the list of things I would need. From the dove cage in the Good Knight Castle I had to select four white doves named A, B, C, and D. They represented the angels A-Uriel, B-Cassiel, C-Raphael and D-Sachiel. The doves were to be two males and two females, then I had to put them in a separate large cage with nesting materials. From each wing tip of the doves I was to remove a long feather and mark each with the letter of the dove the feather came from. Then I was instructed to program eight clear quartz crystals, the size of my little finger, with thoughts of awakening the ancestors to help me with an ancient fertilization ceremony of the Purple Orb. Each pair of crystals were marked the letter names of the white doves. I then collected small plastic bag of dirt and lavender seeds from the labyrinth. I was told to have Lady June, who was part Hawaiian, to bring me something that she owned from Hawaii. She gave me a red woven cotton scarf with a hand painted picture of Goddess Pele exploding from the top of a volcano. Once I had all the items together I called twelve of the most powerful Angel-Knights to walk the labyrinth focusing on an image of me finding the Castle of Skulls and awakening the Purple Orb.

During their walk Michael and I sat inside the Tower of Wisdom dividing up all the materials into two leather pouches, one red, one blue. I then walked the Medicine Wheel labyrinth, wrapping the sacred cloth around the two pouches and tying everything together not to be disturbed again until I stood atop Haleakala, the volcano on Maui.

On March 29th Lady Linda and I flew to San Francisco for a five day stay to help us adjust to the time change. Linda hadn't been back to San Francisco since she split with her ex-husband Richard, twenty-five years earlier. She never had the chance to really see San Francisco, so we had fun doing all the touristy stuff - like seeing the Golden Gate Bridge, Lombard Street (the "crookedest" street in the world), Alcatraz Island and going to Fishermen's Wharf for dinner. We loved watching the talented street entertainers. The singers, and dancers were nice, but there was one guy drawing the largest audiences and he made a lot money.

The man would hide in the bushes and startle people, as they would come off of pier thirty-nine. A huge crowd of people would form across the street to watch the funny antics of the men, women and children he would scare and harass. The locals called him the "Bushwhacker." Every fifteen minutes he would cross the street and pass the hat, then return to the pier for his next set of victims. He was making a hundred dollars easy every time he passed the hat. He wouldn't let you just put in a dollar he wanted fives and tens and got it because his show was great. It was like watching candid camera on steroids.

From watching this scene, Michael gave me a vision of using a third of the land at the Good Knight Kingdom as a scare zone for haunted adventures at Halloween. What I was learning from watching the Bushwhacker would later become scare tactics that I could teach the volunteers. I had to laugh. Michael was always working, even on vacation. He never took a holiday. Always strategizing and seeing opportunities.

The next day the weather was great - eighty-five and sunny. Linda wanted to see Yosemite National Park in the Sierra Nevada Mountains. So we made reservations in one of the lodges and off we went in our short pants and tee shirts. After all, it was warm in SanFran and we were going to

Hawaii, so that's all we packed. After about five hours of driving we started hearing weathers reports on the radio, of different passes being closed because of a surprise blizzard that had hit the area. I couldn't believe it because it seemed way too warm for snow. However, as we drove up the mountain it got cold quickly and started to snow. As we entered the mountain passes what started out as a few inches on the ground turned into areas with 4' to 8' of snow piled up on both sides of the road. Then there were signs warning us of avalanches. Linda panicked and started worrying me about going back.

Lovely.

We finally made it to the lodge and it was beautiful. Because of the blizzard most of the guests had cancelled their reservations. That was great news for us. Our room was upgraded to the presidential suite and we were given a free ticket for a horse-drawn sleigh ride. Needless to say, the first thing we did was run down to the gift shop and buy some warm clothes.

I said, "Now aren't you glad I didn't listen to you and turn around?"

That night after dinner we went on the sleigh ride. We bundled up under a buffalo fur blanket and rode off along the mountain trails. The snow was still coming down and it was so romantic. The ride ended at a bonfire with about thirty other people that had gotten snowed in. We sat around the fire, listened to stories, and drank hot buttered rum drinks. It was hard to believe that just few hours earlier we had been in sunny San Francisco and that in forty-eight hours we would be swimming in the warm waters off Hawaii.

It was nice to see Linda enjoying herself. She was worried about Dawn and Meghan. Michael showed me that Spencer was becoming more dissatisfied with the marriage and that he was sleeping around. Soon Dawn would find out and all hell would break loose. I didn't want to think about that. It was a shame, but Dawn had to decide when she'd had enough. I just felt bad for Meghan.

The next day the sun came out and the roads were cleared so we toured Yosemite. It was beautiful. The mountains were covered in snow and all the waterfalls were frozen in place. It was an incredible sight to see. We hated to leave but we had to get back to San Francisco that evening because our plane left for Hawaii in the morning.

When we arrived in Maui I thought how it truly was a paradise. I spent the first two days with Linda on the beach or snorkeling by myself in the crystal-clear waters. All the fish and rock formations around the island were outstanding. I could spear a fish and the restaurant in our hotel would cook it for our dinner.

When the time came for me start searching for Sgt. Ki-Ki, I learned that he lived on the other side of the Island in a town called Hana. The next day we were on the road to Hana, a fifty-mile drive that took us three hours. It was a beautiful death-defying drive filled with dozens of hairpin turns through the jungle and along narrow coastal roads, but we made it.

Linda went shopping in Hana while I met with Sgt. Ki-Ki. He was living in a small two-bedroom house overlooking the ocean. His wife had died several years earlier and all his kids had grown and moved to the mainland. It was good to see my wise teacher again. When I told him what I was doing he was shocked that my life had taken me down that path. Although he added that he had always felt a great presence around me. "You always had a force surrounding you that I knew was positive and greater than imaginable," he said.

"Can you tell me where the Castle of Skulls is located?" I asked.

"I have never heard about it but there is a practicing Great Kahuna that lives very near here that I can take you to see. He may be able to help," he replied.

"Well Michael said you could help me. Taking me to someone who can is still on the right path!" I said. "So let's go!"

We drove for quite a while until the road ended. Ki-Ki started to walk into the thick jungle growth. It looked like it hadn't changed in a million years. I was a bit hesitant but figured he knew what he was doing.

"What about snakes?" I yelled through the bush.

Ki-Ki replied, "The mongoose on the island ate all the snakes over a hundred years ago. Don't worry."

After a short while we came upon a small shack in the middle of nowhere. An old man with long gray hair was sitting on the roof of his house dressed in a tattered red Hawaiian shirt and shorts. He spoke something in native Hawaiian and Ki-Ki answered.

The old man looked at me and blurted out, "Go away boy. You don't want to disturb the sleep of the ancestors, do you?"

I said, "No, I am here to awaken the Purple Orb in hopes of discovering the secret of the Golden Dove Egg."

Hearing that he jumped off the roof like a young boy in his teens. Running over to me and looking me directly in the eyes he said, "I'm Big Daddy Molokai, do you have what it takes to feed the Purple Orb?"

I looked at the old fellow. He had to be in his mid-eighties, about five-foot-tall and couldn't weigh more than eighty pounds soaking wet. I thought it was odd he would have the name "Big Daddy," but to each his own.

I reached into the satchel I had slung over my shoulder and pulled out the pouches wrapped in a red scarf and handed it to him. Big Daddy started to untie the leather binding, but I put my hand on his to stop him saying, "The angel who told me how to make the red and blue pouches inside said the cloth could not be unwrapped until I was standing at the highest peak of Haleakala's crater."

The old man stopped and just held the red package as if it contained a most sacred relic. He said, "It is very powerful, what you have here. You will find the House of Bones you seek in the Shadow Lands, the place that the Goddess Pele visits this time of the year."

He motioned for us to come sit on chairs around a burn barrel as he continued, "The Hawaiian Government has built a Polynesian Cultural Center in the middle of a rain forest on the site of an ancient mystical village called "Haleokeawe" which was devoted to the Goddess of Wisdom. It is said that "Haleokeawe" is a house made of coral stone blocks that contains the bones of ancient warriors who safeguard a Purple Orb that holds a great and a powerful spirit that no man can ever claim."

Big Daddy stood up quickly and said, "Why do you wish to claim it, if no man can?"

Ki-Ki and I stood up as well as I said, "I have only been sent to wake it up. I hope to send a very special woman to claim it."

He closed his eye, smiled a peaceful smile and walked away saying, "I see, my son, I see. Good luck to you on your spirit journey my friend."

Big Daddy went into his house and came out with a small coconut shell that he carved and drilled holes into. He had wrapped cord through the holes and stuck beautiful bird feathers in the cord.

He said, "Leave this on the mountain as a gift to the Goddess Pele, it will draw her to you, but be careful she doesn't throw you off her mountain when you ask for her blessings." The old man climbed back on top of his roof and waved good-bye.

I drove Ki-Ki back to his house and thanked him for his help. He said, "I have been wondering what life had left for me? I was about to give up on life and then you knocked on my door. Now I have become part of your great quest. Thank you." He smiled showing the few teeth he still had remaining. We hugged and I left.

When I finally tracked Linda down she wasn't too happy with me having left her to fend for herself for three hours. So I took her for a nice dinner and tried to forget about the dangerous ride back we'd have to take to get back to our hotel. Turns out that it was actually better driving it in the dark. We couldn't see that we were driving so close to cliffs with a hundred-foot drop.

On our last day on Maui we drove to Haleakala's crater. Michael wanted me to perform the ceremony during the last ten minutes of sunset. Haleakala means House of the Sun and it is said in legends that the Demi-God Maui stood on the highest point of the mountain to lasso the Sun to slow its passing in the sky so that humanity would have more day light.

As we drove up the winding road we passed through a thick cloud layer and the air started to get thinner. Once we broke through the clouds we parked the car and stood on the edge of a cloudy cliff. It felt like we were standing on top of the clouds. It was one of the most beautiful ethereal sights I have ever experienced. We returned to the car to finish our trek to the top.

The view from the top was otherworldly. Looking down into the island's caldera, one could gain some perspective on how the Earth was formed and of just how fragile this eggshell we live on is.

It was Charles Darwin who said "Nothing, not even the wind that blows, is so unstable as the crust of this earth, and that brings us to Haleakala a shield volcano."

I learned that a shield volcano is a broad, domed-shaped mountain with long, gently sloped sides. If you were to fly over the top of a shield volcano, it would resemble a warrior's shield, hence the name. Shield volcanoes can cover large areas and their eruptions are less explosive than the other types of volcanoes. The lava tends to pour out of the volcano's vents, creating the low layers of lava that are characteristic of these volcanoes. I also learned that the Hawaiian Islands are actually the tops of gigantic shield volcanoes rising from the ocean basin.

When we parked the car we still had another hundred feet to climb to get to the summit. It was very cold and windy, and the air was so thin it was hard to breathe. Linda had to return to the car, but I kept going. When I reached the top, I was tired and gasping for breath. I untied the red cloth and the two pouches. Michael said that the blue pouch was to be used in a sky ceremony. I tried to light some sage for purification. However, the air was too thin and there was not enough oxygen to support a flame. It was cool to see that the white-tipped wooden matches I brought would ignite but then just fizzle out without a flame. So all I could do was wait for the sun to begin to set beneath the clouds. It felt like I was standing on top of the world. I wedged Big Daddy's offering to the Goddess Pele between several rocks so that it wouldn't blow away and I felt Michael enter my body as we began. He spoke through me, but I couldn't understand anything he said.

Michael dumped the contents of the blue pouch onto the red scarf with Goddess Pele's image. Picking up the four dove feathers Michael turned to the north. The wind was blowing from the north to the south, but when he released the feather it sailed off into the north, the opposite way the wind was blowing. When he turned to the south the wind shifted and began blowing from the south, but when he let go of the feather, it flew off into the southern sky. When he turned to the east the wind shifted again, blowing from the east and when he let go of the feather it flew off against the wind toward the eastern sky. I knew then that we were actually standing at the edge of an alternate dimension, or universe. He told me, "An alternate universe, also known as alternate reality, commonly abbreviated as AU, is the occurrence of canonical facts about the setting or characterization of a particular fictional universe being explored in a non-canonical way of being."

But that didn't help me understand a thing about was happening, so I just went with it.

When Michael turned west the wind stopped completely. We held the last feather out toward the setting sun in a clenched fist. He said a few words, I believe in Latin, and then he opened the fist. There was no wind blowing from any direction. As we stood there for a moment, it was like all time had come to a complete stop. He blew on the feather and it took flight into the western sky. Michael then picked up the White Sage bundle and matches. He blew into the leaves and struck the match on a nearby boulder. This time it lit and the sage caught fire! Smudging with the sacred smoke to the four directions, he then tossed the sage wrapped wand into the caldera as it continued to smolder.

Picking up the red scarf and the remaining contents of the bundle, he tossed the four crystals into the four directions followed by the dirt and lavender from the Medicine Wheel Healing Labyrinth. We stood there watching the last light of day slip beneath the clouds in the western sky. The scene felt like we were standing on the surface of the moon. By the time I climbed down and returned to the car it was totally dark and the temperature felt as though it had dropped twenty degrees in ten minutes. Linda had turned on the heat in the car and fallen asleep. The drive back down the volcano's winding road was a long one.

On our way back to our hotel we stopped for dinner. Linda never asked me what happened on the mountaintop and that was a good thing, because she would have never believed it. I did wish she could have made it up to the top as a witness to Michael's controlling the elements, but then again, I was there and still found it hard to believe.

That ceremony took place on Wednesday April 3rd, so I only had a few days left to find the Castle of Skulls. Later that night when we went to bed Michael said, "If this thing we did today works out, you and Linda will return with a very special woman who will witness everything Linda didn't and she will leave with the spirit of the Purple Orb."

The next day we flew to the island of Oahu. We stayed in a Waikiki beachfront hotel located just a mile from Diamond Head. This island was very different from the more rural lifestyles on Maui. Honolulu, the capital of Hawaii, is nicknamed Little Tokyo for good reason. It was the perfect location for east and west to meet. I could see why Michael chose this place and the ancestors of these islands to open the gates to future wisdom. We took all day Thursday to get our bearings and to plan the places we'd like to see.

Friday morning April 5th, I woke up raring to go. I only had two days to find the Castle of Skulls and I was getting antsy. I wanted to start looking immediately, but Linda wanted to spend time on the beach and see the sights she had planned out. I relented and we went to pearl Harbor first. Michael had each of the twenty-four Angel-Knights bless and program amethyst crystals that he wanted me to leave behind. So far on the trip we hadn't left any, but when we visited Pearl Harbor we tossed twelve into the open hole on the deck of the Battleship Arizona. You could see the ship lying just below the surface of the water. The ship still weeps for the four hundred men whose remains were trapped below deck. "Tears" still appear, as a steady drip of oil makes its way to the surface of the water. It was hard to believe that this was the sight of so much death and destruction.

The following day we went to Hanauma Bay. As a diver I had heard for years that if I ever got to Oahu, I had to snorkel in its pristine waters. The bay is a two-thousand-year-old shield volcano that collapsed in the middle, forming a caldera that sits below sea level. Over time, the ocean has eroded one side, opening a mouth that lets in the saltwater and an abundance of sea life. A shallow carol reef also formed inside. It was unbelievably peaceful, like diving in a gigantic aquarium. The reef covered over two thirds of the bay, and schools of fish, from an inch to over four feet long were all around me. At the mouth of the bay we saw two humpback whales breaching. Michael had me deposit three of the Angel-Knight crystals at a special location on the right side of the bay called the Witches Brew, where there was a cauldron of swirling blue water moving in to a deep hole. He had me drop three more crystals on the left side of the bay in a location called the Toilet Bowl. It was a large blowhole. I tossed them in and the surge of water would spit them back out. I had to throw them in three times but finally they were accepted. As I stood at the Toilet Bowl I was reminded of the stories of my birth in the Chicago toilet bowl. It's funny what comes to mind when you're on a spirit quest. So I stood there also thinking about all the Native American Indians I have met, and the special spirits each possessed.

Sir Edward and Lady Linda at Waterfall

It was now April 7th, Easter Sunday, and our last day on Oahu. We finally went to book a tour to the Polynesian Cultural Center only to find out that there were several on the island. I remembered that Big Daddy said the location I was seeking was in the middle of a rainforest. The only way to get there was a bus tour that explored the island and stopped at the Cultural Center for an hour.

"Take it!" I said. It's the one."

When we joined the tour, the bus was full of some of the nastiest Caucasian Americans I have ever had the displeasure to be around. For three and a half hours all they did was bitch, moan and complain. They complained about the bus, the bus driver driving too slowly, and the bus driver driving too fast. They complained about the food at their hotel and all of the Asians on the island. Talk about ugly Americans - these folks were one for the record books.

Our driver hit all the average sight-seeing tourist stops, the overlooks and a few shops, as they obnoxious Americans continued to complain. By the time we arrived at the Polynesian Village I was ready to climb out of the window to get away from those negative people. They were steaming with an ugliness that came from the influence of dark spirits who were trying to infect Linda and me. When we got off the bus the driver said that the bus would pull out of the parking lot in one hour sharp, and that if we are not back by then, the bus will leave without us.

The village and its employees were great. They gave an amazing tour by splitting the group up and taking ten passengers each in golf-cart type trolleys. We rode all the way through the rainforest to a sacred waterfall were locals offered us a cliff diving show, but still I could see no Castle of Skulls. I asked some of the divers if there was a building in the park called Castle of Skulls or House of Bones, but each replied that they had never heard of such a place. I was getting nervous about the deadline Michael had given me. It looked like my time was going to run out.

I looked down at my watch. We only had twelve minutes to get back to the bus. I felt like such an idiot. Here I had come halfway around the world to deliver a package for Michael and it appears I would fail. We got on our golf cart and the driver started back to the bus. Linda and I got stuck all the way in the back. The front seats were taken by some of the complainers from the bus and I was not looking forward to the ride back.

All I could think was, "Great, I failed and now I have to listen to their bitching all the way back to the hotel."

The trip back to the bus took a different route than the way we came in. As we were riding through the jungle I noticed a large square looking building about fifty yards away. I yelled to the driver who was trying to describe points of interest to the passengers, who were busy bitching about sweating in a rainforest. Go figure!

I yelled to him, "What is that building up on that hill?"

He said, "It is some kind of archeological dig, but I don't know much more than that."

A wave of energy washed over me…*I found it!*

Linda must have seen the "aha" look in my eyes because she said, "Ed, don't you even think about it."

So, I sat there frozen, like a good little boy forbidden from taking part in one of the most important assignments of his life.

Michael piped up, "What are we going to do Eddie boy?"

I thought, "Why didn't you help guide me to this place when we first got here and I had more time?"

He said, "It was yours to discover, plus everything has led to this choice and this moment in time. What are you going to do?"

I told the trolley driver I had unfinished business in the jungle and to tell the tour bus driver that if I'm not back by the time he must leave, I will find another way back to my hotel. Linda's mouth was hanging open like she couldn't believe her ears.

I pushed her chin up to close her mouth, kissed her on the lips and said loud enough for the complainers to hear me, "Don't worry darling now these assholes will really have something to bitch about. I'll see you in a few minutes." I jumped off the back of the cart and went running up the hillside.

I could feel Michael enter my body as I ran and I felt like I had the strength of ten men. When we reached the building, it looked like a large square cube formed out of blocks of white coral stone. I don't remember much else about the structure. I only remember climbing onto the stone roof and looking for a hole to drop the red pouch into. There wasn't one. As I felt along the stone I found one that was loose. There was enough room for me to slide my little fingers down either side. I made several attempts to raise the stone, but it kept falling back into place. With Michael's help I finally got it out.

Michael said, "Hurray" then he spoke some words I could not understand. He told me to empty the contents of the blue pouch into the small square hole, and said something like, "I seek to release Prudentia Purpura Orbis of Sophia Deus."

There was a clap of thunder and heat lightning over my head. The force of which knocked me off the roof and on to the ground.

Michael said, "Run, get back to the bus. I must stay here." I took off running. I was on autopilot. I had no idea where I was going, but thank God something was steering me in the right direction. I came out of the jungle right behind our bus. Not missing a stride, I stepped onto the steps of the bus and apologized for my delay.

I said, "You should have left without me."

The bus driver smiled saying, "You were the last one I'd leave behind."

Nine pucker-faced complainers, including Linda were staring me down. I said in a commanding voice, "What?" Then leaning over to the bus driver, I said, "Now they really have something to bitch about."

He smiled again.

I smiled too because I did it, but boy did I pay the price. It was an interesting ride back to the hotel to say the least. Linda was upset because I embarrassed her, so she wasn't talking to me. The complainers never said a word the whole trip back because I called them on their bullshit. It was a win-win situation for me. So, with my mission accomplished I took a nap when I got back to the hotel.

The next morning, we flew back to San Francisco for a couple of days to catch back up with the time zones. Michael was still gone from my consciousness, but for some reason I was drawn to drive Linda out to the town of Carmel. It was a lovely town and I was hoping to catch a glimpse of Clint Eastwood who was the Mayor. During one of my police undercover investigations into gun running by a terrorist groups, I had an art show in a Washington D.C. nightclub owned by Billy Rice, a friend of Clint Eastwood.

When I came in one evening Rice and Eastwood were browsing through my artwork. When Billy introduced me as the artist, Clint who was also an artist said with a Dirty Harry squint and shit eating grin, "I hope you didn't give up your day job to paint this bullshit?"

To which I replied, "Just to have you squint, Clint, at my bullshit, made my day." I laughed he didn't. I moved out of the room so Clint and Billy could finish talking. A short time later I overheard a conversation where two guys were discussing whacking Rice over a deal in Atlantic City that went bad.

I called Detective Bender and the two wise guys from New Jersey were picked up leaving the club an hour later. Both were carrying pistols. The next day Rice was interviewed by Detective Bender and was warned about the hit. The warning gave Rice a chance to work things out with the New Jersey mob. From that day on I felt Billy Rice suspected me as the police informant.

Nevertheless, I always wanted to let Eastwood know what I was doing when we met, was my real day job. And that if we hadn't had that conversation, I wouldn't have been in the right place to overhear the conversation about the intended killing of his friend, which ultimately saved his life.

While in Carmel, Linda was shopping for some unusual things at a gift shop that specialized in fairies. I spotted a beautiful gold and silver crown. It was the perfect crown for the Pistis Sophia angel I placed over the Knighting Circle at the castle. In paying for it, I asked the clerk if there had been any Clint Eastwood sightings lately in town. She replied that he was normally seen having lunch at a nearby bar he owned called Hogs Breathe. I thanked her and off we went to see what adventures awaited us in this charming town.

Once in the Hogs Breathe we looked around, but no Clint. It was a really a cool bar and restaurant so we decided to stay for lunch. Halfway through our meal my attention was drawn to a young girl with long black hair who had walked in. She had a beautiful golden aura trimmed in purple. I had never seen a double aura before. She sat across the room from us. I caught her staring at us several times. I was wondering what she saw in us, as I could see her inner glow. She was obviously very mentally powerful. We sat around a little longer, but Clint never showed up so we paid our check and left.

When we arrived back at our hotel in San Francisco and unpacked the car I couldn't find the bag with the crown. Linda said, "I bet you left the crown in that restaurant." It was much too long a drive back to Carmel to retrieve the crown so I just chalked it up to the fact that the castle wasn't supposed to have it.

We spent a couple more days in California driving south to see the Hearst Castle nestled in the hills at San Simeon. It was a true American Castle. I could have put the entire Good Knight Kingdom in Mr. Hearst's Neptune swimming pool. It's amazing what you can build if you have money. It almost puts my dreams to shame.

We stayed overnight in a nearby hotel then drove further down the coast to Santa Barbara. I wanted to plant four crystals on the beach where Grandfather and the Sun Bow Walkers held their last ceremony.

I know Michael told me to put the Walkers behind me, but my thoughts often went to them. They had touched me deeply with what they had done. I could not imagine what they had gone through walking across the United States and the mental anguish they had to endure with the demons present along the way. They had to walk over mountains through freezing snow and ice storms. Then across deserts in blazing heat. And if that wasn't challenging enough, they had to do it with Tom-Tom pulling everyone down at every turn. I actually saw him as the most challenging obstacle they had to overcome on their Divine Quest to fulfill the Prophecy of the Eighth Fire.

When Linda and I arrived in Santa Barbara I asked some locals where on Eastern Beach the Sun Bow Walkers had held their last ceremony. I was lucky to find two people that were there that day. On that spot I planted four quartz crystals in tribute to their massive human accomplishment. And I wondered if any of the Spirit Fest '94 crystals they took from the castle had made it this far.

When I finished, Michael returned to my consciousness and said for me to dig two of the crystals up and to drive to the Western Gate, seventy miles away. He said, "Leave the crystals at the light house, one to honor Grandfather Commanda and one to honor Tom-Tom for being the guiding lights who touched the hearts of so many on the journey." When we arrived at the Western Gate, I learned that its true name was Point Conception. It was believed to be a Divine Gateway where Native Americans thought the souls of the dead could pass between the mortal world and the heavenly paradise.

Michael said, "Deep down inside, Grandfather knew it was not necessary to walk the remaining seventy miles since the Eastern gateway was reached on day thirty."

It was truly a divine setting. After leaving my last two crystals behind at the lighthouse all I could think was that maybe Tom-Tom was right. If Grandfather hadn't accepted Michael's dare that day the walkers might have made it all the way to the Western Gate, but we will never know.

Chapter Fifty-five

Virginia Renaissance Festival

When I arrived back to work in Maryland I was greeted at the castle gate by Sir Gregory who had great news. On Easter the four doves we took feathers from laid four eggs, two white and two a yellowish golden color. He had removed the two golden eggs and the hens were sitting on the other two. As I walked into the castle my attention was drawn to the Sophia statue mounted above the Knighting Circle in the center of the room. She was wearing the gold and silver crown I had purchased in Carmel, California.

When I asked how the crown got to the castle, Sir Gregory said, "One of my students, Tammy West who used to live in Carmel, was visiting friends last week. And get this – she was in the same restaurant as you and Linda, where you left a bag with this crown."

"Do I know this girl? Have we met?" I asked.

"No, and she didn't know it was you. Although she told me she felt the presence around you. What happened was, the waitress you had saw that you forgot the bag and ran outside with it, but you had already disappeared. Tammy saw all of this happen and then overheard the waitress telling someone about this sweet couple from Maryland and the man being the Blue Knight at a castle there. Tammy couldn't believe her ears but spoke up anyway. She told the waitress that it was all incredible because she attends classes at that same castle. One thing led to another and the waitress asked Tammy if she would bring the bag to you. Last night she was here at Master's Studies Class. She brought the crown and asked that I give it to you. I heard clearly that she should put the crown on Sophia's head."

Hearing that wild story, I said, "Tell her thank you next time you see her. It really is all about being in the right place at the right time. It was a miracle."

I wanted to meet Tammy and thank her personally, but Michael said, "Tammy's waiting is not yet full and our presence will frighten her away at this time. I am holding her in the wings."

I told Sir Gregory what Michael said and he agreed. He shared that Tammy was recently divorced and her ex-husband mentally abused her throughout the marriage. They lived in the Monterey-Carmel area for several years, but her husband made the decision that she and their two kids would move back to Baltimore. The move from California had broken Tammy's heart and she hadn't yet recovered.

Sir Gregory said he did a card reading for Tammy over a year ago. In the cards he saw that she would divorce her husband and a whole new spiritual world would open up for her. Since that reading, Tammy had divorced and was now dating a retired cop from Baltimore. Gregory went on to say that prior to her trip to California, three weeks earlier, he had done a second reading for Tammy, and the cards showed it was time for her to return to Carmel to begin her own divine quest for happiness.

"That's what sent her to recover the crown, you left behind," Michael added.

Gregory closed his conversation by telling me that Tammy and Len, the cop, were now planning to marry. I immediately got a ping in my heart and a kick to the stomach letting me know that this wasn't a wise move for Tammy. I sensed that it would be like jumping out of the frying pan and into the fire. However, that was none of my business. I had my own problems brewing.

With me out of town, April's First Wednesday Club gathering fell in the middle of the month. Michael had me construct two more black crystal talisman Transmitter Boxes, one for each of the Golden Eggs. On the back of one box was written the words, Blue Princess and the other, Purple Princess. During the gathering Michael presented the box marked Blue Princess to Lady Mary-Uriel for safekeeping. He said, "The doves are nesting on the white eggs and it appears the Angel-Knights are nesting as well."

While we were gone many knights seemed to have paired up. Irish Kevin had fallen to the seductive powers of Lady Bonnie. Lady Justine was with Sir Bolton, a new knight with Hebrew teachings, who had come forward. The two Lady Barbaras were with Sir Thomas and Sir Anton respectively. Plus four other Good Knight volunteers were all talking about getting married. I couldn't believe what had come over the knighthood, but I also couldn't fight love, or hormones.

Then there was Lady Mary and Sir Robert; the only two that I saw who would last if they got married. However, Sir Robert still had a lot of maturing to do before that would work. I knew from being married to Linda that it is hard to straddle the two worlds of Angel and Knight. I felt like these knights were heading for disaster.

Michael pointed at Lady Justine saying, "If you continue on this course, you are will bring forth the Princess of the Northern Lights. Justine's eyes widened as Sir Bolton's jaw dropped. He went on to say, "Lady Dawn will bear the Princess of the Eastern Sunrise."

Turning to Lady Mary he said, "You will decide the legacy of your child or children. God has sent two golden eggs one will produce a Princess of the Southern Cross and the other will be the Princess of the Western Sunset." I was shocked to hear that my daughter Dawn played any role, since she was hardly ever around. Plus Spencer's influence on Meghan had made her too weak to fill the position as the M.V. child Michael was sent to find.

On April 27th Dawn and Meghan showed up at our house with all of their clothes. Spencer had gotten mad because Dawn couldn't borrow any more money from Hester or us, so he had kicked them out of the house. She was worried that he was seeing another woman. I told her that could be the best thing for her future and that she needed to move on with her life. Dawn tried for weeks to call, but Spencer wouldn't answer the phone. We registered Meghan in elementary school and Dawn came with me to work. Now what Michael said months earlier was starting to make sense, but with Dawn away from Spencer I couldn't understand how she was going to conceive a child. Michael revealed to me that Dawn and Lady Justine were already carrying the children, but they just didn't know it.

Dawn really took to working at the castle. She helped Lady Mary with the accounting, answered the phones and worked with Sir Robert on small construction projects. Dawn spoke with friends in Pennsylvania who told her that Spencer was seeing another women. She was devastated and wanted to go home and have it out with him, but I saw her doing something she would regret. So I asked Sir Robert if there was any chance that Sir Johnny could join us at the Virginia Renaissance Festival in May to help keep Dawn's mind off of Spencer and the other woman. I reminded Sir Robert that Johnny owed me one. I knew that Johnny's "Don Juan" demeanor would feed Dawn's ego. They always had fun and joked around whenever we had a party. When Robert called him, Sir Johnny jumped at the chance to serve and attend a new festival.

Once Johnny arrived, I sat down with both knights for a talk. Dawn was at a low point and needed to be watched, because the first guy who gave her some attention now would sweep her off her feet. I told Johnny and Robert to pay attention to her and build her confidence whenever they saw the opportunity to do so. However, I strongly reminded them that she was a married woman, so their efforts should go no further than a platonic relationship. They both agreed this was just a "rescue" mission and they understood completely.

On May 9th the Virginia Renaissance Festival began. Sir Robert, Lady Mary, Sir Johnny, Lady Dawn, Sir Gregory, Lady Justine, Lady Linda and I were the knights who were selected to attend from the volunteers available. We rented a large blue van and off we went to Burke, Virginia. It was a very long ride. When we arrived, Lady Justine shared her good news. Michael was right again! She was pregnant and the baby would be due in September.

I was so happy for her. She had often talked about wanting a child, but I was worried about her choice of husbands. Sir Bolton was a bit of a spoiled Jewish rich kid from upstate New York. He was a party guy, very flirtatious, and not the marrying kind. Michael told me everything would work itself out and that Lady Justine would find the happiness she sought.

After a round of congratulations, we all pitched in and set up a small Good Knight Encampment at the Virginia Festival, which was a beautiful medieval theme park. In the center of the village was a large lake with a huge pirate ship. It seemed to be a blend between knight and pirate shows. We set up our tent, props, our angelic knighting circle and Linda's ceramics for sale. The patrons were hungry for the fairies, angels, dragons and fairy crowns that Linda created. My wooden swords were also a big hit. We kept a line at our knighting circle of children all day. The parents just loved that their children were receiving a lesson that would keep them safe. And everyone loved taking a magical adventure tour through the forest next to our camp where I placed some of our fairy scenes and the Sword and Anvil puzzle. All was going well and we met some wonderful children and their families.

Then it happened. Ever hear of the movie *Where Angels Go Trouble Follows*? Well it must have been written about us, because right after lunchtime that first day someone from management dropped by the camp to tell us we couldn't sell any of our products. He said it conflicted with the other vendors who were paying for their space.

I explained to management, "You invited us to come to the festival as an 'act' on your schedule. Since you are not paying us as entertainment, the charity has to generate some revenue and furthermore, we were given the okay to sell all of the merchandise connected to the *Good Knight Story* fairytale."

While the management was meeting on the subject I noticed several people from the Maryland Renaissance Festival secretly trying to take photographs of our camp and volunteers. I went over to pose for their cameras and invited them to come over to our camp and take all the pictures they wanted.

One girl told me, "You know anyone one caught working at this festival isn't going to be invited back to Maryland's festival."

"We are a charity. This is the Child Safety Awareness Outreach Program that we do at schools and festivals all over Maryland, Virginia and Washington D.C. We will go anywhere we are needed," I replied.

"The new management said that there would be no exceptions. Just so you know," she relayed as she and her crew walked away - not very pleased with us.

I sent Sir Johnny and Dawn out to see if they could spot any other "outlaws." I was surprised to learn that quite a few of the actors from the Maryland festival were there in costumes, but not working. When they came by our camp to say hello, they told me they were fired on the spot just for being at the festival in costumes.

The Virginia festival management came back with the decision that we couldn't sell any of our products. They welcomed us to rent the space; it was six hundred dollars a day. I told them that we would finish out the day, but there was no benefit for the volunteers to work the festival for free and that we didn't even have six hundred dollars' worth of items in our inventory.

They asked us about why, as volunteers, we had to make money. I explained that normally schools and festivals pat a fee to the charity for us to do the program, to cover the operating expenses and giveaway of materials. We, as the charity's performers never got paid - that's the volunteer part of the equation. I explained that all of the money brought in went straight to the outreach fund, to allow us to continue to present the program. And that as a matter of fact, no one in the organization was paid for their time. That's how the charity stayed in business. I added that, just because an organization is a charity, doesn't mean everything is free - it takes money to operate the business. Money has to come from somewhere to keep the lights on, print our safety materials, provide props, etc. For some reason, this group and many others thought that as a charity we were supposed to give materials and programs away. That's all well and good if we had a grant to paid for them, or they were sponsored by an individual. Heck, just look at the way PBS uses materials to get high dollar donations. The folks' mind-set at the festival was just plain crazy.

As we were closing up the camp it was decided we would not come back. We had already discussed the festival being too far away from our home base to make it work, so it all turned out well.

One good thing that came out of the day was that Dawn found the inner strength and made up her mind. She felt good about herself and was having fun that day. She was tired of putting up with Spencer's crap and so she decided to file for divorce. It was bittersweet. It is always sad to see someone's marriage breakup, but I was hopeful about this new start for Dawn and Meghan.

In the weeks after the Virginia RenFest event, Lady Bonnie and I were invited back on the Jim Bohannan's radio talk show. Throughout the years we have seen the ebb and flow of energy around our work. When we are shut down in one place, we soar in another. When the producer called to have us on, he told Lady Bonnie that Sir Jimbo wanted to keep his promise to make us a special feature on his radio program two times a year - and more when there was a headline abduction case somewhere in the nation.

The night we went on was interesting. One of the listeners, Margret Davies, was a producer for the Oprah Winfrey Show in Chicago. She called into the show to ask a question, but didn't get chosen to talk right away. So she was hanging out on the line, waiting while the Jim interviewed me.

During our interview Jim asked me to describe what happened to me as a child when I drowned in Florida, and afterwards the feeling of the presence of an angel in my life. I told the audience the angel had been guiding me to protect children as a youth and that it was important to the angel that I become a police officer so that I could learn how to prevent child abductions. I then talked about the abduction of Adam Walsh and the information I uncovered on Otis Toole. I went over the *ABC'S of Safety* and said that it was believed that the man who abducted Adam used the "B-Bribe Trick" to lure him out of the Sears Department Store in Hollywood, Florida. I ended by saying that the angel told me the time had come to put all that I had learned in my life into a direction that would help children. I told them about how I took an early retirement from the police department, withdrew all my pension funds, and created the non-profit with two friends from a federal task force that I had served on - Admiral Elmo Zumwalt and Special Agent Dennis McCarthy.

Jim then asked me to talk about being guided to write *A Good Knight Story*, the fairytale that then took on a life of its own. I shared how the books were being used by teachers in schools to prevent abductions all over the country. And that from that, how The Good Knight Network started receiving requests for the Blue Knight to go to schools and knight the children, so that they could go out and protect other children, just as they did in the fairytale.

When we went to commercial break, Margret Davies was still on the line. She asked the producer to open the studio line so that she could talk to me. She asked if we could explore producing a documentary about what the Good Knight Child Empowerment Network does to protect children. She also said that she and Oprah were firm believers in the influence that angels have on humans. I told her that we would welcome any and all help in getting our message out.

Two days later it had all been arranged - boy does Hollywood move fast! We blocked out the rest of the week for the Margret and her production crew to film us. This meant coordinating with several school administrations for programs that were already scheduled. They had to go into overdrive to get filming permissions and photo releases for all of the students who would be involved.

Chapter Fifty-six

Eyes of a Demon

During the research and scouting for the documentary filming, Margret Davies, the producer, said that she found an old stone watchtower in Washington, DC that looked like a castle. She wanted to get some shots there for the piece about the Blue Knight with some children.

Lady Bonnie-Gabriel contacted parents of the children who had appeared in the *ABC's of Safety* video to see if they wanted to participate - meeting us at the location the next day. Everyone signed on and the kids were super excited.

The kids were so cute. They all acted like they were making a movie. After about an hour of filming, a U.S. Park Police Officer pulled up. He watched us for a while then got out of his car asking if we had a permit to film on federal property. The producer said no. I immediately noticed something dark and sinister come over the officer. It was the strangest thing. I could see in my mind's eye black orbs, like hornets, buzzing around his head.

When the officer found out there was no permit he announced that he was arresting us and seizing the all production equipment as evidence. It was obvious that a very dark force was at work taking over his mind and body. The darkness was obviously trying to stop the documentary on the Good Knights from being made and it was working through this man. I was now seeing first-hand how negative spirits, which are trapped in this dimension, can influence humans.

Some of the children became frightened and started to cry. I could feel Michael slipping into my body just about the same time I saw the darkness slipping into the officer. We were both being positioned - set up to demonstrate a clash between a Son of Light and one of Darkness. I was reminded of what the hierophant had said to me about how the darkness spreads. Now that I was seeing it with my own eyes and I was ready. The only problem was this guy had authority - and a gun.

He ordered, "Everyone sit on the curb!"

He went to his car. We all heard him call for back up, juvenile services and a police wagon to transport his "prisoners." The situation was getting out of control. I could not believe what an ass this cop had become. He was dealing with impressionable children that would now be marked for life by his behaviors.

Michael reached into the black leather pouch on my belt and pulled out my badge and police identification saying, "Sergeant can I speak to you for a minute?" He got out of his car and we walked across the street.

Michael said, "I'm a retired D.C. police officer who established a charity that empowers youth to avoid crime, violence and victimization."

The cop's eyes were black with anger. The man looked possessed and erupted saying, "I don't care who you are. You're breaking the law."

Michael put one hand on the officers shoulder and one on his heart saying, "These people are filming a short news piece for the Oprah Winfrey Show about what the charity does to help prevent crime. They are not filming a movie. We didn't know we needed a permit to film a news piece. Would you please give us a break? These kids are scared to death."

I could immediately see the darkness lifting from the man and his eyes sparkled blue again. He shook his head and smiled saying, "Uh, excuse me, I've got something else I must attend to." With that the officer walked back to his vehicle and drove away.

When I walked back over to the film crew Margret wanted to know what was said to calm the irate officer down. "I saw what you did, but what did you say?"

Michael replied, "We all have our demons. He was like most people caught in a blind rage, which is just an open door for other dark forces to enter and influence the mind. He just needed someone who cared enough to switch his heart light back on."

When Margret returned to Chicago she said that she was going to talk to Oprah's people about having me tell my story of working with Archangel Michael on Oprah's Angel Network. "This is all so fascinating and I wouldn't have believed it if I hadn't seen it with my own eyes. You touched that man's heart and he transformed immediately, like you broke a spell or something," she said.

No sooner did Margaret return to Chicago than I received a call from a woman who worked with the network. She wanted me to tell her my story.

"Where do I begin? It's a long one but in a nutshell---"

I told her about the promise my father made to Angel Michael if he would help him escape as a POW, my drowning as a child, the beautiful celestial woman who asked if I would return to life, the angel's dream of the life I could live if I returned, the angel starting to communicate with the buzzing in my ears, not being able to see or hear the angel, but in my mind knowing exactly what he said and what he looked like. I gave her a brief history of the Native American Indian takeover of the BIA and Russell Means having to survive, Spirit Fest '94, the writing of *A Good Knight Story*, the book saving lives, and me bringing the book to life by creating the Angel's Blue Armor.

When I started to tell her about Master Daniel Watson having a vision where Archangel Michael told him to fashion a special Sword of Swords she stopped me.

She said, "Your story isn't something we would be interested in." And she hung up.

I don't know what I said that turned her off or if everything I said turned her off, but it was obvious that my manifestation of Angel Michael wasn't hers. Plus, when I look back on my life it does seem pretty impossible to believe. It's more like a dream than reality. I thought, maybe the angel is still dreaming and I'm just caught up in that dream?

The very next day I received a call from Margret. She said that the decision makers who reviewed her piece at the Oprah Show didn't think it was right for the show. "What did you say to the woman who called?

I told her, "I just told her some of the things that happened in my life and she abruptly said she wasn't interested in that kind of story. Then hung up. Do you recall the cop we met, who seemed possessed all of a sudden? He was an example of how the forces of darkness will stop at nothing to keep the work of the Good Knight Network silenced. Thank you for all your hard work and consideration. Unfortunately, it looks like the darkness won this time."

She said that she wasn't giving up on the feature. And that if she hadn't seen the evil come over that out of control cop that day, she might think I was crazy too. She said she had decided to take the film right to Oprah. She felt that my story was so much more believable than many of the other stories Oprah producers had featured.

We didn't hear anything from Margaret for a few weeks, but one day out of the blue she showed up at the castle. She told us that she had quit working for the Oprah Show and taken a job with America's Most Wanted. Since she owned the footage she took of us, she was re-editing the film for John Walsh. She had taken out any reference to angels and the producers liked it. The piece had been accepted and scheduled to air at the end of June.

Chapter Fifty-seven

America's Most Wanted

The month of June was exceptionally hot and humid that year. I already sweat just standing still, so any movement I needed to make outside was killing me, and Robert and I were outside working on structures the majority of the day. Needless to say, water breaks were constant. On one of the breaks we took to go inside to cool off, I overheard Lady Bonnie talking to Margaret on the phone. She had called to say that America's Most Wanted was hosting an event at the Mall across from the U.S. Capitol, in late June. The event was to honor the tipsters who had helped in the apprehension of wanted fugitives since the show began. They wanted to feature the Good Knight Network at the event because the piece they were doing on our work was scheduled to air on the tipsters show the following week.

Bonnie held the phone out and asked me, "Do you want to do it?"

"Is the Pope Catholic? Of course, tell them yes," I replied.

Over ten years earlier Michael had told me that John Walsh and I would cross paths and I was to present him with a special sword. With that said, I was faced with the choice of giving him one of the Angel Swords from Brother Daniel or one of the swords that Sir Robert-Cassiel had forged.

On the day of the event it was one hundred and five degrees. It was so hot and humid that the man who was supposed to wear the McGruff, the Crime-Fighting Dog costume, refused to put it on. It was a day full of political speeches and self-indulgent pats on the back for lawmakers. The event had very little to do with honoring the tipsters. They had created the event to celebrate.

In preparation for the event, I brought two swords with me. I figured I would make up my mind about which one to present after getting a read on John Walsh. It wasn't a hard decision at all. Here I was in that incredible heat, strapped into Michael's Armor, and doing our program every 45 minutes for three straight hours in the blazing hot sun for a new audience each rotation. And then I heard John Walsh make comment aimed at me from the podium in front of hundreds of spectators, saying, "You better watch out, because you could be arrested for dressing like that."

I just smiled and waved. For some reason he really thought that line was funny because he repeated it several times that day to the audience, Senators and FBI agents. It seemed he had an instant dislike for me.

The true test was for me of course. Was I going to take his silly comments personally and say, "Screw it. I'm not giving that jerk a sword." Or would I realize that it wasn't about me at all? Decisions, decisions, decisions!

It was obvious to me that I was threatening John Walsh's ego, because that is normally when the bully comes out in someone. Bullies typically react to others with violence or a passive aggressive put downs. At least he didn't call me eccentric. Michael's armor was a constant reminder for me not to be so thin-skinned. I did wonder though, why he didn't have a problem with a guy in a dog costume, but he did with the image of a knight. My final decision was to take a deep breath and forge on.

When the time came for the presentation of the sword I chose to give him the one forged by Sir Robert. On camera Michael knighted John Walsh saying, "I dub thee Sir John Walsh, an Angel-Knight, and I present you with the first sword, The Sword of Adam." Referring to it as being the sword of his son.

When I passed John Walsh the sword, I knew that Angel Michael had placed the spirit of Adam Walsh on the tip of its blade, but I dared not tell John. I could only hope that he wouldn't just stick the Sword of Adam in some dark closet. But a gift is a gift, and what John chose to do with it was up to him. I had done my part.

The Blue Knight and John Walsh

Later that day, Margret came up to me and apologized for the wise cracks John Walsh had made about me. Apparently, there were several more things he said that I didn't hear. She also said that Walsh was now against airing the documentary on the Blue Knight, saying that it wasn't in keeping with the integrity of the show. He was the only one who had a problem with it though. She went on to say that she fought for us, feeling that the nation needed to know what great work we were doing on behalf of children and families.

"Please don't apologize for something you had no control over. It was all actually perfect. John's rudeness helped me decide which sword to give him," I said.

"You know that if the cop had seized all of our equipment and arrested us that day, this piece would not have happened," she said.

I nodded my head then Michael replied, "I see your understanding has grown. You now know that there is more going on here than meets the eye. There are unseen forces of light and darkness on a collision course in this world. You have seen how quickly the darkness will attack the light through any available insecure human vessel. What we are doing is not supposed to happen, yet it is happening. However, the darkness is doing everything in its power to discredit and stop us. But we have already won because of your persistence and we now are going to reach millions." He bent down, kissed Margret's hand and said, "You are my hero."

When the America's Most Wanted piece aired later that month, the charity's phones started ringing off the hook. There was renewed interest in the books, videos and programs. We were receiving requests for programs all over the country, but mostly in areas where children had already been abducted. It was sad that people would call us in after a child had been snatched, but rarely were we called in as a prevention measure. Michael's intention was to have this program be a proactive approach to help safeguard the children.

I later had the realization that the demon agenda during the filming and decision-making process to include the piece, was to tweak John Walsh's ego, hoping that I would lash out in return. If I had done so it would have given Walsh the excuse he needed to cancel the scheduled airing of our segment on his show. I was so glad I didn't let my demons rule me that day.

A few nights after my father saw America's Most Wanted show he called me. "Ed, I had a dream. Archangel Michael came to me and said, 'It's time for the prodigal son to return home.' In the dream Michael was flying over a classroom full of children and you were in blue armor teaching the children the *ABC's of Safety*. Michael told me to talk to my bishop about the program. What should I do?" he asked.

I told my dad, "When we are asleep, our brain is at rest, but our mind is wide-awake, so that's when angels can speak to us without distraction. Our brain is part of our physical body and like a computer that stores information, but our mind is the essence of our soul or spirit. When we are awake our minds are normally too distracted by all of our other senses to hear heavenly thought. You just heard well Dad."

"Well, I called the Pastor at St. Michael's Academy in Chicago about bringing the Good Knight Child Safety Awareness Program to town. I told him I wanted to sponsor the school," Dad told me.

"Dad please, we will take care of it," I told him. "I will make a program happen out there when we come to visit you. I am sure something will come up that will fall right in line with Chicago!"

At the time my father was seventy-five. He was working for minimum wage at McDonalds as a senior citizen greeter and handyman. The cost to bring the program and materials to that school would have been more than he made in a month, but again he insisted. I listened, but of course I was not going to let that happen.

Chapter Fifty-eight

Walking the Halls of Congress

After all the dust started to settle from the notoriety we received as a result of the *America's Most Wanted* piece I was asked to put my diplomat hat on. That's a pretty funny thought though, because I am far from diplomatic most of the time. I keep it real and true, and if people don't like it, I'm okay with that.

Despite my concerns, Lady Justine had set appointments for me to meet with Congressmen and Senators to gain support for a bill to mandate that the *ABC's of Safety* be taught in every elementary school in the country.

"You are going to trust me to talk to these people? You realize I will say what Michael needs said," I told her.

"Oh, I am going with you of course and so is Bonnie. We will help keep you in check," Lady Justine said.

"Keep me in check? Are you feeling okay? How long have you known me?" I asked as I laughed and walked away.

The morning of the first round of appointments Linda had me wear my best dark blue suit. As we were all piling in the car, Michael stopped me. "You can't wear that. Tell Sir Robert to meet you at your trailer," he said.

I looked at the girls and said, "I forgot something in my trailer." I grabbed Sir Robert on my way up and Michael had me suit up in the armor.

The looks on the girls' faces when I returned in the armor was priceless, but neither of them said a word to me. They actually did know better, because they had felt Michael's energy before when he was on a mission, and this was certainly one of those times.

It was an interesting experience walking the halls of the U.S. Congress in Michael's Armor, seeking support for the legislation mandating that the ABC's of Safety be taught in every elementary school in the country. Some of our meetings saddened me, not because of the reaction to the armor, but because of the total disregard for children and their safety. For some it simply didn't matter. Officials like Edward Kennedy, Joe Kennedy and Joe Biden were strong supporters of the concept and loved the whole knighthood idea and child-mentoring strategy. And then there were many others who just saw me as an eccentric fool.

I had to explain why I wore the armor several times. I told them that after I wrote the book the children requested for me to appear in the armor to bring the book to life. I went on to say that the armor was just used to grab the children's attention, which is the most important part of any lecture. However, many of the legislatures were closed-minded and couldn't get past the unorthodox nature of what I was doing to protect children.

I heard more than once, "I'd like to help, but son, children don't vote."

That one comment spoke volumes for me about the people we elect to represent us. It also fueled my resolve to persevere.

Many times, I was described as eccentric. It was often said with a laugh, as if it was some sort of compliment, but I knew it was just a polite way of saying that they thought I was crazy. I wasn't tiring of being called that, I was only getting tired by people hiding their true thoughts behind the word. I believe you should say what you want to say.

It made me think about how one word could have so many meanings, both positive and the negative at the same time. As a compliment it could mean that I was extraordinary, uncommon or unconventional. Who wouldn't want to be seen that way? But, as a put down it could mean they saw me as bizarre, freakish, weird, abnormal, or peculiar. People do like to hide behind their words. This made it clear to me that this was the kind of bullshit the Indian who gave me the buffalo skin was talking about.

All in all, I felt the effort we put forth at the meetings in D.C. was very positive and promising. We made great contacts and received good leads on new partnerships. Only time would tell if our efforts went anywhere on behalf of the bill's sake.

The following week I appeared before the Maryland assembly in Annapolis in full regalia as well. I looked out over the crowd and yes, again there was some disbelief at the way I was dressed. People just didn't know how to take it. Was I poking fun and trying to make a mockery of the legislature? Or was I crazy? Or just plain damn well what was I? I was beginning to understand more of what my old partner, Denny McCarthy, must have been going through when he voiced his objections to me wearing the armor in public.

One senator on the panel opened his mic and asked, "What are you doing wearing a costume here? Have you no respect for us and your state?"

Michael spoke very clearly to me, "Just take a breath and look at him calmly while you listen to me. Here is your creed to live by and don't you ever forget it:

I dare to be a Good Knight
I dare to stand alone.
I dare to have a purpose bold,
And dare to make it known.
Honor, respect and courage,
Together are my creed.
As a humble peaceful warrior
I am sure to succeed!"

Thanks Michael! I needed that.

After hearing the creed and taking a deep breath, I spoke. "If I came dressed as a farmer or fishermen there would be no weird looks at me today." I pointed to the Great Seal of Maryland that was painted on the wall of the hearing chamber and continued, "One side of our state's seal depicts a farmer and fisherman standing on either side of a Coat of Arms, But if you turn the Great Seal of Maryland over to its front, you will see the portrait of a knight in bluish silver armor on a horse, holding a sword up high, protecting the farmer, fisherman and their families." My point must have been well taken because I actually received a standing ovation.

I continued, "Life is art, just like that painting of the Great Seal. And with my life I intend to paint a masterpiece as I continue my quest to empower Maryland's youth. I wish you could see me in that right light, but what's really important is how the children see me."

Michael continued through me, "The way I see it, Marylanders have choices. They can play it safe and be common, ordinary, uninspired folk, quite the opposite of the word 'eccentric.' But the path that my life has taken is different. You see, I've been to the crime scenes of abused and murdered children. I know that the abuse could have been avoided if the children had known the signs that are there to warn them they are in the presence of a child sexual predator. This Marylander has put down his fishing pole and shovel, preferring to pick up the sword of our forefathers. I feel that I have a divine obligation to protect children from the evil predators that are preying upon their innocence, and upon our ignorance."

I paused, seeing many blank faces in the audience, and then continued. "Don't you think we all have that obligation to protect the little ones?" I let them know that I was abused when I was a child and that swore at that time, I would grow up and try to prevent the same from happening to other children.

I outlined how the Good Knight Network was providing Child Safety Awareness Programs to all the elementary schools in Prince Georges County, but that it wasn't not enough. I said that I believed all Maryland County school systems needed to adopt the program and become a positive model for the rest of the United States as well. The charity's goal was to start with Maryland, and then go state by state until we had created a blanket of protection for all of America's children.

Now that I had finished all my meetings with lawmakers, it was time to set an agenda for the rest of summer and the fall. At our Monday meeting, Sir Gregory told us he had received a call from the Maryland Renaissance Festival management. They were calling to inform us that they would in fact be inviting us to return to their festival that year, but that our site would be moved again. This time down to the bottom of the hill in the wet area that I rejected two years earlier. They also informed us that we could no longer sell any of our items since our space was being donated. The festival was a juried venue for vendors and artisans, who had say in what others could do and who could get in. The vendors were still complaining about the charity taking money away from their sales.

"They said the Blue Knight is the most loved and most hated character at the festival. King Henry loves you. Queen Ann Bolyn hates you. The patrons love you; the vendors hate you," Sir Gregory relayed.

"Wow, what to do? It makes me sick. Don't call them back yet. I want to think about it," I told him.

When I got home I told Lady Linda about what the Festival representative said. Linda asked, "Can't we just stop fighting the negativity at the festival? This is ridiculous. Life's too short for all the bull crap and bad will. I don't understand why we seem to always be under attack."

"I am tired of all the turmoil as well. The trouble is we don't fit in. Nobody can figure out our motive, so that leads them to believe we must be bad people. For the life of them they can't believe one person, let alone a whole group, could care so much about an issue that we volunteer our time, blood, sweat, and tears. They can't fathom it's possible that we are people who are so benevolent," I replied.

On my ride in the next day, Michael said that we should focus on building the Good Knight Kingdom, because we didn't know how long we would have the headquarters museum and offices. When I arrived at the castle, I told Sir Gregory to let the festival know we could not move again because we didn't have the volunteer staff to rebuild, and we would send a crew of volunteers down to remove all of our building materials from the former site. We could definitely use the lumber at the Good Knight Kingdom in Beltsville.

Michael emphasized to me that this was just a chapter closing, and that there was nothing more we could learn from the festival, so we had to move on.

It must have been a month of closures as far as planetary alignments go, because that day I found out that Spencer was trying to get back together with Dawn. Apparently, his relationship with his girlfriend fell apart. For a guy who wouldn't return a call from his wife for months, now he was on the phone begging for her to come back to him. It only took a week of sweet talk, promising to be a better person, and Dawn and Meghan went back home. I told her he would promise anything, but once she went back to him he would return to the same selfish person he always was. I felt bad for Dawn. She was a lot like Linda, not wanting to give up on an abusive husband.

Linda's first husband was a nice enough person, but when he drank he got very nasty. He had a terrible childhood and always took it out on Linda. One evening he tried throwing Linda out of his moving car on Suitland Parkway. The next day Michael made him an offer he couldn't refuse and he never bothered her again. I just hoped that Spencer wouldn't lead Dawn down the same suicidal path Linda went down. Michael and I wouldn't be around to rescue her.

During one of Angel Michael's presentations to the knights, Sir Bolton asked, "How do we know when we are talking to Sir Edward and when we are talking to Archangel Michael?"

I answered, "You can normally tell by the answer."

Sir Gregory said, "I can tell because Sir Edward's eyes get bright blue when Michael is speaking. The same way as when Sir Edward channels each of the Seven Celestial Sisters."

Just then Michael started to speak, "I am not Sir Edward and Sir Edward is not me, but together we are the Blue Knight. When we are wearing the blue armor always consider yourself talking to me. You'll figure it out from there."

Afterwards, Sir Bolton came to me and said that he and Lady Justine wanted to get married and they wanted my blessings since I was the First Knight of the Order. I quickly gave my blessings. Who was I to stand in the way of true love; especially when a child was on the way?

I said, "It is true love, right?"

Sir Bolton then asked, "Will the Blue Knight marry us in a ceremony at the castle?"

Michael refused to comment instead he told me to do a card reading for Sir Bolton, which he accepted.

"Meet me here tomorrow and I will do the reading," I told Bolton.

The next day I had him walk the labyrinth. When he was finished I sat down with him in the Tower of Wisdom for the reading. He shuffled and cut the cards, then handed them to me. The first two cards out were upside down Jokers. That is a sign of split or multiple personalities. The next two header cards were the Jack of Clubs and Queen of Clubs.

I said, "This is weird, the cards say that you can't make up your mind if you prefer men or women is that true?"

He said, "I've decided I'm straight."

He revealed that he told Lady Justine that he used to be gay, but decided the gay life style wasn't for him and he wanted to do the right thing by her for the baby. I continued to turn the cards, but they warned me not to perform the wedding ceremony nor should the wedding be held at the castle. Then the cards went blank and stopped talking completely. I guess there were some things about Sir Bolton's past I was not to see.

"The cards have stopped talking. The energy needs to rest. We will address this later," I said.

Later that day after Sir Bolton left, I sat down with Lady Justine to talk. She confirmed that she and Sir Bolton had spoken about his sexuality. I told her the warning I got from his cards and that from my perspective he could switch back to being gay just as fast as he turned straight. I also said, I see no problem with that fact, but that she needed to be aware of it and accept him the way he is, or not. I told her that Michael said that the Blue Knight couldn't marry them, but no one would stand in their way if they still wanted to get married. That evening when I discussed the matter with Lady Linda, without the personal particulars, she quickly said, "Then let's have the wedding here."

Lady Linda loved Sir Bolton. He was a very handsome and flamboyant man who looked a lot like a dark-haired Brad Pitt; plus he was always flirting with her. Linda always dreamed of having a southern mansion and hosting a big wedding for Dawn, but that never happened. This would give Linda the chance to throw her big wedding party. I presented the offer to Lady Justine and Sir Bolton and they loved the idea. Since they were both Jewish I recommended the Rabbi that spoke at Spirit Fest '94 perform the wedding ceremony.

It was settled! Linda and I would host a Jewish wedding at our house on the Fourth of July. I must say Lady Linda outdid herself with the food and decorations. Lady Mary had all the female Angel-Knights bring a dish and the guys supplied the beer, wine and champagne. We moved everything out of my home office and decorated it like a wedding chapel.

I was so happy for Lady Justine, she had worked so hard for the charity over the years and I knew she was having a difficult time living in the white house with Mary, Bonnie and Sir Gregory. Especially since Lady Bonnie had stolen her old boyfriend Irish Kevin and had moved him into the house, causing even more tension with everyone.

Since it was the Fourth of July we ended the evening by shooting off the rest of the fireworks that Irish Kevin had brought me during our first house party in January. I reminded everyone that Michael had said that this was the year our first Goddaughter would be born and that Lady Justine was carrying that little bundle of joy with her tonight.

Sir Bolton spoke up and revealed, "Lady Justine had a sonogram two days ago. Michael was wrong, the child is a boy." A hush fell over everyone standing on our back deck overlooking the water.

I grabbed the grand finale fireworks, "Cake of Rockets," to lift everyone's spirits again.

Before lighting the fuse, I, Sir Edward, said, "I may not always be right, but I am never wrong." I bent down to light the fuse and then Michael stood me back up saying, "Plus we still have a few months to change a *he* to a *she*." Everyone laughed.

It was a beautiful display of sparkling lights and a great way to end the wedding celebration.

Chapter Fifty-nine

Lancelot and Guinevere

Lady Justine wasn't the only one having trouble at the White House. Lady Mary and Sir Robert were having a rough time as well. She was torn with her position as the Blue Princess and having a relationship beyond Robert being her bodyguard. Michael had setup the same scenario with them as was written about in Arthurian legend between Sir Lancelot and Lady Guinevere. When Lady Mary accepted the golden egg in the blue talisman crystal box, Michael also gave her a special ring called the Eye of Oden. The ring also represented the first of the four rings of power. The Ring of Air was very old, white gold with a blue sapphire and belonged to my great-great grandmother. Wearing the Ring of Air set Mary apart from all others in the order. Michael said that the time would come when the Rings of Water, Fire and Earth would find their way into the order as well.

Lady Mary came to me and said that Sir Robert was pulling on her heart strings because he wanted her to give him more than she had to offer. I told her that if he couldn't serve her without having her, that perhaps I should have him return to Michigan.

I could see that this was a true test of love for her. Would she give in to her physical emotions or rise above her earthly consciousness and fulfill whatever her divine spiritual birthright was to be?

It was her choice to make. I told her that sometimes God's gift of free will feels like more of a curse, but that I felt it was given so that one couldn't say they were manipulated into doing something they didn't want to do. It's all about choice and choice is all about the fairytale. Again, I reminded her that the Angel-Knights were an order, not a cult. No one is going to tell anyone they must do something against their will. The choice was hers.

Sir Robert had spent the year so far thinking that he was losing Mary. One day while I was restructuring the labyrinth from a circle shape to that of a heart, when Sir Robert came to me. He confessed that he didn't know what to do about Lady Mary. I told him that he couldn't lose someone he didn't have, and that as long as she wore the Eye of Oden, he would never have her completely. I explained that he was breaking her heart and he should seriously consider returning to Michigan for a while.

I told him that with him gone, she might decide she wanted to be with him, but as long as he stayed she would be torn. That's just her nature. I could see in his eyes though, that he thought I was trying to trick him into leaving. I reminded him that we were all being tested and that the last thing I wanted was to lose him. I tried to tell him how important he was to the future, but he wasn't listening. He began to cry. I told him that I would be proud to have a son like him and that I was looking out for his best interests. I only wanted him to have a wife that wasn't going to be overbearing like his mother.

I promised Michael that I wouldn't interfere. And I knew I would probably regret one day helping Sir Robert. I held him like I had wished my father could have held me all those years we were apart. His sorrow was great. So great in fact, that I gave in and decided to give him the secret to winning Lady Mary's heart.

Holding Sir Robert, I said, "You probably won't understand this, but please try. If you had Lady Mary now, she would just become another dominant mean-spirited woman in your life, like your mother and sister. If you leave now, revisit the lessons in the Book of Wisdom. Then when you return in several months more confident, you will have what she needs to see in you. Absence truly does make the heart grow fonder, and that's what she needs to make up her mind. Plus, she will have matured, finding a greater respect for you. If you stay, you will eventually wear her down. In a few years you will marry and pop out a couple of kids, but there will always be something lacking in the relationship.

He dried his eyes and replied, "And what is that Sir Edward?"

Grabbing Sir Robert by the shoulder, I shook him a couple of times and said, "The level of love and respect that Michael was hoping you two would gain for one another this go around. It's what your journey is all about. It's what your life has been missing and there is only one way to gain it. You must leave now so you can return victorious."

If I had a son I would have loved him to be someone as strong and sensitive as Sir Robert. Other than his anger issues he was a true Prince Charming. Better yet if I was to sum him up, Sir Robert looked and acted just like the Dread Pirate Roberts in the 1987 movie "the Princess Bride." Unfortunately, the character's mannerisms were also his downfall. His approach to winning Lady Mary's heart was just like Wesley in the movie, responding regularly with the phrase "As you wish." However, Lady Mary was one of the most indecisive individuals I'd ever met. I think that's why Michael always said, "She is almost perfect in every way. Mary means bittersweet and she is that."

I told Sir Robert that it's hard to offer Mary an "as you wish" when she doesn't really know what she wants.

He said, "I can't leave. I'm afraid I will lose her forever."

"Okay," I said, "it's settled then."

Michael told me to go to the prop department and get a rubber pink pig puppet that we used at times in safety programs when presenting to preschoolers.

When I returned with the pig on my hand, Michael treated Sir Robert as if he was a small child using the pig puppet to get his message across. In a tone of rebuke he began, "I've given you a chance to redeem yourself in the eyes of Lady Mary and become a champion of true love and respect. You have rejected our guidance and have chosen to become like a pig, accepting any scraps of love that are thrown your way. If you stay you will earn your keep by helping dismantle the entire labyrinth, doubling its width and height." Handing the puppet to Robert he continued, "While you labor, wear this rubber pig on your side, it will remind you of what a pig you have become, wanting our Blue Princess all to yourself."

Sir Robert became angry and said, "And if I don't"?

Michael smiled while passing him the pig and said, "Then I guess you won't. There is a lesson to be learned here son. When you stop learning it is time to leave the knighthood and never look back. It is not just Mary's respect you need to earn here. You will never elevate if you don't learn to respect yourself. You believe you can't do anything right and I believe you can't do anything wrong."

To be honest I have never seen anyone embrace his or her inner pig so well and work so hard. Sir Robert admitted that he could see the logic in what Michael and I had said, but that he just couldn't bring himself to follow our advice. I could see that there were times when he wanted to punch me out and then there were times he wanted to hug me. I told him to punch me if he thought it would help, but he was too busy beating himself up to take me up on my offer. Thank god, because he would have probably knocked my head off. The guy really didn't know his own strength. I armed wrestled him once and he almost broke my wrist.

Chapter Sixty

ERU's Armor

It was now several years since Michael and I created his blue armor from that bull buffalo hide. He told me then that I could only wear his armor for seven years, plus one day. We were coming up on that anniversary, so I figured that I better start looking for a replacement. Since we had made the first armor, humanity had been introduced to the phenomenon of the World Wide Web. I was getting visions of what the next armor would look like, but had no idea what I was going use to make it from this time around. I remembered the Hierophant telling me back in the eighties that the day would come when all we'd have to do is sit at a computer screen and anything we wanted to know would be at our finger tips. The manifestation of the internet in our lives certainly made my search for a new suit of armor much easier. Sir Johnny gave me a list of websites to try that all his RenFest cronies used to outfit their weekend warrior play at reenactments and such. I was surprised at how many companies were actually selling leather armor online.

Michael also wanted me to fashion a suit of female armor for the Blue Princess. As I was shopping for leather armor on the Internet, I also found a link to a company in Hollywood, California, that made metal, leather and plastic armor for television and motion picture productions. When I called and told them what the Good Knight Network did to empower youth, they said that the company would donate the two sets of armor to the cause, but they only came in black leather. I gladly took them up on their offer. I knew I could paint both suits in blue, just as I had done the buffalo leather. Prefabbed armor pieces sounded like music to my ears - no more having to stuff Linda's bra as a mold for the breastplates!

A week later both suits of armor arrived at the castle. Michael told me to take them to the Tower of Wisdom and to walk the labyrinth. I was to call on Master ERU for instructions on what would be needed to construct his armor.

"His armor? Master ERU has armor?" I asked. I was shocked to hear that the new suit would be the Master's. "Why not your armor? What is going on?" No answer. So I headed out to the labyrinth as directed.

During the walk, ERU never spoke to me, but I received a vision. I saw a tall man with long white hair and beard wearing a blue suit of armor much like Michael's. He had a large sword and was surrounded by dark knights that were slashing at him with swords and spears. *It must be Master ERU in his battle dress,* I thought. His armor was gleaming blue and gold with the same black circle, trimmed with angel wings and a white cross on his breastplate just like I painted on Michael's. In the center of the cross was printed the letters "ERU" in black. In the vision, three of the dark knights charged him, with one blow from his mighty sword he knocked them all down and ran to a nearby stone building.

A beautiful, tall, and slender woman, with long wavy black hair, unlocked the door to let ERU inside. He held her close, in a fatherly manner. I felt that this was ERU's daughter, Queen Kei Sophia Pistis. She had been wounded. Blood was trailing down from under her breastplate onto the armor that covered her left leg.

She was also wearing blue and gold armor with markings similar to his. ERU then barricaded the door as the dark knights began trying to break it down. Everyone then froze in place. After a short time, I realized that Master ERU was replaying a scene of some long past event in my head. He wanted me to study the markings, runes and symbols on both blue suits of armor so that I could recreate them on the two that I was to complete. So, I burned the images into my mind. The vision ended just as I reached the center tower. I then heard to leave both pieces of armor in the tower, to go gather the supplies, and to come back for the armor when I was ready. It wasn't Michael who "told" me that, and at that time I wasn't sure who it was, so I just listened.

Once I had all the supplies and the armor pieces ready, I set up an area outside in the shade to do my work. I used the same blue metal flake automobile spray paint and 14 carat gold leaf paint as I did with Michael's Armor. The only difference was that the angel wings around the circle and equilateral cross were painted on and not raised. I painted the letters "ERU" in the center of the white cross on the new breastplate. On each shoulder I was shown to draw the symbol for Jupiter and on the back plate I was to paint a large white Ankh trimmed in black. Special markings were added in black on the white surface of the Ankh. The skirt at the bottom of the breastplates were not to be dragon scales, as they were on Michael's armor. The skirts for ERU and Sophia had eight blue leather strips about 2" wide and 20" long that came to a point instead. ERU's gold helmet looked Roman, with a visor and horsehair brush that ran across the center of the crown from the forehead to the back of the neck. The horsehair was black with a dusting of white. The artistic creation was completely channeled. I had stepped outside my being so that the birthing of this new armor could take place.

As I was working I could sense that my time as being one with Michael was coming to an end. Michael was preparing for me to use the next seven years to attract and merge with the consciousness and spirit of the Grand Master of Atlantis so that we could build the Star-Gate the Hierophant had talked about. It took me two weeks, but the new suits of armor were complete.

The next time Lady Mary was at the castle she tried hers on. I loved the Armor of the Blue Princess. It was trimmed in swags of bright, ornate, gold chains, that produced a unique sound when she walked. She wore a medieval blue and gold tunic under the armor that came down mid-thigh. Her knee to her thigh was covered in armor, painted to match the breastplate. Below the knee she wore blue knee-high boots. Hooked to her shoulder pieces was a blood red cape. Atop her long golden hair was placed a diamond-encrusted, eight-pointed crown. I saw that when the Blue Princess suited up, all who viewed her splendor would simply bow their heads.

Master ERU's armor was not as nice as Michael's Armor. Most people who viewed it didn't notice, but I did. Maybe it was because I cut every piece and wired it altogether. Like I said, the new armor didn't have dragon scales. It was also a bit more uncomfortable because it had a back plate which held in a lot of body heat. Another problem was that I had to be buckled inside tight, like a horse wearing a saddle. Michael said it was all about being able to contain the Ascended Master's energy. One really good thing about the new armor was that my body would relax because I was strapped in so tight, like wearing compression bandages. It took my mind off of safeguarding my back all the time. Although, when I took the armor off, I'd normally wind up with some pain from the old pinched nerve and slipped disc in my lower back. The armor weighed over 80lbs. The compression it offered me was both a blessing and a curse. Because it held me in and made me feel secure, I would do foolish things while wearing it because I felt so strong inside. I wouldn't feel the repercussions of those actions until after the armor was unstrapped. That's when I could tell that my back problems were getting worse.

Most of all, wearing the new armor, I lacked Michael's full presence, which I missed. I knew I was going through a transitional phase but I had no idea where this thing was going. Michael was still with me but said I was evolving. When I asked him where we were going from here, he told me to read Ephesians 6: 10-11:

"Finally, my brethren, be strong in the Lord and in the power of His might. Put on the whole armor of God, that you may be able to stand against the wiles of the devil. We do not wrestle against flesh and blood, but against principalities, against powers, against the rulers of the darkness of this age and against the dark spirits of wickedness in Earthly places."

Chapter Sixty-one

Castle of Zeus

Michael said that we needed to prepare the Kingdom to receive Pandora's box, which was once at RenFest and was now sitting in storage at our headquarters. He said that over the next three years the box would help many people purge themselves of dark spirits that were influencing them, to help finish something Master ERU and the Sons of Light had started 25,000 years earlier.

"How is it going to reach so many people if we are no longer at RenFest?" I asked.

In answer to my question, Michael gave me a vision of the building Sir Robert and I were to build between the two gates on Rhode Island Avenue. It would be called the Castle of Zeus. Once you entered the castle, volunteer scare masters would open hidden trap doors and windows thrilling the guests as they walked the maze-like corridors past very scary scenes of the seven deadly sins. Halfway through the building guests would pop out of a hidden door into a fenced in area outside the front of the castle on Rhode Island Avenue. In that area the Grim Reaper would dare the visitor to find the hidden passage back into the castle. He would also be entertaining the people waiting in line to buy tickets. His job was to be comic relief, much like the ambusher I saw at Fishermen's Wharf in San Francisco earlier that year. The design of the exhibit was to be a maze that walked the viewing guest through rooms depicting life size scenes of the seven vices that tempt humanity. The purpose was to stimulate their senses towards the vice that mostly affected them. Now that I had the blueprint in vision form, I got to work. I was also supposed to use incorporate what I had learned about creating a haunted house from Brother Ken.

Using chicken wire, I built strong spring-like body frames for the demons. I covered the wire with bubble wrap as skin, attached latex evil looking masks, hands and feet, then finished them off with appropriate clothing and props ordered from a costume company. All the scenes were mounted against the same long wall, separated by partitions. That would create a maze effect of walking into different rooms. I mounted pressure switches and motion sensors along the path to activate strobe lights and air blasts to disorient the brave souls who dared to proceed down these Halls of Hell. On the other side of that main wall we constructed a long corridor control room that ran the length of the building with peepholes, hidden windows and trap doors. This way we could have three Angel-Knights operate the entire attraction from behind the wall.

Once the figures were set in place, we ran a strong wire from each flexible demon, through the wall and into the control room where the wire then attached to a main wire in the ceiling. To animate the demons, all we had to do was pull the main wire and all seven rooms would come alive. The harder we pulled the wire the faster the creatures would move.

What we lacked in finances we more than made up for in imagination. We used what supplies we could scrounge to make this happen and then we finished off the haunt with some of the most spine-tingling music and sound effects I could find. The vision was birthed with the help of Sir Robert's carpentry and electrical skills. The hard part was done!

Sir Robert was proving to be an electrical genius when it came to running the wiring and placing the outlets we needed to activate all the devices I put in place. He was also coming to understand the meaning of what the order of Angel-Knight was all about: sacrifice, selflessness and integrity. In many ways I was glad that Sir Robert didn't return to Michigan. (Shhhh! Don't tell him I said that!)

This attraction became the Good Knight Angelic Kingdom's main face to the public. The ninety-foot-long castle had 18' towers on each end. In the middle of the structure was a shorter 10' castle face façade with a hidden entrance and exit. On top of the castle were eight colorful battle flags, waving in the wind. Painted over the center-arched doorway of the castle was a sign that read: "Eight Encounters of the Scary Kind." The strategy was to have patrons enter through the west tower, buy a ticket, and then weave their way through a maze of rooms, viewing the first four demonic exhibits at work.

The First Encounter: The Demon Belial, Prince of Wrath. On the wall a sign read: "Evil personified, the Great Adversary, vindictive anger, angry revenge, inspires mankind to selfishness, brutality, murder and mayhem."

The scene in this 6' x 8' room was the human Seth who was now voluntarily possessed by Belial, manifesting a massive red bull's head with great horns. He was shown attacking the Archangel Raphael, who was sent to help Queen Sophia Pistis heal Atlantis. In the scene, the great angel has been impaled on a wooden stake through her back, where she will remain for all eternity or until a hero rescues her. A pointed bloody stake protrudes through her chest and yellow tunic. Blood flows down her long white wings, as the demon appears to be trying to behead the angel.

The Second Encounter: The Demon Mammon, Prince of Greed. The sign on the wall read: "Inspires injustice, idolatry, the love for money over all other things and wanting too much of everything."

The demon in this room had a twisted human like face and wore a brown three-piece business suit. He was standing in a courtroom surrounded by overstuffed bags of cash and gold coins. He laughs while filing foreclosure documents in court to have families removed from their homes after the banks he represents has given loans to people they know can not afford to repay. Outside a nearby window was a man, his wife and two children, now homeless and forced to sleep on the street. They are foraging through trashcans for food.

The Third Encounter: The Demon Asmodedus, Prince of Lust. The sign read: "Inspires domination and sexual perversion. He has the need to seduce and feed on the body, mind and spirit of his victims. He sucks the life out of everything he come in contact with."

The demon in this room was depicted as a vampire with blood dripping from his sharp teeth and lips. He was dressed in a black tuxedo, standing in an upright old wooden coffin. The bottom half of the coffin was closed, but the top half kept slowly opening and closing exposing the handsome face of this seductive demon. On either side of the coffin were his human victims in cages, waiting to be sucked dry of their life force. When the viewers would least expect it and while the coffin lid was closed, a scare master behind the wall would open a trap door that the vampire was mounted on. When the lid opened again, the live vampire would reach out to grab at anyone viewing the exhibit at the time. When the lid shut, it would then reopen to reveal just the mannequin.

The Forth Encounter: The Demon Succubus, Princess of Envy. The sign read: "Inspires chaos, arrogance and jealousy; the want to have what everyone else has without earning it."

The demon in this room was a green, prune faced darling, wearing a bloody wedding dress with a sharp crescent sharped sickle in her hand. On the walls of her room are pictures of celebrities with their eyes scratched out. In the corner at her feet is the body of her best friends' husband. Because if the demon couldn't have him, nobody could.

After viewing the demon envy, guests would pass through a hidden wall and find themselves outside in a fenced-in area confronted by the Grim Reaper who was dressed in a dark hooded robe with blazing red eyes. The Angel of Death would dare the victims to find the passageway back inside the castle.

The Fifth Encounter: The Demon Belphegor, Prince of Sloth. The sign read: "Inspires indifference, extreme laziness and apathy. He breeds a lack of emotion, thoughts of discouragement, and failure."

Belphegor tricks humankind with inventions that will make their lives much easier, and will take them away from their hard jobs. But this is just a trap, in order for humans to abandon activity, relaying on machines, and thus abandoning their bodies and minds to wallow in laziness."

In this room the walls were lined with clocks. Children were lying on the floor watching televisions while a giant happy clown sleeps in a large bed in the middle of the room. Every child wears a red easy button on a belt around their waist. Far off voices of parents tell the children to stop watching television and do something. The children push the easy buttons and robots enter the room and do homework, pick up clothes, do the dishes and many other chores for the children. The only thing that makes the sloth clown happy is to see the children waste the greatest gift life has to offer, "Time."

The Sixth Encounter: The Demon Leviathan, Prince of Pride. The sign reads: "Inspires feelings of superiority, self-importance and rebellion. Influencing you to be arrogant, while raising your prideful self up, and putting others down."

False pride plays on the human ego and is at the root of all the deadly vices that plagues humanity. In the center of this room was Arch-demon Leviathan, facing off against Archangel Michael in sword fight that has lasted since the dawn of time. Since my seven years wearing Michael's Blue Armor was now over, I strapped the armor onto one of the wire mannequins. When the scare master on the other side of the wall pulled the main wire in the control corridor, these two battling forces came alive. I coated both blades with grains of flint, so that when the swords struck one another, sparks would fly from the blades.

The Seventh Encounter: The Demon Beelzebub, Prince of Gluttony. The sign read: "Lord of Flies who inspires us to over indulge in everything whether it's food, drink, drugs or self-persecution, as in a glutton for punishment and self-pity."

The bald fat-headed demon in this room was morbidly obese and looked to weight four hundred pounds. He was seated at a table covered in beer cans, wine and whiskey bottles. In the center of the table was a large pizza box. When the wire attached to his arm was pulled he opened the box with his left hand exposing a rubber pizza prop with human ears, fingers and eyeballs mixed in with other normal toppings. There was a syringe sticking out of his right arm. With his right hand he picked up a slice of the pizza and stuffed it into his huge gapping mouth.

The Eight Encounter: Down the corridor and on the left guest walked into the East Tower that houses the eighth encounter. The room was all black and the floor, walls and ceiling had been dotted with white phosphorescent paint that in the black light looks like stars. Against the back wall was the mirrored box of Pandora. Floating above and around the box were the Skulls of the Heroes that had also been dry brushed with phosphorescent paint so they would glow in the dark. A mirror was placed inside each of the seven skulls, so if the viewer looked into the eye sockets or through the teeth of the skulls they would see their own reflection.

The demon head had been removed from the mirrored box and it was replaced with the true image of HOPE - an infant child, sleeping, waiting patiently to be born free from the vices that plague humanity. For me the child represented, M.V., the little princess I have been searching for my entire life. The mirrored box had become a metaphor shield for the protection of the Children of Tomorrow. All who entered were to realize that they were passing through the real "Pandora's Box" and being purged of the vices that haunt them.

Michael had me create special talisman throughout the maze of rooms, which would absorb the negativity and evil from everyone that passes by them. It was an experiment to see if we might relieve people of the weight of their negativity, and to see if they'd go revisit the same vices they had left behind in Pandora's box when they returned to the outside world. The main purpose was to draw the dark spirits that influenced the humans, into the mirrored box. When the negative energies moved into the box through the two-way glass on top of the box to go after the infant locked inside, they became trapped and couldn't find their way out.

At least that was the plan.

After their haunted adventure was over, the guests would return to their cars or enter the Angelic Kingdom if it was open for a festival or programs. The attraction was rated PG-13, although any child was permitted to enter with a parent if the parent chose to allow it. As children went through, the live action scares were tailored to match the maturity levels of the visitors.

Chapter Sixty-two

Tears of Sophia

Michael had been showing me a vision of two meteor stones that he called the "Tears of Sophia" falling to earth that said he wanted me to find.

"Two tiny stones are going to fall to earth and you want me to find them? Will there be any more direction ahead of time on this new quest?" I asked. He didn't respond, probably because I was being a little sarcastic. But from time to time he had been bringing my attention to a circle on the map of the United States that formed cross hairs, like you would see in a riflescope. That could be anywhere I thought. Then one day while watching the weather on TV I saw the map illuminating where the states of Utah, New Mexico, Arizona and Colorado come together. The Four Corners area!

"Bingo!" I thought. Michael said that if I went there I would be guided to the location of the two stones he was seeking.

As fate would have it, in August a professor at University of New Mexico in Farmington saw the *America's Most Wanted* piece and sponsored our program for the city. When I arrived and met with Professor Joseph Keating and his wife at their home, he said the whole town was excited about the program. He had purchased twenty-five sets of our program kits to be given to schools and community groups in and around Farmington. He had already arranged for twenty-five volunteers to be at my presentation so that they could observe how I presented the program, in order to offer it in schools and at festivals around the state over the next several years. It was a breath of fresh air to find someone that really understood the need to get this message out to the public.

He told me, "When I was a child and was playing in a park one day, a man approached me with a picture of a dog. The man said that he was trying to find the dog and asked if I would help search a nearby wooded area. Once I went into the woods I realized that I had been tricked, but it was too late and the man assaulted me. I never told anyone because I was embarrassed until he heard you on the Jim Bohannan show talking about the H trick, - Help."

The Professor said he had been thinking about calling the charity to see how he could help over the years, but just never got around to do it until he was watching *America's Most Wanted*. He said that show put a face on what the Good Knights were doing, and he had to finally take a stand for the children. I must say the professor's story moved me deeply and I wondered how many other people had heard me over the years and were just waiting for the right time to act.

The professor's wife, Brenda, was a cowgirl through and through. She cooked up the best steak and fries I have ever tasted. After dinner she brought out a black Stetson cowboy hat that she bought for the Professor for his birthday. He was a New York City boy and never wore it, so she gave it to me.

She said, "Not all good guys wear white hats."

I gladly accepted the hat and said in a poor imitation of John Wayne's voice, "Well pilgrim I guess now I need to mosey on over to a shoe store and buy myself a pair of black cowboy boots to match my new hat."

I was just joking, but on the way back to my hotel she made her husband stop at a western outfitter so she could pick out the perfect pair of black boots to go with the hat. She said, "You might have been joking, but this cowgirl doesn't. I am country all the way. And by the way, we don't call them cowboy boots here, we call them snake boots since New Mexico has so many rattlesnakes.

While we were looking for boots, I told them about the spurs I wear with the armor and the story about Brother Daniel and the rattlesnakes during his treasure hunts in Mexico. I also confided to them that I was going on a quest to find two meteor stones out in the desert after I did the program.

Brenda said "If you go walking out in the desert you might want to put the spurs on as well." She reminded me of my wife, Linda, very caring. We left the store but before they dropped me at my hotel she made Joe stop and buy me two gallons of water and ten long Slim Jims to take with me on my search. Now you are all set and safe!

The next day the turnout at the University for the Good Knight Child Safety Awareness Program was great - we had about four hundred people in attendance. Families came from all around the area. This was the first time I wore Master ERU's Armor in public. Wearing it was different. I could always count on the angel stepping in to say a few words, but that never happened. Michael's presence was around me, but he never entered my body or my consciousness that day. I felt that he was preparing me for something new.

The mentoring program made a huge impact. It was just different from all the others I had done. It was going to take some getting used to, standing alone. It made me feel sad thinking that Michael and I would never bond together as one ever again. I felt alone and a little frightened not knowing what the future would hold. Michael didn't seem to have emotions or an attachment to me like I had to him. Perhaps that comes from being immortal? I felt like I was just another lab rat that he had to put up with as he introduced his experiments into humanity of this age. I guess I was, but regardless, I forged on because this is what I had been guided to do.

At the end of the program I called Professor Keating up on stage. I told the audience that he was a true champion who had gathered twenty-five volunteer youth mentors who will be providing Good Knight programs at area schools and festivals over the next couple of year. I asked the twenty-five to stand saying, "Dr. Keating helped me reach all of you with this life saving message. Remember kids fall victim to crime and violence because they don't know they are being deceived. The people that are hurting children are looking for two things before they strike, vulnerability and opportunity. If you remove only one of those factors from the equation the predator will seek an easier target. By teaching children the ten tricks, if the kids are ever approached they will know how to respond and stay safe. Without knowing the tricks, they will be easy prey. It is just good common sense and it really is that easy."

I turned to Professor Keating and stood toe to toe with him. In my right hand I held the Sword of Truth and with my left hand I inner locked fingers with the professor's right hand. I stared deep into his blue eyes as the sword burst into flames and said, "By the power vested in the Sword of Truth I do hereby dub thee Sir Joseph Keating, the Angel-Knight of Foresight." Everyone in auditorium gasped as the flame slowly made its way up the blade to the tip.

I then called Sir John's twenty-five volunteers up on stage. Having them line up side by side, I pulled the short sword from it sheath on my right leg and gave it to Sir John Keating to dub his knights, as I told the audience that these volunteers had pledged to take the Good Knight mentoring kits back to their schools and neighborhoods to teach others what they had learned here today.

"Your heroes," I said as I waved my arm in their direction. The room erupted in applause.

I ended the program by telling the audience that I was also in New Mexico on the search for two black meteor stones that landed out in the desert near the four corners monument. As soon as it came out of my mouth I asked internally why I said that. But then I continued and gave special thanks to Brenda Keating for preparing me for the journey. At that time I had no idea how important she was to the success of that mission.

Governor Susana Martinez was at the assembly. She loved the positive message and said that when the sword busted into flames it was one of those moments that takes your breath away. She presented me with a proclamation making August 28th officially Good Knight Child Safety Awareness Day. She also wanted to adopt the program in all elementary schools in the state. I told her that I was working on a plan that would allow the charity to send out youth mentoring kits free of charge to any school or organization that wanted to present the programs.

When I returned to my hotel room I received a call from Lady Mary. She said that she had some great news, Lady Justine had gone in to labor about the same time my program started and about an hour later she gave birth to the cutest baby girl. I was so happy for Lady Justine. Mary said Sir Bolton is passing out his "It's a boy" cigars to everyone saying that the cigars represent his son's penis that fell off. I felt bad for him. He so wanted a son.

Michael, you were right!

After they got married and Lady Justine moved out of the white house, the couple rented a nice two-bedroom house in Annapolis on the water. I was so glad that things were working out for them. I had had my doubts in the beginning.

I asked if they had named the baby yet and Mary said, "Yes, they named her Anna Urania, Princess Anna of the North."

The next morning, I put on my new black hat and snake boots, rented a car and went driving toward the four corners area. Not too far from Farmington I passed a sign for the Aztec Ruins. When I did, Michael said, "Turn around and park." He then guided me around the ancient village. I learned that early explorers and scholars believed the Aztecs built the ruins in ancient times. However, after further investigation it was determined that the sacred site was built by the ancestral Pueblo Hopi peoples that had inhabited the area.

The centerpiece at Aztec Ruins is a four hundred and fifty room structure built in the early 1100's, known today as West Ruin. In the central plaza of West Ruin lies the Great Kiva, a circular semi-subterranean structure used for ceremonial purposes. In the surrounding fields are an elaborate complex of roads and buildings, including other smaller kivas. The Hopi people trace their culture to the ancient Anasazi or Star People. They believe their ancestors traveled to earth from another dimension. I was really beginning to understand why Michael was always reconnecting with the spirit of the ancient ancestors who lived in North America.

Not knowing what to do or where to start my search, I sat on a wall to meditate. I could feel the spirit of the people who worshiped there. Then the spirit of Eagle Hunter, the old Hopi medicine man that gave me the buffalo rawhide skin came to my mind's eye. He beckoned me to follow him. He walked to the Great Kiva, stopped, then jumped inside. I walked to the edge and looked down, but he was gone. The sub-terranean walls were stone blocks. I knew he wanted me to follow, but I had no idea how I would get out again if I lowered myself into the circle.

It was a very warm bright sunny day. There were three families touring the ruins at the time, so I would have to wait for them to leave before trying anything. I put my spurs on and started exploring the surrounding desert area. There was a lot of brush, but no sign of any rattlesnakes, thank God. If there were any, I was hoping they were traveling off in another direction after hearing my spurs. I respect snakes and they have their place. Snakes do hold back the rodent population. I've caught my fair share of snakes in my life and had even had a few as pets. Garter and black snakes are one thing, but I had no interest in confronting any rattlesnakes.

Forty-five minutes later as the last family had driven away, I was able to drop down into the large circular pit. When I hit the ground, my spurs jingled followed by the sound of a nervous rattler over in one dark corner. When my eyes adjusted from the sun to shade I could see that indeed it was a rattlesnake curled up, frightened and ready to strike. I wondered how in the world a snake finds its way into this hole in the ground. With no weapon to be found I took off one of my boots to use if it came near me. I just wanted to search the kiva for the meteor stone and get out without getting bitten.

The pit was about twenty feet across and eight or nine feet deep. The floor was a sandy soil. I couldn't see anything on the surface of the ground other than anthills. The ants themselves, were large, red and hairy. Nothing else was there. Everything around and within me was telling me I was wasting my time looking anywhere but under that damn rattlesnake for the stone.

Really? I thought.

I couldn't tell how large the snake was since it was all curled up. Trying to devise a plan, I laid the spurs on the ground and I took off my other boot. This gave me two shots at the snake if it came at me. I knew enough about snakes to surmise that if it had been in this hole for a long time, it was hungry, thirsty and desperate. That's not to say that the snake could eat me of course, but it would likely strike at anything that moved in such a state of duress.

I said to myself, "Self, this is probably is the dumbest thing you have ever done."

Then I realized that I have actually done dumber things.

The first rule of thumb in hiking or survival is, get yourself a long pointy stick to shove in the eye of an attacking animal, or in my case, to stab an attacking snake. Strike one! I had not prepared for this. So I asked Michael if he could help me, but received no reply. I felt he was waiting to see what I was going to do next. "Some guardian angel I have," I grumbled, "I feel like I'm right back in that Chicago toilet."

I sat on one side of the pit and pondered the many lessons the Hierophant had given me all those years ago to see if any of them fit into this situation. The one about shape shifting or becoming an animal came to mind, but what kind of animal could I become that wouldn't frighten the rattlesnake more than he was already. I knew a mongoose or eagle kills snakes, but I wasn't going to grab it in my mouth or with my hand.

Then I heard the voice of the old Hopi medicine man in my head saying, "Stop all the bullshit before you get bit. You need to charm the snake with love cowboy."

Okay I had seen snake charmers on TV sitting in front of a cobra, then they would lean forward and kiss the snake on their hooded head. But my momma didn't raise a fool. I wasn't going to get that close to a rattlesnake. I sat there focusing all my imagination and strength on my arm becoming a sexy female rattlesnake. It reminded me of the time I was on the police department working undercover and had to manifest myself looking like a woman in order to catch the guy who was stabbing prostitutes. Back then, with the help of several ladies, I was able to pull it off. I learned from the Hierophant then, that with a strong will everything that can be imagined can be obtained.

I also thought of when Aaron, the brother of Moses, turned his staff into a serpent for the Pharaoh. Then Pharaoh's magicians turned their staffs into snakes. It was a war of powerful wills, but Aaron had the stronger belief, and maybe an angel nearby who helped his snake devour the other snakes.

With all that in mind I decided to sit on the ground next to the wall. I held my right arm out from my body as if it was a female rattlesnake. I slowly eased over onto my right side and laid my right arm on the ground. I started moving my arm and hand like a serpent moving across the sand along the wall. The rattlesnake watched my hand sway back and forth.

The first rule of a criminal investigator is to keep an open mind. I was trying, but I did feel ridiculous in that hole in the ground. If some family pulled up and looked in this kiva what would they think?

"Get out of your head Ed! This won't work unless you believe 100%," I yelled out loud to myself. I put everything else out of my mind and elevated. Rule one of a Magi is to believe everything is possible, so I did. I imagined my arm had become a sexy female rattlesnake slithering along the wall ever so slowly. I looked at the real snake and projected my thoughts that my shadow snake was real. I noticed the real snake was no longer looking at me; it was following the movements of my shadow snake along the wall.

I moved my shadow snake closer until my snake was right alongside the real rattlesnake. The snake was now darting its tongue franticly in the air as imagined that the female snake was doing the same. Then I moved my shadow snake forward slowly and the real snake followed. As the real snake moved behind my shadow snake, I moved slowly along my side of the wall until I was where the rattlesnake had been. Sure enough, in the sand was a black round meteor stone about three quarters of an inch in diameter. I grabbed it and quickly jumped to my feet. Wasting no time, I jumped up and scaled the wall. Thank God I'm tall. A few inches shorter and I would never have made it out in one leap. I was so focused on retrieving the stone I forgot my boots and spurs in the kiva.

That was awkward.

I looked back inside the hole. I could see my boots, but not the snake. I thought, "Crap that snake is now in one of my boots." There was no way I was getting back in that snake pit without a weapon. On the other side of the ruins was a clump of trees where I found a strong tree limb about five feet long I could use as a spear or club. Now armed, I slid back down the wall into the pit trying to make as little noise as possibly. Still no sign of the rattlesnake, so I knew it had to be in one of the boots.

I eased the limb over to the first boot and spun it around so I could get a good look inside. The snake wasn't in that one. Next, I slid the end of the spear under the spurs that I had buckled together. Lifting the stick on an angle the spurs easily slid down the branch to me. After putting them in my back pocket I began maneuvering the last boot so I could see inside.

The snake wasn't in there either.

My eyes immediately began darting around the pit looking for holes where the snake could be hiding. There were none. Puzzled, I tossed the boots out and climbed back out of that hole in the ground.

Walking back to my car I wondered what happened to that snake; then I heard laughter behind me. I turned back towards the ruins and saw the spirit of Eagle Hunter walking away from the Great Kiva.

Son of a beehacker! He must have been shape shifting to match wits with me, his humble apprentice. I was glad that he was amused and that I was never in any real danger. Finally, I understood why Angel Michael had nothing to say to me during the whole ordeal.

From there, Michael told me to drive to the Four Corners Monument. I still had to locate the second stone. When I arrived at the monument, I did a spiral search looking for the second black stone. There were plenty of rocks out there, but no black round stones. It was so hot and I was truly appreciative of the water Mrs. Keating had given me. I noticed a guy with a set of binoculars watching me from the monument.

I searched and searched, moving through the area always looking for rattlesnakes. It was getting late and the sun was now setting. I drank all the water and had eaten the Slim Jims. Now hot, tired, thirsty and hungry all I could think was someone else had already found the other meteor stone or that it was buried in the dirt. The old fellow who had been watching me came up to my car, as I was ready to drive away. He asked me what I was looking for so intently.

I couldn't tell him about Michael's quest, so I told him that I had a dream and, in the dream, I was supposed to find to two special black stones. One would be in a kiva at the Aztec Ruins and the second would be at the spot where the four states come together. I showed him the black stone I found in one of the kivas at the ruins.

The man laughed and said, "You have been looking in the wrong place." He went on to say that where the Four Corners Monument sits is really in New Mexico and that in 1886 a government surveyor made an eighteen-hundred-foot mistake. The true point where the four corners meet is about six hundred yards due west of where this marker sits.

"Ooookay! Makes sense! Thank you," I said.

"Don't stay too long after the sun goes down. Critters come out then," the old man warned.

Being six foot five gave me a stride of thirty-six inches or one full yard. I put my spurs back on, pulled out my trusty OD green army compass and started counted off my paces. When I got to six hundred I started the spiral-searching pattern again. As a rookie cop I had learned to search for evidence in that manner. I was also thankful for my grandmother teaching me how to search for those four-leaf clovers, because now I was searching for a small black stone which fell in one of four states that was the size of the tip of my index finger. Sight wasn't going to be the only sense I needed to use to find this puppy!

The sun was setting and the temperature was dropping fast. The old man's warning that the creepy crawlers come out at dusk was spot on. I thought my eyes were playing tricks on me when I saw the ground in one area moving. I had disturbed a nest of tarantulas which were each about the size of my hand. I also saw a couple rattlesnakes crawling off in the opposite direction. Again, I was so very glad that Brenda Keating had given me the cowboy hat, snake boots and two jugs of water. I realized how unprepared I was. It was obvious I had more than just angels looking out for me during that mission.

The sun was at such an angle that it was casting shadows across the landscape and knew I had to give up. All the small stones were looking black now and I didn't want to trip with the large spiders crawling about. Just when I was about to give up a ray of sun shone through a cactus plant and on to something shiny. I did a double take. To my right a saw the black meteor stone. I couldn't believe my eyes. I found the second stone in Utah, *I think.* That second stone was just a little smaller than the one I found in the Great Kiva. I felt good driving back to the hotel because I was bringing home the Tears of Sophia. This gave me high hopes that we were on the right track, and that one day Pistis Sophia would come to the Good Knight Kingdom to claim them.

When I arrived back in Maryland on Sunday night I couldn't wait to see Lady Justine's new baby, Anna, in the morning. I always melt when I see a baby. I love their little hands and feet. Oh, and those angelic faces! I guess it's been part of what keeps me searching for the special child with the initials M.V. All babies pull on my heart strings. They are so innocent and vulnerable. I felt like I failed in some way not being able to protect Meghan, but Dawn had blinders on when it came to Spencer. We can only offer information and guidance to empower children. What they do with it is up to them. They have the free will to choose either side and we must above all else not enable them, but empower them instead. I had learned a lot from Grandfather Commanda and the Sunbow Walkers about how people are put in place for many reasons, but most of all that everyone is brought in to our lives to learn from.

When Linda picked me up from the airport, she told me Dawn called to tell her she was pregnant again, due in the winter. My heart sank on one hand, but on the other I was happy. I remember Michael starting off the year saying that Dawn would have another daughter and she would become an important direction on our journey of discovery. I just didn't think it would work out this way.

It was odd that I would get Dawn's news on the eve of me seeing Princess Anna for the first time.

Monday Morning, Lady Justine brought Anna to the headquarters office to meet me. Sir Gregory and Lady Bonnie planned a little welcome home luncheon for me that I turned into a little welcome to the world party for the new little Princess. She was so precious, with a full head of dark brown hair and big blue eyes. It was love at first sight. I knew I would be connected to Anna for the rest of my life.

Chapter Sixty-three

Michigan Renaissance Festival

During September's First Wednesday Club gathering, I briefed the Angel-Knights about the trip to Farmington. I told them that the Governor was ready to take the program statewide if we could supply her volunteers with the resource materials. I also told them about how sweet the Keatings were and that I could never have found the Tears of Sophia if it weren't for them. I explained how I used the Hierophant's lesson on shape shifting to manifest a shadow rattlesnake. It lured what I thought was a real rattlesnake off the first stone in the pit; just to learn later that the real snake was also a shadow snake manifested by the spirit of Eagle Hunter, the Hopi medicine man who gave me the buffalo rawhide so many years before.

Michael had me give the two black meteor stones to Lady June-Zigagael with instructions to have the first stone set into a silver ring called the Ring of Nothingness. The second meteor stone was to be set into a golden ring and mounted into a brass chainmail headband called Crown of Creation.

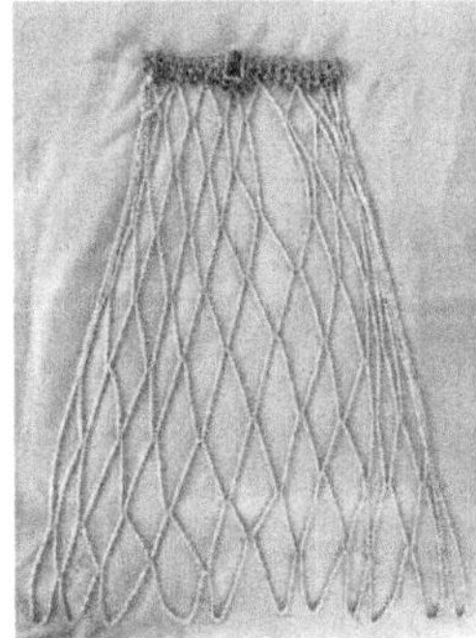

The Headdress

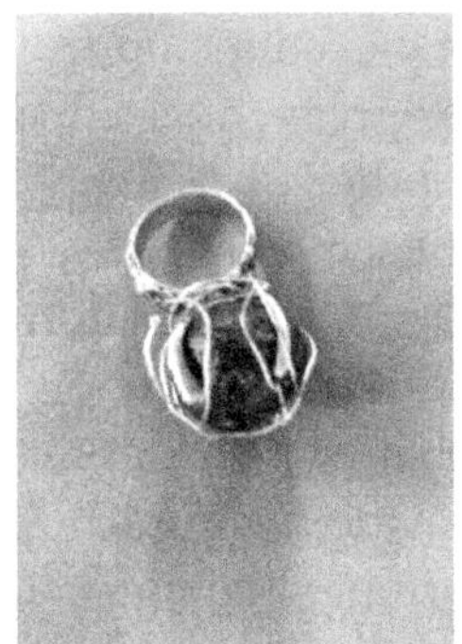

The Ring

During that gathering Michael revealed how dangerous it was creating the Castle of Zeus and collecting all that negative energy and spirits in Pandora's box in that building. He said that we each needed to create crystal shrouds of protection to shield us from the negativity or it could destroy everything we had built. Everyone was told to bring a pure white cotton single sheet to the next First Wednesday Club gathering.

Also, during this meeting, Lady Bonnie informed us that we had been receiving hundreds of orders for the Good Knight program materials and that requests for the Blue Knight to appear were still coming in. "We need help packaging and mailing the materials. We also need volunteers to help at the Michigan Renaissance Festival on September 14th and 15th. Anyone who is available please connect with me after the meeting to coordinate," she said.

Sir Robert was the first to volunteer because it was a chance for him to return home. I asked Sir Robert and Sir Johnny to coordinate the entire weekend event.

Last on the meeting list it was decided that the charity would hold our first Halloween event at the Good Knight Kingdom grounds to premier the Castle of Zeus haunted attraction to the public. Our tickets for the event would be $8 for adults, $4 for kids under twelve and children under three would be free. We would offer a light-hearted spooky adventure rated "G", a medium scary adventure rated "PG-9" and a very scary adventure rated PG-16."

The event would run every Friday, Saturday and Sunday from 6:00 p.m. till 10:00 p.m., starting October 18th through the 31st. I put Sir Gregory Peterson and Lady Barbara in charge of recruiting volunteers from Maryland University for our October haunted event. Barbara had been in Dr. Peterson's Master Study class and met Sir Anton there. They fell in love and planned to marry by year's end. Another happy couple! It was good to see like-minded people find one another. We were all happy for them.

When we left for Michigan Lady Linda and I drove our car since we wanted to visit my father and Henrietta in Chicago after the festival. Lady Justine got a large panel van donated so that Sir Robert and Lady Mary could transport the Sword and the Stone, the Knighting Circle, swords, armor, flags, sales items and props. Sir Thomas drove his van with the other volunteers.

The Michigan Renaissance Festival event was the nicest and most professional festival we had ever attended. Everywhere we went there were signs and banners welcoming the Good Knights to the festival. They gave us our own open-air pavilion where we set up the knighting circle and a shop to sell our books, videos and ceramics.

We were treated like royalty. The festival's King and Queen would announce as they passed through the village, to be sure and visit the Good

Knight's Camp to be knighted and learn how to stay safe from strangers. It was such a breath of fresh air to be welcomed with such respect and admiration.

That festival was Lady Mary's first time in public wearing her Blue Armor. She looked heavenly, and Michael truly enjoyed walking her around the fair telling all the children that Lady Mary was the Good Knight's Blue Princess. It was also nice to see that Sir Robert wasn't pushing her so hard. He had asked her to marry him, but she was in no hurry, feeling we had important work to do.

For the two days, Sir Johnny, Lady Eleanor, Lady Leah, Sir Thomas and Lady Bonnie would take turns telling a short version of the Good Knight Story and go over the *ABC's of Safety* with families in the King's Theater next to our camp.

Lady Mary and I would be called in to autograph activity books and knight the children in a magical ceremony. By the end of each day our arms were aching. Lady Mary used the Shekinah sword with seventeen points and I used the very heavy Excalibur Sword. We set a record that weekend knighting 1,200 Good Knights. At close of business on Sunday, the owners of the festival came to our camp to thank us for our service. They invited us back the next year in the hopes that we could make it. What a welcoming difference!

It had been several years since we had seen my dad and his wife Henrietta. Apparently there had been a crackdown on doctors over prescribing drugs, so Henrietta wasn't getting her diet pills anymore. This made her very irritable with mood swings. It was hard to spend time with her and even harder still to see how she treated my father. It was one of those situations where nothing Dad did was ever enough for her.

We did get a break when my father and I went to meet with the Bishop at St. Michael's Academy. He was a delightful old gentleman who loved to talk about Angel Michael. He freely admitted that Archangel Michael talked to him all the time. He was a priest and could get away with it. Me on the other hand was always seen as odd, crazy or eccentric when I shared my relationship with Angel Michael.

I gave Bishop Carol a copy of the Good Knight Story. I told him the story of my drowning in Florida and having the vision of Angel Michael who wanted me to help him protect children. I explained how Michael guided me through the military so I would gain discipline, and then how I became a police officer so I would learn how children become victims, so that I could teach them how to avoid child sexual predators as I do today.

Bishop Carol said that he believed that Archangel Michael chose me for a very special reason. My father told Bishop Carol about the deal he and his buddy made with Saint Michael when the Nazi's in World War II captured them.

The Bishop said, "We were all part of God's plan to protect the innocent." He then walked us around the school and showed me the auditorium. That day we planned for the Good Knights to return for a presentation. I knew it was going to be very special program.

When I took my father home, Henrietta was in one of her dark moods saying that if it weren't for her my father would be a bum on the street and that she put a roof over his head.

I told her that wasn't necessarily true saying, "If it wasn't for you my father would probably have found someone who really loved him instead of just becoming an unappreciated companion." She flipped her head in defiance as I continued, "My father is always welcome to live with us. If you don't lighten up you are going to pop a blood vessel and give yourself a stroke. If you have a stroke you will need him to take care of you."

Michael told me that Henrietta being cut off from the drugs made her a perfect breeding ground for dark spirits to influence her behavior. Unless dad left the situation, things could get worse for him.

Linda and I took Dad out on the porch to talk to him out of Henrietta's earshot. Dad told us that they would be watching TV and right in the middle of the show Henrietta would say she was tired of looking at him, demand that he leaves the house to go sleep in the garage.

I told him, "Her mind is going, due to all the years of taking pain and diet medication."

Linda let him know, "You are always welcome to come live with us."

He declined of course, saying, "I would feel bad leaving her in this condition."

I knew then that my father was a far better man than I could ever be. I could never stay with someone who demonstrated so little respect for me. We felt bad leaving him there to live in that kind of stress, but again, he was just exercising his free will, and we honored that.

On the drive home Michael told me that my father had never fully recovered from the Post-Traumatic Stress Disorder he suffered during the war. He was just happy to be alive.

Chapter Sixty-four

Where the Darkness Meets the Light

When we returned to Maryland I went back to work on setting up the Haunted Kingdom. Michael wanted us to call the event "Where the Darkness meets the Light." The labyrinth area was finished, so now all we had to do was cut trails through the Forbidden Forest and assemble scary scenes along the way. Sir Gregory went to the local Police and firehouse to look for volunteers. When I met with them, I took them through the Castle of Zeus so they could get a feel for the way we designed the scenes. I explained that I wanted to also create an experience to show people the effects of drunk driving, playing with matches and other fire hazards.

The guys from the fire department had a large tent that we set up over the trail in the Forbidden Forest to serve as the Castle of Fire. Sir Robert and I partitioned off a maze path in the tent, much like we did in the Castle of Zeus. This divided the tent into six large rooms to be negotiated as you walked. In the first room we built a large dollhouse and furnished it with everything you would have in a real house, but to scale. We had pictures on the walls, carpets on the floor, beds, couches, chairs, tables and lots of dolls. These were all things donated from local thrift stores.

The Doll House Exhibit

Room one: As you passed by the front of the house and looked in the doors and windows everything looked beautiful, but as you followed the path and went past the back of the house, everything was charred, making it look like someone fell asleep smoking a cigarette and destroying everything. I had a fog machine underneath the display that would send puffs of smoke up through the rooms and red flickering lights that made the house look like it was still on fire.

The Three "Bes" Exhibit

In the middle three rooms I asked the volunteer fire fighters to set up their own scenes that best fit the message they wanted to convey regarding the themes of "Be Smart, Be Prepared and Be Safe." They gave our guests the basic fire safety message.

The Drunken Driver Exhibit

From the Castle of Fire, guests journey further through the haunted forest until they come across a car that had hit a tree. The car was smoking and looked like it was on fire. A fireman stationed there told people not to get to close because the car might explode. A police officer was also in the scene, talking to the drunk driver.

The local Police department brought us a 1989 four door white Buick that had been in a collision with a telephone pole. No one was hurt in the accident, but the car was pretty smashed up. Sir Robert, the tow truck driver, and I added more to the smash with sludge hammers and the frontend of the tow truck. I asked the tow truck operator to help position the car as if it hit a tree on the path in the Forbidden Forest. We then mounted red strobe lights inside the car, front and back. We also placed one under the car along with a fog machine to look like the accident had just occurred and was ready to blow up. On the hood of the car I mounted a standing four-foot red devil dressed in a white tee shirt and jeans with a Jack Daniels bottle in one hand and a syringe sticking in his other arm. Around his neck was a necklace of miniature bottles of booze.

The Grave Yard Exhibit

In keeping with the haunted season, we ended the tour with a trip through our graveyard that had funny sayings on Styrofoam tombstones like, "I was Fred, now I'm dead,", "Here lies Billy Blake; he stepped on the gas instead of the brake", Benny Slick; I told you I was sick" and "Here lies Eddy Moore, four shots from a forty-four. Eddy is No More!"

Visitors then followed the path, past an old white picket fence with freshly dug graves and a coffin half-exposed that a zombie slowly crept out of, while other zombies come out from behind the trees. After being startled by the walking dead a she/male transvestite with a roaring chainsaw came running down the path chasing one of our female actors. As visitors made their way toward the exit gate an incredibly real looking wolf man jumped out from the bushes with a fake human arm it was feeding on.

The charity put out a casting call to neighbors and students at Maryland University for volunteers to work the event, and as a result, found some of the greatest people to support the charity's effort. We held acting lessons on weekends, training all the actors in the art of the ambush, scare, creep and crawl. I did not want the haunt to be gross or disgusting. We were looking to shock, thrill and add a dash of startling fun to people's lives. No actor was allowed to touch a guest. I set up the trail in the Forbidden Forest so that it would surround a central location in the middle, where a handful of actors could strike out at several places along the paths. This gave the guests the feeling that we had forty monsters when we only had twelve.

Since the Castle of Zeus faced Rhode Island Avenue, Sir Robert and I created several life-size wire-frame heroes and monsters on top of the roof between the two towers, so that the cars and people passing by would see what we had to offer. There were Superman, Batman and a knight in shining armor. They were battling Frankenstein, the Wolfman and a fire-breathing dragon. We created the illusion of smoky fire with a red strobe light and fog machine mounted in the throat of the dragon.

Over their head, and between the colorful flags on the roof, we flew Casper the friendly ghost and his three scary uncles. I attached wires to each mannequin and ran the wires down to a slow-moving rotisserie motor with an offset wheel. As the motor turned, the wheel would pull and release the wires which animated all the characters. As is always the case, I was still working on scenes right up to the moment we received our first families.

When families came through the Ticket Tower entrance they had a choice of turning left into the "Darkness" of Castle Zeus, which would take them through the "Pandora's Box" experience and the Forbidden Forest exhibits, or they could turn right to enter the "Light," which took guests on a path full of light scares for those just looking for fun. Along the Light path guests met their first costumed actor, Macaroni the Magical Wishing Mouse, from *A Good Knight Story*. Lady "Black-Eyed Susan" always played Macaroni Mouse in a costume created by Lady Linda. The kids always loved meeting Macaroni.

In keeping with our goal of teaching through all of our presentations (entertainment with a purpose), the mouse told the guests to beware of people trying to trick them. The path wound past ten small child-sized houses, all painted different colors. On the front of each house was a word corresponding to one of the ten tricks used to manipulate or abduct children. In, or around, the house was a regular person dressed in normal street clothes. Each of these actors would engage the children in conversation trying to get the kids to leave with them. Parents received the shock of their lives through learning how trusting and vulnerable their children really were with strangers. Most kids think a stranger is an ugly, mean, scary person.

The path led on to the Castle of Light and the Labyrinth of Miracles. Angel-Knights, Lady Eleanor-Haniel and Sir Thomas-Sachiel greeted the visitors and set them on the quest to walk the Labyrinth in search of Cinderella, our Blue Princess.

Sir Robert lit up the walls of the seven-ring labyrinth with twinkling white mini-lights. It made for such a magical setting. The children walked the labyrinth seeking the whereabouts of Cinderella. It was so cute hearing the little ones calling out her name, "Cinderella, Cinderella we are here to save you."

Cinderella would be found in the Tower of Wisdom. She gave each child a gold wishing ring from a small treasure chest, giving instructions that the child must make three wishes for other people. The wishes could not benefit the one making the wish. For example, they couldn't wish that their mother receives a million dollars, because that wish would also benefit the child. It made the children really think about helping other people. The fourth wish made on the ring was to be for the owner and it could be used for anything. The kids and adults really loved those wishing rings.

Leaving the Castle of Light, the visitors were then guided by Angel-Knights, Lady Leah-Israfel and Sir Adam-Camael to the Good Knight Castle, in the center of the Kingdom for refreshments. Guests were taken upstairs, past the upside-down Christmas Tree chandelier and the exhibits representing the major religions of the world, and into the main exhibit room. Once inside the room the children could view the white doves, and the Angel Sophia Pistis flying over the Knighting Circle. There they could also watch the short *ABC's of Safety* video and be knighted by Lady June-ZigZagael.

Our guests were then taken back outside to a hill overlooking the Forbidden Forest and were given a choice of sitting on bleachers to watch the action of people being ambushed by monsters while walking through the forest or they could go through the Police's Drunk Drivers Crashed Car exhibit and Fire Department's Castle of Fire exhibit.

It took about ninety minutes to tour the entire Haunted Kingdom. All the actors and patrons had a great time and they didn't want the fun to end.

That first season the charity took in about $2,200 a weekend, which was a good thing now that we had a monthly mortgage to pay.

Chapter Sixty-five

National Tour

The first part of November Linda's mother, Hester, went into the hospital for testing. The dye they used destroyed her kidneys, so she was placed on dialysis for the rest of her life. Hester had to be taken to the Dialyses Clinic four times a week so she had to move in with us so that Linda could take her to the appointments. Once we made this decision, we felt some concern about the coming winter, knowing that if we got snowed in again like we did at the beginning of the year, there would be no getting her out and she could die. I asked the Angel-Knights to put orbs of white light around her and Linda. Hester's husband, Bill, didn't want to move in with us. Their house had been burglarized several months earlier and he didn't want to leave their home unoccupied.

On November 12th, I left to start the Good Knight Child Safety Awareness National Tour. Linda had to stay back home with Hester. The tour was scheduled: New York City at a synagogue on the 13th, Chicago and Saint Michael's Academy on the 15th, then two public schools in Oklahoma City on the 18th, Excalibur Hotel and Casino in Las Vegas on the 19th, a community center in Houston on the 22th, a festival in Los Angles on the 23rd and 24th, two elementary schools in Atlanta on the 26th, an elementary school in West Palm Beach on the 27th, and I was then to fly home on the 28th, so I could celebrate our anniversary with Linda on the 29th.

My itinerary looked simple on paper when Lady Bonnie-Gabriel gave it to me, but I was truly on a dead run for that two weeks. In many cases, I had just enough time to land at the airport, grab a cab or rent a car, drive to the location, suit up, most of the time in a restroom, present the program, return the car and get to the airport just in time to fly out to the next location.

The whole tour was a bit of a blur, except for two appearances: The Excalibur Hotel and Casino where Michael and I were the special guests of the King and Queen during their medieval show. It was during the hotel's grand opening and Archangel Michael was able to flame the Sword of

Truth for over three thousand guests in attendance. During my stay the hotel manager had the Sword of Truth on display in the lobby where I was autographing Quest of the Good Knight activity books for hotel guests. The management was so impressed with the efforts of the Good Knight Network that they collected all the coins in their many fountains during my visit and donated the money to the charity.

The other memorable event was my visit to Saint Michael's Academy in Chicago. That was the only event where Michael moved into ERU's armor and joined me in a presentation. And it was the first and only time my father would see one of our complete shows and the reaction of the children. The kids at the school were different than any group I had ever worked with before. Those children knew that the Archangel was talking to them. I had never seen an audience so spellbound. When the Sword of Truth burst into flame the whole room became electrified.

During the knighting ceremony my father came up on the stage with the kids to be knighted. When Michael touched the sword to his shoulder Dad broke down and started to cry saying, "Sir Edward I am so proud of the life you have led. I don't know what I ever did to deserve such a caring son."

A reporter from the Chicago Tribune interviewed my father that day and wrote a wonderful article with the byline, "The Prodigal Son Returns." That day was one of the proudest moments of my life.

I could tell that I had passed an important milestone with Michael; there was a distinct contrast to the past seven years of working with his energy and consciousness. On the flight home, I realized he had been detached from me ever since we hung his armor on display in the Castle of Zeus. I didn't know it at the time, but the display that Michael had me build was really a threshold to hold back Hell.

It was so nice arriving home on Thanksgiving. Linda was excited to have me back and made me promise not to ever do another cross-country tour like that again. She didn't have to twist my arm on that one. We had a nice dinner together at home because for our anniversary celebration we had scheduled to go on a cruise to Saint Maarten on the Maasdam in December.

The news was on the TV the next morning while we were drinking our coffee and talking about the upcoming cruise. When the weather came on, the map showed graphics of tornadoes all over Maryland and the newscaster said, "Get ready we might be in for it."

That's all Linda needed to hear. She was in a panic.

December rushed in with a freak storm that hit the castle grounds hard. A tornado touched down on the property, uprooting trees and destroying sections of the perimeter wall and exhibit buildings. The only places that seemed to avoid damage were the labyrinth and the Castle of Zeus.

During the construction of the Good Knight Kingdom Michael insisted that in every hole dug I had to drop in an Astral Crystal Beacon, a specially programed quartz crystal and a copper penny wrapped in aluminum foil. He showed me that it was necessary to create a new vortex on the Earth's crust that would link with the planet's three electromagnetic grid systems. He showed me in a vision what we had done, but it was all very high tech and above my level of understanding.

During the storm the Good Knight Angelic Kingdom had acted like a huge magnet or lighting rod, drawing in negative ions and electrical charges that would normally spread out over the area. He also said that the imbalance of these electrons had the capability of interfering with human behavior and mood patterns, which could be dangerous for the Angel-Knights. It was like spirit being exposed to radioactive material.

Michael filled my mind with visions of special elements, numbers, letters and words that I didn't understand. He talked about solar winds from the sun. Electrified molecules that become excited, giving off negative and positive charged electrons and protons, which produce friction, then combined it all with hydrogen and oxygen that produce water molecules in the ionosphere and magnetosphere. To make a long story short he explained that how Earth gets its weather patterns and that we could be drawing too much to our site. He gave me the image of the great storm we call the red spot on Jupiter. I wondered if and why he was creating a mini version of that at the kingdom. It must have had something to do with his intention of sending the dark spirits to Jupiter which were trapped on Earth.

All this added up to the creation of geomagnetic storms that can change the direction of magnetic field lines and create strong shifts on Earth's energy grids on the ground. It is those magnetic grids that keep the planet from wobbling on its axis.

This all felt like TMI. All I wanted to know was, "What all this had to do with electro-magnetism, and how could me dropping foil wrapped pennies and crystals in the holes affect the weather?"

I, like most people, didn't know an atom from an element or proton from an electron so I didn't understand the science behind it. Michael tried to explain it to me saying that the Earth, and all things on it, are like a macrocosmic scientific experiment in a gigantic petri dish where matter is constantly being created. Everything you can see, touch or smell in the universe is composed of atoms. Atoms are the building blocks of all physical matter.

Within an atom there are three subatomic particles called protons, neutrons, and electrons. The protons and the neutrons make up the center of the atom called the nucleus; the electrons fly around the nucleus in a small circular orbit or cloud, like the planets orbit the sun. The suns or stars orbit the black hole in the center of a galaxy and the galaxies orbit around the center of the universe. And the universes orbit around the center of the source of everything I call the Creator.

He said that electrons carry a negative charge and the protons carry a positive charge. The cloud that holds the positive and negative together, yet apart is the electro-magnetic energy force field or Will of the Creator. It is that force that holds everything in balance until an unforeseen force in the experiment tips the balance and creates some new form of matter.

By now my head was swimming, but I was beginning to get the picture. It sounded to me like God was conducting an experiment and had no idea what the outcome was going to be. So much for, "God knows everything."

Michael continued, "Edward, remember atoms are alive with energy and everything that is alive, is made up of atoms. When you programmed those quartz crystals with meditative thoughts, those thoughts will echo forever. Then when you wrapped the crystals and copper pennies in aluminum foil you created a battery that is activated when you dropped them into the moisture of the earth, which is also electrified. Each packet becomes an astral homing beacon drawing in whatever we need during our experimentation period." He ended by saying, "Trust me, the Angelic Triangle that we have surrounded the property with is one of the most powerful areas on the planet. It is a mini version of the Golden Triangle that surrounds God."

Okay now I was right back to my original question, "What do I do to restore the balance?"

Michael said, "Take a cruise."

I felt like I was in an old Abbott and Costello movie skit, "Who's on first?" I asked. "You know of course we are going on a cruise?"

"Yes, I do, and I am going to show you what to do on the cruise," he replied. Michael showed me that I was to create 144 Astral Beacons, then drop them in the water like breadcrumbs to mark a trail along the voyage Linda and I were about to take. He told me to drop 72 on the way down to Saint Martin and 72 back to our homeport. And during any cruise we took in the future, we were to do the same thing. He also told me to number and date each beacon and mark the drop sites on a map.

Before we left for the cruise Dawn came down from Pennsylvania to take care of Hester. On December 8th, our ship left out of Norfolk, Virginia. Michael had me start dropping the first Astral Beacon, labeled #1-12/08/96, in the mouth of the Chesapeake Bay, where it meets the Atlantic Ocean. The second was at Cape Hatteras.

***Special Note from author:** As of 2014 Lady Linda and Sir Edward have taken twelve cruises so far out of departure ports as far north on the eastern seaboard of the United States as Bayonne, New Jersey. It was important that they always traveled south through the Sargasso Sea, where Atlantis once stood, down through the Bermuda triangle, and West Indies, to Venezuela. After August 29th, 2005 when hurricane Katrina devastated the gulf coast Michael had Sir Edward start dropping Astral Beacons in the Gulf of Mexico from Cuba to the Panama Canal. Their last cruise started on September 28th, 2014, where they left out of Fort Lauderdale, Florida. Sir Edward dropped beacon number #1726-09/28/14. When they reached Costa Maya in Central America he dropped beacon #1727-10/01/14 and returning to Fort Lauderdale on October 5th, dropping beacon #1728- 10/05/14.*

When looking at the map now, years later, it is amazing how well Michael has peppered the eastern and southern waters off the coast of the United States. He told Sir Edward at the time that it would be important in the future for the Angel-Knights to focus on storm systems and try to have them change course. He had no idea how important that would be at the time. Over the years we have learned that if you have the right people who have acquired "The Knowing" those humans working with their angelic counterparts could influence the weather.

In total, 1,728 astral beacons have been dropped. Michael then showed Sir Edward 144,000 humans scattered all across the globe activating all the crystals within the earth's crust with their mind producing a White Light Frequency that elevated the collective consciousness of our entire species. Humanity rose above its nature to want to dominate one another and a new wisdom of life was born.

I asked Sir Edward if Michael said what all of it meant? All he said was, "A dream come true." - Lady Sophia

We ended the year with a wonderful Christmas visit from Dawn, Meghan and Spencer. Linda and Hester were happy. Dawn looked like she was ready to pop. We joked that a Christmas baby would be nice. Spencer and Dawn seemed to be doing better. Although, Hester confided in us as Spencer, Dawn and Meghan drove away that Dawn borrowed another five hundred dollars from her.

Linda almost blew her lid with the news. But what are you going to do?

Two days later we got the call; Dawn was on her way to the hospital. Linda got her cousin to stay with Hester so we could drive to Gettysburg to be there for Dawn.

We sat all through the day and night. That baby girl just didn't want to come out and greet the world. I wondered if she knew how much turmoil was waiting for her on this side of her mother's navel.

It was obvious Meghan wasn't too crazy about sharing. Being a first child makes you selfish. I remembered how my brother Billy resented having to share with me. Meghan always called Linda and me Mamaw and Poppop. While sitting in the lobby waiting for her sister to born, Meghan came to us saying that her new sister can only call us grandma and grandpa. I told her that she was going to share us with her sister. But the energy coming from her and the look in her eyes, I could see trouble brewing already.

Dawn hadn't truly decided on the name yet. We all put in our recommendations. I was still hoping to find the child with the initials M.V., so I suggested Mary as the first name. It means "Holy Wish" and the middle name of Veronica, meaning, "Child of Truth."

Michael had already said that Dawn's next child would grow up to serve as one of the Princesses of the Four Directions so I felt a name that meant, "A holy wish for Child of the Truth" would be fitting.

Lady Linda wanted Angelica, which means, like an Angel and Spencer wanted Brianna, which means, strong. I was just happy to see that little baby happy and healthy after waiting so many hours for her to arrive.

Angelica Brianna finally joined us in the afternoon after sitting in the waiting room for nearly twenty-two hours.

It was a great way to end a very nerve racking, but successful year. We had seen the birth of two new beautiful directions, Princess Anna of the North and Princess Angelica of the East. I had to stop and wonder how long would it be before the next child would be born, and would she be one of the children to come from two golden dove eggs?

The End

APPENDIX

Book of Wisdom
Part Two
Lessons 30 – 53
As channeled from the Hierophant to Sir Edward-Michael

Remember:

All lessons were channeled. Some language or grammar may not be as we are used to reading in this age. The Hierophant's language is an ancient one. Channeling and translating varies from individual to individual and language to language as well.

Read each lesson several times. The more you do, the Greater Understanding will be made known to you, like invisible ink appearing.

Important notice: Many of the drawings, figures, charts and power symbols Sir Edward channeled while receiving these lessons have been omitted from the book to avoid misuse and confusion for the reader. If you wish to interact with Sir Edward, Lady Sophia and other Angel-Knights and learn how to join the formal lessons visit so-sophia.com and view links to our Facebook experiences.

Begin Open Channel

Lesson Thirty:
   Queen of Spades, received January 8ᵗʰ, 1991
   Book of Wisdom, channeled from Hierophant

"The more you know, the more 'Knowing' will come to you." ERU

My Dear Brother Hermit and Teacher,

What is love?

There are hundreds of definitions for the word, countless actions to express the word, and an endless caravan of books written on the subject of love. And yet love has as many interpretations and expressions as there are people. Because love is a paradox, we all know what love is, and at the same time we all don't know what it is.

So, what is love?

Love is a tender force centered in our being! Think on it for a moment. It is gentle, easily impressed and enjoyed. It's sensitive, soft, compassionate, caring and temperate. It is also a force, active power, strength, energy, compelling, overpowering, a field or vibration.

Humans are emotional beings. No two of us act or think the same way. So sometimes things get a little weird when it comes to relationships. One wise fellow once wrote:

> *"We are all a little weird, and life's a little weird. And when we find someone whose weirdness is compatible with ours, we join up with them and fall in mutual weirdness and call it love."* — Dr. Seuss

Let me tell you a story about long lasting love:
One afternoon a woman came to me asking for help.
"What is your problem?" I asked. "The house where my family and I once lived, I rent out to others. Each time I do so, within a month later, the renters move out saying that the house has a ghost in it. I believe it to be my dead son." She replied. "Is the house occupied by any renters now? Is anyone living there now?" I asked. "No!" She replied. I said, "Then take me to your house."

An emotional woman and the ghost of her dead son could end in a tragic state of affairs, so I suggested we ride separately to the house. The sun was setting when we arrived. She unlocked the house and lit the lamps

377

in each of the rooms. As she was a woman of means there were many rooms in the house, but very little furniture, since she was renting the house out.

I asked for an article of clothing that her son had worn. She left the room and promptly returned with a pair of gloves. As I held them, a numbing feeling began to occupy my fingers. It crept up my arms and became a heavy weight in the center of my chest. I felt my heart aching. I walked back-and-forth through the rooms of the house. When I reached the back door, I knew this was the point of beginning.

I could see, in my mind's eye, a sixteen-year-old boy busting with energy. He was full of joy and love. I described him to his mother, reflecting his state of bubbly happiness. I said he would enter the house through the back door, come into the kitchen and taste the food being prepared for the daily meals. He would then move through the dining room and enter living room. As he did so he stayed to the far-right side of the wide-open archway that separated the two rooms.

I asked why he never entered the room in the center or right side of the archway? I was told that there was always piece of furniture that once blocked that part of the opening. As I continued through the house all I felt was happiness and love. I walked down a hallway and entered a small room. It was his bedroom. I could see him entering the room and diving, spread eagle, onto the bed. I saw where each piece of furniture had been placed. I touched the walls and knew exactly where each athletic achievement hung. The room was filled with love and excitement of his youth.

I told the woman of the things that happened in the room, which she verified. "Well!" She asked, "Is my son here?" I sat a spell and contemplated; not knowing exactly how to tell her. "No. He is not here," I replied. Then she continued, "If he is not here, what is it that the renters are experiencing?" I said, "Your son had a great love for life, none like I have ever seen coming from a human being. That is probably why our Father has called him home. It is this love of all things that this house is permeated with. Your renters don't see ghosts. They feel what they interpret as a presence or ghost. Furthermore, what they feel as a presence is not a presence at all. It's the residue of your son's electro-magnetic energy of happiness that has infused itself throughout every part of this house. So, it is his love that is felt and nothing else."

She was in shock. So I said, "You were hoping that I would bring your son into communication with you. "Yes," she said, sadly. "Do you love your son?" I asked. "Of course, I do," She retorted.

Then it was time for the hard truth. I asked, "Do you realize that your strong desire to have your son here with you is binding him between two worlds? In essence, he is being held in limbo. It is his desire to go on to his reward verses your desire to have him here with you. This is painful to him because he loves you very much. His heart energy is breaking." The woman began to weep. I could tell she was feeling her son's heartache.

I continued, "Now if you want the best for your son you must let him go. There is nothing wrong with remembering him or keeping him in your prayers. However, desiring to have him here now with you is contrary to the nature of a spiritual being. Your son needs to move into the afterlife. Do not fret, for he is in a far better place then you are. He's on his way to the Father with a great story to tell and he knows it."

I passed the woman my handkerchief then continued, "And you will see him again, but only after your waiting is full. If you must worry, worry for the living. Remember this, to worry will not change anything. It is only in praying, then doing, that things can be changed. Turning the love you had for your son toward those who are still with you is the most positive path for all concerned."

I sat with the woman for a short time while staring into the blue flame of the candle that sat on the table between us. It was a good thing we rode separately. She said she was going to stay in the house for one last time that night. She confessed that she felt it was time to sell the house so others could create happy memories in it.

Background on Hauntings

I will touch here for a moment on the appearance of someone long dead, as found in, haunted houses, castles, etc.

When I'm called upon to investigate such manifestations, the first thing that I wish to know is where do the apparitions take place. Then I examine that room or area for certain signs. There are two things that I look for in a room. Those items are: cut glass or crystal objects that may produces a prism effect when light is passed through, and marble. The marble acts as a recording substance like a music recording tape or floppy disk. The prism light acts as the recorder's switch. Like a recorder, it needs power to run.

What kind of power? Where does that power come from?

The power comes from what powers everything in the universe, the Electro-Magnetic Energy of the Creator. In the case above, it came from the emotions of the woman's son that still permeated the house. The house was alive with his being that was still trapped in the house because of his love for his mother. We all have frequencies of power. These electro-magnetic frequencies are transmitted during the emotional expressions of fear, hate, love and desire.

Now to create a new scenario:

It's a beautiful day. The light streams in through the window. As it passes through the facets of the glass it produces a rainbow of color on the marble fireplace. A mother is sitting nearby rocking her child. Her mind is wandering; she is not paying attention. Suddenly her baby begins to choke. The mother jumps up screaming "My baby, my baby!" The baby recovers and begins to cry. The mother embraces her baby and it begins to cry harder.

The event has now been recorded for all time. It lies like a dragon waiting to be unleashed. Many years or centuries later when conditions are right, the dragon will be set free. Some people are more sensitive than others. It is that sensitivity that triggers the recorded past event. Then the stories begin. Some will say they have seen a woman rocking a child. Others will say that they've heard a woman crying out, "My baby, my baby!" And yet others may say that they have heard a baby crying or a woman sobbing.

Those who know no better, start to weave tales of horror and terror. The tales turn into morbid ghost stories that become bigger and more involved until they are no longer related to the facts of the original event.

What is an apparition?
Apparition is Latin - "Apparition" meaning to appear; to be evident; to serve; to attend. Today it is used to refer to ghosts, angels, poltergeist or the manifestations of demons. It has also been used to mean the materialization of the dead, astral bodies and inanimate objects such as UFO's and phantom ships.

So, when one uses the word apparition, the reference usually relates to any paranormal appearance; though the most common is that of a ghost. Yet there are also true supernatural beings, which have never been embodied on this physical plane. These are referred to as apparitions as well. Some appear out of love for mankind with a desire to be of help. We have covered some in this lesson as a true story I've shared. They are all bound together with an underlying theme of love.

As we have discussed already, love can be expressed in many ways. People have been abused, hurt or even died out of love. Those forfeiting their lives out of love have been recorded in histories all around the world, from the Sons of Light, in the days of Atlantis, to the crucifixion of early Christians, to the Knight Templars, to the Salem Witch Trials, to the men and women who fall on the battle fields of today. It is found in every age and in every nation from the beginning of time to the present.

Some of these deaths have been deemed good and some evil, depending on who is writing the history books. The truth is told when the heart is weighed as you tell your tale in the afterlife. Remember, in the next dimension there are no deceptions or motives, only the pure light of Truth. When two armies go to war, there are good soldiers on both sides praying to the same "God" for victory. Although they are both fighting for a different cause and principle when it comes down to living and dying in a battle, most all soldiers are fighting for the love of guy next to them and those at home.

What I am here to tell you is that love is a great power that can be used in many ways. And like any great power it can be used for good or evil, to create or destroy, raise or debase. It all depends on whose hands the power of love is in. How strange is it that we all know love, and yet, we do not know "Love" at all. When you think you understand what Love is, write it down for your students as I have for you.

End of Transmission

Begin Open Channel

Lesson Thirty-One:
   Jack of Spades, received February 8ᵗʰ, 1991
   Book of Wisdom, channeled from Hierophant

"The more you know, the more 'Knowing' will come to you." ERU

Beloved Hermit and Teacher,

One bright summer's day after breakfast, I was summoned and informed that I was to go on a long journey. I was told to take one of my pupils with me. The trip would take several weeks and our course would take us through some very rough mountainous regions, so we should prepare accordingly. On the seventh day into our journey, while stopping for the mid-day meal, my pupil began to curse the stones upon which we had been walking.

I looked up from my cup to ask why he should be doing this thing? He replied, "The rocks and stones are keeping me from a speedy journey. They bruise my feet and cut my hands. They are useless and bring me grief. They have no value, but to bring me sorrow and pain."

I began to laugh. He retorted, "It is not humorous!"

If you have not traveled this way, would you have appreciated how much someone had gone through to reach you by this very same way? The answer is "no!" Because you cannot appreciate someone's pain until you go through it yourself. That is why those who suffer in life have such a great love for life and are more understanding to the sufferings of others.

Thus, the stones have taught you a great lesson in life. But stones have other lesser and greater uses. They are needed to give shelter and heat, cure illnesses, heal wounds, protect against evil or bring good luck. If it were not for the stones, where would man be? How many lives have stones saved?

There are stones of every size, shape, color, texture and power. But, most important are the powers within the stones themselves. They enhance and bring forth individual powers as they also awaken the powers locked in nature's bosom. By understanding the stones, you become in tune with nature, not cursed by her. Therefore, it is now time for you to become in tune with nature.

Here are the stones, their names, powers and symbolic meanings. Many of their uses go back to Atlantis. Unfortunately, the methods of their uses have been lost in the shadows of time. As a seeker of the "Knowing" you should try and collect as many of these stones, crystals and gems that I describe in this lesson. Once the "Knowing" you seek has been achieved, and you are able to receive influence from the higher consciousness you may be shown how to use these earthen gifts for your own advantage and for the benefit of all mankind.

The Stones that make up the Treasures of the Magi are:

Agate or Achates: Mercury rules this stone. Thus, it puts a stop to thunder and lightning. It drives away evil air, soothes the mind, disposes to solitude, promotes good eyesight, eloquence and secures the favor of princes and the wealthy. It presides over the liberal arts, poetry, music, astronomy and mathematics. Signifies joy, courage, happiness and prosperity. It is victory over one's enemies.

Amethyst: This gem gives peace of mind and serenity, yet, it is ,ruled by Mars. It attracts love. When bound on the navel or made into a cup from which one drinks, it prevents drunkenness. It is also said to sharpen the wit, turn away evil, render the barren fruitful, and as a potion it was thought to expel poison. It is said to be the stone in the ring given by St. Joseph to Mary the mother of Jesus. The Romans engraved it with the head of Bacchus.

Ammonite: This is a fossil or stone of meteoric origins. Placed under your pillow, it will give you prophetic dreams.

Aqua Marina: Gives relief to depression and brings out or gives hope. Sometimes it causes inconsistency.

Beryl: This is a stone of the planet Jupiter, said to rule over propagation and preservation of the human species. It is said to preserve wedded love and act as a medium for magical vision.

Bezoar: A precious redstone said to be found in the bodies of stags. This stone possesses magical properties against poison and contagion. It is worn as a pendant around the neck, from a ring, or crushed and taken internally.

Bitumen: Was carved into images used in sympathetic magic.

Carbuncle: This gem drives away poisonous vapors, preserves health, reconciles differences among friends and is said to have fire within. It is a great talisman stone, a symbol of Divine love, faith, hope and charity.

Let us stop here for a while and review what we have covered thus far. As you can see there are many properties attributed to each of the stones. We will continue the list with our next lesson.

End of Transmission

Begin Open Channel

Lesson Thirty-Two:
    Ten of Spades, received March 8th, 1991
    Book of Wisdom, channeled from Hierophant

"The more you know, the more 'Knowing' will come to you." ERU

Dear Hermit and Teacher,

As we already started our alphabetical list of the stones, their names, color and powers, it is only fitting that we should complete that list since the true importance is in you hearing these ancient names and descriptions. Even those words will add power to your consciousness.

Before we continue on, let me inform you that the names of many of the stones have changed since the days of our forefathers in Atlantis. As nations and empires have risen to change the name of the days, months, years, zodiac signs, plants and animals, so too have the names of some of these stones and gems changed. Even so, some of the ancient names have been given to different stones of our days. But notwithstanding, there is power to be found in the bones of our mother earth, so let us now continue.

Chalcedony: Chalcedony is called "The stone of Saturn." This is the mystical stone of priesthood and is used for contemplation of Divine Things. It gives one triumph over evil powers and hallucinations.

Chrysolite: This stone is brought to reconciliation. Some say prevents madness and fever, but when covered with pure gold or gold foil and placed under a pillow it is said to protect against bad dreams and terrors of the night.

Chrysoprase: This is good for weakness of sight, rendering a possessor joyful and liberal, but it brings an executioner's death to the owner. Its color is green and gold. *You may not want to collect this stone.

Chintamani/Tektite - an ancient wish fulfilling jewel. It is said to have been created during the planetary impact event where Lucifer is cast to Earth from Heaven out of the eyesight of God.

Red Coral: Red Coral stops bleeding, preserves houses from thunder and children from evil spirits, goblins and sorceresses. Protects from the evil eye, evil spirits, witches, misfortune, violent dreams, and curses. It also confirms understanding reason and prudence.

Carnelian: This is one of the stones of Saturn. It increases the flow of saliva in babies, brings joy to the bearer and dispels evil thoughts. Helps with depression and hyperactivity.

Colorless Hyaline Quartz Crystal: This crystal prevails against unpleasant dreams; dissolves enchantments and is a medium for magical visions. It also relieves headaches, raises emotions and mental faculties. *This crystal can be programed for just about anything and is a very useful tool for a practicing Magi or Healer.

Diamond: This is the "Stone of Mars," the gem of April and stands for purity and fortitude. It protects against enemies and snares, proves faithful to engagements, purifies the blood and protects against epidemics.

Emerald: This is the gem of May and gives faith in God and faithful friendships. It a good preservative against decay, promotes childbirth, arrests dysentery and heals the bites of venomous animals. It is the most grateful of all jewels to the eye and reflects images like a looking glass. Nero, the Emperor of Rome, is said to have had one of immense size through which he observed the combat of the Roman Gladiators. It also heightens understanding and gives eloquence.

Garnet: This is the gem of January, giving perseverance and consistency to its owner. It also gives the bearer faith, hope, charity, loyalty, frankness and friendships.

Jacinth or Hyacinth or Zircon: This gem is for March; it gives moral beauty and goodness. It's the "Stone of the Sun" and preserves someone when drunk, cures coughs, ruptures, and melancholy. It also protects from lightning and the plague. It is said to bring wealth, health, and wisdom and induces sleep.

Jade: This is the stone of Divine Revelation, truth and purity.

Jasper: Prevents bewitchment, nightmares, epilepsy, dropsy, fever and yet strengthens the mind and speech.

Lapis Lazuli: This stone confers love, tenderness and an air of gentleness.

Lignite: This stone preserves children from witchcraft, stops nose bleeds and restores lost senses.

Lodestone or Herculean Stone: It is said that this stone lets you hear the voices of the gods, so one can learn of great things. This is a great stone of magic for the accomplishment of one's desires.

Malachite: This is a green stone that brings hope and success in business.

Moonstone: This stone returns the wearer to childhood innocence.

Onyx: This is a negative stone which brings the bearer sadness, sleeplessness; and when sleep does come, evil dreams, quarreling, fear and discord. The stone calls forth specters, phantoms and shadows.

Opal: This gem is of October for a pure life and hope. It is not a good stone to possess unless it is your birthstone. It is called the stone of tears, for it destroys love and turns accomplishments into disasters. For those who claim it as a birthstone it gives beauty and wealth, turns pale in the presence of poison and brilliant in the company of a friend.

Ruby: The gemstone of July, it brings success and devotedness to duty. This gem is of the sun. It brings happiness and good thoughts, action, respect and beauty. It is said by some that it quenches thirst and relieves headaches.

Sapphire: This gem is of September bringing divine love and mercy, and records repentance in man. This gem is under Saturn's influence and thus gives power, vigor, peace and good feelings to the body. It absorbs poison and contagions from the body, defends against wickedness, and consuming passion. It symbolizes justice, loyalty, beauty, nobility and truth.

Tanzanite: It resonates or vibrates at a high rate which makes for a quick but gentle connection with angelic realms, spirit guides, and higher consciousness. Tanzanite gemstone energy is highly protective, an aspect in keeping with tanzanite meaning that is invaluable during spiritual healing.

Topaz: This is the gem of November bringing divine providence and fidelity. The sun also rules this stone. It is said to render the wearer invulnerable. But, most important of all, it is called the stone of virtues because it draws so many virtues unto itself, even as it draws gold.

Turquoise: This is the gem of December for fervor and piety in God's service. It is used to prevent accidents or getting tired and drives away misery.

Tourmaline: This stone becomes electrically charged when exposed to heat or friction. Further it is said to polarize light. Best used for casting spells of a good nature.

When I finished my teaching to the young lad, I asked, "Now, my brother, are you eager to curse the stones upon which you tread?" My pupil spoke not a word, but rose to finish his journey, forever searching for those special stones.

End of Transmission

It should be noted, some of the stones and gems on the original list are no longer available on earth and others are very hard to find. For that reason, they have been left off the list in this book and we are the only keepers of the complete list. We have been able to recover most and used them in the foundation as we experimented with the creation of the Star-Gate chamber. I suggest that all seekers of the "Knowing" follow our lead and collect as many as you can find. They could be useful to you in the future. Grand Master ERU calls them "Treasure of the Magi" and if you set them up in various patterns around yourself during meditations a powerful force field will envelope your body. It is something well worth their collection to experience what they have to offer.

Begin Open Channel

Lesson Thirty-Three:
Nine of Spades, received April 8th, 1991
Book of Wisdom, channeled from Hierophant

"The more you know, the more 'Knowing' will come to you." ERU

My Dear brother Hermit and Teacher,

It has been many lessons since you have taken a test on the many subjects we have covered in the last thirty months. So, let us cover tests and testing that can be used to develop your psychic sharpness or check others for psychic ability.

The way in which you execute the test determines the type of ability that you are testing for, even though you use the same materials in each test.

Test "A-1" -- Precognition

Take a deck of Zener Cards. Shuffle the cards thoroughly, then place the deck of cards on a table or flat surface face down. Have a pencil or pen and a pad of paper at hand. You are now ready to begin.

First relax, clear your mind of all subjects and concerns. You may use progressive relaxation if you wish. Now concentrate on the top part of the deck. Become receptive to its identification. Whatever the card is that comes to mind first, more often than not, that is the correct card, write it down on your pad of paper. Now take that card, don't look at the face, and lay it face down as the beginning of a new pile. Now clear your mind again. Concentrate on the top card of the deck. The first card identity that comes to you, write it down.

Now what if the impression that you received on the first card and the impression you receive on the second card were the same? Don't worry about it! This can be brought about by one of several causes. One, the first time you tried, you may have bypassed the first card only to perceive the second card. Two, you may not have cleared your mind adequately after your first perception and the first card's identity was repossessed. Continue through the deck. After each attempt, place the subject card face down on the second pile. When you've gone through the whole deck, turn the second pile of cards over the bottom card. The first part is now face up. Now check the cards against those that you've written down to see how many you have correct.

Number Correct	Rating
1– 5	Laws of Chance
6– 7	Possible Ability
8–14	Workable Ability
15–25	Definite Ability

If your score is an 8 to 25 correct range, work with your ability daily. Make that ability a part of your existence. Use it. Exercise it. Try and predict the outcome of national events before they take place.

Also pay more attention to, and heed, that little voice in your head that tells you to do, or not to do something. That ability could save your life one day.

Test "A – 2" -- Precognition

For this test you will need a die, glass or cup, pad of paper and a pen or pencil. Prepare yourself as you did for test A-1.

Now to start, write down on your pad the first number from one to six that comes to mind, or that you think the die will roll. Shake the die in a cup or glass and roll it out on the table. While shaking and rolling the die out do not concentrate on or think of the number that you wrote down. Each time you write down the number and roll the die constitutes one set. Run thirty-six sets before marking your score.

Number correct	Rating
0–6	Law of Chance
7–9	Possible Ability
10–18	Workable Ability
19–36	Definite Ability

If you practice and master it you will be ready to take a trip to the local casino to test your skill.

Experiment: Decide how much money you want to put at risk - say seventy-five dollars. Call down the Angels of the Four Directions to accompany you and your money on a mission to double it. Your mission is only to turn seventy-five into one hundred and fifty dollars. Take four quartz crystals about the size of your little finger. In gold, write the direction East, and name of the angel Michael, on the first crystal. Then do the same with the other three crystals for Gabriel, Raphael and Uriel. Now write a statement of intent on white paper.

"I, your name, call upon the Angels of the Four Directions to help me increase my wealth by doubling these seventy-five dollars. I ask that it be turned into one hundred and fifty dollars through an honest wager on cards or dice. If you help me double my wager I hereby promise to give ten percent of my winnings to the poor."

Now sign the paper, lick your thumb and put a wet thumbprint over your signature. Put the money, your statement of intent and the four crystals in a black sock. Tie a knot in the sock and twirl it around your head, six times clockwise and six times counter clockwise. Now put the sock in a drawer for forty-eight hours.

During that time, your angels will let you know if you are ready to go on a Wager Quest or not. If they say you're not, put your money away and practice some more. If they say you are ready for the experiment only play the seven-five dollars from the sock, no more, no less. If you wish to start with less money in this experiment feel free, but don't start with more than seventy-five dollars.

Test "B-1"

As a part of this test you will need a pad of paper, pencil, a glass or cup and a die. Prepare yourself by relaxing. Now randomly pick a number from 1 to 6 and write it down your pad. Concentrating on that number, roll the die and try to make that number you have chosen come up on the die. Do not touch it except with your mind.

Test "B-2" -- Psychogenesis

In this test you will need a clean white piece of cardboard approximately four inches square, a piece of coat hanger wire about twelve inches long, and a pen or pencil. Some construction is also required.

First, take your piece of cardboard and drawn X from corner to corner with three-inch diameter circle in the center.

Second, take your wire and bend it so that the top is about six inches above its circular base.

Third, take the cardboard square and place it on the base.

Fourth, now thread your needle and hang it from the top of your wire, so that the needle is over a quarter of an inch above the center of the X on the cardboard.

You're now set to run your test. Concentrate on the needle. Think of a layer of warm air covering your face or chest. This is an extension of you. Direct that warm feeling toward the needle to make it move back-and-forth. When you have achieved this make the needle stop. Then make the needle swing in a circular motion or pattern. Do not blow on a needle or try to make it now by any other means.

Test "B-3" -- Psychogenesis

In this test you will need a cork one inch in diameter, a needle and a glass or ceramic punch bowl or basin filled with water.

Cut off approximately one-quarter-inch of the piece of cork. Then push your needle into it.

Place the cork with a needle into the basin full of water. Feel the warm air covering your face or chest, as you did in test B-2.

Direct that warm feeling, as an extension of yourself, to move the needle around the basin at your will. Again, I remind you, do not blow on the needle to make it move.

As in all long tests, it is time for you to take a break. We will continue in your next lesson.

More importantly it is my hope that these tests will be of benefit to you in your development, as well as helping you to locate others having these abilities.

End of Transmission

ADDED NOTE—*Sir Edward and I have found that the use of certain Essential Oils can jump start certain student's skills. Once you have attempted these tests cold turkey, try putting a drop of lavender, lemon, sage or wintergreen oil on your thumbnails. When you are ready to test, smell the oil and see if it makes a difference in you scores. The oils relax the mind and can help open the third eye up wider.*

Begin Open Channel

Lesson Thirty-Four:
Eight of Spades, received May 8ᵗʰ, 1991
Book of Wisdom, channeled from Hierophant

"The more you know, the more 'Knowing' will come to you." ERU

Dear Brother Hermit and Teacher,

Now that you have taken your break and have had a taste of fresh air it is time to carry-on with the tests. I hope you enjoy and learn from these tests. Every time you test yourself, your powers grow.

A wise man once said, "We do not know the strength of the steel until it has been tested." How true that statement is! Now it is time for your next test. This test will require some construction and materials that may not be easy to obtain. But once you have built the device it will serve you for many years.

Test "B-4" -- Psychogenesis

Items needed for this test are a watch display dome with stand, a three-inch needle, a cardboard tube one inch in diameter and one and one half inches long, a thin piece of metal such as in a tin can. Cut the metal into one and three-quarter inches in length by three eighths of an inch in width.

Take the strip of metal and in the middle put a dent with a punch or nail, but be careful not to punch a hole in the strip. All you want is a dent. Next, make two cuts in the side of the tube, opposite to each other, one half inch wide and one quarter inch in from the end. Now push the metal strip through the cuts so that it almost blocks off one end of the tube.

Now either by driving the needle, or drilling a small hole to hold the needle, put it perpendicular to and in the center of the stand for the watch display dome. Place the paper tube over the needle so that it is balanced by the dent in the piece of metal.

Use the same steps you have used in test "B-2" and "B-3" to make the cardboard rotate on the needle. First have it go one way and then the other. Remember focus and relaxation is important.

Test "C-1" -- Telepathy

What you need for this test is a pen or pencil, pad of paper, and another person. You should both be seated in comfortable chairs. The subject and you should take a few minutes to relax. Have the subject concentrate and relive in their mind's eye the happiest thing that ever happened to him or her. As you sit in your chair try to become a part of them, let their thoughts come into your mind. Be receptive! Write down whatever comes to mind, whether it is a picture, taste, emotion, fragrance, or feeling. Whatever it may be, no matter how illogical or disjointed it may seem, write it down.

After about five minutes break, read to the subject what you have written down to see if there are any relationships to what they were thinking.

Test "C-2" -- Telepathy

This time you will use the same items as in test "C-1" with the exception that you will have a subject in possession of some photographs or pictures from a newspaper or magazine that you have not seen. You will be seated with your back to the subject. Both of you relax for a few moments. Then have the subject concentrate on one of the photographs or pictures.

Again, become a part of the subject and let whatever they are seeing flow into your mind so that you may see it. As soon as you get the picture write it down on your pad of paper. When you are finished, read to the subject what you have written down. Then look upon the picture or photograph to see how well you have done.

You may also try electric drawing to help your focus. While concentrating on the image being sent, let your strong hand start making lines and circles on a clean white sheet of paper. If an image appears, compare it to the picture the subject has focused on.

Everyone has the gift of telepathy, you just need to find out how your mind can express it.

Test "C-3" -- Telepathy

To run this test, you will need a Zener deck of flashcards, a pad of paper, pen or pencil, two comfortable chairs, a small table such, as a card table and another person. Set one chair so that it faces the table and the other chair so that it has it's back to the table. The person in the chair facing the table will shuffle the cards and place the deck face down. They will pick up the top card and say, "card number one" and concentrate on it for about one minute. Then put the card face down as the beginning of the second pile. In this manner they will go through the complete deck.

The person in a chair facing away from the table is to write down the first impression of the card they receive when its number is called.

After the run is complete, check for the number of hits or correct answers you have.

Number Correct	Rating
1-5	Low Chance
6-7	Possible Ability
8-14	Workable Ability
15-25	Definite Ability

Test "D-1" - Psychometric

This test takes some preparation. First of all, three people will be involved. The person giving the test must receive an article, the inductor, from a third person who knows the history of the object and has not had any contact with the person taking the test.

When the test is over they can meet. In fact, the third person should not even be in the building where the test is given until after the test is completed.

The subject should take a few moments to clear his or her mind before receiving the article from the person giving the test. Relax using the guidance given in Lesson One. It should be used before taking any of these tests for better results. Always remember to relax the mind and body so the spirit can soar.

The subject shall handle the inductor to receive its impressions. As the impressions, or statements are revealed to the subject's mind they should be written down or dictated to the person giving the test.

After the test is completed, the third person should be contacted for verification of the information received. Remember no matter how silly or disjointed the information that the subject receives, make an accurate record of it.

Test "E-1" -- Remote Viewing

Remote Viewing is also called Psychic Sight. This test also involves some preparation. It will require three people, the person giving the test, the subject and the third person. The person giving the test will have a photograph of the third person to show to the subject. The time of the test will be arranged in advance. For conversation sake, let us say that the test was given at 10:00 PM. At that time the third person will be at a place where they have access to a telephone.

They will stay in that area for one half hour. Where they are at that time is not to be prearranged nor is the person giving the test to know where the third person is or what they are doing or what they are wearing at the time.

At 10:00 PM (or a time you designate) the person taking the test will be shown a photograph of the third person. The subject will concentrate on the photograph, but may not touch it. The subject will then try to see where the third person is, what they are and wearing, and where they are located. At twenty-five minutes later, the subject will stop writing or dictating and relax.

At 10:30 PM (or thirty minutes later) the third person will call in and tell the person giving the test what they are wearing, doing and where they are located. This information is to be recorded and checked against the subject's information.

Please don't give up if you don't get results the first few tests. You are like a baby trying to learn to walk, before you've learned to crawl. It will come when your waiting is full.

End of Transmission

Begin Open Channel

Lesson Thirty-Five:
Seven of Spades, received June 8th, 1991
Book of Wisdom, channeled from Hierophant

"The more you know, the more 'Knowing' will come to you." ERU

Dear Brother Hermit and Teacher,

I recall a hot summer day long past. I was seated beneath an ancient Gingko tree whose boughs I had sought as protection from the sun's burning rays. I was meditating to cool myself when a sweet voice broke my concentration.

"Who are you my dear sir?" It questioned. "Are you ill good sir?" she continued. "Let me fetch a cool cup of water for you!" My mind began to clear. The heat returned. I beheld a beautiful woman approaching with a cup of cool water. My mind and vision were clear now.

"Take this water and drink slowly," she said. I thanked and blessed her for her kindness.

"Who are you my dear sir?" she inquired again.

"A simple teacher," was my reply.

"What do you teach?" she pressed.

"I teach of Love and Good, Energy and Life, and the Mysteries of the Universe, which are hidden from the eyes of man," I replied.

"Teach me sir, some of the Mysteries of the Universe," she begged.

"Look up to the sky and tell me how many stars you see?" I said.

She laughed and said, "The heat must have baked your brain. There are no stars up there! Has no one told you that, good sir?'

"I am sorry, dear lady. I cannot teach you anything. For you do not believe what you do not see. The mysteries that I teach are truly hidden from the eyes of man. During the day some see no stars, some see one star and viewing through the 'Knowing' some see the same stars in the heavens day or night," I replied.

She turned and left, likened to an angry child cursing me under her breath. I tell you this, my brother Hermit, you will meet many people during the course of your life. Those that you talk to about the 'Ancient Mysteries' will react in different ways. Some will call you mad and crazy. Others will say you are wise and a great teacher. But, I tell you this, I do not think twice about what they say, for their wagging tongues will return to laud you later on in their lives.

Remember Sir Good Knight, you are a very rare person and important to the future. Archangel Michael chose you because you have the best chance of helping him succeed. If you listen well and follow his lead, you will reach heights beyond your wildest expectations. Just continue to do good works and be yourself regardless of what others think of you. Just follow your heart and the path you must walk will be made clear.

That leads us to another important topic, "Identity." In the world community many humans are losing their identity. Everyone wants to be like everyone else in order to be accepted. You cannot be an individual and also be like everyone else. You must choose one or the other. The Creator made us individually different for a reason. Like the snowflakes that are all different, so is true for people. No two humans have the same fingerprints, destiny or interpretation of life.

If you are a street cleaner, then put your heart into being a street cleaner; be proud of your work and proclaim your position with zeal.

If you are a priest, nun, evangelist, or holy man, wear the clothing that represents your faith.

If you are a soldier, police officer or knight in shining armor, wear the uniform of your profession in service with pride and truth.

If you want a part in the great play of life, dress and act the part, or do not take the part at all.

Woman cannot be man, priest cannot be sheep and police cannot be criminals without society rotting away and vanishing into the past. Be yourself, do not throw your identity away to be like the masses.

In nature, each maintains its identity. The Oak tree is a stately tree. Its wood is hard, it grows slowly and its leaves have special characteristics all belonging to the mighty Oak.

The Blue Spruce is a conical shaped tree, soft wooded and has needles for leaves. Now what if the mighty Oak decided it wanted to be a Blue Spruce, and to do this it gives up its leaves to bear needles. In this it loses its beauty, ability to give shade and its identity. It is now worthless and loses its might!

Before you were born into this world you viewed and reviewed the life you wish to live on this planet. You chose the state to be, male or female, master or slave, the picture of health or the epitome of suffering. So why would you wish to change your decision? It was chosen for a purpose. Now live that purpose.

So many people become zombies, caught up in being like the other guy they never live their own dream or fulfill their own destiny. Let me continue to tell you of the fate of my homeland. Too many Atlanteans became too much alike and we lost our true identity. We were too proud and a people who thought nothing could overwhelm our great social culture. We were wrong. Don't let that happen to your world.

Atlantis and the Walking Dead

When the Sons of Darkness took power over all the land they brought down heavy taxes and burdens upon the shoulders of the good people of Atlantis. The laws of the land became one-sided and unfair. The innocent suffered while criminals and ne'er-do-wells prospered.

When Seth began his rise to power, he did so under the premise to help others. He was a poet with words and convinced all who knew him that he was true and just. All the while in secret, his ego took over the small spark of good in him. He lusted for power over the land and community in which he loved. Once he got what he wanted, he could not stop. The ego grew and he wanted to build an even greater power to conquer the entire world. He was filled with greed as he thought to build his empire. This empire, as great as he envisioned would require many slaves. They would work the fields to feed the armies, build the barracks to house them and raise the ships to transport them into battle.

He called upon his magicians, alchemists, commanders and the wise men of his royal court to start work on his great evil plan.

First, they needed to raise an army of warriors, mercenaries and slaves. They decided to place a tax on merchants and their wares that were brought into Atlantis. With these revenues they purchased warriors and mercenaries. Now they needed slaves. So, they took many people on false charges. Thus, anyone who broke the law was condemned to slavery.

Soon the numbers of slaves were so great that Seth feared an uprising. Again, he called his council together, as to address this situation. His alchemist had a solution. He had the guards bring in an unruly slave. He then gave the slave a cup of wine that had a certain drug in it, to drink. The slave drank it. Soon after, his stomach began to burn, he seemed to be suffocating, his heart weakened, he became stiff and fell to the floor.

"I do not need dead slaves, you idiot!" screamed Seth. "He is not dead my king," the alchemist said. "All I have done is captured his will. He hears you! He sees you! But he has no emotions or will of his own. He is "Walking Dead."

We can put this in the food of the slaves. Once their will is taken from them, a few guards can control the many. We can also use this on the "Thing" creatures that we have problems controlling.

"Those under influence of this drug, we will call Zomba meaning "Child of Seth." Thus, Zombies are your new race of children that will serve the darkness without question."

"So shall it be written, so shall it be Law," Seth decreed.

When the Sons of Light were given this ill news, they were sorely afraid. But eventually they found that if a man missed his daily dose of the drug the effects would wear off.

Seth also found that if he gave the drug in smaller doses he could use it to weaken the will of those he wished to seduce. This is but one of the many evil uses he made of something that could've been helpful to mankind. Seth was evil and every good thing that he touched was used for evil means.

He used a great crystal to destroy entire cities and empires. When the life generator was invented to create food for the hungry, he sent zombies and soldiers out to find pieces of flesh and bones from the prehistoric monsters, from which he created monsters to unleash against the world. It was only by removing all of Atlantis that the world was to be saved from his evil scourge.

It is important that we know the history of the "Knowing" so that it can be preserved.

The "Knowing" is the Light that burns within the hearts and minds of the Sons of Light. The time will come when my teacher, Grand Master ERU, will return to earth to help you and the Good Knights rebuild the Star-Gate. So learn well these lessons and make ready yourself to bring the Sons of the Light and Angel-Knights home.

I tell you this so you and your students don't throw away your identities just to be like the masses. You, my brave knight, be who you are! Like the single star that shines brightest during the day, you are the only one, the sun of creation, in your personal universe. Those who savor and nurture their true identity will be looked up to in the end, when all others have lost identities and have become zombie slaves to their egos.

Now go away to your place and meditate on what has been spoken this day. When is the last time you have gone to your Secret Sacred Place?

End of Transmission

Begin Open Channel

Lesson Thirty-Six:
   Six of Spades, received July 8th, 1991
   Book of Wisdom, channeled from Hierophant

"The more you know, the more 'Knowing' will come to you." ERU

My Dear Brother Hermit and Teacher,

Let me start this lesson with the three M's - Mystic, Mystical and Mysticism. A definition of each is our first step on the Path of the Magi.

Mystic
One who comes to feel he or she has direct contact with the Creator, direct insight into truth and/or the nature of reality. A mystic is a person who seeks by contemplation and self-surrender to obtain unity with or absorption into the Deity or the absolute, or who believes in the spiritual apprehension of truths that are beyond human intellect.

Mystical
Mystical is an experience through exultation of the mind and/or soul. Having a spiritual meaning or reality that is neither apparent to the senses nor obvious to the intelligence, involving or having the nature of an individual's direct subjective communion with the Creator or ultimate reality; an experience of the "Inner Light."

Mysticism
Mysticism derives from the Greek word Mueo meaning to "Initiate" into a mystery. A belief or doctrine that knowledge or truth comes from a spiritual illumination which cannot be explained by ordinary processes of reason and implies a direct communication between the Creator and man through the inward perception of the mind.

The belief that union with or absorption into the Deity or the absolute, or the spiritual apprehension of knowledge inaccessible to the intellect, may be attained through contemplation and self-surrender.

During your meditations of late I have noticed that you are trying to find explanation of the overwhelming experience that you have had while calling down the "White Light."

It is a mystical experience, brought about through the frequent calling down of the White Light for the benefit of those ill or in need. The more you use the power, the greater the power becomes. But, there are conditions that you may not be aware of that evolved before this mystical event took place.

For some time now, you've been trying to develop certain psychic abilities. Some of these powers have been relatively easy, while for others they have come slow and painstaking. Unknown to you, an awakening has been taken place. An awakening, for the most part, that is not realized until an event takes place to draw your attention to it. You began preparing yourself for a new experience by learning to relax.

Relaxation has been repeated throughout many lessons. How many times have I started a procedure with the word "relax?" How many times have I stressed, "you must relax?" This has been likened to preparing the soil for planting. With good preparation of the soil, a magnificent garden will grow.

Then you were showered with the development of procedures for the awakening of your psychic abilities. These, as well as many symbols, words, numbers and stories that were revealed to you are like seeds that were planted. There has been so much planted in your mind, body and spirit that it will take you a lifetime to realize the magnitude of it all! As any farmer or gardener can tell you, planting is a slow, tedious process. And it must be done out of "Love" or nothing will grow very well. The plant will grow when its waiting is full. It can't be rushed or the plant will be weak and flawed.

Then through meditation, contemplation and quiet recollection you took care and watered your seeds. It is in doing for others out of love that the seeds began to grow. And better yet, by your good works that your plant began to spring forth into the "Light of Day."

Now through introversion, looking deep within yourself, going the way to your place, you are becoming aware of the true flower of your development. One day your creativity will produce a glorious Heavenly Kingdom where the land meets the sky.

Even more beautiful than this, you are coming to experience the ecstasy and rapture of mysticism. Calling down the White Light is a force that has allowed you to experience the All.

According to ancient alchemist you are the Philosopher Stone, an appropriate symbol for the Mystic Warrior of Peace. When you are observed from the standpoint of the Hermetic Arts it is not hard to understand. According to the Hermetic Mysteries, it was taught that the base metal, lead, could be changed to gold.

Man, in his base, beastie, loathsome self, is symbolized as lead. To this is added suffering and purification, understood to be sulfur. This is mixed with knowledge and wisdom, known as quicksilver. Lastly, we add three drops of the "Royal Tincture" - Compassion, Inner Awareness and the White Light. This mixture is then placed into the Fires of Desire.

Once removed from the fires, these ingredients are hung in their correct proportions on the three sacred bones of human success, the funny bone; remembering to always keep a good sense of humor, a wishbone, never forgetting to dream and a strong backbone, always taking good care of your body.

When wrapped within the full armor of "Divine Destiny" the individual undergoes a "Transfiguration." The base lead becomes the purest form of the Golden Man. That is the metaphor for you becoming a true living "Philosopher Stone."

This, my brother Hermit, is the overwhelming experience you have tasted. You are evolving into a Mystic's Mystical Force of Mysticism, as you walk the "Path of the Magi."

You may have just started out feeling like you could not work miracles. But, just the thought of being able to execute one small feat would intrigue you. So you studied and pressed yourself to develop. When you were utterly frustrated, events or happenings would take place. Then you would ask yourself, "What did I do this time that I did not do before?" Thus, you continued with highs and lows, successes and failures, or joy and frustration. But, most of all, you found that when you tried to use these abilities for others your powers grew and grew. The more it was used to help others, the stronger they became.

Now, one day, when your waiting was full, you came to a new experience. You were at one with universe and the Creator. You knew all things, but could not express them in words. You were a part of the universe and the universe was a part of you. You became a part of the force and the force became with you.

Like Master ERU told you at the beginning of each lesson, "The more you know, the more 'Knowing' will come to you!" What that means is that you have attained the Seeds of Knowledge from these lessons. Those seeds will sprout within your mind and you will know things in the future that you have never learned. That is the wisdom of knowledge growing inside you. You won't know how you know, you'll just know. But remember, "When you think you know, you don't, and when you know you don't, you do." The answer to that riddle is, "Just keep your mind open and keep learning from everything around you, because what you know will change."

Hierophant's Warning

Use these powers wisely or they will be taken from you and you will forget you ever had them. They will be replaced with a deep dark black hole filled with nothingness. You carry two very great responsibilities, knowing when to use the powers and when not to use them.

Some people would violate and misuse these powers by using them for personal wealth, casting negative spells, for sex and self-indulgent fame. Do not go there. The lessons cannot be used for ill-will and that negative energy will just turn on you. All you deserve will be provided if you stay righteous and humble, with your feet planted firmly on the true "Path of the Magi."

I tell you this, if you abuse these powers, they will be lost to you forever. And when you have lost them you will feel as though a part of your being has been cut away from you. You shall then be blinded to good and your heart will be filled with sorrow. And you will wander aimlessly in a blur of darkness.

I beg you my dear brother and all those you teach, please heed my words. Because I am your teacher, I am responsible for your actions, good or bad. Through your deeds I may elevate or decline.

Remember, only through your good works will I ever find my way home.

End of Transmission

Begin Open Channel

Lesson Thirty-Seven:
Five of Spades, received August 8ᵗʰ, 1991
Book of Wisdom, channeled from Hierophant

"The more you know, the more 'Knowing' will come to you." ERU

Dearest Brother Hermit and Teacher,

By now you have come to know my love for nature. I spent much of my time on earth in my gardens and in the forest for many reasons. They are quieting to the mind and spirit. It is a peace that comforts and soothes my mind, which is found in few other places. Herein you too will feel refreshed and charged with new life. We learn from flowers and plants, great wisdom and knowledge. Mysteries of the Universe can be found in the simplest flower or leaf.

And last but not least there is the healing found in the flowers, plants and trees of the gardens and forest. As I have already discussed much of this with you over past years, I will continue with what I have learned in regard to healing by plants. In turn, Master Hermit, I ask that you update this lesson as you reach greater levels of understanding so that your students may grow even more powerful than their teacher. A dark-haired woman who will embody Wisdom will come into your life one day. That day depends on many things. With her, she will bring an ancient knowing of the plant essences and their healing oils. She will teach you and all your students as well.

Hierophant's List of Herbs:

Aloe: The Aloe plant has many medical properties. When the juice or jelly from within the spikes or leaves is applied to burns it relieves the sting and helps to heal the burn quickly.

Angelica: Angelica powdered, then mixed with water and drank warms the inside and causes one to sweat. It protects the body against the cold weather. It is said to be good in curing pleurisy and diseases of the lungs.

Aniseed: As long as man has known about plants, he has used the seeds to stop the pain of hunger. The oil was used to cure stomach problems.

Caraway: Caraway seeds are eaten to relieve stomach cramps and gas.

Carrots: Carrots when taken with each meal raw, breaks down the fat buildup in the blood's circulatory system. It is also said, when taken faithfully, carrots reduce the growth of tumors and possibly cancer. The same effect is found in drinking fresh carrot juice.

Chamomile: Chamomile taken as a tea is good for the spleen and it dissolves stones in the body.

Cherries: Cherries are a fruit that have a property to relieve those who suffer from Gout. One is to eat twenty-five to thirty cherries the first day and eight to ten each day thereafter for thirty days.

Chervil: Chervil dissolves blood clots and helps pass kidney stones. When smashed or bruised leaves are applied to the area, it brings down swelling.

Chives: Chives crushed up are used to stop bleeding.

Clove: Clove has a long history of culinary and medicinal use. The oil was used as an expectorant and antiemetic with inconsistent clinical results. Clove tea was used to relieve nausea. Clove oil is used in dentistry as an analgesic and local antiseptic. It is used topically as a counterirritant.

Comfrey: Boil the root to make a tea. The drink is said to relieve all internal pain, breaks up phlegm and as an ointment is used for sprains and back strains.

Croton Teglium: Croton Teglium is a plant from which we get all Croton oil. One drop on a lump of sugar evacuates the bowels more forcefully than any aperient and or laxative. It is also said to be an active agent against leukemia.

Dill: Dill, whether you eat the seeds or prepare them in a tea to drink, relieves stomachaches.

Fennel: Fennel as a tea is thought to be good for the eyes and breaks down fat cells in the body.

Foxglove: From this plant we get Digitalis. It cures dropsy, a puffed-up body filled with watery liquid caused by weakened heart muscles. The leaves of the foxglove strengthen the heart muscles and the fluid drained away restoring the person's health. Too much is dangerous.

Garlic: Garlic it is said to rid the body of worms and melancholy. The ancient Hindus valued the medicinal properties of garlic and thought it to be an aphrodisiac. Garlic was used in Ayurveda medicine and held to increase virility and strength. The Charaka Samhita, 2,000 years ago, suggests garlic for the treatment of heart disease and arthritis. In ancient Chinese medicine, garlic was prescribed as an aid for respiration and digestion, most importantly diarrhea and worm infestation. Garlic was also used to treat sadness or depression. Fatigue, headache and insomnia were treated with garlic. Garlic was used to treat male impotency, or said another way, to increase virility.

Golden Rod: Golden Rod used as a tea helps keep the body well. As a lotion it is used in curing ulcers and used to wash the privy parts in venereal problems.

Hollyhocks: Hollyhocks dried, powdered and mixed with hot red wine to reduce swelling of the tonsils, prevent miscarriages and kill worms in children.

Indian Tobacco or Lobelia: Indian Tobacco or Lobelia, when smoked, relieves asthma and congestion of the respiratory system. It is also used to stop infection in war wounds.

Jessamine: With Jessamine only the flowers are used to make the oil which is used to soften the skin and revitalize weak limbs.

Lemon Balm: Lemon Balm tea is said to prolong life. Lemon Balm was dedicated to the goddess Diana, and used medicinally by the Greeks some 2,000 years ago. In the Middles Ages lemon balm was used to soothe tension, to dress wounds, and as a cure for toothache, skin eruptions, mad dog bites, crooked necks, and sickness during pregnancy. It was even said to prevent baldness. As a medicinal plant, lemon balm has traditionally been employed against bronchial inflammation, earache, fever, flatulence, headaches, high blood pressure, influenza, mood disorders, palpitations, toothaches and vomiting. A tea made from Lemon balm leaves is said to soothe menstrual cramps and helps relieve PMS.

Licorice: Licorice is used for dry cough, shortness of breath and constipation relief. Licorice root contains many anti-depressant compounds and is an excellent alternative to St. John's Wart. As an herbal medicine it has an impressive list of well-documented uses and is probably one of the most over-looked of all herbal wonders. Licorice is useful for many ailments including asthma, athlete's foot, baldness, body odor, bursitis, canker sores, chronic fatigue, depression, colds and flu, coughs, dandruff, emphysema, gingivitis and tooth decay, gout, heartburn, HIV, viral infections, fungal infections, ulcers, liver problems, Lyme disease, menopause, psoriasis, shingles, sore throat, tendinitis, tuberculosis, ulcers, yeast infections, prostate enlargement and arthritis.

Madder: With Madder, crush the leaves and roots together and apply to the skin where there is a problem, as in scales or freckles, for it will clean the skin and relieve these problems. Useful for all problems with the urinary tract, particularly where the urine becomes alkaline. It has been used for rickets, slow-healing broken bones, inflammations, and lack of appetite, diarrhea, dropsy, jaundice, blood purifier, and fever. Externally, a decoction of madder can be used for skin problems, especially tubercular conditions of the skin and mucous tissue.

Mandrake: Mandrake roots contain a powerful narcotic that acts on the nerves to relieve pain and induces sleep. Antibilious, cathartic, emetic, diaphoretic (increases perspiration), cholagogue (increases the flow of bile to the intestine), alterative, emmenagogue, resolvent, vermifuge (expel intestinal worms), and deobstruent (relieving obstruction), counter-irritant, hydragogue.

Nutmeg: Nutmeg is used as a tea to calm the nerves and produce visual illusions.

Parsley: Parsley opens obstructions of the liver and spleen. Fresh picked leaves placed on the eyes takes swelling away.

Rosemary: Rosemary sharpens the senses and improves the memory. In time it will be found useful in stopping the breakdown of brain cells.

Sassafras: Sassafras is said to strengthen the blood. Made into a tea, the brew can help with detoxification and in a tonic helps promote longevity.

Sesame: Sesame seed improves the memory and concentration. Ground and boiled and made into sesame seed tea it is said to cure a hangover with ten minutes.

Sunflower: Sunflower seed is said to make memory and concentration sharper. The sunflower is a sacred plant that appears in many Native Indian myths and stories. Sunflower has a special place in Native Indian Medicine. The seeds were used for treating the pain that females experience with menstrual cycle; it was thought to help due to the Sun having a daily cycle, which keeps us warm and helps to grow food and medicinal plants. Ancient men ate the seeds for strength in love; sunflower seeds are a good source of arginine, which helps boost sperm count. The plant contains one of the best sources of phenylalanine, helpful in the control of pain, and is a rich source of vitamin E.

Tamarisk: All parts of this young tree are used. It is best known to stop bleeding and to work against the hardness of the spleen.

Thyme: Thyme is very good for improving eyesight. As an ointment it is used to reduce pain and swelling of the testicles. Thyme has many helpful actions. It has been used as an antiseptic, anodyne, disinfectant, anti-tussive, anti-inflammatory, rubefacient, demulcent, aperitif, carminative, diaphoretic, depurative, digestive, diuretic, expectorant, fungicide, nerve agent, pectoral, sedative, stimulant, and vermifuge.

Willow: The inner bark of the willow tree contains a chemical called so Salicin, a painkiller related to aspirin. It is also said to help rheumatics and people with weak hearts. Chewing the inner bark does this.

Wintergreen: Wintergreen oil is used to break a fever or cold. In addition to being used as a flavoring, wintergreen and its oil have been used in topical analgesic and rubefacient preparations for the treatment of muscular and rheumatic pain.

Woodruff – (Sweet): Sweet Woodruff used as a tea, relieves headaches. Sweet woodruff is thought to possess tonic properties and also has noteworthy anti-inflammatory and diuretic actions. The chemical substances coumarone and flavonoid enclosed by this herb are responsible for its positive effect in treating phlebitis and varicose veins. In addition, sweet woodruff has also been employed in the form of an antispasmodic and is administered to children and adults alike to cure sleeplessness or insomnia.

Yarrow: Yarrow, when used in the form of an ointment, is said to have the ability of healing wounds. Ingested it can reduce the fever of a cold.

On the "Path of the Magi" the pupil must have a working knowledge of the many mysteries of the universe. I have started you with this simple list of ancient remedies and cures, to help feed your knowledge. I could go on and speak volumes, but if you are a true healer you should explore this world on your own.

Hierophant's Warning: As there were combinations of herbs that made up the zombie drug that robbed men of their free will, there are also many combinations that promote good health. Before using any of the substances discussed in this lesson, I would first advise that you consult with your modern-day medical physicians and guides before trying any of them. What may be one man's medical cure could be another man's illness.

I do, however, recommend that you collect samples of all the herbs I speak of today, because the Ascended Masters used and respected them all; therefore, like the "Treasure of the Magi" stones, the "Magi's Garden Herbs" have power and respect with just possessing them. It is your link to a very powerful past.

End of Transmission

Begin Open Channel

Lesson Thirty-Eight:
 Four of Spades, received September 8th, 1991
 Book of Wisdom, channeled from Hierophant

"The more you know, the more 'Knowing' will come to you." ERU

My Dear Brother Hermit and Teacher,

With the seasons, the earth goes through changes. Each of these changes is distinct and represents a stage in the development of man. The physical relationship is obvious, so let us discuss the psychic and mystical development.

In the spring the earth is reborn. The earth smells good and alive. The plants issue forth blossoms and their greenery. All comes to life.

With man, he begins his quest for knowledge and understanding. He observes with his eyes, listens with his ears, and begins to seek with every part of his being. And by reading the Ancient Books of Wisdom he acquires that knowledge.

As the summer begins, changes take place. The plants and trees begin to form their fruit.

So too is it with man. He begins to realize his abilities as changes begin to take place within him. He becomes aware that he has the power to change things.

With the autumn comes the harvest time where in the labors of Mother Nature are seen, appreciated and used.

In man, the fruits of his labor ripen to the execution of his newly developed abilities to help those in need. The beauty of his Divine Nature is truly fulfilled.

Then comes the winter when all things rest. This is also the time for man to rest. It's time to step back and look at the accomplishments and failures. A period to evaluate the good he has done, and where he has fallen short. It is also a time for man to set his goals for the next year's cycle.

Not only does man follow a yearly cycle, but he also follows a seven-year cycle.

Every seven years your body is completely recycled. And a reoccurrence seems to take place. There are events or attitudes that seem to last forever. As you look back you will see that they rarely exceed a seven-year period or multiples of seven years.

Be aware that all things in the universe follow cycles and laws. When you come to an awareness of the cycles and laws you will know how to change things.

During the course of these past lessons, we have given you the alternatives to arrive at the same place. Yet, without the laws there is no order. Even in the cause-and-effect of things, the altering of things, or the changing of things there must be order. Without order no power, force, or change can survive with anything less than disaster. Take time to review the Ancient Laws of Wisdom that you have received so far.

Now my faithful student because of your patience in seeking out the knowledge of the "Knowing" you have ascended to the great "Doors of Oneness." As Jesus said, "I and the Father are one," you and the Creator are also one in the same. How can this be, you might ask? The answer is simple, when Jesus began seeking the great knowledge of the Universe, the Archangel Michael guided him as he guides you now.

Once Jesus gained the "Knowing," the Creator's electro-magnetic energy flowed into parts of his body that increased his power and understanding. The seeds of wisdom that have been planted in your mind will grow in time and you will find your Divine purpose as Jesus did. I speak of the real Jesus not the one of legend. Jesus was not the only Son of God. Just as Mohammad was not God's last prophet. The creator would never limit to one human, the great gifts intended for all his children who seek to know and do good things for others.

After contemplation of this degree, the Order of Wisdom will recognize you as a Magi of the Third-Degree. This will be the highest level you can attain within the Ancient "School of Wisdom." Some of the deepest mysteries will be revealed to you, as your lessons draw to an end.

You may count yourself among the fortunate, for many have fallen along the way. They were not ready for such wisdom as this, or they thought they could use this wisdom to become materially wealthy, or to seduce their friends. Those with that attitude have not only failed in their studies, but have had the power turned against them. They cast darkness and lies towards the righteous to draw attention from them, denounce the Wisdom Lessons and to make themselves feel a little better if for only fleeting moments. These poor wretches have ended up in a state far worse than that in which they began.

You are now becoming a Master. And as a Master you are looked up to, so conduct yourself as one who is wise and learned. Teach those about you who are worthy. Waste not your time or wisdom on those who are obstinate in their ignorance, nor argue with them. Be calm and at peace.

Forgive those who have wronged you or bring harm upon you, for they shall suffer a far greater misfortune. Seek no revenge for you will lose the power.

Once I had a student that I held very close to my heart. A second student, who had not been my student very long, and who was treated with such kindness as the first, was jealous of the first. He resorted to slander of me to the first student and slander of my first student to me. Being not ignorant of this play, I waited to see what the results would be.

The first student left, falling prey to the words of the second student. He let a lie become his truth.

He married had a child and accomplished little in his life. The second student left of shame and guilt. Some years later he sent me an epistle admitting what he had done and asking my forgiveness. Unknown to him I had forgiven him when he left the first time, but now I told him. Ten years later he came to inform me that he was dying of an illness far worse than leprosy.

I hold no malice for what he did, nor do I seek revenge. His crime was not against me. It was an offense against the wisdom he had attained, for he knew the truth.

Revenge is a disease. Once you let it take hold, it is not only almost impossible to destroy, but you will lose every ounce of ability you ever developed.

Lastly let me speak of feelings. It is said, "A Magi sees with his ears, hears with his eyes and feels with his heart."

Let your heartfelt feelings, be your guide on your Divine Quest. If your heart tells you not to do something, or not to say something, follow the advice of your heart. If you have a strong heartfelt feeling to do something, which is not in conflict with the Ancient Laws, do it. Be aware of those feelings that inform and educate you. They are your communication with the Universe and the Creator.

Do not confuse those feelings with your own ego or personal desires, for they will lead you astray.

Special Note from the Hierophant—

Master Hermit for your next First Wednesday Club gathering I want you to find the most meaningful words of wisdom of your day. Add them to this lesson for you club's members and students.

I did as my teacher asked and I am wiser for the effort. Now, I invite you to research wise quotes of your day to use personally or to share with your students.

End of Transmission

Begin Open Channel

Lesson Thirty-Nine:
   Three of Spades, received October 8th, 1991
   Book of Wisdom, channeled from Hierophant

"The more you know, the more 'Knowing' will come to you." ERU

My Dear Hermit and Teacher,

This is a special day. Every year on October 8th, the Pleiadean earth sister the Constant Walker or Gaia ascends back to Heaven for a review of Earth's experiment with the Creator.

There have been years that the human experiment that we are part of hasn't fared too well, but she was always allowed to return to help our experiment continue.

As you know the essence of the Creator is the great Electro-Magnetic Consciousness. The EMC runs within everything throughout the great void known as the "Time Space Continuum." It is the force that brings things together and forces them a part. It's what selected all the elements that came together to make up the earth and allowed you to develop and enjoy earth as the paradise it truly is. Much like you do with your hands when you create or experiment with things.

One day humans will learn how to infuse EMC into the things they build. Then humanity will be invited to join the other advanced forms of intelligent life that exist in the other dimensions found within the seven universes of creation, also known as the Macrocosm.

It is hoped that humanity fares better than when they developed an understanding of the simple equation that ended with $E=MC2$. The first thing man did with it was to use the knowledge for a senseless bombing, in 1945 of God's children.

The Creator is the Electro-Magnetic juice of life itself and its divine reason for being. Remember everything has a Divine Reason and Purpose! When you, in the physical world, start to die, your body will waste away returning to stardust, but when you die the EMC juice within lives on and returns to the Creator from whence it came. However, while in life it grows and records what you experience in your life.

Every spark of life is important because of the awareness it gathered during its human story. This means your life matters. It is matter. It creates matter. As it does, your story expands along with it and your EMC grows ever larger. Each story is unique and the awareness you gather while you are alive will seek its own level and key. That key will gain entrance for you into the levels or dimensions of that place humans call Heaven that you can comprehend.

Remember when Jesus said, *"In my Father's house there are many mansions"*?

You can only enter the levels or mansions your awareness can comprehend. The "Keys" you receive are your levels of "awareness" that are achieved during your life. You only get one chance at this. So, this is your time to grow!

It is time for you to wake up and stay awake. The great net of illusion that was thrown upon the earth thousands of years ago is able to be broken. You have the ability to break it and free humanity from the deceptions that have been programmed into their existence. Humans have been led to believe false concepts and notions. Humanity is far greater than you have ever imagined. Believe it or not, the biggest things that hold someone back from moving forward on a positive path are negative childhood memories. Let us explore the depths of the memories of our childhood.

Childhood Memories

I ask that you put your mind into a relaxed state. As you have learned from Lesson One. Now think back five years at how you felt about life, your job and friends, are you happy? Move slowly back in five-year increments until you reach age four.

Now at age four how do you feel?

Move to age ten. How do you feel and why do you feel that way?

Moving further along into your life, at age sixteen, how do you feel and why?

Now move to age twenty-one, how do you feel and why?

Stay hovering between the ages of your life when you were the most impressionable, review your life and pick out times of great joy and times of great fear and anxiety.

Bring as many of these remembrances to light as possible, then return to your rightful age and create an outline on paper of your childhood memories, the good things and the bad, that you remember.

Now that we have discovered the source of your problems we need a miracle to help you get over those problems that are deep-rooted in your sub-conconscious.

Labyrinth of Miracles

Now that you have the powers of astral projection, journey with me to the Sacred Labyrinth of Miracles in Atlantis, where Queen Kei Sophia Pistis is waiting for you. It is truly, a beautiful sight to behold.

As we start our journey we float through time and space until we hover over a special fortress devoted to the Magi. It is neither a Kingdom nor Queen-dom, it is Wise-dom or Wisdom.

We land near a smooth calm reflecting pool at the foot of the Star-Gateway. Passing near the Temple of Isis, through the Valley of the Kings and a Great Pyramid, we fall under the watchful Eyes of the Universe.

Progressing further through a hidden door in the side of the pyramid we find ourselves in a lush green garden. The sun is setting and the Labyrinth of Miracles lies before us. It is lit up with a canopy of small white orb lights, suspended in air like ten thousand fireflies.

The entrance to the heart shaped labyrinth is through the top of the heart. There are seven rings to the labyrinth's maze-like configuration. Each ring is made up of three-foot high blue-gray stone walls. The tops of the walls are planters filled with colorful flowers and blue lavender bushes in bloom. The smell is sweet and awakens all of our senses.

In the center of the labyrinth is a sixteen-foot blue-gray stone tower, outlined in tiny white orb lights. It is the "Tower of Sophia," Guardian of Wisdom. There is a faint sound of music in the misty air and angels sing high above us. As we enter the labyrinth, on our journey to the center, you are given a choice. Do you turn right toward the north or turn left toward the south?

Remember which direction you choose, if you want to find your way out. I will walk with you no matter which direction you choose, for you have now been made blind and cannot see your way without my descriptions.

Even blind, your feet know which way to go. You are seeing through your third eye now. Arcing thirty steps forward you turn right, then right again. Now arching another sixty-five steps you turn left, then another quick left.I will describe the scenes before you. The outer walls of the labyrinth are five-foot-high with stone statues of twelve hooded Magi holding shepherd hooks with a brass lit lamp swinging in the breeze. Their robes are alternating gold and silver in color. There are holes in the hoods where the faces would be. One clear quartz crystal illuminates the faceless space.

The twelve Magi stand upon the outer wall guarding the hours on this Great Clock of the fourth dimension. Now picture a clock in your mind. One of the numbers is flashing. What is it? I must guide you to that corresponding Magi, for he stands here for you. As I take you to your statue, I asked that you feel your way up his robes to the hood until you feel the tiny crystal. Break it loose and hold it in your hand as we continue your journey.

After about ten minutes of arcing right and left turns, we stand at the threshold of the Great Tower of Wisdom. You are blind, yet your third eye can see everything I have described. You knock and Queen Sophia's clear sweet voice says, *"Enter."* I take you inside and sit you in one of two-throne chairs in front of a small cascading waterfall. You hear the water falling and a gentle breeze blowing a cross your face. Kissing your hand, I leave the tower in the hope that you can remember how to find your own way out.

Rising out of the pool of water at the base of the waterfall is a purple mist. As the mist flows out and across the floor it forms the figure of a tall beautiful woman with long dark hair. She is dressed in a silver breastplate and gown. Upon her head is a silver crown containing eight bright shining stars.

Queen Kei Sophia Pistis speaks, *"Beloved child of knowledge, you can't change how people treat you or what they say about you. If you allow someone else's words and actions to control you, you give up your power. All you can do is change how you view it through observation. Reactions are not thought through thoroughly. Responses, if needed, are done with a clear mind. So, take a deep breath, clear your mind, and move on. Life is too short for the pains you are inflicting upon yourself! What is in the past is there for a purpose. Learn from it and move toward a brighter future."*

As you breathe, you are taking in the pure healing essence of the "White Light."

Queen Sophia says, *"Give me your list of childhood memories. We will carve your good memories in stone so that they will be with you forever. We will write your sad memories in sand, so the winds of time will erase them never to affect you again."*

You can feel a release of your old pains.

"Now hand me your crystal." She says. Taking the crystal and dipping it in the pool of water at the bottom of the waterfall, she gives it back saying, "If you truly want to be free of what haunts you put this crystal under your tongue and find your way back home. When the crystal melts and becomes a part of you, your worriers will be gone. Become the hero of your life story."

You follow Queen Sophia's instructions. As soon as you place the crystal in your mouth your full vision returns. You are sitting in the beautiful tower alone. The inside of the tower is decorated as if for a Christmas celebration, with tiny multi-colored orb lights outlining the roof and all the corners of the room. There are evergreen garlands, large sparkling snowflakes and door-sized mirrors on the twelve walls that surround you. There seems to be no doors only large mirrors where the doors should be. Then you remember what I told you, "What direction should you chose right or left?" Walking through the mirror in that direction you find yourself home, free from all the things that once haunted you. Now never let them invade you again.

The path to a happy life is found in the Queen of Wisdom's words, *"You can't change how people treat you or what they say about you. All you can do is change how you respond to it. So, take a deep breath and move on! Become the hero of your own life story."*

Now that you are free from the things that haunted you in the earth dimension it's time to learn about the other dimensions within the great macrocosm.

The Nine Dimensions

The time has come for you to expand your knowledge by perceiving all nine dimensions of the macrocosm. Once you are aware of them you will learn how to probe them. The path to all dimensions is to go within you.

First Dimension: The core of the Earth is the first dimension, and the source of harmony, bliss and being grounded.

Second Dimension: The world above this and just below the earth's surface. The second dimension is the source of telluric powers and elemental beings.

Third Dimension: is the existence on earth, in linear space/time.

Fourth Dimension: is a nonphysical, archetypal zone where feelings, dreams, and all connections to Gaia, Mother Earth, and higher dimensions are available. Planets manifest fourth dimension archetypal patterns that express their own distinct versions of the Sun's energy and stimulate behavioral patterns on earth. Use of mirrors can help to create gateways to the higher dimensions. Remember you must go inside to go out.

Fifth Dimension: The Pleiades are the fifth dimension of orbital patterns and cycles of your solar system and Pleiadean spiral. The Pleiades is home of the Seven Celestial Sisters. Use of lasers lights help to stimulate the fifth dimensional experience.

Sixth Dimension: The Sirius star system is the sixth dimension of your world and it creates geometrical light constructions out of the physical forms in third dimension that are shaped by forth dimension archetypal feelings and their creative patterns in fifth dimension. There are the morphogenetic fields behind physical patterns on earth. It might also be considered the first level of heaven.

Seventh Dimension: cannot be described it words since it is inconceivable, but I will try. It is a multi-universe of time and space where beings of multi-dimensional energy systems are able to travel through many levels or Heavens. This is where the Angels of the Four Directions reside closest to the Creator. They have the inconceivable ability to move in all four directions at the same time. The seventh dimension is the gateway to the eighth dimension.

Eighth Dimension: Probability Initiation space. All probable patterns realized come from the eighth dimension. Seventh dimension Archangels exist here so this is considered the highest level of heaven.

Ninth Dimension: Hall of Records or God's Library where the Book of Life or Consciousness of God resides. The Will of God exists here. Some might call it the Holy Spirit or the Electro-Magnetic Energy force of the Father-Mother Godhead. This is where archangels ascend to communicate with the Creator. The highest point in ninth dimension is the Omniverse and Omega Point from which all existence started. This is the Electro-Magnetic Pulse of all Light Matter, the Father-Mother Godhead. The Ninth Dimension is from where everything comes from and will return.

I know that what I have given you in the outline is somewhat confusing, but I am trying to explain an enigma. Something that is unexplainable. In time, as your knowledge grows, the "Knowing" will make more sense of it for you.

End of Transmission

Begin Open Channel

Lesson Forty:
Two of Spades, received November 8th, 1991
Book of Wisdom, channeled from Hierophant

"The more you know, the more 'Knowing' will come to you." ERU

Dearest Hermit and Teacher,

Now that you are about to enter into the inner sanctuary of the "Temple of Wisdom," it is time to take your rightful place among the Sons of Light and Magi. There will be others there with you who will help you through their psychic abilities in order to expand your knowledge. But you, and you alone, must call forth what has been taught in these lessons from the Book of Wisdom, so that you may take that next great step. No one can take this for you.

Prepare yourself by drinking plenty of water to flush your system, and stay away from smoking and alcohol for three days before you proceed.

The preparation

I ask that you go to your quiet secret place to study. The room should be aired out and smudged ahead of time. Light one candle and set up an angelic altar.

About fifteen minutes before the appointed time, begin to relax your mind.

The Beginning Step One

When you are ready to begin, face west making the sign of the cross in the air before you, and call upon the Archangel Raphael saying:

"Archangel Raphael, come forward to be my witness and my aid that what I do is right, just, and for the betterment of mankind."

Then turn to the east. Make the sign of the cross in the air before you, and call upon Archangel Michael saying:

"Archangel Michael, come forward to be my witness and my aid that what I do is right, just, and for the betterment of mankind."

Now make now turn to the north. Make a sign of the cross in the air before you, and call upon Archangel Gabriel saying:

"Archangel Gabriel, come forward to be my witness and my aid that what I do is right, just and for the betterment of mankind."

Lastly turn to the south. Make the sign of the cross in the air before you, and call upon Archangel Uriel saying:

"Archangel Uriel, come forward to be my witness and my aid that what I do is right, just and for the betterment of mankind."

Now you will face the East and make the Star of David in the air above your head as you say:

"(Yod - Hey - Vau - Hey) you are great above all things, holy is your name, hear my cry and plea, for what I ask is not in vain, but for the betterment of mankind."

This completes the first step.

Before you proceed you must be relaxed and at peace within and with all things in your life. If you harbor any ill feelings toward another, are angry, are upset, in fear, or have any negative emotions or feelings within your being, I ask that you not go into part two.

The reason for this is because you are about to experience the most exciting part of your development. I tell you this, love cannot enter where there is hate and good cannot be brought about when one holds negative feelings within. It is not only for you that I ask, it is for the sanctity of the Holy Temple. Sit quite now and meditate. Listen inside and ask, "Am I Ready?"

If the answer is "no," wait a few days until you have freed yourself of any and all negativity, then proceed.

If you receive the answer "Yes" please continue.

Step two

Using the relaxation method, you learned in lesson one, relax your mind, body and spirit. Project yourself and ask that you be taken to the Temple of Wisdom. It will be interesting how far you can reach on your own.

Remember everything you see and hear. When you return to your body write it all down. It will be needed in the next lesson if you progress, when I will take you for an audience with the Creator.

End of Transmission

Begin Open Channel

Lesson Forty-One:
Ace of Diamonds, received December 8ᵗʰ, 1991
Book of Wisdom, channeled from Hierophant

"The more you know, the more 'Knowing' will come to you." ERU

My Dear Brother Hermit and Teacher,

Before we proceed make sure the Ancient Laws of Wisdom you have been given so far are carved deep into your memory. They are the seeds of your powers and the means by which you should live your life, if you choose to stay on the "Path of the Magi."

Please take this time to review the past forty lessons again to see if there is any additional information on any subjects you may have forgotten. It is important that you be prepared for the last ten lessons. If you haven't gained an adequate level of understanding and proficiency, you will be lost.

Like my teacher, Master ERU told me, *"It is not enough that you know this knowledge, you must become the Wisdom of this Knowledge if you are to succeed."*

Now please review from the past lessons below before you may dare continue. If you do not feel you are ready to enter the temple, stop here until you are.

Great Temple and Symbols

From lesson four: Let us speak of the symbols of our wisdom school and of our forefathers of Atlantis. The most powerful symbol is the Ankh. It originally represented "Eternal life through the Divine Creator," and was called the "Gate-way of the Soul."

Let it be known that all the current religions of man in your modern world have borrowed from the spiritual beliefs of the ancient past. Many of the stories found in the Old Testament can also be found in ancient texts dating several thousand years earlier from other cultures.

Since the beginning of time, the great guardian of humanity has been the Archangel Michael. If he could say one thing to you it would be, "Stop all your religious disputes. They are just different views of the same thing, the Great Unknown. So stop acting like you know IT. You are all right in your limited beliefs, but know this; the Creator of all things has no religion, only children. Serve his children and you serve the All."

There is power and energy in everything humans believe in, past and present, even if it is a lie, if man believes it. It's the truth until man doesn't

419

believe it anymore. That is the power of the will and mind of man. So don't discount anything, ponder all beliefs and find your own truth. Truth is as different as the human fingerprint and no two humans have the same fingerprints or absolute truth. If you want to come closer to the truth study all the religions of man. Your heart will tell you what's "Righteous" and what "Not."

Remember: *"When you think you know you don't, when you know you don't, you do!"*

In Egypt, it was a sandal strap or tie that became the symbol of "Life," although life was written in symbols. The Ankh was usually pictured in the hands of the gods or goddesses. Then in the period 1375–1350 B.C. it was used in Egypt as a sign for the God Aton. This was the first introduction of monotheism, the belief in one God, in Egypt. The total graphic symbol of this one God was the Sun on whose lower edge was supported a small vase and whose rays terminated in the hands of children.

The children were holding the Ankh, which represented everlasting life. The Sun disc represents Re or Ra, the Father of the Gods and the "Creator of All Living Things." The vase represents the Heart, which is synonymous with the Soul or Spirit, for it was a Heart that was weighed in the final judgment against the Feather of Truth on the Scales of Justice and Balance.

The "Tau" a T-shaped cross is the Ankh without the loop or Eye of God. It is also the 19th letter of the Greek alphabet and the last letter of the Hebrew alphabet, Therefore, it represents the end of all things, or the end of the world. It is also believed that it is this seal with which the Order of Righteousness will be spared during the "Great Judgment on the End of Days." Among some Christians it is believed to be the symbol of The Christ. Although, frequently disguised, it is found in the paintings, monograms and stained-glass windows of many churches throughout the Christian world.

Let us go on to the symbol what is referred to as the "Anchor of Hope." If you were to ask a minister or priest what the symbol means they will say that it is a symbol of their hope and faith in Jesus Christ. It is actually made up of two glyphs or symbols. The upper part of symbol is the Ankh. In this instance the Ankh represents the Christ. The spurs at the bottom represent the virgin birth. The miracle of the birth of the Christ and his virgin birth represent faith and hope to millions of the faithful thus the significance of the symbol.

In astrology, we have Love for the sign representing Venus, which, besides being the second planet also means, "Love of life." In alchemy it stands for the element Copper. For many thousands of years, the symbol has come to have many meanings. You shall come to realize as we continue, that the symbol has great power.

Now, let us study the symbol of the Ankh. In the crown or loop is the "TETREGRAMMATION."

"Ankh Power Symbol"

From lesson eight: Remember our discussion about the Ankh? The Ankh is an appropriate symbol to characterize the student. As you look at the symbol, it might bear a resemblance to the human figure. Within the symbol itself, we see the "A" or the Alpha, the beginning and also the "O" or the Omega, the end. The A & O represent the brain in the physical body; the organ that is created first in the womb and the organ which stops functioning last to indicate physical death.

"Then God said, 'Let us make man in our image, in our likeness' … So, God created man in his own image, in the image of God he created him; male and female he created them.'

Is the above quote referring to our brainpower being one and the same with the Creator? And isn't it interesting that below the A and the O are the arms of the Ankh or the glyph meaning "The Infinite?" The glyph is a symbol for our ever present, imperishable spirit, which cannot be destroyed. As in the Christian cross there are four "stars" or points, which represents faith, hope, charity, and love. Remember the meaning behind the symbol for it has always been with us always and is a powerful talisman for human kind.

"White Light"

From lesson five: The "White Light" is a highly concentrated form of Electro-Magnetism within the universe where positive energies are stored. The "White Light" can be called upon by anyone with a strong will and understanding of its use and Divine nature. It should not be confused with the light you are drawn to when you die. If you, as the dearly departed, see a white light, look to the right of it and you will see the "Golden Light of Oneness." That is the path you want.

The "White Light" is used for healing and protection from negative energies or death. White light cannot be used to harm, nor can it be harmed in any way. For this reason, negative or dirty energies can be sent to the "White Light" for purification and transformation.

The "White Light" can only be brought down and placed in a person once to help that person, but it can be brought down and placed in quartz crystals, which can be used by a person many times. The symbol from ancient times that best represents the "White Light" is a long crystal. Are you surprised that the symbol would be a crystal or that your own Washington Monument embodies the power of the "White Light"?

Its ornamental channel, called a compound glyph, is topped by a triangle that is representative of the Creator. The parallel lines extending earthward are the shaft of the extended forces of the Trinity or the "White Light" descending to man who is symbolized by the square at the bottom of the cliff. The "White Light" is sent to all of mankind and is diffused throughout the earth to benefit all matter.

Many years prior to your birth my Good Knight, The Creator sent an open channel of healing energy to a man in the East who had lost his way. He began to teach and spread this energy to heal mankind. He called it Reiki. The very same woman you will seek in the future to write your life's story for the world, the one who also has the Knowing of the plants and the oils, was born as Wisdom. She wields a great power of healing. Things will begin to come together for you when she places the Crown upon her own head. All seekers should obtain from her this healing frequency she possesses.

Put all I have just told you together. I know, it's a lot.

Are you ready?

Now, if you dare – Beware - You are entering the third and final level of the Ancient School of Wisdom. In your mind, let yourself follow me to the Great Temple of Atlantis. As you pass through the Great Temple's Doors, you will notice an inscription over head, "Laws of One," to the right you see a tongue meaning "Speech" or "Command." But when this is combined with the glyph on the left it reads:

"By Command of the Creator, the Angels of the Four Directions have established the Great Laws of Wisdom and thereby bring Order throughout the Universe."

Once inside the Ancient "Temple of Wisdom," on your right you will see on the table a bright white tunic with an equilateral red cross on its breast, put it on. Now on you left is another table which contains seven cloth belts - blue, red, white, green, purple, yellow and black - choose one and tie it around your waist.

In front of you are two very large black doors with a large golden Ankh carved into them. Pound on the doors with your fist three times. Then wait.

If the doors don't open for you within five minutes, return the belt and tunic to the table and return home. You are not ready. Try again after forty-eight hours and careful review of you lessons once again. This is a big step and you must be ready for it. Once inside your life will change forever.

If the sacred doors of the temple open, close your eyes, then step inside. Take a deep breath then open your eyes and behold in front of you in the center of the room is the "Throne Altar" it's a waist high red equilateral cross lying flat on the floor, in the center of altar is a circle supporting a huge golden Ankh. In the center of the loop in the top of Ankh is a burning "White Light."

There are twelve large numbered rocks or stations, like the numbers on a great clock. You are now witnessing all time and space. Walk around the outside of the rocks and count them as you go. From one of the rocks you will feel a pull: One, Two, Three, Four, Five, Six, Seven, Eight, Nine, Eleven, Twelve. Now go to the rock that you felt the pull from and have a seat. If you did not feel a pull, sit on numbered rock that corresponds with the crystal you choose in the Labyrinth of Miracles where you met Queen Sophia Pistis.

What number rock are you now sitting on?

Say its number over and over again in your mind so you do not forget it. Remember it because that number represents the hour of time that will be important to you in the future.

Spend ten minutes pondering all the lessons you have learned thus far on the "Path of the Magi."

You need not say a thing, but if you have questions ask them now, any two you might have, for you are in the presence of your "Creator."

The Creator will answer only one of your questions. If you do not hear the answer immediately, it will come to your mind within the next twenty-four hours if it was proper.

Look up. Swirling above you is a great Host of Heavenly Angels. You can feel the breeze created by their wings.

Relax, just relax. You have joined with your Creator and you didn't have to die to get here. Think about your life. Be thankful.

When you are satisfied with your Divine audience, stand, bow to the All Mighty and without turning your back to the Creator, leave the "Great Temple of Wisdom" without a word.

Do not stop to remove the white tunic it is yours, and you should visualize yourself wearing it whenever you, use your powers of Astral Projection. You now wear the robes of the Magi.

Consider yourself one of the privileged few that have ever been granted a seat, as a "Point of Light," on the "Time Space Continuum."

End of Transmission

Begin Open Channel

Lesson Forty-Two:
   King of Diamonds, received January 8ᵗʰ, 1992
   Book of Wisdom, channeled from Hierophant

"The more you know, the more 'Knowing' will come to you." ERU

My Dearest Hermit and Teacher,

Please ask yourself one more time, are you ready? Are you at peace within? Are you ready to use the "Knowing" for the betterment of mankind?

If your answers to these questions are all yes, then you are ready to go on to the next great step.

"I pray that you be filled with peace and the 'Knowing'"!

Full Moon "White Light" Ceremony

The Full Moon "White Light" Ceremony is a proud tradition of the Sons of Light that has been carried on, unbroken, for over twenty-five thousand years. Since you and your knights are seekers of the ancient knowledge contained in the Book of Wisdom you are welcome to join our gathering in this great tradition under each month's full moon; and at no other time as a group since it would be a waste of your time and effort.

During the full moon is when we should all gather because, "When we are together we are a part and went we are apart we are together."

The Sons of Light have chosen to make direct contact with the All and meditate during the light of the full moon to send good energy out into the world. In balance, the Sons of Darkness always gather under the new moon, and then ask that their attacks be launched every month during the full moon. That is why there is so much craziness, crime and violence during each full moon cycle. These times have been set aside to help maintain balance in the universe and to give humanity free will to choose its path in life. Choose wisely for you shall exist forever within the choices you make.

Continue if you seek to do "GOOD" in your world. If you seek to do "EVIL" in your world, well get behind me my beloved for the truth is, "Good is only as good as evil is evil. Some evil people make other evil people look good, just as some good people make other good people look evil. How many times have you judged a good man out of ego and fear?

How many times have you been deceived by an evil man you thought was good?

Before you start the ceremony, you need paper and pencil to write petitions.

Now think about people in the world or around you that need goodly acts, help, and comfort in their lives. In your first written petition document what you want to request for them. Pick someone that really needs help in his or her lives.

Now in a second petition document write down your needs or requests. You will be using these petition documents in the formal ceremony ahead.

What you are about to do is likened to making a phone call to the Creator. The "White Light" you will be calling down will be your direct line and private messenger to the "Almighty."

Calling Down The "White Light"

It is time now, to begin calling down the "White Light." Make sure that you are within twelve hours before or twelve hours after a full moon cycle. You can contact us individually or as a meditation group.

Hold your hands in the open receiving position and tip your head back slightly as you call the "White Light" down.

Visualize the small ball of "White "Light" beginning to form at the ceiling or six feet above you head as if you are outside in the moonlight. The "White Light" looks like a sparkler and is beginning to descend. As it does so, it is growing larger and larger. It is now a foot from the ceiling and is the size of a tennis ball. It is continuing to float downward. It is now about two feet from the ceiling in the size of a softball. The "White Light" is descending slowly and is now three feet from the ceiling and the size of a basketball.

It's continuing to grow larger and larger as it descends. It is now at chest level. You can feel the warmth of the pure white light as it grows. Now it is beginning to enter into you and feels good. You're being filled with the white light and you feel at peace. You have never felt so good in all your life. When your filled with the "White Light." Cross your arms over your chest and tip your head downward.

Using your mind now, go deep within the "White Light" that is within you. It is with this that you enter into the Oneness of the Fifth Dimensional Consciousness.

When you reach this point, take out your petition documents.
Start with the first petition and say:
First Petition

"I petition for my brothers and sisters who are in need of help in body, mind and spirit and temporal needs."

Read now your request for them here, and then continue.

"Let this not be my will, but thy will be done oh Lord God the Creator of all things."

Second Petition

"I petition for myself that you strengthen my body, mind, spirit and temporal needs and…."

Here read your special requests. Be clear with your hopes, wishes and dreams then continue.

"Let this not be my will, but thy will be done oh Lord God the Creator of all things."

During this part, acknowledge what you did not expect or even ask for, is sometimes given to you. Some of our brothers and sisters have received visions during this time that normally cannot be expressed in words, only in pictures. After the ceremony you should draw or write down what you see or hear for further review later. It should not be overlooked.

Open your arms and raise your head to the ceiling, full moon or sky.

Now the "White Light" is leaving you to form a large ball in the middle of the room or a few yards away from you. It is beginning to rise, as it does it is getting smaller and smaller. Continue the process until you reach the point where the ball of "White Light" has disappeared.

Now say, "I thank you archangels as my witnesses I grant you leave to depart."

This concludes the "Full Moon White Light Ceremony."

End of Transmission

Begin Open Channel

Lesson Forty-Three:
  Queen of Diamonds, received February 8th, 1992
  Book of Wisdom, channeled from Hierophant

"The more you know, the more "Knowing" will come to you." ERU

My Brother Hermit and Teacher,

As a third level Magi you are now being taught those mysteries which most schools of ancient knowledge forbid their students to learn. It is only when their students become masters that they are allowed to enter the Holy of Holies in the temple and receive the Creator's Divine Knowledge.

However, be aware! For this knowledge with its mysteries that I am about to cover, if used in folly, can be hard to deal with, not only to you, but to those around you. This is an awesome power I'm about to relate to you.

No student who isn't ready should experiment with it alone for the warnings connected with it are very real. You may think that these words of warning do not apply to you. Well, let me assure you nobody escapes a punishment for careless or misuse of Kundalini.

Heed my words; *"One should only attempt this under the watchful eyes of a Master."*

There are no exceptions!

Before we can proceed, please review the below part of Lesson Twenty-Two. It is important for you to remember the name and location of the Chakras.

Review of the Location of the Seven Chakras

1. The Muladhara or Root Chakras is located at the base of the spine.
2. The Umbilical Chakra is found over the naval as referred to as the sacral chakra, which is sensitive to feelings or emotions. It also increases control over internal processes.
3. The Solar Plexus Chakra seems to be over the spleen in much of your modern world's people. Its function is the dispersion of vitality that comes to us in the sun it is known as the solar plexus.
4. The Cardiac Chakra is self-explanatory. It is located over the heart and controls the subtle winds.
5. The Throat Chakra controls the etheric and communication.

427

6. The Third Eye or Brow Chakra is on the brow line in the middle of the four head and have power over elemental beings and intuition.

7. The Crown Chakra is located on top of the head and appears as a rainbow predominantly violet in color that resembles the aura. This chakra brings ultimate understanding of Nature's Great Mysteries and connection to God.

The first and greatest of all mysteries is the "White Light." Now we will cover the second great of all mysteries, the Kundalini, or Serpent of Fire.

Warning: modern religion has banned the mysteries of the White Light and Kundalini labeling them satanic in nature. That is not true. It's all part of the Divine. The White Light is the pure positively charged energy force of the Creator and the Serpent of Fire is the Root negatively charged energy force within humans. When those two forces meet within the crown Chakra, a great awakening could occur; like magnets, they are opposing poles, both needed for balance. That is why modern religions don't want it practiced. They equate it to "Eating the fruit of the Tree of Knowledge." They would prefer everyone go through them to commune with God and the Heavenly Hosts.

It not satanic, but it can be harmful to awaken the Serpent of Fire without a Magi or Yoga master present to guide and control the energy. If the energy gets out of control it could initiate a insatiable sexual drive. That is another reason why the church has banned it.

What is Kundalini?

1. The evolutionary energy residing in the human body.

2. The biological basis of all forms of spiritual experience, religion, genius, insanity, and higher consciousness. Kundalini is the nucleus of vital energy and the repository of physical, spiritual and sexual force within the human body. It is a spiral of fire, the feminine creative power, awakening to rhythmic movement.

It is most commonly referred to as a Serpent Fire because it is crimson in color and causes the temperature in the body to rise as it moves. It has also been told in stories to burn the flesh, both inside and outside the body.

You have actually seen representations of Kundalini if you have gone to medical facility or have been around people in the medical profession. It is a medical seal or symbol known as the Caduceus.

Where is the Serpent of Fire located?

The head of the Serpent of Fire starts with the last hollow of the spine just above the Coccyx in the area called the Sacrum. It is likened to a small serpent lying in a spiral of three and a half coils between the sacral area of the spine, over Cowper's gland, and the Leydig Center in the testicles.

When awakened, it will be directed to and through different Chakras in the body.

Preparation for awakening Kundalini

Before you awaken Kundalini, you should be in perfect health. This is very important, as the body will undergo great strains and pressures. An ill or sick body may bode well the experience.

During this period of development and preparation one is expected to abstain from smoking, alcohol, narcotics, drugs or stimulants and sex, as they will block the Serpent of Fire from rising.

Work patiently on the improvement of your character. Help those in need around you. Lift the burdens of others upon your shoulders. Devote your time and energy to doing works of charity.

Meditate on the divine nature of things. You must be at oneness with the Creator. It is written, *"Seek first the Kingdom of God and His Righteousness, and all things shall come unto you."*

In your meditations asked to be surrounded with the Will of the Creator; *"Not my will, but thy Will, O Lord, be done in and through me."*

The power can only be use for good. If it is used for selfish purposes it will turn on you. Thus, you must only use it for and in the name of others, never for yourself.

Let that what you seek be, that the law of the Lord God, which is manifest in the powers of Christ, may be manifested through you.

You will now come to know that the last forty *and* two lessons have been prepared for these mysteries. If you have followed them faithfully, you're prepared to go on. For everything that we have covered has had meaning for your total development and elevation to Master.

Now is the time when you're waiting is full. Over the next month think about whether or not you are ready for this next step. If there is any doubt, don't take it. You only have one chance to succeed. If you fail, you will fall so don't take this step until you know you are ready.

End of Transmission

Begin Open Channel

Lesson Forty-Four:
    Jack of Diamonds, received March 8th, 1992
    Book of Wisdom, channeled from Hierophant

"The more you know, the more 'Knowing' will come to you." ERU

Dear Master Hermit and Teacher,

It is imperative that you use the will to arouse the higher potentials of the Serpent of Fire and force it through the Chakras centers one by one.

I might mention here to picture the Chakras in your mind's eye likened to sunflowers facing the ground. When the Serpent Fire touches them, they will turn their faces skyward.

It is only through a determined and long continuous effort of the Will that brings a Serpent of Fire to the first of the Chakras. Where upon the blossom rises its head to a full and glorious awakening. Once the tremendous force of the Kundalini awakens the first Chakra, the experience will move on to the next. As Kundalini moves upward, each Chakra that it touches with its life-giving energy turns the blossom skyward.

The movement of the Serpent of Fire must be slow and controlled. That is because there is an enormously increased sensitiveness throughout the whole body, which, in itself, demands that total control be employed at all times.

The proper progression of the Serpent of Fire is in its ascent through the solar plexus, spleen, cardiac, throat, third eye and lastly Sahasrara.

Remember the Serpent of Fire's movement must be upwards after it is awakened. If on the occasion of its awakening it moves downward it will excite and intensify the undesirable forms of passion to such a degree that is almost impossible to resist them. They will then become lost and you could turn to lustful thoughts and actions. So, be aware.

Know that by deep meditation you can raise the forces in the body to awaken the Third Eye. This can be intensified by external conditions, such as, the influence of soft music or chanting.

One other method to awaken Kundalini is the Altar Method. Have a Master take an aluminum rod, the Staff of Alta, one inch in diameter and twenty-four inches in length. The Master must place the end of the Staff of Alta at the base of the spine and draw it up the line of the spine to the base of the skull. This is to be done very slowly, smoothly and with great intent.

The Serpent of Fire will follow after the Staff of Alta naturally.

You are a very special person, it is my belief in your goodness that has allowed you to receive and learn these Ancient Secrets. I ask that you use them wisely. The Powers of Wisdom consume those who would misuse them, and from that there is no escape.

For forty-four months I have given you the basis of the knowledge and wisdom of the Magi so that you may, in your lifetime help Archangel Michael and the Sons of Light rise up again and shed light on the world in this, it's darkest hours.

In parting, if you do not know a Master that can work with you, seek out a Master of Yoga. Ask him or her if they know how to awaken and control the Kundalini. Remember the Serpent Fire is to be awakened with caution, awareness and respect. Only use it under Archangel Michael's command and for those you seek to become the Angel-Knights."

After channeling this lesson, I returned to bed exhausted, just to be awakened an hour later by Michael who said to contact the hierophant again, he had more information for the Hermit. This is what he said:

"I have bestowed upon you the Second of the Great Mysteries for your safekeeping. It is my fervent hope that you and your students have studied, practiced and applied all your former lessons up to this point. At the request of Archangel Michael, I have taught you these ancient lessons to the best of my knowledge and abilities as taught to me by my teacher, Ascended Master ERU.

Lastly know that you must have a "Strong Will" to control the Serpent of Fire, yet passive enough to adapt. When you use the power to help others, let it be through the Solar Plexus or Third Eye, only on one Divine occasion should it be used below the Solar Plexus and that is under the strictest guidance from Angel Michael. That will be if you are to bring down of the "Golden Light of Creation."

End of Transmission

Begin Open Channel

Lesson Forty-Five:

Ten of Diamonds, received April 8th, 1992
Book of Wisdom, channeled from Hierophant

"The more you know, the more 'Knowing' will come to you." ERU

Dear Master Hermit and Teacher,

You have used the "White Light" and awakened Kundalini for the betterment of yourself and mankind. As one about to become a Magi you must realize that with these powers comes great responsibility, dignity, compassion, and understanding. And with that, you must be able to control your emotions and desires, something most humans cannot do! You have risen to a level where you can no longer harbor hate or revenge. If one becomes angry or mad at you, compose yourself, for you are above this.

What can they do to harm you? In reality, they can do very little, when you stop to think about it. However, if it does get physical, walk away. If you are attacked, use their energy to defend. There are many marshal art techniques like, "Aikido," that can be easily learned. You are now a Peaceful Warrior. If the world around you seems to be falling apart, do what you can to stop the aggression and hatred altogether. You are a very special person. Remember that!

You (and your students) have come to know the "Oneness" with Creator and are now guided in a righteous way of life. Most seem to know and hear more clearly that voice within that helps one through those tough events in your life. Follow the guidance of the voice within. Just make sure it's the higher consciousness and not your egos talking. It also is a fact that those who have used their powers to help others have reaped great benefits from it. I commend you. You are well on your way of delivering the Son of Light.

The time has come to increase your powers of telepathy. It is not enough that you go with the world. You must grow with the world. So let us move aside the veil and probe the depths of your mind.

Telepathy
As you know, the Electro-Magnetic Energy Consciousness of the

Creator is in each of us. It is what super charges us and gives us the ability to be self-aware. Truly the Creator is in you and me in equal proportions. The Creator is the one mind. Now he is in you and me and there is no separation of his mind so we are of one mind. When I address the mind within me, I address the mind within you, because we are also of one mind.

The person I wish to address can be in the next room or many thousands of miles away. There can be no interference or problem in this communication for there is only one harmony between the Divine Mind in me and the Divine Mind in you.

Now I hold in my mind the image of the person I wish to communicate with. Then I visualize a light forming in the area of the Cardiac "Heart" Chakra. It then ascends up to the Third Eye or Brow Chakra. And I send my message on a stream of light to the Third Eye of the person I wish to communicate with. This is how you send thought waves.

Pick a partner, sit them across the room from you and practice sending images to their third eye. Have them write down what they receive. Start with letters and numbers. Remember practice make perfect in every lesson I give you. If you don't practice, don't expect to grow your powers.

This leads us to another form of mind and will control. You may have noticed that when Archangel Michael takes control of the classes he puts you into an altered state of awareness. I will now teach you how this is done.

Hypnosis
The word Hypnosis comes from Greek Hypnos meaning "Sleep." Hypnosis is the act of placing a subject into of a state of consciousness in which a person is highly responsive to suggestion. Its use in therapy, typically to recover suppressed memories or to allow modification of behavior by suggestion. During hypnosis a person cannot be made to do anything against their will.

Before we begin let me serve you warning. Hypnosis is not a game or a toy, nor should it be taken or use light heartedly. Physical or mental damage to the subject can occur if not use wisely.

Many people ask to be hypnotized to lose weight, stop smoking, increase or deter their sexual activity, increase their memory or recall past lives and to contact spirit guides.

Prior to trying to change a habit it is best to learn all you can about the process. You never take anything away from someone without putting something in its place. You cannot leave a void without causing a serious problem.

Example: let us say someone has a smoking habit. You do not

hypnotize them and tell them to stop smoking. You tell them that every time they have the urge to smoke, instead of smoking, have them suck on a lifesaver, chew gum, tooth pick or drink a glass of milk; water or juice and the urge to smoke will go away if the person truly wants to stop smoking.

The reason is that sucking is instinctive. In the womb the fetus sucks its thumb; afterbirth it sucks on a bottle or its mothers breast; as a youth it drinks soft drinks out of a bottle; therefore sucking on a cigarettes is instinctive replacement.

When you tell a person to stop smoking, you are in fact trying to stop an instinctive habit. This can cause one or more psychological problems, which can give rise to violent type activity. That means to handle the problem is to keep the instinctive habit of sucking, but change the developed habit, smoking. So, you exchange cigarette for a lifesaver, gum or a drink of water. Also, if you use this method to stop smoking, do not expect one session to cure the problem. Tobacco has a drug in it that creates a chemical dependence and since it gives pleasure, the brain releases the chemical dopamine.

What is Dopamine?

The brain is awash with chemicals, but Dopamine is the molecule behind all our sinful behaviors and secret cravings. Dopamine is the chemical that controls the pleasure point in the brain. It releases during pleasurable situations and creates the desire to seek out more pleasure. Many objects or acts create this cycle of release which could link to addictive behavior: food, sex, over shopping, stimulant drugs, etc. Dopamine can be responsible for that little voice in the back of your mind that says, "I can quit anytime I want. I could quit tomorrow." But tomorrow never comes.

Self-Hypnosis

Self-hypnosis, or hypnosis which is self-induced, and usually is preceded by session with a therapist. Self-hypnosis is formal "self-talk."

Remember you are asked to start each lesson from the Book of Wisdom with a relaxation process that is geared to put you in a post-hypnotic altered state of awareness. The suggestions to open your mind are in each lesson and when the written lesson is over, your mind continues to receive information from other worldly sources. The lessons never really stop. They are always playing out in your mind with your guardians help; particularly during the REM sleep cycle. REM stands for rapid eye movement which occurs during deep sleep.

What you have passed through by the end of these fifty-three lessons is the equivalent of a four-year doctorate degree in the compound

Knowledge of the Universe. You, under self-hypnosis, have used each lesson to open doors to data that transcend the words on the blank pages I gave you. It is all about conceiving the inconceivable. There is so much in the world and universe that humans have a hard time conceiving because in the great scheme of thing there is much more going on. To humanity, earth is the largest thing going. But to the cosmos it is but a speck of dust. As for size, we could fit 30 million earths inside our sun. Now can you conceive the size of the earth as it relates to the size of our moon? Think about it using a bowling ball as the scale size of the earth. Which would be closest to the size of the moon, a marble, golf ball, tennis ball, grapefruit or a soccer ball? You now have a picture in your mind. Remember it or write your answer down.

Now can you conceive the distance your scale model Earth and Moon are apart? Would the scale distance from one another in feet be, 5', 10', 20', 30' or 40'? Remember or write down your answer. I will give you the correct answer soon.

Through self-hypnosis you and your student have projected into other dimensions, but it doesn't stop here. The seed of knowledge that you have received will grow within your mind forever if you choose. Just never stop pondering the great question of questions.

Ancient History of Hypnosis

In the days of Atlantis, hypnosis was practiced by the priests, magi and physicians. It was known to be a godly art. The priests used it to cause illusions and to bring man into closer harmony with the Creator. They used it also to show that they were given the power to help people.

The physicians employed it to help their patients overcome pain, whether from an illness or surgery, and to heal them. By using hypnosis, they were able to remove brain tumors successfully and work medical miracles. The Magi used it to teach and educate their students. It was used as a medium to enter the mystical states of mind, to take steps into past and future and to work miracles.

Those Priests and Wiseman who were of the "Laws of Wisdom" used this power to explore the world of the mind as well as the spiritual. They extended their knowledge and fields never before known. Through this tool they learned how to capture energy in crystals, pass energy through crystals to cure and to do surgery. Knowledge of the laser was discovered through the media of hypnotism and our communication with our more advanced cosmic brothers and sisters. However, more important is the fact that it caused a relationship with the Creator in which we came to know the Creator more deeply than people before us.

Like all good things, the Sons of Darkness used hypnotism to turn men into monsters. They crushed the poor peasants will, deformed their bodies, twisted their minds and even killed them by means of hypnosis. As in everything they touched, they used it for the dark force. Seth became so powerful that if a person were to look him in the eyes they would fall into a deep mindless trance.

When Atlantis was removed from the planet, the knowledge of hypnosis went out to all the colonies. Every corner the world came to know the use of hypnosis. The Babylonian sages and the Egyptian priests became masters in its use. The Roman historian Diodorus Siculus wrote in the first century B.C., "The ancient Egyptian priests threw each other into trance." Thus, even Rome recognized the power the Egyptians had knowledge of.

We will soon come to a time wherein we learn how to apply this knowledge and create a hypnotic state commonly referred to as a trance. Practice your powers of Telepathy over the next month so that you are ready to learn the art of Hypnosis.

Now review your perception of the size and distance of the earth and moon. It is time to comprehend the correct visual so that you have a better understanding of the size and distance of your earth ship as it speeds through space. If the earth was the size of a bowling ball the moon would be the size of a tennis ball and they would be about 30' apart. Think about that the next time you look up at the full moon.

End of Transmission

Begin Open Channel

Lesson Forty-Six:

Nine of Diamonds, received May 8th, 1992
Book of Wisdom, channeled from Hierophant

"The more you know, the more 'Knowing' will come to you." ERU

Dear Hermit and Teacher,

In hypnotism, you as a hypnotist must be firmly confident in the method you are using to induce a trance, positive in your attitude toward your subject and definite in your approach.

The subject should trust you, be relaxed in your presence, and feel comfortable, warm and free of sudden noises.

A person who has eaten within an hour's time before the session is much easier to work with than someone who is hungry. Feeling hungry distracts the mind.

Monotonous rhythmical sensory stimulation or chemicals usually produce the trance state. This makes up the four classifications in which the method of induction can be accomplished.

1. Auditory: This induction is brought about by a soft persuasive voice using such words as tired, relax, sleep, heavy, numb and bored.
2. Visual: This method is executed by having the subject stare at a point of light, flashing strobe, the tip of the candle flame, a pencil point, or a ball.
3. Tactile: Having some kind of physical contact with the body of the patient.
4. Chemical: There are a number of drugs and essential oils that can be used by physicians to induce a trance state in a patient.

Let us now look at some of the techniques for inducing a hypnotic trance and some of their developers. I am giving you the names and background of some who have passed in case you would like to try and connect to their consciousness. Perhaps you could channel them for further guidance and assistance.

Doctor Friedrich Anton Mesmer a German physician who was the inventor and creator of Mesmerism.

In Mesmerism you place your hands on the shoulders of the patient. Then bring your hands down the extremities of the fingers holding the thumbs a moment and repeating this process two or three times causing the subject to pass into a trance state.

Doctor James Esdaile (1808-1859) was a Scottish surgeon and director of Hooley Hospital in Calcutta, India. He was a pioneer in surgical operations using Mesenteric trance. Esdaile would put his subjects to bed in a darken room. He would direct them to close their eyes and try to go to sleep. He would then make passes over the subject, from head to toe, with his hands and never contacting the subject's body. Periodically he would breathe gently upon the head and eyes of the subject.

Dr. Louis Braille (1809–1853) would use a highly polished lamp case to induce trances in his subjects, that he would hold in his left-hand about a foot from the patient's eyes. It was at such an angle above the eyes as not to be seen without straining the eyes. Then using the third and fourth fingers on his right hand he would move the lamp case towards the subject's eyes. This would cause the subject's eyes to close involuntarily.

Now let us speak of the techniques that I was taught by my teacher Master ERU:

First: I air out the room in which I plan on hypnotizing my subject. I also make sure the room is warm.

Next, when the subject arrives, we sit and talk for a while. This allows the subject to become at ease with me. During the course of discussion, I explained what I am going to say and do. I also tell them that I will leave the trance open. Meaning, they are aware during and after the session knowing all that is said and happens. In other words, they will have total recall. I then asked them to tell me when they are ready to be hypnotized.

When they are ready to proceed I make sure that they are seated comfortably. I then light a candle and place it about three feet before them, dim the lights in the room and I sit myself near the subject.

I begin the induction by telling the subject to stare at the top tip of the candle flame and listen to my voice. Then I proceed by talking them through progressive relaxation as found in lesson number one.

When I complete the progressive relaxation I say, "You are very tired now and all that you want to do is sleep. Your eyelids are so heavy that you have to fight to keep them open. Close your eyes now and go to sleep.

I say, "Sleep, sleep, sleep, sleep, warm soothing sleep, you have no cares, no worries, you just wish to sleep. All your cares have vanished. Your mind is clear and your only thought is to sleep."

Once the subject's eyes are closed say, "You are now sound asleep. It feels so good to rest and sleep. You never realized you were so tired. Now you are going to go deeper and deeper into this sleep. You hear nothing but my voice. You will do and understand what I tell you. And you will, upon awakening remember everything that happened to you while in this trance."

Since smoking cigarettes is one of the most damaging habits in your modern time we will focus this lesson on replacing that habit. I would say: "I want you to light up an imaginary cigarette." Pause, and wait until they do what you've asked. "Now I want you to take a big long puff of your cigarette." Pause again until the subject has done what you've asked. Say, "Taste how good it is. Now take another puff of your cigarette. It doesn't taste so good this time." Pause for them to adjust to the taste. "Take another puff of your cigarette. It tastes rotten now." Pause again. "Take another puff of your cigarette. It tastes sickening now. The taste is beginning to make you feel a little queasy. You don't like the taste of the cigarettes anymore. You want to stop smoking. You never want to smoke another cigarette again." Pause for a moment. "Now put out your imaginary cigarette. Taking an imaginary glass of water and drink it. The water has washed away the nasty taste of the cigarette." Pause until the subject drinks the water. Say again, "The water is washing that bad taste away and you begin to feel good again. You don't ever want to smoke cigarettes again. If you ever want to smoke a cigarette it will taste rotten. Now if you get the urge to have a cigarette, instead of smoking you will drink a glass of water or suck on a hard candy or chew gum and the urge to smoke will leave you. You will feel good again. Do you understand?" Wait for a reply. "Now I'm going to wake you up and when you awaken you will feel as though you have had a good refreshing nap. You will feel good, whole and healthy. In fact, you will feel better than you ever felt before." Pause again then ask, "Do you understand?" Wait for a reply.
"I will now count from one to five and when I reach the number five you will be wide-awake and feeling great. One, you are beginning to wake up. Two, you are almost awake, three, four and five you are wide-awake." When you say five, clap your hands together once. After your subject has awakened, wait a few minutes and ask how they are feeling.

In this scenario, you have altered the habit of your subject. You have changed their thought processes to reject an act, which could be harmful to their health; if not their very life.

Stop now, for a moment and think of what we have done in the scenario. We've entered into an instinctive habit to attack a developed habit without injury to the instinctive habit. Remember the instinctive habit was sucking and the developed habit was smoking. We left the sucking habit intact while changing the cigarette for a drink of water, lifesaver candy or chewing gum. We have in fact altered a person's life, their thinking, attitudes and other habits subsequently related to the smoking habit.

Do you see, you have the power to change things in your life and in the lives of others? These things are acceptable in the course of events. But it is not acceptable to use these powers to satisfy an ego, to alter time or to do harm to another.

End of Transmission

Begin Open Channel

Lesson Forty-Seven:

**Eight of Diamonds, received June 8th, 1992
Book of Wisdom, channeled from Hierophant**

"The more you know, the more 'Knowing' will come to you." ERU

My Dear Brother Hermit and Teacher,

Let us take rest from these most involved disciplines for one more relaxed. As we become in harmony with nature the world around us becomes an awareness that cannot be explained by science or the scholarly.

As one sees the Cirrus Clouds in the sky, you know that it forecasts rain within forty-eight hours. So too, we must see, hear and feel the significant in the nonsensical details of nature all around us. For these hold profound intimations to us because of our discipline. It gives us insight into the future, expands our knowledge and gives us a broader intuitiveness into all things.

Animals are more aware of such things and react to them. When we see mass migrations of animals running away from an area, other than seasonal migrations, it is usually a warning of impending catastrophe. By being aware we could save our lives and the lives of others.

It is our "lot" in life, as a Magi and Son of the Light, to be of service to others. Master Hermit you were born to serve the greater good. As a child your natural instincts drew you to become a Boy Scout helping people, as a teen, an Army soldier safeguarding your country and as an adult, a police officer protecting and saving lives.

All of these choices were selfless service. You made those choices while you were surround by selfishness, people who took and never gave. That's why you were chosen for this Divine Quest and to learn the sacred "Knowing" these lessons offer. That is your "Lot" in Life.

Most of people have heard the expression "Cast your lots to the wind" or "This is my lot in Life." But the majority of people do not even know where the term "Lot" came from. It too, had its origin in Atlantis. Originally it was a stone. Later it was a coin with the head of Atlas on one side and the symbol of the sea on the other.

If the coin was tossed or flipped and the head of Atlas landed face up, the answer to the quarry was "Yes." But if the head of Atlas was facedown the answer to the question was "No."

According to the Ancient Law you were only allowed three questions a year. To use the casting of Lots more than three times of year was prohibited. The only ones in Atlantis who were allowed to cast Lots more than three times a year were priests and the Magi.

The casting of Lots has been used throughout the whole of history in every country in the world. Only the Lots themselves change over times and countries. Some of the Lots used throughout history have been stones, coins, bones, dice, yarrow sticks and disks.

In the Christian's Bible there are many references to the casting of lots. Here are just a few:

Leviticus Chapter 16: *"The Lord spoke to Moses and said … he shall cast Lots to determine which one is for the Lord and which is for Azazel."*

Proverbs Chapter 16: 33 *"Lots are cast into the lab, but they are disposed of by the Lord."*

Acts Chapter 1: 26 *"And they drew Lots between them, and the Lot fell upon Matthias; and he was numbered with the eleven apostles."*

John 19:23-24 *"Then the soldiers, when they had crucified Jesus, took His garments and made four parts, to each soldier a part, and also the tunic. Now the tunic was without seam, woven from the top in one piece. They said therefore among themselves, "Let us not tear it, but cast lots for it, whose it shall be," that the Scripture might be fulfilled which says: "They divided My garments among them, and for My clothing they cast lots." Therefore, the soldiers did these things."*

Method of Casting Lots

Take the smallest denominational coin you have that has a head on one side. Relax and concentrate on a question that requires only a "Yes" or "No" answer.

When the question is fixed your mind. Flip the coin letting it fall to the floor or ground. If the coin is facing heads up, the answer is "Yes." If the coin is facing head down, the answer is "No."

If the coin stands on its edge the question is not answered and should not be asked again. Do not ask more than three questions in one sitting. Do not catch the coin. It must hit the ground.

Since this lesson is intended to be light, let us discuss light.

With the increase or decrease of the vibrational rate of light waves, we perceive it in forms of color.

Now these colors, or frequencies of light, affect whatever they come in contact with. It makes things grow, multiply, heal, become active or come to rest. They control our attitudes, emotions and activity, in many cases.

When you experience several cloudy days, where you do not see the sun, you feel sluggish, tired, low and irritable. Then when the sun comes out you feel happy, strong, and active.

Our bodies absorb light. The pituitary interprets these waves and activates the appropriate glands. Which in turn control our state of being. The light of the sun is made up of all the colors of the rainbow; therefore, it yields to us all the positive attributes necessary for life. If a living thing is cut off from the light for any great length of time it will suffer and die. The sun is our greatest source of Vitamin D.

So too, we can stimulate our being by different colors of light to cause certain manifestations to take place. The following are the attributes affixed to the different colors of light.

Ultra-Violet Light is said to cure certain forms of cancer and destroys impurities in the blood.

Violet Light is for healing the Aura, casting out spirits, for protection and exorcisms.

Blue Light helps to control our RH blood factors, lowers blood pressure and retards strength in reaction time. It destroys adrenalin, activates insulin and oxidation of tissues. It makes the body relax, increases Alpha Waves, gives a cool soothing feeling and relieves anxiety. It reduces crying and heightens activity in babies. It also reduces neurological pain. It has great penetration powers and makes a person friendlier.

Blue Fluorescent Light is used for premature babies and is helpful in curing Jaundice. It causes hyper-activity in many children. This light gives off x-rays, which also causes irritability.

Television Light produces x-rays, which causes hyper-activity.

Vita-Light increases calcium.

Green Light simulates accuracy in work and is soothing. The use of green tinted lenses and glasses reduce eye tremor.

Pink Light makes a person look younger and stimulate sexual drive. Too much can cause people to become irritable.

Red light is stimulating to muscular strength and reaction time is increased. It causes anxiety as well as a feeling of warmth. It increases sex hormones, causes muscular constriction and arousal, as well as increasing adrenaline and inhibiting insulin.

White Light, regular white light, is cool feeling, stimulates boredom and disinterest. It is said to destroy tumors when used with light-sensitive drugs or dyes and can destroy certain forms of cancer.

Colors are also associated with sound or diatonic scale: the seven tones: "C"- Red, "D"- Orange, "E"- Yellow, "F"- Green, "G"- Blue, "A"-

a Purple and "B"- Violet.

How to Use Light

When light is used as a therapy, the source should be between thirty and forty inches from the subject. The subject should be relaxed with eyes closed while concentrating on a particular color in their mind's eye. Exposure should not exceed one half hour.

In Atlantis the use of light and colored lenses was a great tool in the hands of the physicians. Many people were healed through this method.

Throughout history there were references to the use of colored light. In the Kabbalah it is written, *"White, Red and Green, are the secret colors used to reveal angels. And they that are wise, intelligent, and teachers shall shine like the Splendor of the Firmament."*

Aristotle did some of the earliest studies and theories about light.

He discovered that by mixing two colors, a third is produced. He did this with a yellow and blue piece of glass, which when brought together produces green light. He also discovered that light travels in waves.

Plato and Pythagoras also studied light.

The Middle Ages

During the middle Ages, Paracelsus reintroduced the knowledge and philosophy of color using the power of the color rays for healing along with music and herbs. Unfortunately, the poor man was hounded throughout Europe and ridiculed for his work.

Most of his manuscripts were destroyed, but now many think him to be one of the greatest doctors and healers of his time. Paracelsus was a man very much ahead of his time. Not only does modern medicine use "Color Therapy," but his other ideas of using herbs and music in healing.

Sir Isaac Newton

A pioneer in the field of color, Sir Isaac Newton in 1672, published his first, controversial paper on color, and forty years later, in his work "Opticks," Newton passed a beam of sunlight through a prism. When the light came out of the prism is was not white, but was of seven different colors: Red, Orange, Yellow, Green, Blue, Indigo and Violet. The spreading into rays was called "dispersion" by Newton and he called the different colored rays the "Spectrum."

He learned that when the light rays were passed again through a prism the rays turned back into white light and if only one ray was passed through the prism it would come out the same color as it went in. Newton concluded that white light was made up of seven different colored rays.

Future Color Laser Light Surgery

Hear the words "Laser Light," and scenes from your favorite science fiction movie may come to mind. This mysterious energy is seen cutting chains off of prisoners, to death rays that blow up entire planets. In reality, however, lasers will soon have a much wider range and applications. You will have machines in the coming years that allow you to watch a movie. The laser light will carry data in fiber optic networks. Laser Lights will be used in corrective eyesight and spinal surgery, and some will even remove unwanted body painting tattoos and body-hair. Lasers will also be be used for healing!

Laser Lights will be made in virtually every color of the rainbow for a variety of purposes. Color Laser Light therapy systems will have several different wavelength frequencies of colors. They will range from green to infrared. You might ask, what color light laser will be best? A lot depends on what you will be trying to heal. Each color reacts differently with the body.

Green Laser Light is very quickly adsorbed by the skin and can be used only to help heal surface wounds such as bedsores or diabetic ulcers.

Red Laser Light can penetrate more deeply, and will generally be used for surface conditions such as burns, acne, and hair restoration.

Infrared Laser Light penetrates much deeper and will be used to help heal muscles, ligaments, and even bones.

Some surgeons will combine laser Light systems of different wavelength frequencies of colors into a cluster to increase their range and uses.

Laser Light will find more and more uses every year from laser pointers in the classroom and surveying, to guidance systems for cars and rockets.

In the future, humanity will discover how to use wavelength frequencies of various light colors and Elector-Magnetic Energy to heat homes and to fly to the stars and back.

There is one light color that has not been mentioned in this lesson! That is the pure "White Light of the Creator," the Divine Light that is called down for healing and aglow in the Great Temple. It is the Light of Perfection, in that this light has all the colors of the rainbow in it. It heals any and all maladies, gives peace to the mind, body, and spirit. It's the Divine essence of light in its purest form. It is like a voice in the darkness.

When the "White Light" touches you, it is ecstasy. It is the Creator touching you and working through your being!

As I said, my brother this lesson was meant to be simpler, relaxed and somewhat removed from the discipline of your former lessons, while giving you food for thought. Sometimes we all need a moment of rest and look back over what we have accomplished and how we have put the "Knowing" to work in our lives.

My brother, you are becoming a Steward of the Ancient Laws of Wisdom. The hardest thing to do is not judge another individual. It has become the root of "all-evil" on earth. Everyone has an opinion based on his or her judgments. Humans judge others based on their limited understand of the one being judge. Weigh what you see and hear for balanced truth, but keep the mouth closed and the mind open, for you shall be judged by your judgment.

End of Transmission

Begin Open Channel

Lesson Forty-Eight:

**Seven of Diamonds, received July 8th, 1992
Book of Wisdom, channeled from Hierophant**

"The more you know, the more 'Knowing' will come to you." ERU

Dear Master Hermit and Teacher,

I know as a police detective you have already developed an acute awareness of your powers of observation. If you hadn't, you probably wouldn't still be alive. But there is always room for improvement and your students need to become more observant as well. It is important as we continue to develop those powers. Observation is the foundation of all development and discipline. Without observation the sciences and their development could only be reproduced haphazardly, if at all.

Remember there is a big difference between seeing and observing.

Observation is a sister to awareness.

Through observations, we become aware.

If you should observe that the date of the first snowfall predicted the number of days snow would fall that season, then you would become aware of the first snowfall each year.

If you observe that the cirrus clouds always appeared within forty-eight hours before rain, then you would be aware of cirrus clouds and the rain to come.

Through observations, you understand, become aware, and make predictions.

Once, while on a journey with his brother, one of my students, Magi Gentile, was asked if he would have any objection to taking time away from the journey to visit his brother's old friend. Magi Gentile told his brother that he had no objections and that it might prove to be refreshing.

Along route, they stopped at a rather large house belonging to the friend, whereupon they were invited in for a cup of tea. In the receiving room of the house, Magi Gentile noticed some Egyptian artifacts in a showcase, books on ancient Egypt and Egyptian grammar on one of the shelves and some papyrus rolls on the desk. After they were seated, Magi Gentile asked his host, "How long have you been studying Egyptology? More particularly their ancient language?"

The man looked at Magi Gentile and asked how he knew he was

interested in Egyptology and particularly it's language.

"Are not the seeds from what your wisdom grows scattered about this room?" Magi Gentile asked.

This opened the door for him to express his knowledge about Ancient Egypt; a discussion that enlightened and educated all. Before Magi Gentile left, he informed his host that if he were to go to all lengths to learn everything he could from reading the ancient papyrus, he would learn a language older than Ancient Egyptian and a history that pre-dates Ancient Egypt.

Many years had passed before Magi Gentile was to see the man again. When they met, the man related to how he had in fact learned a language far older than Ancient Egyptian and discovered a lost continent situated in the middle of the Atlantic Ocean.

How did Magi Gentile come to these conclusions and predict the outcome, you might ask?

The objects in the man's house told him of his interest. The books on grammar expose the depth of his studies; a fact that in the Sais Egypt was a deposit of text on the most Ancient History, brought there by our forefathers. Magi Gentile knew that they would speak of Atlantis, its history and language.

Thus, through observations and awareness Magi Gentile was able to make a prediction, which later became fact. As you can see, there was nothing mysterious in what Magi Gentile had done. It was basic logic founded on some simple observations.

Can you now appreciate why it is important to develop your powers of awareness and observation?

Some ways to help you develop your powers of observation are as follows.

Experiment in Observation

Walk into a room and take a glance around. Then sit down, close your eyes and try to recall everything in the room. After you finish, open your eyes and look around to see what you have missed. Close your eyes and have someone remove something for the room. When they are ready, see if you can discover what has been removed.

Through practice you can increase your powers of observation and awareness. This is one of the most important aspects of being Magi. Through our powers of observation each Magi must write his own Book of Shadows based on the observations and lessons learned.

It was the custom in ancient times, that the Magi had their books buried with them when they died. Thus, so much knowledge of the past became lost, and valuable information is gone forever. But in those days it was said, "It is far better my knowledge die with me than it should fall into the hands of the vulgar and wicked."

Master ERU changed all that when he shared his Book of Shadows with me and I have shared my Book of Shadows with you. Now you must someday write your own book for your student teachers. That book must chronicle your life, your growth in the Spirit of Truth, the wisdom you have uncovered and how you used your powers for good.

Because you have committed your life to the Divine Quest of the Archangel Michael, yours will be the Book of Light and Shadow. The purpose of your book is to shine light into the dark recesses of humanity's shadow in the hope of bringing forth the return of the Angel-Knights and Sons of the Light.

If you absorb all that you will learn, your perspective will change and you will grow closer to the Truth. Become all that you know and then you will know what you have become.

The Twelfth Ancient Law of Wisdom: **"Forgive those who wrong you or bring harm upon you, for they shall suffer a far greater misfortune."**

End of Transmission

Begin Open Channel

Lesson Forty-Nine:

Six of Diamonds, received August 8th, 1992
Book of Wisdom, channeled from Hierophant

"The more you know, the more 'Knowing' will come to you." ERU

Dear Brother Hermit and Teacher,

I have come to know you as if you are part of my own family. I know the struggle you have gone through as well as the sacrifices you have made to your commitment in pursuit of the "Knowing." For this I have heart-warming pride in your accomplishments.

Let me give you some small Seeds of Wisdom to take with you. Heed them for I give them to you out of love; so share them with the world.

Heed these Seeds to Succeed:

1. Love one another, for you are your brother's keeper.
2. Get out in nature, it is part of you.
3. It is your resistance to 'what is' that causes your suffering.
4. Render whatever services you can do for those in need, and accept no reward for the good you do.
5. Allow yourself to experience joy and love.
6. Anything is possible. There is no such thing as failure, only learning opportunities.
7. Hold no revenge or hate in your heart for those that rob or wronged you.
8. If you cannot speak well of a person then please do not speak at all.
9. Be humble and boast not of your abilities for you will surely lose them.
10. Don't compare yourself to other people or other people to you.
11. Have compassion for those who suffer and try to find understanding for their plight.
12. Don't be afraid to ask for help to overcome difficulties.
13. The only thing that never changes is the fact that everything will change. Embrace the change.
14. Much of what matters today won't matter in a year, and what matters in a year won't matter at all.

15. It is always a small matter, how much you are in pain, for you will miss the pains of life one day.
16. Challenge yourself, get enough sleep, and meditate often.
17. Understand and be grateful for your fears they are but warning. Face your fears and do it anyway.
18. At all times be at peace with your Creator, for without the Creator you would not be.
19. Take care of yourself and exercise your Mind, Body and Spirit.
20. If you don't get something you want, it just means something better is coming.
21. Laugh and be an optimistic, always keep an open mind. When it is closed, the "Knowing" is no more.
22. Do not worry, for all it brings you is aging and despair.
23. It is only a problem if you think it's a problem. Look around you, a solution is at hand.
24. If you want things to change, you need to start with changing yourself.
25. Pray for the dead as well as the living, for they will be a gift in your house in your hour of need.
26. Accept what's out of your control; never let yourself become a victim.
27. Honor the slave as you would a king, the poor as you would the rich, and the weak as you would the strong.
28. This too shall pass and let go of desire, you will receive all that you deserve.
29. Clothe the naked, feed the hungry, help the sick, and befriend the forgotten and forlorn.
30. Touch someone and spend time with friends and family you will miss them when they are gone.
31. Memorize the Ancient Laws of Wisdom and observe them on a daily basis. Make them part of your life each and every day.

What I have given to you and your students, I give out of love. Now I ask that you do something for me. I asked that you use this knowledge to serve mankind and do good works in memory of me. I want that you should rise up and do more than I have done for mankind, so that what I have taught you shall live on long after we are gone, in your Book of Light and Shadow.

I know that you and Archangel Michael have a strong bond and a long road ahead and it will not be an easy path to tread. It is my hope that these lessons should help illuminate your way through the darkness. I ask that you place me in your prayers even as I have placed you in my prayers.

It is time for you to take your last test. Upon completion of the test, which consists of one simple, but complicated question. Only then will you be raised to the level of Master Magi.

End of Transmission

Begin Open Channel

Lesson Fifty:

**Five of Diamonds, received September 8th, 1992
Book of Wisdom, channeled from Hierophant**

"The more you know, the more 'Knowing' will come to you." ERU

Dear Master Hermit and Teacher,

We have traveled long and far together. As I have said before the "Knowing" starts with these lessons and because you have studied hard they will continue to feed you information every time you review them. These lessons from the Book of Wisdom have been given to you in the form of cards. Once a week you should shuffle a deck of cards until the voice in the back of your mind tells you to stop. Then cut the cards into four piles. They need not be equal. Number the piles one, two, three and four. You will then see one of the numbers in your mind blinking. Let us say it's the number two. Turn over the top card in the second pile and say it's the Five of Diamonds.

Your guides feel you need to review that lesson because you will need that knowledge in the near future. If you don't receive a number, one through four, shuffle the cards again and lay out four piles. If you still don't receive a number, a lesson review is not needed at that time. It is important that all of these lessons become ingrained in your subconscious.

There is so much more to learn in this world of ours. So, seek out the answers to the questions that have haunted, or challenged your imagination. Remember, the world is full of magic and unanswered mystery.

As we enjoy the beauty and natural structure of minerals and gemstones so also did our ancestors before us. Even 25,000 years ago when humanity was going through the Stone Age. Stones, especially the sharper and harder varieties were used for hunting, for defense, carving out hieroglyphs and for religious rites. Softer minerals and stones could be ground up and used in some instances for medicine to be ingested.

Archaeologists feel that gems and crystals were often carried in the form of an amulet or talisman to ward off bad spirits and protect the wearer.

Priests and Magi used gemstones for health purposes in Atlantis and crystals were used as giant transmitters of light, energy and information. You also learned that the great outer wall of Atlantis City was composed of gold, silver and bronze. The respect and adoration for the precious metals and stones were our greatest gifts from the Creator. The precious materials represented the spiritual, mental and the physical nature of man.

Though we first used crystals, precious metals and gemstones in Atlantis, the Egyptians have left us many colorful paintings to show the many uses of stones. In Egypt, Gold, Lapis and Carnelian decorated many pharaohs' costumes and thrones, but it also was seen abundantly in temples and tombs.

Malachite is a bright green mineral consisting of copper hydroxyl carbonate. It typically occurs in mass in fibrous aggregates with azurite and is capable of taking a high polish. It is known for its healing properties and was used in great abundance by the Egyptians.

Metals like copper, gold, and silver were considered conductors for vibration or energy forms that would promote peace, love and wisdom within sacred places of worship, on statues of gods or, in the case of Atlantis, throughout entire communities. It is known fact that royalty wore certain gems to promote strength and leadership.

Headdresses and crowns give the wearer wisdom and health as well as a beautiful appearance. Imagine how carefully the gemstones must have been placed within the crowns in order for these characteristics to be brought forward and enhanced. Many Magi wore crystal straps that crisscrossed their chest to fine-tune their intuitive reception.

Gemstones of Aaron's Breastplate

Aaron was the brother of Moses, and became the leader of the Leviticus tribe of Israel that was appointed as priests. The book of Exodus records the Creator's directions concerning the breastplate of the high priest:

Exodus 28:15-17

"You shall make a breastplate of judgment, the work of a skillful workman; like the work of the ephod you shall make it: of gold, of blue and purple and scarlet material and fine twisted linen you shall make it. "It shall be square and folded double, a span in length and a span in width. "You shall mount on it four rows of stones..."

Exodus 39:10-14

"The first row was a row of ruby, topaz, and emerald; and the second row, a turquoise, a sapphire and a diamond; and the third row, a jacinth, an agate, and an amethyst; and the fourth row, a beryl, an onyx, and a jasper. They were set in gold filigree settings when they were mounted. The stones were corresponding to the names of

the sons of Israel; they were twelve, corresponding to their names, engraved with the engravings of a signet, each with its name for the twelve tribes

The Hebrew names for the stones on the breastplate have proven difficult to identify with any certainty with existing gemstones. Different translations of scripture identify different stones. The following gemstones are those mentioned in Exodus (positioned right to left as the Hebrew language is read):

Row 1.   Reuben Sard – Hebrew - Odem
Simeon   Peridot – Hebrew - Pitah
Levi   Emerald – Hebrew - Bareqet

Row 2.   Judah Turquoise – Hebrew -Nopek
Dan   Lapis Lazuli – Hebrew -Sappir
Naphtali   Moonstone – Hebrew -Yahalom

Row 3.   Gad Hyacinth – Hebrew -Lesem
Asher   Agate – Hebrew -Shebo
Zebulon   Amethyst – Hebrew -Ahlama

Row 4.   Issachar Chrysolite – Hebrew -Tarshish
Joseph   Carnelian – Hebrew -Shoham
Benjamin   Jasper- Hebrew -Yasepeh

Aaron's crown and breastplate covered two extremely important chakra areas energy sites, the heart and mind of man. In the presence of the Ark of the Covenant the stones would light up and sparkle during ceremonies and communication with the Creator.

In Atlantis, the Ascended Magi used Quartz Crystal Astral Beacons in the construction of sacred structures and as a way of controlling weather patterns that threatened to destroy our lands. You will need to learn how to make the beacons and use them in case you are called upon to create an Atlantean Microcosm to bring the Sons of Light home.

Quartz is the most recognized type of crystal on the planet. In fact, many people envision quartz crystals when they think of crystals, even though there are many different types of crystals. Quartz can be clear or have inclusions or bubbles and come in various colors. Visual clarity normally isn't important to quartz's energy quality and its ability to amplify energies and thought.

A Quartz crystal is a very powerful stone. It has been called the

"Universal Crystal" because of its many uses. It enhances energy by storing, amplifying, balancing, focusing and transmitting energy. Quartz also enhances thought since thoughts are also a form of energy. Because it directs and amplifies energy, it is extremely beneficial for manifesting, healing, meditation, protection, and channeling. That makes quartz crystals particularly good for programing for a particular purpose. Due to its ability to balance, quartz is excellent for harmonizing and balancing one's environment.

Quartz is a stone of clarity, which dispels negativity. It can be used to purify the spiritual, mental, and physical planes. Quartz enhances spiritual growth, spirituality and wisdom. Because it clarifies thought processes and emotions, it can increase inspiration and creativity. Most of all quartz crystals wrapped in gold, silver or copper have the ability to record and echo human thought and emotion indefinitely.

Creating Astral Crystal Beacons

In the making of Astral Crystal Beacons always remember to make them in sets of four. The maximum that can be made in one sitting is one hundred and forty-four. For this lesson we will make one set of four.

Items needed:

1. Start by selecting the quartz crystals you wish to use. Each crystal should be no smaller than first joint of you little finger.

2. Place the crystals in a bowl or cup and sprinkle a 50/50 mixture of baking soda and baking powder over the stones.
3. Cover the crystals with warm water and let them sit for one hour to cleanse and clarify.
4. While you are waiting, cut four 2" x 2" square pieces of aluminum foil.
5. Collect four copper pennies with dates no later than 1966.

Assembly Instructions:

a. Lay the foil out on a table to match the true compass direction of north, south, east and west.

b. Now call in the Angels of the Four Directions, Gabriel 1st.

c. Cast your Lot or first penny on the table. Do it until it comes up heads, then place it heads up on the foil in the northern position. Then do the same for Uriel, Michael and Raphael.

d. Take the first crystal out of the water and touch it to your forehead and state your request. Do the same with the remaining crystals. For example: "I ask that the Creator bond with this Astral Crystal Beacon to amplify my request to block any dangerous weather patterns from crossing this line and bringing harm to life and property." Or, "I ask that the Creator bond with this Astral Crystal Beacon to support this wooden beam that supports this sacred structure."

e. Now wrap the crystals and pennies in the foil.

f. Take the Astral Crystal Beacons to the building site and drop them into hole underneath support beams or to areas of land and water where you intend to build an Electro-Magnetic Barricade and drop them in a line that you don't want crossed.

Remember of you are trying to stop storms from affecting a particular area you may have to create a barricade several hundred miles long. Atlantis was ringed with Astral Crystal Beacons, which is why Archangel Michael was able to transport the entire continent to Jupiter.

To activate the crystal Beacons is going to take tremendous willpower, so always be mindful of the thirteenth law of wisdom. You should review the lesson on willpower before you program anything.

The Thirteenth Ancient Law of Wisdom is: **"At its essence, willpower is the ability to set aside your fears and resist short-term temptations in order to meet long-term goals."**

End of Transmission

Begin Open Channel

Lesson Fifty-One:

**Four of Diamonds, received October 8th, 1992
Book of Wisdom, channeled from Hierophant**

"The more you know, the more 'Knowing' will come to you." ERU

We cannot talk enough about crystals. Next to life itself crystals are our greatest gift if you know how to use them. We have already discussed that the human body is full of crystals that help us stay healthy and well balanced. Isn't it only logical that the body of the Creator would want to enjoy a four-dimensional body that would also be full of crystals? Everything in the cosmos is layers of the Creator's body.

The best way to explain it is: In our beginning, the Creator who lived in the fifth dimension had an electromagnetic four-dimensional thought. That thought manifested as four-dimensional Mega-Star that because of its electromagnetic field collapsed into itself forming a four-dimensional black hole with a three-dimensional outer surface called a hyper sphere. Under immense pressure from the electromagnetism the black hole then began spewing out all the three-dimensional matter that now makes up the known universe. In that one thought was everything that we are part of. The Creators now wait to see what the children are going to do with it.

In time, science will discover that the electromagnetic field that covers our plant is held in place by the crystals within the earth's surface. Without your planet's magnetic field, the sun's solar winds would turn the surface of the earth to match that of Venus and Mars, dry and lifeless. It is the consciousness of the Creator flowing through the crystal that allows earth to enjoy magnetosphere that keeps our oxygen rich atmosphere from drifting off into space.

What are Crystals?
Crystals are pieces and products of Mother Earth. They are grown within the mantel and are living energy. Because of the matrix and sacred structure, they have been said to be and to hold, the keys to the multiverses. Each crystal is unique and has a different gift or aid to help shift vibrations. They can be used for healing, power, knowledge, meditation, protection, understanding, just to name a few. Crystals have been used in all ages of man.

Can Crystals Affect Us?

Crystals can balance the body's energy system and boost the chi of a body. Placing crystals on the chakras of the human body can heal and rejuvenate the body, mind and energy system.

The woman you will call Wisdom who I have told you is coming weaves Reiki and Earth energy with crystals to heal and empower. She will show you grids of crystals to lay upon and around the body.

Every Crystal Has Different Energy

As you were instructed in earlier lessons, you should now have a complete Treasure of the Magi. Your box should have at least one of each crystal I told you about. Take them out and feel their vibration. Play with them. There will be many people who write books about what to do with each crystal and which powers they have. I tell you this—each crystal is as unique as your fingerprint and they will work differently with different people and different at certain times. Don't get hung up on what people tell you about crystals. FEEL them!

Cleaning Crystals

After purchasing a crystal you need to clean it. There are many ways to do this.

- Under running water
- In the sunlight
- In the moonlight
- Plant it in the ground

Just don't put crystals in salt like some people say unless you thoroughly know the properties of the stone. Salt can erode some other minerals.

If you ever get the chance to have the channel of an Ascended Master charge your crystal, it will not need to be cleansed. Pure love and light will beam through the matrix and no negativity can ever affect it.

All crystals on Earth link to the sacred geometric structure of the Multiverse. My Master ERU had all sacred geometric figures, such as Metatron's cube in crystal form. He carried them in a red cloth pouch tied at his waist. Once he sat me down while by the river and told me the tale of Metatron's Cube and how the great angel came to wield it. It originated from the Flower of Life. Metatron is the great angel, as I know you know, who is in charge of creation. With the sacred Cube, God created the cosmos according to a geometric plan. Once God was finished with the cube, he entrusted it to Metatron. When the perfect righteous and just human comes into your fold and attracts Metatron, Michael will tell you.

Miraculous events will take place as the Cube my Master ERU carried will manifest in this age. This of course will only happen if the person is just and TRUE.

My brother Hermit I speak to you about crystals once again, because if the Sword of Truth and the Stone of Enlightenment have found its way to you, the Rainbow Quartz Crystal (another piece in the sacred geometry set) in the pommel of the sword will be crucial in the creation of the Philosopher's Stone that you may be called upon to manifest in the future. The Philosopher's Stone will help you manifest the gold you will need to fund the message that the God Sword brings to the children of earth.

Remember when you know less than there is to know, you know very little. Be humble with your knowledge and practice all the ancient laws always and your "Knowing" will grow.

The Fourteenth Ancient Law of Wisdom is: **"When you think you know, you don't and when you know you don't, you do!"**

End of Transmission

Begin Open Channel

Lesson Fifty-Two:

Three of Diamonds, received November 8th, 1992
Book of Wisdom, channeled from Hierophant

"The more you know, the more 'Knowing' will come to you." ERU

Dear Master Hermit and Teacher,

The time has come for our last lesson together. Over the past several years I have passed on to you the great "Knowing" of the ancient Magi of Atlantis. I have updated it with history and events to help you further understand the basic information. You should do the same in passing the lessons on to your students.

You have now risen to the level of Magi and Master. Your final examination comes in the form of answering one simple question. You have until you begin writing your Book of Light and Shadow to answer it, but I would not wait too long. We have covered many topics over the past fifty-one months. We have covered Love and now it's time for you to cover Hate.

In the days of Atlantis, we were surrounded by hate from the Sons of Darkness. As wise as our leaders were, we could not comprehend those who hated. They waited too long to rally our forces and fight back. That level of hate is growing again in your time. You experienced hate first-hand as a child and were shown visions of hate unleashed on the native people of your country, what it did in Europe under Adolf Hitler's rise and you have felt it as you try to deliver the Good Knight safety message to children.

You know the history of the hatred, persecution and murder of the Native Tribes in America. You saw their desperate last stand attempt at the Bureau of Indian Affairs Building in Washington D.C. Many of them still curse and hate the Americans from the grave. Their hate holds them captive on the earth plane. The day will come when you and Angel Michael will call forth those tortured spirits and ask for their forgiveness. It will not be easy for them to set aside their hate, but if your love and passion is true, your apology will be accepted and their spirits will be released to journey back to the Creator.

With that in mind I ask that you use all the "Knowing" that you have received from the blank pages I gave you years ago. Look deep into the

Book of Wisdom and write your students a lesson on hate, like the lessons I have given you. The final lesson, Fifty-three, will come from my teacher, if, and only if, you pass this test and your lesson has merit.

The Question of Questions: "What is Hate?"

Before answering this question, review the Tenth Ancient Law of Wisdom: **"The Powers of Wisdom consume those who would misuse them, and from that there is no escape!"**

End of Transmission

I remembered what Michael said years ago that I would one day stand before Russell Means and a host of American Indians. I was sure that I still had a lot to learn before I would find the words of forgiveness necessary to release the trapped earth-bound spirits of our ancestors.

Begin Open Channel – My Inner Channel

Lesson Fifty-two was the shortest lesson of all, but at the same time it was the longest. The hierophant wanted me to use everything I had learned from all the lessons and write my own lesson on "Hate" for the First Wednesday Club. Where do I start? I thought. I created a 5-D gateway and asked for guidance and this is what came through.

Lesson Fifty-Two+:

**The Black/White Joker,
Book of Wisdom November 9th, 1992, from Sir Edward-The Hermit**

"The more you know, the more 'Knowing' will come to you." ERU

Dear First Wednesday Club Members,

The Hierophant has asked for his last lesson, that I write a lesson on, "What is hate?" I ask that before the class starts you write your definition of what hate is. I would like for it to become part of the new Book of Wisdom that I will be adding to my Book of Light and Shadow. I would like for the children of tomorrow to have the benefit of your views on hate since understanding hate comes from the lives we have led and the hate that has affected each of us. Some of you have hated and/or experienced hate, so what is hate?

Hate - A Hard Lesson to Learn

Just as love signals attachment, hatred signals detachment. I have loved and been loved during my life by my family and friends. Many in my life have also hated me with no apparent reason other than my mere presence rubbed them the wrong way.

When I was a young boy I was attacked by a group of boys that beat, tortured and humiliated me. I was scared to death and, my best friend, Frankie was afraid we were going to be hung. The Ku Klux Klan murdered his father two years earlier. I will never forget the animated look in those boys' faces who were torturing us. They were out of control and enjoying every minute of it. We didn't seem like human beings to them, just some inferior subspecies that didn't deserve to breathe the same air that they were breathing.

Now, after years of reflection, I know that what those boys really hated was their perception of us. Most of all they were acting out the fear and anxiety passed on to them from their parents. Therefore, their hatred was born of fears and ignorance, two very dangerous combinations.

As for Hate, I can't say I've ever really hated anyone. I might not like someone, but I never hated, like those boys hated Frankie just because he was black and me just because I was Frankie's friend. I have had many reasons to hate certain people, but I didn't. Like the janitor I investigated who kidnapped, raped and murdered a little girl whose body I found under a tarp which was twisted from the weight of her attacker or the satanic cult member who butchered the two second graders at Bird Neck Elementary School in Virginia Beach. I can't hate them because I would become what they are; just another hater in this world. Life is all about choices and I chose to be a forgiver, not a hater.

I hope to answer this question for the Hierophant, but mostly for the one person that I **hope** to meet one day. She is a special child with the initials M.V. To me "**HOPE**" means, **H**elp, **O**pen, **P**eople's, **E**yes. It is my hope that this book will illuminate her path so she can accomplish her Divine Birthright.

What is Hate?

Before I can answer the question, I must explore what hate is to me, since it means different things to different people. Hate is the intense emotion to despise, dislike, distrust, disgust, detest, contempt, loathe, execrate, and abhor something or someone.

It's amazing how many words we have that describe, "Hate," but I can only think of one word that describes, "Love." I can think of many words that describe the feelings of love; pure, passionate, true, painful, joyous, adoring, hot, burning, insane, patient, amazing, beautiful, everlasting, bright, enduring, unwavering, blissful, astonishing, shameless, aching, raw, intense, right, tender, romantic, eager, strong, stunning, scary, giddy, rich, daunting, consuming, non-judgmental, ecstasy, freeing, boundless, delicious, divine, honest, illogical, sensual, devoted, enveloping, stirring, cherishing, deep, challenging, and surprising. However, many of those words could also describe hate.

It is easy to hate because all you have to do is shut down and close yourself off from love, forgiveness and understanding.

Great religious texts offer varying opinions on hate. Look some up and see what you find

We are told that the Bible is the definitive "Word of God," but that's just a perception of our ancestors' programing. The first two volumes, Old and New Testaments, of the Bible are full of inconsistencies that allow hateful people to justify great atrocities against humanity. Some Christians used it to justify killing Muslims and some Muslims are using it to kill everyone to include fellow Muslims all based on a perception.

Michael proclaims that in the future the "Final Testament of Man" will be written by seven authors in the hope of giving the world a better perception on humanity's true purpose in life. He said, "Only those who elevate and dare to stand in the Shadow of the Spirit of Truth will find their stories in the Creator's "Book of Life." He said all the haters would find peace in the sad lives they lead

As a professional investigator, when I trace Hate back to its roots I find myself on the door steps of the seven deadly passions as described in the Bible:

1. **Lust** - "But I tell you that anyone who looks at a woman lustfully has already committed adultery with her in his heart" (Matthew 5:28)

2. **Gluttony** – "for drunkards and gluttons become poor, and drowsiness clothes them in rags" (Proverbs 23:21)

3. **Greed** - "Having lost all sensitivity, they have given themselves over to sensuality so as to indulge in every kind of impurity, with a continual lust for more" (Ephesians 4:19)

4. **Laziness** –"The way of the sluggard is blocked with thorns, but the path of the upright is a highway" (Proverbs 15:19)

5. **Wrath** – "A gentle answer turns away wrath, but a harsh word stirs up anger" (Proverbs 15:1)

6. **Envy** – "Therefore, rid yourselves of all malice and all deceit, hypocrisy, envy, and slander of every kind. Like newborn babies, crave pure spiritual milk, so that by it you may grow up in your salvation" (1 Peter 2:1-2)

7. **Pride** - "Pride goes before destruction, a haughty spirit before a fall" (Proverbs 16:18)

For all the reasons listed above it is imperative to support your life and those around you with virtue and virtuous behavior.

It is when we lose control of these negative passions that lead us down the path to Hatred. It's obviously a flaw in our psyche and a lack of virtuc.

So, let's travel up the positive path of the virtues to see how we can counter the negative passions.

1. **Chastity-** Abstinence. It is the embracing of moral wholesomeness and achieving purity of thought through education and betterment. Chastity is the ability to refrain from being distracted and influenced by hostility, temptation or corruption. **Chastity counters Lust.**

2. **Temperance-** is restraint and constant mindfulness of others and one's surroundings; practicing self-control, abstention, moderation and deferred gratification. Temperance is prudence to judge between negative actions with regard to appropriate actions at a given time. **Temperance counters Gluttony.**

3. **Charity-** Generosity, personal sacrifice; Charity is also sharing Love, in the sense of an unlimited loving kindness towards all others. It is the definitive vibration of human spirit. **Charity counters Greed.**

4. **Diligence-** cautious and steadfastness in belief, upholding morals even when alone. **Diligence counters sloth or laziness.**

5. **Patience-** serenity and unflappability. **Patience counters Wrath.**

6. **Kindness-** is compassion and friendship for its own sake. Empathy and understanding. **Kindness counters Envy.**

7. **Humility-** Modesty, control of ego, putting other's needs before one's own.. **Humility counters Pride.**

Angel Michael tells me that life is like a game of chess and we are playing against ourselves. It's a series of moves and counter moves. Now you know how to counter some of the negative moves you make in life.

"Hate is trying to control something that's out of control. Love is the surrender of all control." ~Sir *Edward Jagen*

Response essays on Hate the Angel-Knights wrote:

"Hate is a powerful force which can be used as an instrument of darkness or evil. It has its own presence and can be experienced and felt by those around it. It can be all consuming. It is the regression of the human brain's elevation to that of the Amygdala. It spawns from intense fear, insecurity and frustration. Fear is the lack of feeling loved or of knowing love. If one truly knows love and believes he/she is loved, then fear cannot control. And hate can never consume where the light of love shines bright." *Lady Lilly, Teacher*

"I've heard people say that hate is the absence of love, but I believe God is the All and where there is God there is love. I know God loves the haters so there must be at least a spark of the love of God present even in hateful moments. And since hate is a presence, like love, it can't be the absence of anything because it is something in of itself. They say that hate is the opposite of love, but I've also heard about studies saying there's a fine line between hate and love in the physical human brain, literally and physically. Hate and love are very close in what they do chemically in the brain and in the physical location of where they play out in the brain. When I have seen people consumed with hate, all I see is self-absorption, so hate seems to be all encompassing or the ultimate of selfishness. I believe God is Love and God created us in His image so we must be love. With the free will we were given, I believe mankind created hate." *Lady Tammy, a health care professional.*

"Hate is the ego being in control in the moment, not allowing the higher self in. When someone hates, it's like they are drawing a line in the sand refusing to elevate, because they think they know it all. Hatred is saying you know more than God. It's lack of awareness. It's refusal to elevate. Hate is blind to all but its rage and self-importance." *Sir Thomas, Marine Biologist*

"On the surface, hate is a strong dislike for something or someone. It really made me think when you sent this because it's really not that simple. It is not truly the opposite of love because fear is, but it is fear based. Maybe it is more a mirror image to love, as it seems to be fueled by the same passion? It is a passionate disdain, driven by insecurity. It ignites terrible and irrational actions when spurned by emotions out of control. But in reality, if not acted upon, it hurts the offender more than the target. Perhaps it is the absence of love? Fear and insecurity made manifest. Perhaps it exists merely to provide contrast, the universal equal and opposite reaction? I wish I had more wisdom to offer, but I very much appreciate the opportunity to ponder this question and will continue to do so." *Lady Mary, Chairwoman, law clerk*

"People hate the things they see inside themselves. They hide away their flaws and seek out others with vehemence in hopes of eradicating their fear of inadequacy with the purging of those they believe embody the traits they try to hide. Eventually the hate spreads and the reason is lost. The hate becomes uncontrolled and without cause like a chemical flame. So, it burns brightly with an indignant pride fueled by the fear of being found out as groundless." *Lady Eleanor, U.S. Justice Dept. Official*

"Feeling jealous over one's success, actions, or even looks can be very hard to deal with when you realize those same people are performing better than you are. It's much easier to hate someone and spread negativity towards them, than taking a step back and realize what we are doing wrong or not doing in our own life." *Lady Justine, lawyer*

"I grew up hating, it's a knee jerk reaction, with emphasis on jerk. Hate was the easy way out from having to show compassion and understanding. There was a time when I had a love/hate relationship with Sir Edward. He said things I didn't want to hear or even give a second thought to. Then my teacher held a mirror up to my face and said, "Who do you really hate? I have not hated since!" *Sir James, Outlaw Biker*

"People hate because they don't know any better and they don't even attempt to learn about what they are talking about. They are scared to hear that what their parents or teachers told them might not be the only side of the story." *Lady Susan, professional dancer.*

"For the most part I feel that Hate is a learned behavior. I think a lot of times people only hate because their parents taught them to hate or society influences them. Sometimes you have to hate others to stay popular." *Lady Que, Mental Health Therapist*

"I guess hate is an intense level and high degree of dislike and hostility. People "hate" what they do not understand. Hate is just another emotion that stems from fear and distrust. All it takes is a little bit of education to help make people more aware and less hateful." *Lady Leah, lawyer, teacher*

"I think the reason why people hate boils down to one essential and simple point, and I know this from personal experience…people hate because they are hurt. They have a hole inside they are trying to fill, but never can." *Sir Gregory, Teacher*

"People often hate other people because of either envy or jealousy.

They see something in that person that they don't like about themselves. Once we learn to love ourselves, we will be more capable of loving others. I believe that hate is just fear out of control. I think Yoda summed it up best when he said, "Fear turns to anger, anger turns to hatred and hatred turns to suffering." *Sir Robert, Health Care Practitioner/Therapist*

Many struggled with the question as you can sense in the below response from Sir Bell. You can feel the angel wrestling within the mind of the human to seek the answer to the question; of which there is no right or wrong answer.

Dear Sir Edward Michael,

Hate seems like an emotion that can manifest when we feel threatened enough that we cannot be with the fear we feel, or be with feeling disconnected or any of the seven vices so it seems like a coping mechanism of the EGO to survive, or to prevent surrender to not knowing.

My understanding of lessons on hate, from the First Wednesday Club gathering, is that we are going to feel negative emotions and it's what we do with that emotion that affects the outcome. For example, I feel afraid that I don't have the wise spiritual answer to your question. Of course, I could answer your question with -- hate is the opposite of love; it's without wisdom, it's without the knowledge of the Angels of the Four Directions. But, you already know that so I imagine you are looking for something deeper and wiser than a textbook answer.

How to explain that? Here's a try – I'm aware I feel not good enough, less than, and ignorant because I am struggling to write to you what I imagine is the wise answer that shows deep spiritual growth. I thought about it, meditated on it, and yet, I am afraid because I'm not sure what to write to you. I feel that anxiety and fear in myself.

Now, what to do with all those negative voices trying to get me to move from fear to hating myself, which is really hating all things, since all things are connected? I'm applying previous lessons that say, it's okay to feel fear, I can say, I don't understand, I don't know, but if somehow, I can be with fear and surrender to it, acknowledge it's there, but keep going and then I feel that's the opposite of hate, "LOVE."

I guess hate is a confused state of mind since I want to hate you for asking the question, but that would be to easy so I will send you "LOVE" and thank you for the lesson and hate myself in the morning for writing this." *Sir Bell, Physical Therapist*

Some got the message loud and clear and weren't afraid to voice it like Sir Leonard:

Dear Master Hermit,

It is intense dislike. To me hate is a deeply felt negative emotion that is felt and carried to such a degree as to want to obliterate that which you truly hate. All hate is ultimately self-hatred. It causes spiritual stagnation at the least and regression at its worst. To hate anything or anyone is to hate something about yourself so deeply that you need to project it to deal with it and thus never deal with it at all. It bleeds into everything we do although we are not aware of it many times. We believe it only affects the hated and not our loved ones or things but because it has no real effect on anyone but the hater it actually bleeds on everything into which they come in contact. All hate is fear based so they are deeply afraid or insecure which causes them to deny and project. It blinds a person to so many of the beautiful gifts offered by the universe. Hate is actually a misperception of a gift given you by the universe to assist you in your spiritual growth. Whatever you hate was given you as an opportunity to "choose again" and move beyond your "self" toward your "SELF." It is always offered as a way to get it right or do it better this time. How cool is that that we are given so many second chances?

Speaking physically the hater floods their body with unhealthy chemicals and energy.

Its funny but as I examined the word and how it played out in my life, the only thing I think I have ever come close to hating was my own behavior.

With deep Thanks and Love,

Sir Leonard-Sachiel
Angel-Knight

After reading a sampling of the essays I received from my lesson's assignment, it is obvious that the meaning of Hate is different for everybody and the same is true for Love.

In closing, I have found that most people hate out of inner fear and frustration. What we fear is the unknown or what we think is known and we'd "Hate" to find out that we were wrong. Humanity has a natural tendency to hate in order to love. It allows us to separate the people we care about from those we don't. We seem to need the comparison to survive. I think its part of us being a microcosm unto ourselves, caught up in the great macrocosm. It's like the stars, without the blackness of the void; their light would be meaningless without the contrast.

Hate is like the basic Law of the Universe. Whereas a negative charge of the Electro-Magnetic-Current needs to feed on a positive charge, it is like a great celestial snake chasing its tail through space and time.

I asked Archangel Michael, "Why did the Creator create hate if hatred is the problem?" Michael replied, "To give humans a choice and to make life more interesting! We all need an adversary."

So, it is with the eternal struggle between love and hate. Love creates. Hate destroys. Good is only as right as evil is wrong. Without evil in this world good people would only have good people to judge, therein lies the problem. The root of "all evil" is judgment. If good people judge, are they really good or just living the lie? Therefore, judge no man, for you shall be judged by your judgment.

End of Transmission

Begin Open Channel

Lesson Fifty-Three:

Two of Diamonds, received December 8th, 1992
Book of Wisdom, channeled from Master ERU

"The more you know, the more 'Knowing' will come to you." ERU

My Beloved Master Hermit-Sir Edward,

I have looked forward for this moment for 25,000 years. You have been long in the making my dear Son of Light and we will have many great adventures together.

I very much enjoyed your lesson on Hate. You covered the topic thoroughly, gave great references, and documented the views of your students. That was very wise since they have been in Michael's control group for the past four years. The "Knowing" shows in their answers, even Sir Bell's response will help future seekers of the "Knowing" because it is human to be confused and frustrated. The Path of the Magi is not an easy path to walk.

When Master Jesus' time was up, and he had to leave the earth plane, he told his twelve most trusted disciples to write down the "Knowing" that they had gained into a gospel. Those gospels would then be incorporated into one Great Book of Wisdom so that no matter who picked the Great Book up, the seeker could relate to one of the twelve writers. You have accomplished that in your lesson. Well done.

The 144,000 Light Bearers

The time has come for your final lesson from my Books of Wisdom. You have studied hard and when I look around, I see you have applied what you have learned to the environment in which you live. Because Archangel Michael's plan is to bring back the Sons of Light you will need to know how to set up a proper defense to block negative attacks from the Arch-Demon Beliel and his Sons of Darkness. They are mounting a move to destroy you now before you have a chance to gain a foot-hold in your world and any chance of bringing the Sons of Light home. The last thing they want is for these fifty-three lessons, from the Books of Wisdom, to fall into the hands *and minds* of the 144,000 Angel-Knight Light Bearers around the world.

There are many prophesies and much has been written about those 144,000 Souls of Destiny over the past 25,000 years. In Revelation 7, John claims the number must come from the twelve tribes of Israel. That is a misinterpretation by scribes with a controlling agenda.

The 144,000 could come from all four corners of the earth or they could all come from one very large city. It's really not about individuals or their faith it's about whom the 144,000 Souls of Destiny, which are to be summoned by Light Bearers, will align with.

There can be 144,000,000 plus Light Bearers, but the "Well of Souls" from Atlantis only number 144,000. It will also depend on the human Light Bearers' ability to project the acquired "Knowing" into three ancient grids that safeguard our Solar System. There are three main grids that operate through and around the Earth. These three Grids hold our place in the Cosmos. Without them, earth would move outside of the ring of life and become as desolate as the other planets.

The Crystalline Grid

The first is the Crystalline Grid, which links all the Crystals in the Earth and the ones in our bodies. The Ancients were aware of the Grid and constructed Pyramids, Temples, Stone Circles and Standing Stones to connect with the Stars and Inner Earth. They help hold concentrated beams, or waves, of Electro-Magnetic energy in place that shields the planet from harmful solar radiation while fueling multi-dimensional Star-Gates for beings to travel from other worlds using astral projection or thought transmissions as their mode of transportation. There is nothing faster than the speed of thought!

The Light Grid

The Light Grid is in the higher mental planes around the Earth as it links us all to our Higher-Inner Self, known as the Fifth Dimension. The Fifth Dimension is where the mind is born and returns to when the human experience ends. Some call the Fifth Dimension Heaven.

The Light Grid is most often used when you meditate or pray in order to connect with other Light Bearers around the world or when you connect to the Creator and the angels. These Light Bearers link to the Light Grid and become of one mind that sheds that light upon the darkness of humanity. Through meditation they link their higher state of consciousness to heal, energize and enlighten the world. This will produce a higher level of consciousness that will allow all of humanity to shift. The shifts in consciousness must occur if the human experiment is to continue.

The Solar Grid

The Solar Grid and Discs around the planet, holds the energy of our Sun and that is what creates life, as we know it. There are Crystals within the Earth that receive and transmit energy and send it through all three Grids, as well as storing, amplifying and focusing that energy. They link to our Solar System, Galaxy and often align to other Star Systems. These energy vortexes are Electric, Magnetic, or Electro-Magnetic having both qualities.

The Electric vortexes are male energy, giving off an emotional and physical negative-charge and stimulating the consciousness.

The Magnetic vortexes are female energy, which give a positive-charge enhancing psychic perception stimulating the sub-conscious.

Electro-Magnetic vortexes combine both energies providing the perfectly balanced charge of the Creators.

What I am attempting to explain is inconceivable to you now, but in time it will all make sense. It is like describing the Big Bang. The explosion was the Electro-Energy, of our Divine Father, flinging all the particles out from the center creating an expanding four-dimensional universe. The Magnetic-Energy, of our Mother, is the glue or gravity that holds those particles and the universe together.

Balance for Happiness

It should be noted that the energy of an individual does not always match up to the gender of their body. There are many humans forced to live out their lives as men trapped in a female body and women trapped in the body of a man. In the future, wisdom will prevail and humans will be accepted for what's really important, how they live their lives.

When humans choose their mates, they use their energy to blend into their relationships. If an Electro-Male individual, regardless of their gender, aligns with a Magnetic-Female, again regardless of their gender, there will be a constant push-me/pull-me in the relationship.

If an Electro-Male aligns with an Electro-Magnetic-Female the female will spend her life dominated by her male counterpart because of a lack of balance in the male energy. He or she is too masculine. The same is true if the roles were reversed because there is no balance in the relationship.

If an Electro-Magnetic-Male aligns with an Electro-Magnetic-Female you have soul mates regardless of their gender. The relationship has the perfect balance of male-female energy in both parties.

That is why it is very important for every human, males and females to get in touch with their other side, or energy. It would go a long way for finding bliss, so take your time to get to know the other person and don't think you can fix or change someone. What you see is normally what you get. That is why the Hierophant passed on the lesson on cross-gender energy for you and your students.

Positive and Negative Forces

In time, we will help you build a microcosm of Atlantis in the hope of trapping the destructive energy of the Arch-Demons that still haunt humanity. They are the negative influences that are infecting those humans with weak minds and wills. These Arch-Demons feed on the raw emotions of human selfishness and hate, just as the Archangels are boosted with human selflessness and love.

It should be noted that these two opposing forces are necessary for the balance within the body and the universe because the Creator's gift to the children is the ability to choose. If either force were removed completely, there would no longer be choice. The best either force can do is to hold the other force at bay and achieve balance. Remember Good is only as Good, as Evil is Evil.

The Power of Polished Silver

You have learned how to create Astral Crystal Beacons that will be the foundation which you will need when you are called upon to build the Great Celestial Wall around Atlantis. It will be the first line of defense. Now you must learn how to swipe the interior of the property of any negativity brought in by volunteers, the knights or visiting guests.

In Atlantis, we found that the Sons of Darkness and their negative force were deeply disturbed by reflected sunlight and moonlight off of highly polished silver surfaces. We also found that the opposite was true when they were confronted by a highly polish gold surface.

We created Solar Reflector Shields for our warriors to take into battle. We also strategically placed the reflector shields on all homes and buildings. As the light from the sun and moon moved through the sky, the light was reflected by the shields and disbursed across the grounds. As the angle of the sun and moon changed so did the reflection, much like the shadow on a sundial. Negativity loves the darkness and hates a positively charged solar beam of light. That's why we were called, Sons of Light.

The problem Atlantis faced was keeping the silver shields from tarnishing which would render them ineffective. In 1835, German chemist

Justus von Liebig developed a process for applying a thin layer of highly polished metallic silver to one side of a pane of clear glass and the problem was solved.

Creating Solar Reflector Shields

You can create Solar Reflector Shields in any shape and size and acquire the items needed at any hardware store. I will give you instructions for the standard size you will need. I have been watching your technology and tool progression through the ages and found these items to be of use:

To create a Solar Reflector Shield you will need-

1. One 12" x 12" silver mirror

2. Eight small quartz crystals

3. One can of insulation foam (Great Stuff)

4. One ½" x 13" x 13" exterior plywood

5. One can of black exterior paint

6. Eight 1" x 1" aluminum foil squares

After cutting the plywood to size, paint it on all sides with two heavy coats of black paint to preserve the wood. This will insure that the Solar Reflector Shields will last for many years.

Cleanse, and then program each crystal with the powers of the Angels of the Four Direction. Ask the angels to vanquish all negativity caught within the watchful eye of the Reflector Shield and purge it from the land. Now wrap the eight quartz crystals in aluminum foil. The foil will protect the crystals during the painting of the device.

Coat the back and inside edges of the mirror with a heavy bead of "Great Stuff" foam, then mount the mirror in the center of the plywood and press down hard. The foam will squeeze out and around the mirror. Add an additional bead of Great Stuff insulation foam around the edge of the mirror and wait fifteen minutes for it to expand.

Press the foil wrapped quartz crystal into each corner of the form. Then press the remaining four crystals in between the first four crystals. You should now have three crystals on each side of the reflector shield.

Let the Solar Reflector Shield rest for a full day then paint the foam black. Once the paint dries, peel the aluminum foil off the exposed surface of the crystals and release their powerful energy.

A Solar Reflector Shield should be mounted square, or turned sideways in a diamond formation, with screws on all four sides of any sacred structure you wish to protect. Mount them high for far-reaching effect and eye level for close combat. Remember you are at war and they will try to invade the sacred space. The Solar Reflector Shields can also be mounted on walls and fences for added protection. Ask your guides where they should be hung and how many you need to protect your desired areas.

If hung correctly, you will notice that the shields will reflect off of each other creating a solar beam mesh or network of sun and moonbeams. This will cloak you and the land from anything negative. Once you have activated the shield, people carrying negativity will find it hard to exist within the beams of solar cleansing.

Master Hermit, you should be warned that people harboring deceit and treachery will become agitated and combative in the presence of the Solar Reflector Shields, but if you wish to prepare a microcosm of Atlantis for the special child you seek, you must first purge the land of people who can't defeat their negative nature. That is why the Angel-Knights must apply all the fifty-three lessons found in this Book of Wisdom to their everyday life. You will lose many who claim they would never leave, but remember if they leave, they were never really here.

Angelic Gateways

An Angelic Gateway is not a toy and you are entering into high-level Magi Angelic Magic! Only attempt this if you have mastered the first fifty-two lessons and can maintain a positive body, mind and spirit.

The mirrors described can be obtained from most hardware stores. If you create an Angelic Gateway don't leave it in place for more than two weeks at a time, with two weeks intervals between assemblies of the next gateway. Remember as long as it is setup, it is working.

Keep a record book of when you set it up and taken it down. Also give reference to what you asked for, i.e. knowledge, wisdom, special healing for someone, travel, love, wealth, etc. Also keep a record of what information has come to you. Some information may not make sense at the time, but could be useful in the future.

The only exception on time setups is if the gateway is being set up in groupings inside a Star-Gate. Then the Angelic or 5-D Gateway can remain set up indefinitely.

Understanding Gateways

The near future holds new innovations in telephones and satellite communications. Soon everyone will have personal pocket telephone where you can actually see the person you are talking to in real time. Also, imagine having a telephone computer that you can ask any question and receive the spoken or written answer. I know that, in 1992, it sounds like something from a science-fiction movie, but it is on the horizon. Why? Because man choose to imagine it and so it will be created.

The universe is ever expanding and so must your mind to keep up. Like you found it hard to imagine the size and distance between the earth and moon. So is it hard to imagine the size of the earth to the sun. How many earths do you think would fit inside the sun? Is it 500, 5,000, 500,000, 100,000, 1,000,000 or 5,000,000? I ask the question to expand your mind, since I must prepare your mind to reach out to the ends of the cosmos and back.

Our sun is just an average-sized star. The largest star in our galaxy is Mu Cephi and it is 1,500 times the size of our sun and there are stars out there 1,500 times larger than Mu Cephi yet to be discovered. I tell you this so you can open your imagination to the endless possibilities available to you through astral communications - 1,000,000 earths will fit inside our sun. That's a big sun. Now just imagine how many of our suns would fit in Mu Cephi?

Within known physics there is nothing faster than the speed of light. How fast is the speed of light you ask?

Well, light travels at a speed of 186,000 miles per second. A traveler, moving at the speed of light, would circum-navigate the equator approximately 7.5 times in one second.

Many of the stars you see in the night sky have burned out millions of years ago, but their light is still traveling toward the earth. Science can measure the speed of light; therefore, it is proclaimed to be the fastest thing in our four-dimensional universe. However, there is one thing faster that can't be measured because it comes from the Fifth Dimension, and that is the Speed of Thought.

Humans project thought every day that speeds through the cosmos in less than the blink of an eye destined for the Creator. It's called prayer. It is so fast that the moment you think with your fifth dimensional mind it's received in the farthest reaches of the cosmos. That's why we call it, "Being of one mind."

Most of those prayers, or thoughts, lack focus and depth, and go unanswered. I will teach you how to create a communication device that will hit the target every time if you apply everything you have learned on the Path of the Magi. With it, you can learn to contact all those intelligent life forms that dwell in the positive dimensions. After the Sons of Light were taken from earth we were scattered throughout space and time. We number 144,000 and Archangel Michael is ready to help bring us home to finish what we started during the beginning of humankind.

The communication device I speak of is the Fifth Dimensional Gateway. If you and the Angel-Knights learn how to master it, I will follow the beacon created and the Golden Man of Fidelity will walk the earth again. We have until 2015 to reconstruct the "Tetragrammaton Star-Gate" of Atlantis before the window closes for delivery of the child Michael has come to safeguard.

Fifth Dimensional Gateway

The 5-D Gateway is a portable device so I recommend to keep it and other sacred objects you have learned about in the Book of Wisdom in a briefcase that locks. You do not want anyone tampering with any of your sacred objects.

To create the 5-D Gateway you will need the following items, all of which can be acquired from a hardware store:

1. Two 12" x 12" silver mirrors tiles

2. One roll of ¾" black electoral tape

3. One roll of 2" Duct tape

4. One can of black spray paint

5. One Gold paint marker or jar of gold leaf paint

6. One personalized statue

7. One white votive candle

8. Four quartz crystals

9. Small glass dish of water

Assembly of the 5-D Gateway
So you don't cut yourself on the glass mirrors use the black electrical tape first. Tape the sharp edge borders of both 12" x 12" mirror tiles. This

is done by cutting the tape in 12" strips, then lay each strip on the edge splitting the tape in its center then fold the tape over the front and back of that edge. Repeat until all eight edges are safe.

Now place the reflecting sides of the mirrors face to face together. Use the duct tape to create a hinge on one of the four sides of your mirrors so the device will open like a book.

Now lay the two mirrors open and face down. Spray the backsides with the black paint. When the paint dries, in gold, paint a 6" Ankh in the center of the top mirror and on the bottom mirror in gold, paint the phrase "Angel Knight Light Bearer." This will be your protective password and will shield the user from any negative interference from being attracted to your beacon. You have successfully created your gateway window into the universe.

Place your gateway on a table, or shelf, leaning the top plate, with the gold Ankh, against a wall at a slight angle so it doesn't fall forward, but so you can see yourself in the mirror. The bottom mirror has now become your altar plate.

Cleanse and purify four quartz crystals and then call in the Angels of the Four Directions as you have learned from the Book of Wisdom. In gold paint or marker, write the names of the angels, giving each their own crystal.

Place a white votive candle in a small glass dish, or saucer, on the altar plate so its edge touches the Ankh top plate.

Place the angelic crystals in the glass dish pointing in the true directions of north, south, east and west. This is very important so you might want to use a small compass for help.

Place an image or statue, that best represents you, in front of the dish nearest you. It should be a statue of a small angel, fairy, knight, or action figure. Just make sure that you can identify with the figure.

Now you are ready to activate your 5-D gateway. As an offering to the Creator, pour clean water into the dish of crystals and light the candle.

Relax your body, mind and spirit while staring past your statue, through the candle flame and into your true image reflecting back at you in the Ankh plate. Stare into your eyes. You may begin to see the four angels, in miniature, manifest as white orbs, hovering over the altar plate and around the candlelight. Do not get distracted by them.

Now focus on your desire or requested outcome. If you are seeking clearer guidance and communication from other worldly intelligence speak it now and "Will" it to happen. You will be probing deep space for one of the 144,000 that best suits your cosmic energy so keep trying until you find a match. As you and the Good Knights open gateways it will become easier for other students seeking the "Knowing" to draw attention to their calls.

Just don't give up.

If and when students do contact one of the 144,000, ask for its spirit code. It will be in three to eight letters, i.e. ERU or ZUMBRYND. When the Angel-Knight Light Bearers make contact, have them print the code on the bottom of the altar mirror plate to be viewed while open. Also, keep a record of all students around the world who make contact. You will need to find 144,000 seekers of the "Knowing." It will be important for use with the Star-Gate in years to come.

Once you have activated the 5-D gateway, walk away. The crystals will continue to echo your thoughts for twenty-four hours. Check back in from time to time to see if you have made a connection. You will start to feel or hear a buzzing in your ears. In time, the buzzing will turn into understandable thought.

The 5-D gateway is like a telephone booth; it may contact you during sleep, so you might want to set it up near or in your bedroom. It also helps with astral projection. If it interferes with your sleep move it to a closet or another room. You must match the power of the crystal through belief. That is key. I ask that you consider the great crystal debate. Crystals will not work for some people for many reasons. It takes a keen mind to unlock their secrets.

The wisdom of the All can be received through the proper placement of certain crystals using the 5-D gateway. All anyone needs is a strong will, an open mind and a forgiving heart.

Pandora's Box

Although the formal lessons from the Book of Wisdom are over, you will still receive instruction on how to create an assortment of devices that will be needed in the future. In time I will guide you in the construction of a Fifth Dimensional Prism Cell, which is also known as Pandora's box. Using special crystals and mirrors that line inside and out of a quadrilateral di-pyramid shaped wooden box. It is a reflector prism cell.

You and the Angel-Knights will be called upon to expose thousands of humans to the Electro-Magnetic gravitational energy of the Prism Cell. People will gladly purge themselves of their negativity and the Prism Cell will become a trap for the darkness of the Seven Deadly Passions of Hatred. Archangel Michael's plan is to restore the positive/negative balance to the earth. This will level the playing field for the return of the Sons of Light and usher in a new age of enlightenment for humanity.

In closing, remember you can only get out of something based on what you have put into it. Therefore, apply everything you have learned and keep learning. When you know less than there is to know, you must ask the question - How much do I really know? Most humans would take the knowledge we have given you and do little with it because that would take a lifetime of effort.

If you stay true to your pledge to Michael and the Constant Walker you will take this knowledge and build a better world. Start by passing the Light to 144,000 children. The children will help reach 144,000 Light Bearers and the Light Bearers will go on to reach 144,000,000 around the world. The time has come to reveal the Fifteenth and final Ancient Law of Wisdom:

"Remember all life is sacred, Respect the Books of Wisdom and the Books of Wisdom will always Respect you."

If you and the 144,000 Light Bearers hold true to the laws you will succeed in the great task you have undertaken.

In the end, hopefully, Michael will finish what he was sent to do in the beginning, deliver the Sword of Truth and the Stone of Light to the Children of Earth. The two sacred objects have been forged into one. You now safeguard God's Sword for the last child of Atlantis. I pray that you find our beloved M.V.

From the story of Atlantis, the Hierophant has shared with you I am sure you have figured out that it was to the people of Atlantis that the Creator sent the gifts of Divine Enlightenment. The gifts came at a time when a Magi student, Seth, who was in league with the Arch-Demon Biel, betrayed his teacher and all but a few Atlanteans bowed down to the Dark Lord Satan/Beliel. The Angel-Knights and Sons of Light are now ready to return. May the Truth be with you always and righteousness by your side my son.

End of Transmission

Note: I have updated the original information I received over the years. As I discovered new methods from those who guided me and I added it to these lessons. I want to make your journey a little easier, just as you will add new wisdoms as you pass the lessons on to your students. So please listen well to everything the Hierophant and Master ERU have to say, it could mean the difference between success and failure.

I didn't know it then, but when I look back now, the powers I learned to control in lessons thirty-one and thirty-two were at the foundation of everything the Angel-Knights and I were to accomplish. Those powers and the use of stones and crystals saved us thousands of man-hours in meditation and brought in several million dollars when our quest needed financing for major program outreach.

Sixteen Ancient Laws of Wisdom

1st Law "The more you use your ability to help another, the more your ability will grow."

2nd Law "The door to the psychic world is not opened with a ram, but with the slightest caress."

3rd Law "The law of love is unchangeable; in that, as you do it to the least of your brethren, you do to your creator."

4th Law "The White Light can only be used once to heal any one person."

5th Law "He who needs no one is no one."

6th Law "Sit quietly, humbly and patiently at the feet of the wise for one day others will sit at your feet and drink from your cup of wisdom."

7th Law "With all of our power and wisdom we have little effect on the macrocosm or microcosm, however the microcosm of our being can have a great effect on the macrocosms around us."

8th Law "Absolute faith emanates only from the inner or spiritual self through conviction. And contemplation alone without absolute faith attending it, will not advance you one iota."

9th Law "Words of power are an individual manifestation."

10th Law "The Powers of Wisdom consume those who would misuse them, and from that there is no escape."

11th Law "Judge no man, for you shall be judged by your judgment."

12th Law "Forgive those who wrong you or bring harm upon you, for they shall suffer a far greater misfortune."

13th Law "At its essence, willpower is the ability to set aside your fears and resist short-term temptations in order to meet long-term goals."

14th Law "When you think you know, you don't and when you know you don't, you do!"

15th "Law "Remember all life is sacred, Respect the Books of Wisdom and the Books of Wisdom will always Respect you."

About the Authors

Sir Edward-Michael Jagen is a U.S. Army veteran, retired Washington, D.C. Police Intelligence Investigator, and dedicated child abuse protection advocate. He is the author of the *Good Knight* fairytale series and the *Good Knight Crime and Violence Prevention Program*, which has been used in the public-school systems as a child protection teaching tool. After official being dubbed, "The Blue Knight of Maryland, by the Governor, he set out on a quest to educate children with the wisdom to protect themselves from those who would manipulate, deceive and/or abduct them. Over the past 33 years Sir Edward and his Angel Knight volunteers have reach millions nationwide. For his many years of public service, he has been awarded The National Jefferson 'Gold Medal' Award, the President's Service Award for Public Safety, the Maryland Governor's Award for Volunteerism and received the Silver Star for Bravery after being inducted into the American Police Hall of Fame. Jagen "retired" in 2014 and passed the mantle to Sophia. He also gave her his memoirs to adapt for publication.

Lady Sophia Key West is a twenty-nine-year veteran health care practitioner with holistic and integrative focus. She is a renowned Reiki Master/teacher/practitioner, Cranio-Sacral therapist, Certified Aromatherapist and wellness guide. A highly sought-after lecturer, Sophia is an acclaimed author of the *Super Book of Family Safety* and Good Knight Child Safety Awareness video productions. As the volunteer COS of the Good Knight Child Empowerment Network Inc, Sophia oversees programs, services and the museum's exhibits. She has also received many awards over her twenty-four years of volunteer service to include the Maryland Governor's Volunteer of the Year Award for 2005, the Volvo Hometown Hero Award and the Presidential Volunteer Service Lifetime Achievement Award for Public Safety from President Bush. Sophia is also working to convert the Diary of an Angel Knight Series into a major motion picture.

Made in the USA
Monee, IL
07 July 2026